Princeton Theological Mon~~~~~~~~ ~~~~~~ ~~ ~~~~~~
(College.)

Dikran Y. Hadidian

General Editor

25

CHRIST IN OUR PLACE

The Humanity of God in Christ for
the Reconciliation of the World

**James Torrance**

# CHRIST IN OUR PLACE

The Humanity of God in Christ
for the Reconciliation of the World

Essays presented to

Professor James Torrance

Edited by

Trevor A. Hart
and
Daniel P. Thimell

THE PATERNOSTER PRESS
EXETER, GREAT BRITAIN
PICKWICK PUBLICATIONS
ALLISON PARK, PENNSYLVANIA

Printed in the U.K.
for
Pickwick Publications
4137 Timberlane Drive, Allison Park, PA 15101–2932
and
The Paternoster Press
Paternoster House, 3 Mount Radford Cresent, Exeter, U.K. EX2 4JW

**The Library of Congress Cataloguing-in-Publication Data**

Christ in our place: the humanity of God in Christ for the
reconciliation of the world: essays presented to Professor
James Torrance/edited by Trevor A. Hart and Daniel P. Thimell.
p. cm. – (Princeton theological monograph series; 25)
Includes bibliographical references.
ISBN 1–55635–009–0
1. Jesus Christ—Person and offices. 2. Salvation. 3. Theology
I. Torrance, James. II. Hart, Trevor A. III. Thimell, Daniel P.
IV. Series.
BT202.C52 1990

232—dc20

90–21238
CIP

**British Library Cataloguing in Publication Data**

Christ in our Place
1. Christology
I. Hart, Trevor A. II. Torrance, James 232
ISBN 0–85364–504–3

Made and Printed in Great Britain for the Paternoster Press and
Pickwick Publications by A. Wheaton and Co. Exeter, Devon.

# Contents

# Foreword

In September 1989 James B Torrance retired from the Chair of Systematic Theology in the University of Aberdeen, concluding some forty years' devoted service to the study and teaching of academic theology. His colleagues, friends and students wish to pay tribute to this distinguished scholar and churchman in the time honoured manner, with the preparation and presentation of a *Festschrift*.

James Torrance was born in China in 1923, the son of missionary parents. After a distinguished academic career in Edinburgh, Basel and Oxford, he spent seven years as a parish minister before joining the staff of New College, Edinburgh in the early 1960s as lecturer in the History of Christian Thought. Here he soon established himself as a popular and respected teacher, and developed his own interests in the theology of the Reformers, Scottish theology and the development of modern theology. In January 1977 he moved to King's College, Aberdeen to continue the tradition of Reformed theological education there. Professor Torrance is well known for his widespread involvement in both academic and church life. His frequent lecturing tours to the United States, Canada, South Africa, and Northern Ireland have introduced his theology to an international audience, and have drawn many students to Aberdeen to pursue research under his supervision. Others will know him better through his extensive involvement in ecumenical dialogue at various levels, as Chairman of the international conversations between the World Alliance of Reformed Churches and the Lutheran World Federation, Chairman of the British Council of Churches' Commission on the Trinity, and Chairman of the Joint Commission on Doctrine of the Church of Scotland and the Scottish Roman Catholic Church. He was also Convener of the Church of Scotland General Assembly's Panel on Doctrine in the period 1982-86.

Professor Torrance's distinctive contribution to Christian Dogmatics has been to call the church back to consider again the implications of the divine covenant of grace established once for all in the saving humanity of the Son of God. It is this same theme of the relevance of christology for soteriological, pastoral, social and other issues that this book seeks to reflect. The essays contained within bear testimony, we believe, to a renewed commitment of Christian theologians to the doctrines of the Incarnation and the Trinity, not out of any misplaced sentimentality, but because it is realized that with these doctrines the Christian Gospel, and with it the church's relevance in mission, ministry and social praxis, either stands or falls.

We would like to thank the the contributors for their willingness to be involved in this project and their patience in awaiting the fruits of their labours. We would also like to thank the following people for their help and support without which the production of this book would not have been possible: Michael Cummings, Conrad Gempf, Rachel Hart, Baxter Kruger, John MacCormack and Mrs Mary Torrance. Finally, we would extend our thanks to The Paternoster Press for their help and encouragement in the realisation of this project.

The editors
Autumn 1989

# Abbreviations

The following abbreviations are used throughout the volume. Additional abbreviations used within individual articles are indicated in square brackets following the first reference in the footnotes.

| | |
|---|---|
| *CD* | Karl Barth, *Church Dogmatics*, GW Bromiley and TF Torrance (eds.), (Edinburgh, 1956-75), followed by volume number in roman, part number in arabic |
| ed., eds. | Editor, editors |
| edn. | Edition |
| *EQ* | *Evangelical Quarterly* |
| ET | English translation |
| *Exp. T* | *Expository Times* |
| *Inst.* | John Calvin, *Institute of the Christian Religion* |
| *SJT* | *Scottish Journal of Theology* |

# James Torrance : An Appreciation

ALASDAIR HERON

Some twenty years ago a Divinity student in New College, Edinburgh, was driven close to distraction by the complexities of Christian Dogmatics. Another student brought her to James Torrance. He calmed her fears, answered her questions and showed her how to cope with the demands of the Dogmatics syllabus. That may appear nothing out of the ordinary - but I know what it meant for that student, for she is my wife and still today remembers with gratitude the trouble James Torrance was prepared to take to listen to her difficulties and to help her to find a way through them. In our family James counts even today as something close to a saint for this reason alone!

These days are long past. My wife is no longer terrified of Dogmatics, has indeed learned from our daughters to treat the pretensions of theological professors with affectionate disrespect. Said daughters had a head-start not vouchsafed to their mother: they grew up in the home of a theological teacher and learned from infancy not to regard theologians as repositories of all wisdom and knowledge. Here too James played a part in the days when he and I were colleagues in New College in the seventies, not least by his willingness to take time off from serious academic work to entertain them, notably by drawing pictures of rabbits in patched trousers and chewing carrots in order to distract the rising generation from such creative pursuits as dismantling their father's bookcases, tearing up his papers or scribbling with crayons on the walls of his office. Have such personal, even trivial reminiscences any place in an academic *Festschrift*? Not, perhaps, according to the normal pattern of this literary *genre*. That pattern would demand strict concentration on the properly academic - e.g. on the scientific character of James' work, the logic of his theological method, his contributions to the

1

advancement of theological thinking. Just such a concentration would, however, risk missing the real heart and core of his character and widespread influence. James Torrance is not and never was a cloistered academic, but a pastor, a guide for the perplexed, a man of faith whose goal and interest was above all the nurturing and guiding of others in the way of that same faith. Theological reflection, theological writing and theological teaching are for him firmly anchored in (and related to) the community of faith, a community far wider and broader than the purely academic. Theology as he understands and practices it is both existential and ecclesiastical. It is not merely a matter of dusty books or rarified ideas or brilliant theories; it is a personal quest and responsibility in the service of the Church, and as such involves not only the mind but also the heart of the theological teacher. It requires and demands *integrity* of the sort portrayed in the metrical version of Psalm 15:

> The man that walketh uprightly,
> And worketh righteousness,
> And as he thinketh in his heart,
> So doth he truth express.

James Torrance is a highly qualified and experienced academic theologian, but he is more than that. He is an honest man, an honourable man and a Christian man. These are not merely academic qualities; they are of even greater worth. 'A king can mak' a belted knight ... An honest man's abune his might' (Burns). We do not need the warnings of McDiarmid's drunkard regarding the thistle to appreciate beyond all couthy Scots sentimentality the value of an honest man in a Chair of Theology. That is what King's College in Aberdeen has been privileged to have in these last years - not a time-server, not a self-advertiser, not a crafty manipulator of university or ecclesiastical politics, but an honest, honourable Christian man who cares for the Church and for the students who flock to him from all over the world, and whose academic work is pursued in order to take up and deal with the issues presenting themselves in that setting as requiring attention.

Where, then, do the roots of James Torrance's theology lie?
What has made him such a valued, appreciated and beloved
colleague and teacher? The answer lies first of all in the man
himself. He is a man so mastered by the Gospel of Jesus Christ
that he lives from the evangelical message of forgiveness and
reconciliation. That is his daily bread, the air he breathes, the
substance and tenor of his teaching. He has not, so far as I am
aware, written any hymns; but had he done so, they would have
been similar to George Matheson's or George Herbert's:

> Teach me, my God and King
> In all things thee to see,
> And what I do in anything,
> To do it as for thee.

> O love that wilt not let me go,
> I rest my weary soul in thee;
> I give thee back the life I owe,
> That in thine ocean depths its flow
> May richer, fuller be.

James Torrance has the rare gift of enabling the simplest
parishioners, the most perplexed theological students to sense
that they are fledglings destined and called to fly in the
atmosphere of the eternal grace of God. The warm humanity of
his personality is not only a natural gift; it is the radiation of
conviction, the conviction of one who knows himself to be
constrained by the love of Christ and can therefore do none other
than express and convey this witness to others as both claim and
liberation.

Had James Torrance done nothing more than impress this message
on successive generations of theological students, he would have
made an abiding contribution. But he has done more. He has
fostered and encouraged pioneering research in the history of
Scottish theology, not least with the aim of uncovering and
disposing of the clouds of melancholic fatalism, of resignation
and determinism, which even today shadow our Scottish Reformed
heritage. A whole series of doctoral dissertations undertaken
under his supervision witness to his activity in this field, as do

3

his own published writings, which are very largely concerned with reviewing and correcting aspects of the tradition of Scottish Reformed theology and showing the difference between the teaching of Calvin and what later developed as 'Calvinism'. That he has more than once been publicly attacked by would-be 'Calvinists' of a conservative sort is an indication of what sensitive nerves he has struck - though his aim in striking them was never to wound but to heal; to allow the power of the Gospel to shatter the fetters of rigorism and legalism which the deeply religious are particularly inclined to fasten on themselves and on others.

The nerve of his teaching is perhaps best caught in a series of antitheses which he has constantly reiterated and impressed on his students through nigh on thirty years: *Gospel* rather than *Law*; *evangelical* rather than *legal* repentance; the *indicative* of grace as prior to the *imperative* of obedience; the primacy of the question, '*who* is Jesus Christ?' over the question '*what* has Jesus Christ done for us?' The combined impact of these antitheses was accurately grasped by a group of students in New College, Edinburgh, in the mid-seventies in a mildly satirical 'Prayer for JBT' which ended: 'Through Jesus Christ our Lord, who is in column one as well as column three.' The hidden reference for the initiate is to James' well-known diagram - a diagram which he not only laid out on the blackboard in many a class, but was also ever-ready to sketch out afresh ('have you seen my diagram?') on the back of an envelope drawn from his filing-cabinet in the inside breast-pocket of his jacket. The point of this diagram, reduced to its simplest essential terms, is that the primary and all-determining reality with which we have to reckon is God's good favour towards us, signed and sealed in Jesus Christ as the love with which we are loved from before the foundation of the world (column one). The imperative of God's Law, God's demands upon us - column two - depends on the primary indicative; and the message of reconciliation - column three - does not introduce Jesus Christ for the *first* time simply as the answer to our failure to fulfil the Law, but returns to him as the Alpha and Omega on whom indicative and imperative alike depend, for in his

4

incarnation, crucifixion and resurrection all the purposes and promises of God are once and for all gathered up and put into effect, 'for us and for our salvation'.

In this emphasis and this shaping of the horizons of rising generations of theological students, James Torrance made no claim to be 'original' or to break fresh ground in academic theology. He was concerned far more to bear witness to the abiding foundation of all Christian faith as the promise leading us forward to the Kingdom of God. In this, he belongs firmly in the main-line tradition of Scottish academic theology - a tradition which has by and large concentrated more on the paedagogical responsibility of the university teacher than on demanding academic originality from him, much less making original research achievements the primary criterion for university appointments. This tradition can be and has been criticized as failing to encourage in Scotland the kind of untrammelled interest in pure thought which has been the glory of modern German theology. The criticism may not be entirely unjustified, but the warning of HR Mackintosh in a famous and much quoted remark more than half a century ago also deserves to be heeded: 'Theology is created in Germany, corrupted in America and corrected in Scotland'. The remark of the Czech theologian Josef Hromadka also comes to mind: after he had studied in more than one German faculty of theology, it was when he came to study in Aberdeen with the elder Professor David Cairns that he 'found the solid ground of the Church under his feet'. Theological work needs its outriders and pioneers; it will in any case find numerous misinterpreters and distorters, in America and elsewhere; Scotland's contribution may well still be that of a solid common-sense, of a reorientation towards what really matters. It is no disgrace if Scottish theology is primarily concerned with the *corrective* and *stabilizing* task, with helping students to find the solid ground of the Gospel and the Church under their feet.

To draw this out a little further; there are at least three distinct tasks which present themselves to a teacher of Systematic Theology today. The first is that of *edification*, the straightforward education of students who need to be informed, challenged and strengthened in their Christian theological commitment. This demands a high degree of personal engagement on the part of their teachers, of contact and exchange between teachers and students. It involves an intensive *pastoral* responsibility of the teacher. Our Scottish tradition of theological education has rightly placed this as the first priority on the agenda of our Divinity Faculties. A Divinity Faculty is first and foremost a 'school of faith', not merely a talking-shop for the batting-around of ideas good, bad or indifferent. The tenant of a Chair of Systematic Theology in a Scottish Divinity Faculty has a special opportunity and responsibility to influence the ideas, the self-understanding and the professional goals of his students. This pastoral and paedagogical task has its own special evangelical and missionary importance, not least because of its essentially *personal* nature.

I have been privileged to see at first hand and from various sides how splendidly James Torrance has filled this role over a good quarter of a century, first in Edinburgh, then in Aberdeen. First as a student, later as a colleague in Edinburgh, later still as external examiner in Aberdeen I could never fail to notice his genuine care for his students and his paedagogical concern that they grasp the fundamentals of the matter. In teaching he is visibly concerned to *communicate* - which is by no means always the case with university teachers who sometimes can seem to be conducting a private dialogue with their material, a dialogue for which the presence of hearers is quite incidental. But then - and there is a direct connection - James Torrance was a preacher before he became a lecturer or professor, and he approaches his teaching with the same seriousness with which he approaches his sermons. It can often enough happen that theological students in the course of their classes suddenly begin to wonder what the material they are studying really has to do with their future vocation as ministers; in James Torrance's classes the question generally does not need to be asked because the connections and implications are apparent. Those who do not recognize them for themselves will have them pointed out anyway!

The second task is that of encouraging *theological research* in the form of independent study, especially at honours and postgraduate level. This research is by its nature generally historical in character, enquiring into the shaping and articulation of theological themes in the more or less recent past on the principle that cutting one's teeth on such history is the appropriate continuation of what has been learned at undergraduate level and the best preparation for further theological work in the future. At this level, the teacher is less an *edifier* than a *supervisor*, responsible for guiding the work by advice and criticism whose intention is to bring the student to the point where he can engage independently in his own constructive work, where indeed he can discern for himself what questions arise out of the material and find ways of resolving them. The special character of such research work, properly undertaken, lies in the fact that it cannot simply be programmed in advance; the methods and results have to emerge through genuine first-hand engagement with the material on the part of the student. The supervisor has the role of *critical enabler* who accompanies the work without seeking to dominate it or to determine in advance what conclusions ought to be reached.

A glance at the statistics of the Aberdeen Divinity Faculty over the last decade can show how popular it has become as a centre for postgraduate study, not least for students from overseas. These postgraduate students, so important for the life of a faculty, are not all working in Systematic Theology - but a goodly number of them are. Nor can there be any doubt that James Torrance's own travels and contacts through the years have been responsible for many of those students coming to Aberdeen.

The third task is that of *critical and constructive theological rethinking*. James Torrance's main interest here has been in the history of Scottish theology, especially in the strengths and weaknesses of the tradition of Federal Calvinism. While he has published less than many of us would wish - and hope that he yet will do - his articles in this field deserve to be required reading in any course on the history of Scottish theology, covering as they do such central themes as the teaching of the *Westminster Confession*, the controversy around 1720 concerning *The Marrow of Modern Divinity*, the notion of the Covenant and the work of John McLeod Campbell. Not that this is his only field of interest - he has, if I see aright, published on those topics because of his awareness that the issues arising are of direct contemporary relevance as well, especially in the Scottish context - for his teaching ranges much more widely with special emphasis on the lessons of the development of modern theology since the Enlightenment for fundamental principles of theological method, and on the interface between theology on the one hand and philosophy, ethics and politics on the other.

Yet another aspect of James Torrance's work deserves to be highlighted: he is not merely a theological teacher but also an active and committed Churchman contributing at many levels to the theological work of the Church as well as the University. The Church of Scotland's Panel on Doctrine, the Scottish Church Society and the Church Service Society have all drawn on his time and talents, as have the World Alliance of Reformed Churches and the British Council of Churches. The value and demands of such contributions are often not widely known or recognized; all the more reason to emphasize them here.

But to return to the point where we began: in James Torrance we do not seek to honour simply the professor or the member of Church committees or the far-travelled ambassador for his faculty in Aberdeen. We honour the man who in such rare fashion integrates all these capacities and qualities, activities and achievements. For myself, I wish to pay tribute to a respected teacher to whom I myself owe much, a colleague with whom it has always been a delight to work, and a friend. It is hard to believe that one so youthful and energetic is now approaching retirement age; I am certainly not alone in hoping that a certain increase of leisure will give him occasion and opportunity to distil the fruits of his experience and studies in further publications.

Part One

# Christ and the Reconciliation of the World

# 1

# Christopraxis : the Ministry and the Humanity of Christ for the World

RAY S ANDERSON

Nowhere have I heard James B Torrance more eloquent than when he stood before church leaders and theologians of the Dutch Reformed Church in South Africa assembled in Pretoria in late August of 1986. There, at the conclusion of a two day conference on church unity, Professor Torrance was asked to give his impressions following the debate on the theological basis for the church's official position on Apartheid. Speaking informally and without prepared notes, he cut quickly to the heart of the matter when he said that the humanity of Jesus Christ was both an act of divine grace and divine judgment. It was an act of judgment against the merging of race, religion and national preservation into a structure claiming divine origin and justification. All such distinctions which seek to align God with one kind of humanity and against another were put to an end on the cross. But the incarnation of God was also an act of grace. For it created a new humanity in which all divisions and distinctions were healed and transformed into a commonwealth where each and every human being is accepted and affirmed as representative of Christ himself. The church can only be the true church, Professor Torrance concluded, where both this judgment and grace determine its existence.

What we heard was a radical reminder that there is nothing so dangerous and destructive as the humanity of the church when it fuses race, religion and political theory, but also nothing so contemporary and compelling as the humanity of God. The humanity of God in Jesus Christ, his birth, life, death and resurrection is both the 'personalizing of persons' and the 'humanizing of man' as TF Torrance likes to put it.[1] When the

---

[1] TF Torrance, *The Mediation of Christ* (Exeter, 1983), pp. 78, 79.

humanity of the church claims divine providence and historical priority for its prerogatives and power of self preservation, it dehumanizes both Christ and persons in the world. The church finds its true humanity in the relation between Jesus Christ and all humanity. The church finds its true ministry in the upholding, healing and transformation of the humanity of others as already grasped and reconciled to God through the incarnation, atoning life, death and resurrection of Jesus Christ. This is the thesis which controls the development of this essay. This is the authentic praxis of Christ's ministry through his humanity: (1) objectively completed through his own vicarious life in solidarity with all of humanity; (2) eschatologically confirmed through his resurrection to be a living and faithful paraclete ever-present alongside of and on behalf of all humanity; (3) historically concealed as a healing and transforming presence where 'Christ clothed with His gospel meets with Christ clothed with the desperate need and plight of men'.[2] This is what is meant by Christopraxis.

## I The Vicarious Humanity of Christ

As the Mediator who stands with humanity as advocate, healer and transformer, Jesus Christ is not merely a principle by which ministry is defined, but, as James Torrance has reminded us, is the very presence of Christ as the ministering one: 'Christ does not heal us by standing over against us, diagnosing our sickness, prescribing medicine for us to take, and then going away, to leave us to get better by obeying his instructions - as an ordinary doctor might. No, He becomes the patient! He assumes that very humanity which is in need of redemption, and by being anointed by the Spirit in our humanity, by a life of perfect obedience, by dying and rising again, for us, our humanity is healed *in him*. We are not just healed "through Christ" because of the work of Christ but "in and through Christ"'.[3]

---

[2]Cf. TF Torrance, 'Service in Jesus Christ', in RS Anderson (ed.), *Theological Foundations for Ministry* (Grand Rapids, 1979), p. 724. First published in JI McCord and THL Parker (eds.), *Service in Christ* (London, 1966).

[3]JB Torrance, 'The Vicarious Humanity of Christ', in TF Torrance (ed.), *The Incarnation - Ecumenical Studies in the Nicene-Constantinopolitan Creed AD 381* (Edinburgh, 1981), p. 141.

This clearly grounds the objective basis for all ministry in the incarnation, death and resurrection of Jesus Christ. In assuming humanity the divine Logos *became* Jesus of Nazareth. Through his own self testimony accompanied by his ministry of service to God and to human need, Jesus revealed the ontological source for his ministry to be that of the Son to the Father in the power of the Spirit. In this way, the criterion for all ministry is placed squarely within the ministry and the humanity of Christ. The doctrine of the *homoousion* as formulated by the orthodoxy of Nicea not only answered the question as to the ontological source of the person of Jesus Christ, but the ontological source of his work and ministry as well.

Attempts to make a distinction between the being of Jesus as Son of God and the saving significance of his humanity qualify the *homoousion* and sever the vital connection between the atonement and the incarnation. The humanity of Christ is left to serve an instrumental purpose only, so that once he has died upon the cross his human life of obedience and ministry as the Son to the Father in solidarity with humankind comes to an end.[4] In its place arises the humanity and ministry of the church as the new instrument by which the salvation of God is presented to the world. Karl Barth, more than any other contemporary theologian, has helped us to see the epistemological and soteriological

---

[4]This seems to be the implication of the statement by Professor Paul Jewett when he says: 'As God, the Son is equal with his Father, though as Messiah he has assumed a servant role and become subordinate to his Father. The basis of the comparison between Man's being, as an "I"/"thou" fellowship of male and female, and God's being as an "I"/"thou" fellowship of persons in the Godhead, is the doctrine of the Trinity, not the doctrine of Incarnation', *Man as Male and Female* (Grand Rapids, 1975), p. 133. Professor Jewett's concern is to show that the subordination of the Son to the Father in the incarnation is not an essential, or ontological subordination within the Godhead. By creating a dichotomy between the humanity of the Son (Incarnation) and the essential deity of the Son, however, the saving significance of the humanity of Christ lacks ontological grounding within God himself. From this perspective, the humanity of God in Christ cannot serve as the continuing basis for the reconciliation of God through Christ, and the church is cast back on its own humanity.

problems with this unfortunate bifurcation. In his own way, James Torrance has now helped us to see the practical problems and even dangers of separating the humanity of Christ from the ministry of Christ. Through the incarnation, both judgment and grace have taken hold of humanity in such a way that grace cannot be received in any other way than through solidarity with the crucified humanity of Christ. More than a mere instrument to effect an abstract forensic atonement, the humanity of Christ brings all humanity under the judgment in order to bring it within the gracious work of renewal and reconciliation through resurrection. The humanity of the church is thus grounded ontologically, not merely ethically, on the humanity and ministry of Jesus Christ.

## II Orthopraxy vs Orthodoxy: an unresolved dilemma

So far we have pointed to what might be called a case for orthodoxy by which the ministry of the church can be called Christian ministry. This enables us to say that all ministry is Christ's ministry. A christological criterion is thus established by which the various forms and methods of ministry can be critiqued. Some have rejected this approach, and call for an orthopraxy by which the criterion for the ministry of the church is more contemporary and contextual than the doctrines of orthodoxy. Indeed, some have even suggested that orthopraxy should replace orthodoxy as a criterion for the ministry of the church today. Orthopraxy, it is argued, takes seriously the condition of oppressed humanity and makes liberation a test of theological method as well as a hermeneutic approach to Scripture. It is in liberation as praxis that the Word and work of God is revealed, not in the confession of orthodox doctrines.

Charles Davis makes the point clearly when he says: 'Religion when maintained as an orthodoxy claims a permanent self-identity, remaining unscathed by social and practical changes. It involves some purely theological center of reference to serve in an abstract way as a norm of identity ... The presupposition of orthodoxy is the contemplative conception of knowledge, according to which knowledge is the result and disinterested viewing of reality by individuals'.[5]   Having said this, Davis is equally critical of orthopraxy as a conceptual alternative to orthodoxy arguing that it is a 'half-hearted compromise' which merely transfers sacral authority from doctrines to social and political strategies.   It is the dialectic between theory and praxis, he contends, which represents the best approach.

If indeed we are now at a point in the discussion where the substitution of orthopraxy for orthodoxy is viewed as naive and even problematical from an ideological standpoint, it is also quite clear that a return to orthodoxy as construed by Charles Davis is equally unsatisfying.   Some are attempting to find a 'middle ground' in the debate by envisioning a 'dialectic' between orthodoxy and orthopraxy.   This is the position taken by Clodovis Boff who suggests that the dual responsibility of theology is that of establishing internal consistency for theological statements (epistemological validation) and correlation between theology and experience (pistic verification). In this dialectic, he suggests that praxis constitutes the 'indirect norm' for theology.[6]

Johann Metz, in somewhat the same fashion, suggests a 'praxis of imitation' whereby praxis itself is not considered to be the primary criterion.   He suggests instead that 'imitation of Christ'

---

[5]*Theology and Political Society : The Hulsean Lectures in the University of Cambridge, 1978* (Cambridge, 1980), p. 130.   The rejection of orthodoxy as an epistemological and hermeneutical criterion is a well-known theme in liberation theology, with varing degrees of emphasis.   The seminal work in liberation theology written by G Gutierrez sets the agenda for this position: *A Theology of Liberation : History, Politics and Salvation* Sister C Inda and J Eagleson (eds., ET), (Maryknoll, 1973).   Cf. also the works of L Boff, *Jesus Christ Liberator : A Critical Christology for Our Time* Patrick Hughes (ET), (Maryknoll, 1978), and J Sobrino, *Christology at the Crossroads : A Latin American Approach* John Drury (ET), (Maryknoll, 1978).   A more recent and more critical view of orthopraxis as a substitute for orthodoxy can be found in the comprehensive work by C Boff, *Theology and Praxis - Epistemological Foundations* (Maryknoll, 1987).   While sympathetic to the concerns expressed in the move toward orthopraxy, Boff suggests that praxis is 'not what explains' but 'what must be explained' (p. 200).

[6]C Boff, *op. cit.*, pp. 199ff.

as a praxis of solidarity in suffering be considered as an apocalyptic form of action for the sake of liberation. As an alternative and opposition to the apathetic structures of human society (including orthodoxy), Metz suggests a 'pathic structure' for Christian presence in the world as a form of social praxis. This, he argues, retains the distinctive element of 'Christian praxis' in a theology of liberation.[7]

Dennis McCann and Charles Strain, in a critical approach to a practical theology, reject Metz's formulation as 'too orthodox' and call for a 'religious praxis' that is less christologically and apocalyptically oriented. Nor are they persuaded by the claims of orthopraxy, which they find no more acceptable than orthodoxy. Instead, they propose a praxis orientation which is guided by a transcending vision for religious values which are intrinsic to human experience itself.[8] This however, seems to throw humanity back upon itself as a continuum on which Christ is placed as the 'exemplar' of religious praxis.

Todd Speidell has reminded us that the risen Jesus Christ provides the basis for an on-going reality of liberation in which we participate, instead of relying upon our own resources to 'imitate Jesus'. Thus he argues that the incarnation provides a christological criterion as a corrective to liberation as praxis: 'The incarnation as the concrete reality of God's liberating presence from above to below provides a hermeneutical correction to liberation Christology. The hermeneutical criterion is Christ as the Son of God, who in the presence and power of the Spirit assumes and heals human existence. This christological criterion may provide a corrective to liberation Christology, which places Jesus on a continuum with us [on] a common pathway to the Father. A christological critique, however, points the way forward to a liberating praxis based on Christ's praxis, which is not a function of liberation that we must imitate, but the reality of

---

[7] J Metz, *Faith in History and Society - Toward a Practical Fundamental Theology*, David Smith (ET), (New York, 1980), pp. 57ff.

[8] D McCann and C Strain, *Polity and Praxis - A Program for American Practical Theology* (New York, 1985), pp. 40, 45, 142.

liberation in which God summons us to participate'.[9]

This brief survey of contemporary options in a praxis orientation toward the role of church in society demonstrates the ambivalence which pervades the thinking of liberation theologians, indeed, of most modern theologians. Defenders of orthodoxy are deeply committed to the normative criterion of truth as revealed through a Divine Logos and expessed in a logical theological formulation. At the same time, they are uneasy over the ease with which these orthodox formulas can be held in abstraction from human suffering. On the other hand, proponents of orthopraxy are radically committed to the normative criterion of human suffering under oppressive social and political structures, quite certain that God's truth is revealed through actions which are salvific rather than credal confessions which are sanctified through dogma. At the same time, they realize that no ideology has an eschatological confirmation, though it promises a historical future, and that liberation without transformation contains the seeds of its own destruction.

Orthodoxy, it is true, can lose touch with humanity through abandonment of the concrete situation for the sake of the eternal verities of theology. On the other hand, orthopraxy may fail precisely at the point where it expects more from human action than it can deliver. Where human actions undergirded by the idea of liberation become the praxiological criteria for a theology of ministry, humanity will inevitably betray its own cause.

In the end, praxis itself must contain an 'idea' and be sustained by ideological means, or it will disintegrate into aimless and inarticulate spasms of revolutionary and radical activity. Praxis as a theory of human life and, therefore, the right life, can be as relentless and ruthless as any doctrine, when pursued for the sake of itself. 'Ideas exist for the sake of life, not life for the sake of ideas', Dietrich Bonhoeffer once wrote. 'Where life itself is made into an idea, real life [created and redeemed life] is more thoroughly destroyed than by an other idea ... Only the life from

---

[9]T Speidell, 'The Incarnation as the Hermeneutical Criterion for Liberation and Reconciliation', in *SJT*, 40 (1987), p. 253.

God is purposeful and fulfilling, overcoming the contradiction between what is and what ought to be'.[10]

### III   Christopraxis: the Contemporary Humanity and Ministry of Christ

Only the life from God is purposeful and fulfilling.  But this life 'was the light of men' and this light is the 'true light that enlightens every man', wrote the Apostle John (John 1:4,9).  Life from God issues from the Word of God which became flesh and who 'was in the world' and who 'came to his own home' (John 1:10,11).  Grace and truth came through him, and his name is Jesus Christ.  This is the praxis of God.  It is the act of God himself, becoming human; and being human, he recognized and affirmed what is human through actions as well as words.  The truth came from above and the grace from below, both revealed simultaneously in his human and historical life as the act, or praxis of God.

This, as we have stated at the outset, is the authentic praxis of Christ's ministry through his humanity: objectively completed through his own vicarious life in solidarity with all humanity; eschatologically confirmed through his resurrection to be a living and faithful paraclete ever-present alongside of and on behalf of all humanity; and historically concealed as a healing and transforming presence in the life and ministry of the church.

This is Christopraxis.  Not a doctrine for which life is sacrificed, but the very being and life of God given for the sake of preserving and upholding human life.  Not an ideology or strategy which fights inhumanity for the sake of becoming human, but the very humanity of God which seeks the transformation of all that is inhuman in humanity.

This life of Christ is vicarious in the sense that he offered his own humanity as pledge for ours by offering up his own obedience to the Father as the faithful Son.  The bond between our

[10]D Bonhoeffer, *Meditating on the Word*, D McI Gracie (ed., ET) (Cambridge, 1986), p. 135.

humanity and his is not a metaphysical or mystical connection but is a filial bond - we are bound to him by the 'Spirit of Sonship' by which we have received his very own Spirit so that we too can cry, 'Abba, Father' (Rom. 8:15-17).

This life and humanity of Christ is eschatologically confirmed through his resurrection to be the true life of the Son of God. As our advocate, he continues to be present with us through the 'paraclete', the Holy Spirit, who continues to pledge the humanity of Jesus as the objective basis for our reconciliation with God and with each other. Christ not only 'sends' the Holy Spirit in his place, but through the Holy Spirit the life of God himself as the sending Father and the obedient and faithful Son encounters the world as a continuing act of reconciliation.

In this way, the vicarious life and humanity of Christ continues to exist in this world as concealed in the history and life of the church, which is his body. Both truth and grace are present in this 'praxis of Christ' which constitutes, as Barth once put it, both the 'heavenly history' and the 'earthly history' of Jesus Christ and his church. Both the doctrines of the church and its own praxis of ministry are thus bound to the reality of Christopraxis. Christopraxis is the act of God in Jesus Christ which occurred once and for all through his life as Incarnate Word, but which continues to occur through the mighty acts of revelation and reconciliation whereby the Holy Spirit glorifies Christ by coming into our sphere of historical and personal existence to manifest his resurrection power and presence (John 16:13,14; Rom. 8:9-11). Thus, revelation as well as reconciliation, true knowledge of God as well as true life with God, true worship as well as authentic ministry, are derived from out of the same structure of reality which I call Christopraxis.[11]

The church finds its true ministry in the upholding, healing and transformation of the humanity of others as already grasped and

---

[11] I have developed the concept of Christopraxis further as a basis for theological education for ministry in 'Christopraxis: Competence as as Criterion for Theological Education', *TSF Bulletin*, (Jan/Feb 1984), pp. 10-13.

reconciled to God through the humanity and ministry of Jesus Christ. This is our basic thesis. We have attempted to show that the humanity of Christ serves as a vicarious basis for the ministry of the church as well as for the salvation of sinners and their reconciliation to God. In the debate betwen orthodoxy and orthopraxy, we saw that there is a fundamental ambivalence in these two approaches, with a move toward a dialectical relation as the only solution. Our argument has been that the incarnation of God in Christ is thus considered not only to be a theological construct for establishing a true doctrine of salvation, but a contemporary praxis of ministry concealed in the historical form and practice of the church as a continuation of the humanity and ministry of Jesus Christ for the world.

The remainder of this essay is devoted to developing the implications of this understanding of Christopraxis as a starting point for a theology of ministry. When we look closely at the ministry of Christ himself, at least three primary aspects of his ministry can be developed as formative for the praxis of the church. Simply put, Jesus is the real *presence* of God with and for humanity; Jesus offers true *service* of humanity to God and of God to humanity; Jesus brings actual *transformation* of humanity through conversion and regeneration in the power of the Spirit.

In pledging his humanity as a vicarious representation of all humanity before God, Christ fulfilled a paracletic ministry. He became and continues to be the *advocate* for human persons under the burden of sin and oppression.

In consecrating his humanity as a two-fold service of God to humankind and humankind to God, he fulfilled a diaconal ministry. He became and continues to be the *leitourgos* for God in the service (*latreia*) of the gospel to the world and for humanity in the service rendered to God.

In yielding his humanity to the Spirit, he prepared humanity for the manifestation of the Kingdom of God; and in so doing, he fulfilled an empowering ministry. He became and continues to be

20

the *redeemer* of humanity, not only emancipating, but empowering human persons.

## A *Christopraxis as Paracletic Ministry*

Despite the variety of forms in which the word *paraclesis* is used in the New Testament, scholars generally agree that the original meaning of exhortation, or encouragement is qualified by the mode of Christ's own presence 'alongside' of and on behalf of those to whom this exhortation or encouragement is given. The specific promise of Jesus to his disciples is that he would not leave them as 'orphans' but would send 'another paraclete', the Holy Spirit to be with them (John 14:16). The intention of Jesus' words is clear. Even as he has been their advocate, standing with them and for them, even in their instability and unfaithfulness, so he will continue to do this through the presence of the Holy Spirit.

If we were to make a distinction between the mode of kerygma, didache, and paraclesis, it would be as follows. Were God to come to me only in the mode of kerygma, that could mean: God has come: be silent before him - my realities and interests do not really matter. The reality of the Kingdom takes precedence. Were God to come only in the mode of didache, that could mean: God has come: the road on which life has brought me no longer is important; he has another way for me. When God comes to me in the mode of paraclesis, it dawns upon me: God has come and he wants to live in my house and my situation. God enters my situation in its concrete historical reality, and he appears in it for that very purpose. Through the paracletic presence of the Holy Spirit, Jesus himself takes up my cause as his own.[12] Through this ministry of Christ in the power of the Holy Spirit, I am not simply addressed with the demands of the Kingdom of God, I am grasped by the love of God as Father, upheld by the intercession of God as Son, and made to share in the inner life of God himself through the indwelling Holy Spirit.

[12] I am indebted to Jacob Firet for the substance of this paragraph. *Dynamics in Pastoring* (Grand Rapids, 1986), (J Vriend, ET from the Dutch, *Het agogisch Moment in het pastoraal Optreden*, (Uitgeversmaatschappij JH Kok-Kampen, 1982)), p. 70.

21

Following this line of thought, the paracletic ministry of Jesus is grounded in the incarnation whereby in his true humanity he becomes the advocate, pledging his humanity on behalf of all others. This advocacy is more than an instrumental one, performed for the purpose of effecting legal atonement. The advocacy is the pledge of his humanity as the continuing representation of human persons to God as the basis for the mode of paraclesis carried out by the Holy Spirit. Thus, the Spirit has no incarnation of his own, nor does the Spirit become incarnate in the humanity of the church as the body of Christ. The church participates in the humanity of Christ as the objective basis for its own fellowship with God.

Yet, as we have seen, the incarnation is the pledge of the humanity of Jesus Christ on behalf of all human persons. Thus Christ is the advocate of all persons not merely those who are 'in Christ'. 'Through Christ' all persons have an advocate with the Father. This enables Paul to say: 'All this is from God, who through Christ reconciled us to himself and gave us the ministry of reconciliation; that is, in Christ God was reconciling the world to himself, not counting their trespasses against them, and entrusting to us the message of reconciliation' (2 Cor. 5:18-19).

This paracletic ministry of Jesus, of course, presupposes the kerygma as the announcement of this act of reconciliation. But even as the incarnation provides the basis for the kerygma in the humanity of Jesus Christ as the ground of reconciliation, so the continued humanity of Christ provides the ground for the paracletic ministry of the Holy Spirit and the kerygmatic message. Christ was present as the advocate of the people who had not yet heard the good news. The good news of the gospel was not only that God had taken upon himself the death that was the human dilemma because of sin, but that the human person, Jesus of Nazareth had been raised from the dead and affirmed to be the Son of God in power (Acts 2:22-24; Rom. 1:3-5). It is not merely through his death, but through his resurrection and life that Jesus continues to be the advocate for humanity before the

Father.

Christopraxis means that this paracletic ministry of Jesus is a pledge of his humanity to and for all human persons in the concrete historical, social, and moral dilemma of their existence. As the advocate for humanity, the criterion for what is authentically human is his own humanity, not a general principle of humanity. In his paracletic ministry, Jesus pledges his own humanity which has already passed through judgment and the penalty of death to and for the humanity of all persons. Jesus is not merely the advocate for the best of humanity, leaving the rest to their own fate. Rather, he is the advocate for all of humanity, bringing every human person into the place where no human distinctive, whether racial, sexual, or social, can serve as a criterion for relation with God or with one another.

Christopraxis in the mode of paraclesis is a summons to humanity to become truly human; it is an exhortation to move out of the place of sorrow and humiliation into a community of reconciliation, peace and dignity. Christopraxis as a form of the real presence of Christ is a pledge of comfort and consolation to the oppressed and broken. It will be the 'worldly' form of the presence of Christ in many cases, or the 'non-religious' form of Christ's presence in the world, as Bonhoeffer came to see it.

For the church, Christopraxis means that actions which involve advocacy for the full humanity of persons have a priority and authority grounded in the humanity of Christ himself. The strategy of paracletic ministry is non-negotiable in terms of advocacy for persons who suffer discrimination, oppression, and human torment of any kind. This strategy is not derived from ideological concerns nor from general principles of humanity itself. The strategy of advocacy as a form of Christopraxis is the strategy of God himself, enacted in Jesus Christ, and through Jesus Christ for the sake of the world. The tactics by which this strategy must be carried out are contingent upon many factors, including resources, short term versus long range objectives, not to mention the specific sense of the leading of the Holy Spirit.

As Barth once said, the church may have to engage in tactical withdrawal from the world at times, but never strategic withdrawal. Jesus himself made tactical moves both toward and away from confrontation with the world, but never strategic withdrawal. Having pledged his humanity for the sake of the humanity of others, he was the faithful paraclete until the very end. The humanity of Christ and his ministry in and for the sake of the world constitutes the criterion for the humanity and the ministry of the church.

## B *Christopraxis as Diaconal Ministry*

The true vocation of Jesus was grounded in his personal being as the Son of the Father. In assuming the role of the servant, he fulfilled this inner life of service and thus revealed the true service (*latreia*) which mediates between God and humankind. He did not become a Son through his obedience and service, but because he was a Son he learned obedience and thus became the source of salvation for others (Heb. 5:8,9).

The root of the diaconal ministry of Jesus is thus found in his ministry of service grounded in his life as the Son to the Father. He is the true *leitourgos*, or minister of God (Heb. 8:2). This *latreia*, or service of Christ, is a primary event in the sense that it is the actuality of community between human beings and God from which all possibility of community proceeds. Here again, we must say that the true diaconal ministry of Christ is not formed by some general principle of servanthood, or service. Rather he is the *diakonos* of God and of human persons because he is the *leitourgos* of God.

This *latreia* of Christ is performed through his true humanity in a two-fold way. First, he is faithful in his service of the Father by extending the gospel to the world. In pledging his own humanity to and for others, as we have seen, he is the bearer of divine love, compassion and mercy toward persons who have no righteousness of their own. Christopraxis is thus more than advocacy, it is a ministry of the grace of God to those who are without grace. It is a ministry of the love of God to those who are unloved, and even unlovable. It is a ministry of the forgiveness and healing of God

24

to those who are condemned and broken. It is a ministry of help to the helpless, of caring to the uncared for, and of food for the hungry, clothing for the naked, and shelter for the homeless. This is the ministry of God himself to those in the world who are 'without God' and thus whose own humanity is distorted and deformed. It is the ministry of one who has already pledged his own humanity, and so it is a ministry with 'no strings attached'. This divine *latreia* has as its goal the humanizing of humanity. Its criterion is not merely human need, but divine love. Its justification is that it is a fulfilment of divine intentionality, not in the response it produces.[13]

The second movement of this *latreia* of Christ is the offering of the true service from human beings to God, of praise, worship, and thanksgiving. The healing of the ten lepers was an act of Christopraxis by which Christ mediated the healing power of God to each of them in their concrete situation. Only one returned to give thanks - a fact noted by Jesus with some amazement (Luke 17:10-19). There is no indication that the divine *latreia* of healing was revoked for the nine who did not return to give thanks. This service of thanksgiving to God Jesus himself offered up as a vicarious intercession and mediation on their behalf. Here he pledged his own humanity not merely as an advocate, but as their priest, offering up on their behalf what they failed to do in their own humanity. Thus the church pledges itself to the humanity of those who are oppressed as well as the oppressors for the sake of the true humanity of both as an act of reconciliation. A service of repentance as well as a service of

---

[13] The comment by Dietrich Ritschl is *a propos*: '... the goal of *diaconia* is not the attuning of those who receive the *diaconia* to the faith of those who perform it. The basis of *diaconia* should not be confused with its goal: *diaconia* in solidarity with the poor and those without rights can be practised without the secret aim of convincing the recipients of the basis of the *diaconia*. The conversion of the recipients of works of *diaconia* to the faith of those providing it is a particular part and additional miracle of the presence of the Spirit of God. It is not the goal of the diaconal activity'. D Ritschl, *The Logic of Theology* (Philadelphia, 1987) (J Bowden, ET from the German, *zur logik der Theologie, Kurze Darstellung der Zusammenhänge theologischer Grundgedanken* (Munich, 1984)), pp. 270-1.

compassion is bound up in the humanity and ministry of Christ through his church.

Christopraxis is the continuing humanity and ministry of Christ expressed through this two-fold *latreia*. This is a diaconal form of service through which the humanity and the humanizing of others is seen as the object of Christ's own ministry in the world. The church has been granted a share in this service of Christ by the extending of its own life in to the world where those 'without God' in the sense of being under torment and bondage are touched with healing and healing actions. This Christopraxis unites advocacy and diaconia so that actions of 'being there' are accompanied by actions of 'bringing there' tangible assistance and deliverance. Christopraxis as the praxis of the ministry of the church takes seriously both the kerygma and didache of Jesus - that the Kingdom of God is given to the poor, the oppressed and the powerless, and that Christ himself is present in the act of ministry to such (cf. Matt. 25:31-46).

## C *Christopraxis as Empowering Ministry*
We have shown that Jesus pledged his humanity as the true advocate of all human beings, and that he offered through his humanity the true service of God for the humanizing of persons as well as offering on behalf of all persons the true worship and response due to God. A third aspect of Christopraxis must also be shown in order to complete the ministry of Christ through his humanity. As Advocate and Leitourgos, Christ is present also in the world through his humanity as Redeemer.

In yielding his humanity to the fullness of the Spirit, Jesus received on behalf of all persons the gift, or *charism* of the Spirit. Following Barth, who developed his theology under the three-fold rubric of God as Creator, Reconciler and Redeemer, we see that Christopraxis includes not only reconciliation through Christ, but redemption as the transformation and liberation of humanity in the life of the Spirit. Christ transformed humanity by receiving the Spirit into his own humanity and by sending the Spirit as the Spirit of his own resurrected life to redeem those who are in bondage and captivity.

26

The Holy Spirit, given at Pentecost, releases the Spirit of Christ himself in the world, reversing the confusion and division of humanity at Babel, enacting the ecclesial reality of liberation and reconciliation accomplished through the life, death and resurrection of Jesus. The ministry of God as Redeemer in his particular work as Holy Spirit, commands and enables us to be what we are and are becoming in and through Christ, to the glory of the Father. This provides a truly evangelical basis for social repentance, whereby the very structures of human social and political existence are opened up for redemption.

Christopraxis means liberation, or emancipation, as the transforming work of redemption actualized in human lives. We realize that here we are touching most directly the key theme of liberation theology as a form of praxis. We use the word emancipation cautiously in this context, for it carries ideological overtones which could easily mislead us. In his penetrating analysis of emancipation and redemption, Johann Metz suggests that: 'any emancipation cast as a universal historical totality is dangerously abstract and contradictory. A universal theory of emancipation without a soteriology remains caught under an irrational mechanism of exoneration or guilt-repression. A history of emancipation without a history of redemption, faced with the concrete history of suffering, subjugates the historical subject to new irrational constraints and either man is forced into a transcendental suspension of his own historical responsibility or he is forced into irreconcilable enmity or finally to negate himself as a subject'.[14] Metz is concerned for a praxis of Christian presence in the world that takes seriously the history of suffering, both of the past generations as well as the present and future. He will not surrender the redemptive reality of Christ to mere 'spiritual' expressions of faith and so turn away from solidarity with and redemption of actual human situations. Nonetheless, he fears that a praxis which has as its 'gospel' emancipation as an historically realizable goal will fail humanity as surely as an orthodoxy which is blind to historical realities.

---

[14]Metz, *op. cit.*, p. 127.

The suggestion by Metz that a 'praxis of imitation' of Christ be viewed as the appropriate Christian presence in the world through solidarity in its 'pathic structures' falls short of what we mean here by Christopraxis as a ministry of empowerment. Metz does insist that there be an 'apocalyptic sting' to this 'imitation' of Christ, thus preserving the eschatological dimension.[15] In this way he seeks to overcome the ambivalence between orthodoxy and orthopraxy. The history of redemption cannot be a history of freedom, Metz argues, without also being a history of suffering. There is much with which we can agree in what Metz offers by way of Christian praxis. There is what Bonhoeffer called, 'participating in the sufferings of God' in a godless world. There is what the Apostle called, 'completing what is lacking in Christ's afflictions for the sake of his body' (Col. 1:24). We can follow Metz in the direction he is taking, when he speaks of a praxis which '... tries to keep the Christian memory of redemption alive in narrative form as a dangerous and liberating memory of redeemed freedom ...'.[16]

But in the end there is little said about a ministry of enmpowerment and the reality of the Kingdom of God as the eschatological and transforming power of the Holy Spirit. Christopraxis means the real presence of Christ as the one who has been raised from the dead and the one who is coming again, but also as the *eschatos* who is even now present in the world. We are now, in this present time, the New Testament argues, given the 'power to become children of God' (John 1:19). The Apostle Paul views this as 'empowerment' not merely 'entitlement'. We are no longer subject to the 'principalities and powers' (Col. 2:15). Through Christ and in the power of his Spirit, there is both entitlement and empowerment. Being children of God is much more than a 'dangerous memory' which challenges the natural and historical determinism which stands over our existence as impersonal fate. It is that too! But it is also a 'dangerous life' in that the Holy Spirit brings the humanity

[15]*Ibid.*, pp. 73ff.
[16]*Ibid.*, p. 133.

of the risen Lord Jesus Christ as the presence of the Redeemer himself, not merely a history of redemption.

Christopraxis as a form of the ministry of the church expects the eschatological presence of Christ to be released as a 'charismatic' experience. This has the danger of succumbing to the temptation of pietism, individualism, and corporate inwardness as a variety of Christian experience. To the extent that this happens, it is no longer 'dangerous' as a manifestation of the Kingdom of God in the form of Christ's real presence. The authentic *charism* which empowers is the charismatic power which redeems humanity from the social, political, and institutional powers which dehumanize. But here too, we must realise as Metz cautions us, total emancipation can become a utopian vision, not an eschatological reality fulfilled in history. If there are manifestations of this eschatological reality of liberation, they may serve as 'signs' that evil has already been 'exorcised' through the presence of the redeemer in world history.

Christopraxis as the critical intersection of the new humanity of Christ with the structures of humanity in this world is not unfamiliar with the phenomena of exorcism, in the broad sense of the word. There is an 'ordinary exorcism' by which dehumanizing forces, both personal and impersonal are challenged and disarmed of their power. What ideological praxis sees as primarily a struggle between an inhuman social order and a human social order is understood through Christopraxis to be a 'power encounter' between the old, unredeemed human order and the new, redeemed order, with Christ himself the authority (*exousia*). This ordinary exorcism has as its criterion not humanity as a general principle, but the person of Christ who, in his own redeemed humanity, pledges himself to human beings who suffer under the old order. The goal of this ministry is not merely deliverance from evil nor emancipation from structures which bind, but empowerment to be truly human under even circumstances and situations which are not yet redeemed. For a praxis of liberation, this is an unacceptable idea, for it appears to compromise the very nature of liberation itself. For this kind of praxis, only the attainment of the idea of

29

liberation in actuality grants the entitlement to be considered human in a real sense. For Christopraxis, however, entitlement is given through Christ's own praxis of advocacy and empowerment. Liberation is thus the goal of that which is authentically human, rather than humanity being the goal of liberation. The empowerment of Christ is to suffer under this tension and even contradiction 'humanly' as he himself does. No warrant should be assumed here, however, for justification of structures which oppose the humanity of Christ as pledged to others. Failure for those structures to recognize the humanity of others is to oppose Christ (God) himself.

This empowerment might take the form of mental, emotional and physical therapy wherein the goal is the humanization of persons through restoration to fellowship with God and the human community. This empowerment might take the form of advocacy for social justice where there is injustice, diaconia which provides for creaturely well being and comfort, as well as the breaking down of racial and sexual discrimination which 'disempowers' persons. If there on occasion be the need for 'extraordinary exorcism' in order to break the hold which evil forces and structures have over human beings, the least dramatic form may be what is called 'demonic exorcism'. While such phenomena, ambiguous as they are, tend to attract attention as 'charismatic' displays of divine power over evil, there is usually little concern for the empowerment of the humanity of the persons supposedly exorcised. Christopraxis as a ministry of Christ in the world does not shrink from such 'power encounters', but values empowerment of persons as a more valid criterion of the ministry of Christ than power over evil itself.

The authentic *charism* which liberates is not the spirit of power, but the Spirit of Christ. The authentic charismatic ministry is one which empowers blacks in South Africa to participate in the franchise of full membership in the human race as defined socially, politically and spiritually. It is a ministry which empowers women to have full parity in every structure of society; it is a ministry which empowers the poor, the marginalized, the weak, and the homeless to live meaningful and comfortable lives as human beings created in God's image. The authentic charismatic ministry is one which disarms the church of its pride and privilege, causing it to repent, and to enact repentance toward God through responsible service toward the world which God loves. Thomas Smail has said it well: 'The charismatic Christian with his world-affirming approach and his awareness of both the demonic and the prophetic should be among those who can catch the vision. God wants to give in local churches structures of relationship that have their roots in the central relationship to himself, but that express themselves horizontally and practically in such a way as to challenge the oppressive structures of society in which the church lives'.[17] Charismatic Christians, Smail continues, should be as much concerned for the socially demonic in the form of oppressive structures as for the personally demonic. Exactly! The incarnation is not a supernatural phenomenon, but a truly human occurrence of the natural in three spheres, in place, power, and time.[18]

If there be an orthodox theology, let it be accountable to this Christopraxis as the primary dogma, seeking faithfully to interpret it on the basis of the humanity and ministry of Christ. If there be an authentic orthopraxy, let it dare to submit its concerns and its agenda for the healing and hope of humanity to the One who is the Advocate, the Leitourgos, and the Redeemer of all humanity. If there be an authentic church, let it be found where Christ has his praxis - let it pay the price of its orthodoxy in its true ministry and so be empowered by Christ himself.

---

[17]Thomas Smail, *The Forgotten Father* (Grand Rapids, 1980), p. 179.

[18]This is a point made well by Dietrich Ritschl: 'The natural affects human existence by limiting it in three ways, in place, power and time. These are more fundamental anthropological constants than the human drives and desires to which so much attention is paid in classical theology'. *Op. cit.*, p. 232.

# 2

# Salvation as Healing and Humanization

JOHN DE GRUCHY

*'To hold out Christ to the world is not only to
hold out personal salvation, but to give to all
their humanity'. James Torrance.*[1]

There are three areas which need exploration in any dialogue
between Christian theology and medicine, each integrally related
to the other. The first is medical ethics; the second concerns the
practice of medicine, the care of the sick, and the healing
ministry of the church; and the third is the more fundamental issue
of the philosophical, ideological or theological basis for medical
science and practice. In countries like South Africa, where first
world medicine encounters third world needs in a situation of
socio-political crisis and change, these areas of dialogue take on a
particularly urgent and demanding character. But as it is the third
area which in large measure determines and shapes both ethics and
practice, this is where we have to begin if we are to engage in
fruitful dialogue and co-operation for the sake of humanity.

## I Salvation as Healing and Humanization

In traditional societies there has always been a close correlation
between religion and healing, priest and healer. This much is
already clear in the Hippocratic Oath which begins and ends
invoking the gods,[2] but it remains true even where
modernization has become a reality. The acceptance of secularized
Western medicine by blacks in South Africa, for example, has not
resulted in the rejection of the more traditional approaches to

---

[1] JB Torrance, 'Interpreting the Word by the Light of Christ or the Light of
Nature', a paper presented to the Theological Society of South Africa, August
1986.

[2] See H Kung, *Eternal Life? Life after death as a Medical, Philosophical, and
Theological Problem* (New York, 1985), p. 154.

32

healing.[3] Modern medicine without traditional forms of healing is, in fact, regarded as inadequate. One of the reasons for the enormous growth of African indigenous churches this century has been their ability to provide this service, and so contribute to the healing of the sick and the humanization of societies of dislocated and dehumanized people.

The felt need for such healing and humanization is found in all communities, however, irrespective of race, culture or class. Consider as an historical example the emergence of Christian Science amongst the middle and upper classes of New England society in the nineteenth century. Whatever its weaknesses, Christian Science addressed a need which was being met neither by the churches nor the medical practitioners of the day.[4] The Pentecostal movement, which started at the turn of the twentieth century, responded to a similar need with its practice of faith-healing amongst the socially disinherited. Similar developments are presently taking place amongst 'fearful whites' in South Africa.[5] One result of such therapeutic religious movements has been the gradual reawakening of an interest in religion and healing within the so-called mainline churches. Today services of healing are not uncommon in many churches, so that within white society as much as within black, and amongst all classes, the work of the medical practitioner is often supplemented or even supplanted by spiritual healers of one kind or another.

However one evaluates phenomena such as faith-healing it is important to recognize that churches which practice some form of spiritual healing are generally in continuity not only with traditional religions, but also with their biblical roots. The

---

[3] See SD Edwards, 'Attitudes to Diease and Healing in a South African Context', and V Buhrmann, 'Some Aspects of Healing Among Black Psychiatric Patients', in GC Oosthuizen (ed.), *Religion Alive* (Cape Town, 1986).

[4] See LD Weatherhead, *Psychology, Religion and Healing* (London, 1951), pp. 160ff.

[5] See ES Morram and L Schlemmer, *Faith for the Fearful: An Investigation into new churches in the greater Durban Areas* (Durban, 1984).

healing ministry of Jesus of Nazareth was a central element of his ministry, just as it was of charismatic Judaism at the time.[6] Moreover, the healing ministry of Jesus was comprehensive - forgiveness, reconciliation and, if need be, restitution, were all part of the healing process. Indeed, in many instances in the Gospels, to be 'saved' means not only being healed of some physical ailment but becoming a whole person in relationship with others.[7]

In fact, the New Testament regards Jesus' and the early Christian community's healing ministry as integral to the proclamation of the kingdom of God, a sign of the salvific purposes of God. Healing was a sign that the kingdom of God had broken into history in Jesus, and it pointed towards the liberation of humanity from the bondage of decay, and its restoration in Christ at the end time. This understanding of salvation as the restoration of humanity is, of course, the very antithesis of how it has been understood in the privatized and individualistic piety of much Christianity since the Enlightenment. It is, rather, consonant with the Hebrew prophets' vision of *shalom* which may well function as a synonym for salvation understood as healing and humanization. For *shalom*, normally translated 'peace', is more appropriately translated as 'wholeness', embracing not only physical well-being but human flourishing in its widest sense, including at its centre, the flourishing of social justice. We shall return to this further on.

In one form or another, the connection between healing and Christian faith has been maintained within the churches and sectarian Christian movements through the centuries. The first hospitals, as we know, were religious foundations. This connection is still maintained in many hospitals and clinics in South Africa as elsewhere which are often as much centres of humanization as they are of healing. Nevertheless, since the rise of modern science and the eighteenth century Enlightenment a fracturing of this tradition has gradually taken place in Western

---

[6]G Vermes, *Jesus the Jew* (London, 1976), pp. 58ff.

[7]D Hoch, *Salvation and Healing* (London, 1958).

European culture. The story of this separation is well known, and needs no repeating.[8] But it is important to remember that the separation of Christian faith and theology from the healing sciences went hand in hand with the privatization of Christian piety and the reduction of salvation to the rescuing of individual souls for life in heaven.

## II Consequences of a Fractured Tradition

Whatever the inadequacies of Fritjof Capra's critique of modern medicine in *The Turning Point*, there is more than sufficient substance to his claim that the mechanistic/dualistic worldview, inherited from Newton and Descartes, has become the dominant ideology not only in modern medicine but also for much of modern psychology, economics, and politics,[9] and, we might add, Christian thought and practice. Capra describes the significance of the Newtonian/Cartesian worldview for medical science in the following way: 'Before Descartes, most healers had addressed themselves to the interplay of body and soul, and had treated their patients within the context of their social and spiritual environment. As their world views changed over the ages, so did their views of illness and their methods of treatment, but their approaches were usually concerned with the whole patient. Descartes' philosophy changed this situation profoundly. His strict division between mind and body led physicians to concentrate on the body machine and to neglect the psychological, social and environmental aspects of illness. From the seventeenth century on, progress in medicine closely followed the developments in biology and the other natural sciences. As the perspective of biomedical science shifted from the study of bodily organs and their functions to that of cells and, finally, to the study of molecules, study of the phenomenon of healing was progressively neglected, and physicians found it more and more difficult to deal with the interdependence of body and mind'.[10] The consequences for the practice of medicine have been enormous

---

[8] See IG Barbour, *Issues in Science and Religion* (London, 1972).

[9] F Capra, *The Turning Point : Science, Society and the Rising Culture* (London, 1982).

[10] *Ibid.*, p. 122.

and are well known.

Put crudely, it has resulted in the treatment of cases rather than people, repair work on malfunctioning parts of the human machine rather than the enabling of the healing of the person, and a failure to treat people in relation to their social environment, cultural and religious values, and the deeper ethical and spiritual needs of their personhood. This judgment is, of course, a generalization yet it is one which is increasingly acknowledged by medical scientists and practitioners themselves. Here we see most acutely the impact of worldview or ideology on medical ethics and practice, and the challenge this presents to theology to get its own house in order and to help provide an alternative basis for medicine.

By way of illustration of the problem, let me share a case history which I received from a hospital chaplain. The chaplain was telephoned one evening by a ward sister and requested to visit a cancer patient who was in great distress and who was asking for such a visit. The chaplain spent several hours with her, listening, sharing, praying, and when he left the patient was at peace, indeed, able to articulate calmly fears of death and work through them. Several other issues relating to her family situation, which were also part of her distress, were also dealt with. The next morning the chaplain enquired of the ward sister how the patient was. The conversation went something like this: 'Sister: "Oh, she's alright; she had a bit of an upset in the night, but she slept it off".
Chaplain: "Yes, I know, I was with her, I just wondered how she had slept".
Sister: "I know nothing of that".'
The chaplain goes on: 'The report of the night staff simply said: "Patient was greatly disturbed. Doctor prescribed valium after which she slept well". This highlights the experience I frequently have as a chaplain. Techniques, diagnosis and procedures are reported on in detail, but our ministry to the person is not seen as of value or effective in the healing process, as in this instance where the sister who called for the chaplain's help was the same

sister who wrote the report'. What is at issue here is not whether the chaplain's visit and ministry should be included in the medical report, but the mindset and worldview which is operating. It is a mindset which can see the value of valium in dealing with human distress, but is unable to see the role which personal care and spiritual counsel plays. The opposite mindset, but one which shares the same philosophical basis, is evident in those forms of Christianity which show concern for the soul but little for the body, and even less for the social environment within which people live.

All of this is a denial of the biblical worldview and its social anthropology, indeed, it is a radical denial of the incarnational character of Christianity and a relapse into something akin to the gnosticism against which the New Testament protests so strongly. The Cartesian split between mind and matter (mirrored in the separation of nature and grace, creation and redemption) found a ready acceptance within the church not least because it was already deeply affected by neo-Platonic dualism, and had not sufficiently resisted the gnostic idea that matter and therefore the physical body is base and inevitably in conflict with the spirit. Hence such aberrations as the disparaging of sexuality, and the regarding of people as disembodied souls who need to be redeemed, even if this means physical maiming or death on the inquisitors' rack. Likewise the popular notion that religion has to do with the spiritual alone and must not become involved in issues affecting society or the body politic, a notion reinforced by such dualistic doctrines as the Lutheran 'two kingdoms'.

Thus, though much modern medicine and traditional Christianity start from opposite ends (medicine concerned about the body alone, and theology about the soul alone), both have to overcome the same obstacle within themselves and within their respective constituencies if they are to recapture the holistic character of salvation as *shalom*. From a Christian perspective this requires that both medicine and theology break free from captivity to the Cartesian and Newtonian worldview and its theological correlates, and come together on a new foundation in which creation and redemption are brought together and salvation is understood as the restoration of humanity in its fullness.

## III Rediscovering the Holistic Paradigm

Capra's critique of modern medicine derives in large measure from the fact that he, as a physicist, regards the scientific paradigm which shapes modern medicine as outdated, and incapable of meeting the crisis within which we find ourselves today. As he points out, modern physics since Einstein has increasingly broken free from the Newtonian and Cartesian model and developed a new paradigm. 'In contrast to the mechanistic Cartesian view of the world, the world view emerging from modern physics can be characterized by words like organic, holistic, and ecological. It might also be called a systems view, in the sense of general systems theory. The universe is no longer seen as a machine, made up of a multitude of objects, but has to be pictured as one indivisible, dynamic whole whose parts are essentially interrelated and can be understood only as patterns of a cosmic process'.[11]

This 'new' paradigm is, in some important respects, an ancient one. It correlates, for example, with many religious traditions in the East and the West, as well as those of Africa, North America and elsewhere. Capra himself regards it as best expressed in the Tao vision of reality. But those who are familiar with the worldview and anthropology of the Bible will immediately recognize that it has affinities with biblical tradition as well. Thus Aubrey Johnson begins his seminal mongraph on *The Vitality of the Individual in the Thought of Ancient Israel* by saying: 'Any attempt at a successful interpretation of the Bible seems bound to take note of the fact that Israelite thinking, like that of the so-called 'primitive' peoples of the present day, is predominantly synthetic. It is characterized by what has been called the grasping of a totality. Phenomena are perceived for the most part as being in some sort of relation; they have a share, or (to adopt Levy Bruhl's expression) they 'participate', in some

[11]*Ibid.*, p. 66.

sort of whole.   This recognition of the mental activity of the Israelites as predominantly synthetic, the awareness of totality, is important.   It is, perhaps, hardly too much to say that it is the "Open Sesame" which unlocks the secrets of the Hebrew language and reveals the riches of the Israelite mind'.[12]

Central to this biblical holistic understanding of reality is, first of all, an anthropology which regards human beings as psycho-somatic wholes, so much so that 'physical functions have close physical associations'.[13]   Secondly, human beings are never perceived in any individualistic way but always in relation to society as a whole.   Thus scholars speak of the 'corporate personality' (Wheeler Robinson) of Israel in terms of which the individual has to be understood.   In fact, this corporate personality is so real that the sins of any member of the society become the responsibility of the whole, and, likewise, the faithful obedience of one person can be redemptive for the whole of Israel.

Similarly in Pauline, and subsequently Irenaean, theology the concepts of humanity fragmented 'in Adam' and restored 'in Christ' express most powerfully the sociality not only of fallen humanity but also of Christ as redeemer.   Indeed, as James Torrance might well remind us, the 'new' paradigm of which Capra writes, is consonant with Irenaeus' concept of the 'recapitulation' of humanity in Christ.[14]   Few twentieth century theologians have developed this theme as significantly as Dietrich Bonhoeffer,[15] and on this basis, particularly focussed on the concept of 'deputyship' (*Stellvertretung*), drawn out its consequences for Christian social responsibility.[16]

---

[12] A Johnson, *The Vitality of the Individual in the Thought of Ancient Israel* (Cardiff, 1949), p. 7.

[13] *Ibid.*, p. 9.

[14] Irenaeus, *Against Heresies*, III.18-19.

[15] See his passing reference in D Bonhoeffer, *Letters and Papers from Prison* (New York, 1971), p. 170.

[16] See CJ Green, *Bonhoeffer : the Sociality of Christ and Humanity* (Missoula, 1972).

The biblical sense of corporate responsibility is extended to the creation as a whole, and therefore demands husbandry of the earth and its resources. Thus, human well-being, or *shalom*, has to do not only with the physical and psychical (including spiritual) health of the individual, but with the health of the social and political order, and the vital balance of nature. Hence, biblical anthropology neither asserts the primacy of the soul or the body, but of life as a whole, what Jürgen Moltmann refers to as 'the *Gestalt*- the configuration or total pattern - of the lived life' as this develops within our historical and cultural environment.[17] Our relationship to God is in terms of this *Gestalt*, so much so that, as the creation narratives and the sagas which climax in the collapse of the Tower of Babel (Gen. 1-11) depict, the breakdown of *shalom* at any point affects everything else.

In other words, the paradigm which has emerged in modern physics, and which is beginning to re-shape science as a whole, is one which relates positively to the roots of Christian theology in the Bible. As such it is not a totally new paradigm, but one which has in a real sense been lost and which needs retrieval and restatement for today.[18] Thus just as the Newtonian worldview led to the separation of medical science and theology, and reinforced the dualism of much Christianity, so the emerging holistic worldview relates modern physics and biblical understanding and makes it possible for theology and medicine to discover each other again and thus jointly serve humanity.

The emerging holistic paradigm, as Capra describes it, and the holistic biblical vision of *shalom*, are not, however, identical. Indeed, there is a critical tension between them. After all, the biblical vision (as distinct from both Tao and modern physics) assumes a transcendent, personal God who is dynamically related to but not part of nature. Moreover, this God shapes and controls

---

[17] J Moltmann, *God in Creation : A New Theology of Creation and the Spirit of God* (San Fransisco, 1985), p. 259.

[18] See TF Torrance, *Transformation and Convergence in the Frame of Knowledge: Explorations in the Interrelations of Scientific and Theological Enterprise* (Grand Rapids, 1984), especially ch. 7.

history according to purposes of justice, righteousness, redemption and therefore *shalom*. Central to the creation narratives is the awareness that social and human failure result from the breakdown of the relationship between God, on the one hand, and human beings and societies on the other. Implicit in this breakdown is the misuse of human freedom, and especially the desire for deification or absolutism. The Bible is acutely aware of evil as a power that corrupts what is good. This means, *inter alia*, that while creation is a whole it is also fallen and not self-sufficient.

The biblical commitment to a transcendent source of life, meaning and value within its holistic worldview, has important ramifications for medical science, just as it has for theology and Christian faith and practice. Firstly, it is this which injects a demythologizing, iconoclastic dynamism into history[19] which, in part, enables the emergence of modern science within the West despite the protest of the church and some theologians of the day. But it is also this which provides a theological basis for a much needed 'hermeneutics of suspicion' which can enable us to discern the ideological biases determining the practice of medicine in favour of the wealthy and to the detriment of the disadvantaged and poor.

Secondly, the biblical commitment to a transcendent God, while allowing and even enabling the development of modern science, places limits on any autonomous or absolute claims it might have. And it does so for the sake of the *humanum*, the well-being of humans and society, or salvation understood as the restoration of humanity. From this perspective, science and technology, like anything else, cannot be autonomous or value-free. By claiming autonomy, and then proceeding to make absolute claims, it becomes a law unto itself free from any ethical constraints. Science thereby plays the role of God, with scientists its high priests. This forces us back to ask the question of the identity of God, or how are we to understand

[19]See H Frankfort *et al.*, *Before Philosophy* (Baltimore, 1971), pp. 241ff.

ultimate reality - which is ultimately the fundamental question on the search for a theology of medicine.

If we are to develop a holistic basis upon which theology and faith can be reintegrated with medical science and practice in the healing process, from a Christian perspective we need to speak of scientific integrity rather than autonomy. By this I mean a commitment to scientific method which takes seriously the fact that science is not an absolute but a servant of human well-being and flourishing. Its integrity as a science is integrally related to its integrity as a truly human project, and therefore an endeavour which relates responsibly to those values which make the *humanus* possible. If medical science proceeds in this way then it correlates with the biblical holistic yet transcendent worldview and the new scientific paradigm, thus enabling medicine to relate creatively to Christianity in the healing process. This has far-reaching implications for restoring the broken link between the theology and Christian faith on the one hand, and the science and art of healing on the other, and doing so in relation to the social context and the crises within which we now live.

The shift from one paradigm to another is a complex phenomenon, and one which has been well described by Thomas Kuhn in *The Structure of Scientific Revolutions*. Of particular interest to us is his observation that: 'The transition from a paradigm in crisis to a new one from which a new tradition of normal science can emerge is far from a cumulative process, one achieved by an articulation or extension of the old paradigm. Rather it is a reconstruction of the field from new fundamentals, a reconstruction that changes some of the field's most elementary theoretical generalizations as well as many of its paradigm methods and applications. During the transition period there will be a large but never complete overlap between the problems that can be solved by the old and by the new paradigm. But there will also be a decisive difference in the modes of solution. When the transition is complete, the profession will have changed its view of the field, its methods, and its goals'.[20] We are, I suggest, in

[20]TS Kuhn, *The Structure of Scientific Revolutions*, 2nd edn. (Chicago,

such a period of transition which, though it will not be the last, certainly opens up new possibilities and opportunities. It is the theologian's task to facilitate this process through supportive yet critical (including self-critical) dialogue. One important place to begin is by examining the question of the meaning of health.

## IV The Meaning of Health
Paul Tillich visited Germany shortly after the end of the Second World War. On his return to the United States he preached a sermon entitled 'On Healing' which began with these observations: 'Recently I spent three months in Germany and what I saw was a sick people, sick as a whole and sick as individuals. Their faces were shaped by burdens too heavy to be carried, by sorrows too deep to be forgotten. And what their faces expressed, their words confirmed: tales of horror, stories of pain and despair, anxieties dwelling in their blood, confusions and self-contradictions disturbing their minds. And if you look deeper into them you find guilt-feeling, sometimes expressed, mostly repressed ... But within this nation I found people who were healthy, not because the sickness was not written in their faces also. But something else was in them, a healing power, making them whole in spite of their disruption, making them serene in spite of their sorrow, making them examples for all of us, examples of what could and should happen to us!'[21] Tillich's observations bring us back to the question of the meaning of health, a question which is of fundamental importance if we are trying to understand the role of Christian faith in the healing process. What, for example, is the Christian understanding of being healthy? Or, to put it differently, what is the purpose of health? As Moltmann points out, the answers to such questions vary greatly in the course of human history, and not all definitions of health are necessarily healthy themselves.

The answer to such questions must surely lie in our understanding of the meaning and goal of life. Health is that which enables us to be fully human in relation to ourselves, our society and our environment.[22] This means that even a person who is

1970), pp. 84ff.

[21]P Tillich, *The Boundaries of our Being* (London, 1973), pp. 176ff.

[22]See R Dubos, *The Mirage of Health* (New York, 1979).

physically disabled, or, indeed, terminally ill, may nevertheless be more healthy than the self-centred hedonist for whom a healthy body has become a fetish. Reflecting on this, Karl Barth insisted that sickness and health are relative terms. 'Sickness is obviously negative in relation to health. It is partial impotence to exercise those functions. It hinders man in his exercise of them by burdening, hindering, troubling and threatening him, and causing him pain. But sickness as such is not necessarily impotence to be as man. The strength to be this, so long as one is still alive, can also be the strength and therefore the health of the sick person. And if health is the strength for human existence, even those who are seriously ill can will to be healthy without any optimism or illusions regarding their condition'.[23] Indeed, if physical health as normally understood becomes a supreme value this really implies, says Moltmann, a 'morbid attitude to health'. 'Being human is equated with being healthy. This leads to the suppression of illness in the individual life, and means that the sick are pushed out of the life of society and kept out of the public eye. To turn the idea of health into an idol in this way is to rob the human being of the true strength of his humanity. Every serious illness which he has to suffer plunges him into a catastrophe, robs him of his confidence in life, and destroys his own sense of value'.[24]

Our understanding of healing, then, implies an anthropology, an understanding of what it means to be a human being, but this in turn implies a sociology, for human beings do not live in isolation from each other. This is central to any religious faith and tradition; it is also implicit within the practice of medicine, usually as an unexamined *a priori* assumption, and often derived from what we now recognize to be an inadequate worldview.

This leads us directly to discern that health and healing are integrally related to our life in society. Recent ecumenical studies on the healing ministry of the church have pointed to the interconnection between health and justice, and reminded us that

[23] See K Barth, *CD* III/4, pp. 357ff.

[24] Moltmann, *op. cit.*, p. 273.

physical sickness is integrally related to an unhealthy socio-political environment, [25] a factor which has become only too apparent in many modern societies, not least South Africa. By way of example, we may refer to the inevitable effect which bad living and working conditions (housing etc.) have to do with our health. Thus social injustice needs to be recognized, as both Charles Dickens and Frederick Engels saw so clearly in nineteenth century England, as a health hazard. [26] It is too easily forgotten that much of the ill-health in our society stems from bad living and working conditions, that is, our inhumanity rather than our concern for humanity. In his Latin American diary, *Graçias!*, Henry Nouwen has this pertinent observation about poverty: 'Poverty is so much more than a lack of money, lack of food, or lack of decent living quarters. Poverty creates marginal people, people who are separated from that whole network of ideas, services, facilities, and opportunities that support human beings in times of crisis. When the poor get sick, have handicapped children, or are the victims of an accident, no help seems available. The poor are left to their own minimal resources'. [27] Thus a concern for health cannot be separated from a commitment to social justice and transformation. Hence the connection in the Bible between social justice and *shalom*. A healing ministry requires a prophetic-critical ministry; the one without the other distorts the gospel of judgment and grace.

But at another level, we are now becoming aware of the extent to which social crises, such as we are presently experiencing in South Africa, affect our health, our well-being, and indeed, our humanity as such. Tillich's observations about post-war Germany are not far removed from our own experience in South Africa, and we may anticipate that they will become even more apposite. What happens around us in society, the social upheavals, violence and crises which beset us, affects us in every dimension of our being. Pastors ministering to those going through divorce, for

---

[25] Cf. D Gill (ed.), *Gathered for Life* (Geneva, 1983), pp. 64ff.

[26] F Engels, *The Condition of the Working Class in England*, first published in German in 1845.

[27] H Nouwen, *Graçias!* (New York, 1983), p. 118.

example, can tell of the extent to which the collapse of relationships is related to the anxieties and stresses attendant upon living in a time of crisis. There also is a clear connection between this and physical illness, and probably not only at the psycho-somatic level. In the process we all lose something of our humanity - we are dehumanized, whether we oppress others or are the oppressed. The need for some kind of 'healing ministry' which relates directly to the equally necessary prophetic ministry, thus becomes particularly acute and urgent in times of social uncertainty, upheaval and crisis.

We need to go one step further, however, and recognize that if ill-health is integrally related to social dis-ease, then it is equally true that being healthy means participating in society in such a way that you contribute to its redemption. Hence the truly whole person may well be the person who gives of his or her time and energy to the struggle for right and justice in society, or in serving other people in need, even if this might be at some physical cost. This in no way implies a disregard for one's physical health, or any kind of ascetic masochism, but it does affirm that there are values which are essential to being human and therefore to being fully whole people. The person working in a clinic in a poverty-stricken area where demand for service may well affect physical health is, from a biblical perspective, more whole and healthy, than a doctor who simply practices medicine for financial gain. And the same applies to other vocations. Such considerations also point to the need for medicine to become much more appropriate to the needs of the poor and deprived, as is gradually happening in some quarters, and this, in turn, raises the fundamental question of the availability of resources to those who need but cannot afford them.

In this paper I have not attempted to discuss such issues as faith healing, nor have I made any suggestions about the practice of religion and the use of its resources in the healing process. I have attempted, rather, to explore a possible basis in the 'new' holistic paradigm upon which we can proceed in dialogue between doctors, theologians and priests, so that these other issues which directly affect both the churches and the practice of medicine can be more fruitfully discussed in relation to our common goals to help create a more humane and therefore healthy society. The gains of medical science and technology need not be surrendered, but in dialogue with theology they need to be reworked on a new basis. Such a new basis is an urgent requirement both for the future of medicine and theology if they are to retrieve in theory and practice the prophetic vision of *shalom*, or salvation as healing and humanization. The transformation of our apartheid society in South Africa so that justice and true reconciliation become a reality is a task to which theology and medicine may thus jointly contribute, but only if their focus becomes the well-being of humanity as a whole.

# 3

# Spirituality and the Doctrine of the Trinity

## JAMES M HOUSTON

My early friendship with Professor James Torrance began in the psychology class that we attended as undergraduates at Edinburgh University. We had to give each other suggestibility tests, which we did with some humour. Perhaps we have continued to question the suggestibility of theological studies ever since. The christological focus of Professor Torrance on 'Christ for us' has contributed significantly to the critique of 'Federal Calvinism' in his native Scotland. [1] His further emphasis on worship as the gift of participation through the Spirit in the Son's communion with the Father[2] renews the focus of the church today on the teachings of the early Church Fathers. This essay is therefore written in appreciation of his own trinitarian emphasis.

Studies on spirituality and trinitarian theology are both much in evidence during the past decade. When we ask why this is, perhaps the first reason is because they are clearly the fresh starting point of all ecumenical effort among Christians today.[3] A second reason is doubtless because they both need to be the focus of renewal for the church, when much emphasis is given to 'charismatic' renewal, without a trinitarian emphasis.[4] A third

---

[1] JB Torrance, 'The Incarnation and "Limited Atonement"', *EQ*, 55 (1983), pp. 89ff. See also 'The Covenant Concept in Scottish Theology and Politics and its Legacy', *SJT*, 34 (1981), pp. 225-43.
[2] JB Torrance, 'Covenant or Contract?', *SJT*, 23 (1970), pp. 51-76.
[3] JB Torrance, 'The Lima Report - a Church of Scotland Perspective', *One in Christ*, 20 (1984), pp. 12-18. See also, TF Torrance (ed.), *Theological Dialogue between Orthodox and Reformed Churches* (Edinburgh and London, 1985); also, L Vischer (ed.), *Spirit of God, Spirit of Christ* (London, 1981).
[4] See RP Hanson, *God - Creator, Saviour, Spirit* (London, 1960) for redress of this balance. For he notes: 'we know God in three different activities and three different manifestations of himself; we find him and know him as the Father who is approaching us in Christ, as the Son who is God entering human history and human life to save us, and as the Holy Spirit who is God in whom

reason is because in the contemporary theological debate over the deity of Christ, all christologies must be tested ultimately by their trinitarian assumptions.[5] Perhaps the fourth reason is that there is much questioning about the nature of theological education, and the divergent split between systematic theology as an academic pursuit and the more pastoral relevance of a spiritual theology.[6] Without the complementarity of both systematic and spiritual theology, we only add to the pluralism today of many theological systems.[7] These are more the product of methodologies than of the experience of the living God. Technique thus threatens to become the Zeus to rival Christianity.

## I  Why Spirituality?

The sudden prominence of 'spirituality' today suggests many things.  Spiritual literature suggests the fact that the discovery of a vacuum in contemporary church life can be filled by reflection on past religious traditions.   For the popularity of 'spiritual classics' now occurring in the Protestant world suggests that the jump from the Bible to the Reformation has left too big a gap in church history, as well as neglecting the communion of saints.[8] The new-found 'spirituality of the Bible' suggests the recovery of the life-giving relevance of the Word of God to Catholics since Vatican II.  The need for 'spiritual direction' suggests the burn-out of evangelicals who have capitalized upon 'a born-again experience' that still remains liable to be 'still-born'.[9] 'Spiritual theology' might also suggest the need to recover the original unity that the early Church Fathers exercised between theology and prayer, faith and life.[10]

---

ye respond to that activity', p. 86.

[5] DG Bloesch, *The Battle for the Trinity* (Ann Arbor, 1985).

[6] R Kereszty, 'Theology and Spirituality: the task of a synthesis', *Communio'* 10 (1983), pp. 314-31.

[7] See for example JJ Mueller, *What are they saying about theological method?* (New York, 1984).

[8] This has been this author's concern in the edition of *Classics of Faith and Devotion*, being published by Multnomah Press, Portland Oregon.

[9] See the popularity of books such as K Leech, *Soul Friend* (San Francisco, 1977) and the many other subsequent books published on this theme.

[10] See for example, C Kannengeisser, 'The Spiritual Message of the Great Fathers', in B McGinn, J Meyendorff and J Leclerc (eds.), *Christian*

'Spirituality' then, with its associates, is perhaps evidence of the need of correctives for the Christian faith and life in the technological and information society of today. It suggests the cry of the heart for a balance between knowing and doing, doing and being, being and experience, indeed between doctrine and living. In an increasingly secularised society, Christian spirituality becomes the whole concern for pursuing, cultivating, and enjoying communion with God in worship, private prayer, the study of the faith, and the whole *practice* of the Christian life.[11]

In times past, 'spirituality' has denoted other movements. In seventeenth century France, 'la spiritualité' was a somewhat derogatory term for an intense type of mysticism, that was often blackmailed as 'quietism' by pragmatic French prelates.[12] At other times, as with the dissolution of the medieval world-view during the fourteenth century, it was identified with a rarefied type of mysticism that was not always clearly distinguished from neoplatonism or even pantheism. 'Spirituality' is still perhaps suspect to those strong, self-determining personalities who major upon a rationalistic type of faith, with a self-certainty of direction. 'Self-abandonment to divine providence' is not for them!

Nevertheless, 'spirituality' as a more vitalised expression of theological thought is much needed today. We may observe, indeed, an intrinsic inconsistency in academic theology that is not seen for example in the physical sciences. For no national academy of science has admitted to its select membership such odd fellows as alchemists or astrologists. Nevertheless, a large percentage of theologians are secularists, whose views of God are incompatible with the biblical revelation of the Father, Son and the Holy Spirit. How is this possible? Certainly the Bible knows nothing of a 'neutral' and merely intellectual knowledge of God that has been allowed to take over in modern theological

---

*Spirituality, Origins to the twelfth century* (New York, 1985), pp. 61-88.
[11] H Rack, *Twentieth Century Spirituality* (London, 1969), p. 2.
[12] G S Wakefield, *Dictionary of Spirituality* (London, 1984).

Christ in our place

studies. Instead, the early Fathers related theology to prayer, and
to the formation of spiritual life in the Father, through the Son,
by the Holy Spirit. Conversion and baptism into the community
of faith were the prerequisites for the *gnosis* or prayerful study of
the Scriptures. Indeed, from the Greek Fathers to the early
Cistercians of the twelfth century, theology and spirituality
remained one.[13]

## II  Why the Divorce between Theology and Spirituality?
The divorce between theology and spirituality only began in the
thirteenth century with the rise of scholasticism in the
universities. While Thomas Aquinas was known to fast and to add
prayer to times when he tackled theological problems, the
experiential knowledge of God was no longer, in his time, an
integral part of the theological method itself. So what Thomas
Aquinas experienced in prayer neither influenced the style not the
content of his theological works. For the assimilation of
Aristotelian philosophy, and perhaps even the immutability of a
God that was more islamic than biblical, overburdened scholastic
theology with metaphysical questions that had very little
reference to the practice of faith.[14] What is not adequately
appreciated is that Thomas Aquinas himself not only had a
profound influence on all subsequent Thomist scholarship within
the Roman Catholic Church, but also upon the Reformers of the
Protestant churches.

Following upon medieval scholasticism, the separation of
theology and spirituality as distinct disciplines was exacerbated
by the intense mysticism of the fourteenth century, and reinforced
by the Carmelite writings of the sixteenth century (i.e., of Teresa
of Avila and John of the Cross). Psychological interest in the
analysis of mystical states focussed attention upon mystical
theology.[15] Then in the Counter-Reformation the exaggerated

[13]This was the character of 'Monastic Theology', as described by J Leclerc,
*The Love of Learning and the Desire for God* (New York, 1985), pp. 191-235.
[14]For a more detailed history see YMJ Congar, 'La Théologie. Étude
Historique' in *Dictionnaire de Théologie Catholique*, 15.2 (Paris, 1946), cols.
346-447.
[15]Thus Jean Gerson (1363-1429) entitles his works *De Mystica Theologia
Speculatia* and *Theologia Mystica Practica*, in contradiction to the rational,

51

role of the confessional led to the emergence of 'moral theology'. This was a response to treating 'moral cases' in the casuistry of confession. Thus disciplines for the 'advanced' Christian life of mysticism, and the 'elementary' stage of morality, were differentiated. By the seventeenth century, the process of specialisation within the Roman Church was complete: dogmatics, moral, ascetical,[16] and mystical theology, were all seen as distinct disciplines. In the Reformed Church, pastoral theology rejected the mystical and ascetical components, while christology tended to overshadow the needs of a more balanced trinitarian theology. For the issues of controversy were those of justification by faith through grace.

Since the Enlightenment, a further divorce has occurred between exegesis and theology. Luther had already flattened the four-fold levels of medieval exegesis into the two levels of literal and ethical interpretation. Then with the rise of historical criticism and the attacks upon the historicity of biblical faith, the separation between theology and exegesis was widened. As Walter Wink has observed shrewdly, 'the conservative ideology was not wholly deceived by the so-called ideology of objectivism, though it was at a loss to know how to overcome it. For it sensed instinctively that the modernist was not so interested in being changed by his reading of the Bible, as in changing the way the Bible was read, in order to conform it to the modern spirit'.[17] The outcome today has been the trained incapacity of the academy to provide a pastoral theology that deals with life-giving realities. Instead, we see everywhere the creeping, moral paralysis brought about by the tyranny of technique and methodology within theological studies. Inevitably, this tends to remove theological scholarship further away from the community of faith.

---

scholastic theology of the times.

[16] C Dobrosielski writes of *Summarium asceticae et mysticae theologiae* for the first time in his work published in Cracow, 1655. At the same time, P Schorrer in Rome speaks of *Theologia ascetica*, published in 1658.

[17] W Wink, *The Bible in Human Transformation* (Philadelphia, 1973), p. 13.

No wonder, then, that the renewed interest in Christian spirituality is a *cri de coeur*, expressive of the spiritual bankruptcy of much theological education. However, it is not just the divorce between theology and spirituality that has occurred. For underlying this rift is a deeper and more profound issue, namely the weakness of trinitarian faith in the West, that may be attributable to its Augustinian heritage.

## III The Augustinian Heritage

Broad though the generalisation may appear, the influence of Augustine's interpretation of the Trinity has dominated Western theology. It is unlikely that Augustine himself, in the composition of his major work on the Trinity that preoccupied much of his life, ever had access to the full texts of either Athanasius or the Cappadocian Fathers on the Trinity. Moreover, he wrote from a Latin mind-set. So he did not appreciate deeply enough the sophisticated polemics of the Greek Fathers against the Arian heresy. To summarize a complex history, it appears that a major difference between the Western Roman Church and the Eastern Greek Church, as Jenson has ably demonstrated, was that in the West theologians argued how the One God was also three Persons, while in the East, they began with the Three Persons and affirmed that he was One God.[18] The contrast brought about significant consequences.

Firstly, Augustine assumed that all men understood the traits of divinity. So unwittingly, the natural theology of a platonic God was the foundation of his thought. That is to say, that God was described as impassible, timeless, and with all those other attributes that philosophers still love to debate about what is consistent with *abstract* notions of Godhead. Building upon this classical, *Hellenistic* foundation, Augustine then tried to justify the Three Persons in One God. Emphasis was therefore placed upon the economy of the Trinity, whose threefoldness was recognized in the divine roles of God in creation, redemption and sanctification.[19]

---

[18] RW Jenson, *The Triune Identity* (Philadelphia, 1982), pp. 114-20.

[19] M O'Carroll, *Trinitas, a theological encyclopaedia of the Holy Trinity* (Wilmington, 1987), pp. 42-5.

Secondly, Latin language had created a 'cast' for this mind-set with Tertullian's usage of one self-equal substance (*substantia*), expressed in three Persons (*personae*). *Substantia* came from everyday speech, as the sheer 'stuff' of reality, that was 'out there'. But it had no philosophical history compared with its Greek equivalent *ousia*, with which Plato and Aristotle had wrestled. While *persona* was the actor's mask through which he spoke his acted role, the Greek equivalent of *hypostasis* implied more emphasis on resemblance than upon role-playing. Thus overall, there was a philosophical innocence in the usage of the Latin terms, compared with the more sophisticated Greek equivalents. Moreover, while *substantia* and *persona* had never been used interchangeably in Latin, *ousia* and *hypostasis* were almost interchangeable in Greek for what 'is'. The nuance of *ousia* emphasized the 'is-ness' of a thing, while *hypostasis* conveyed what was distinguishable about that thing. In Greek theology, the nuance was sharpened to avoid the heresies that either the Trinity lacks three Persons or that there are three Gods. The Cappadocian Fathers did so in identifying - not individualistic traits - but personal relationships. That is to say, God as Father is the Source of the Son's and the Spirit's Godhead. The differing ways in which each is for and from the others are their *hypostasis*.

Thirdly, Augustine never did grasp, as he confesses, 'what difference the intent was between *ousia* and *hypostasis*'.[20] Indeed, it was only later after the Council of Chalcedon (451 AD), some twenty-one years after Augustine's death that the term *hypostasis* was generally accepted in the West. But it was then incorporated within Augustine's framework.

Fourthly, Augustine built up his trinitarian theology by using human analogies. Basically this involved a platonic definition of God, with the biblical characteristics of Father, Son and Holy Spirit. Later when Boethius presented a correct trinitarian dogma, there was still incomprehension of the Greek theologians'

---

[20] Augustine, *On the Trinity*, 5.10.

54

teaching. Meanwhile, the collapse of paganism in the West coincided with a general acceptance of Augustinian trinitarian doctrine in its society, so that the function of trinitarian theology, which was in the East established to refute Hellenism and its inherited heresies, was not enforced for the daily needs of the West.[21] In other words, there was no need to defend the Gospel's God over other claimants. One consequence of this was that the platonic assumptions of God's timelessness and impassibility remained unquestioned in the West. Another implication of this was that all attributes of God were identified with his *one substance*, and none were predicated from the threefold identities. To all intents and purposes, Augustine states that relations within the Godhead are irrelevant to their being God, which is really a contradiction to the whole Nicene theology. 'This Trinity', says Augustine, 'is of one and the same nature and substance, not ... more in all than in each other, equally in the Father alone or in the Son alone as in the Father and the Son together'.[22] Again he says, 'whatever is said ... of God himself is said at once triply of the Father and of the Son and of the Holy Spirit and singly of the Trinity itself'.[23] It is as if God is God, in spite of the Trinity!

What Augustine was doing for the sake of simplicity, was to reject the dialectics within the relations between the trinitarian identities, as being themselves expressive of the character of God. Thus he flattened the mutual structure of the divine identities into one identical possession by the identities, of an abstractly simple divine essence. Since the original purpose of the trinitarian dogma of the Greek Fathers was that God's relations with man are internal to God's own character, the 'relational concept' of God was introduced to define the distinction of the hypostases. The destruction of this interpretation of the Greek Fathers in the West left trinitarian theology with only a modal emphasis.[24] For

[21]On the contrast between Western and Eastern teachings on the trinity see T Hopko, 'The Trinity in the Cappadocians' and MT Clark, 'The Trinity in Latin Christianity', in McGinn, Meyendorff and Leclerc (eds.), *Christian Spirituality*, pp. 260-76, 276-90.
[22]Augustine, *Letters*, 170.5, quoted in Jenson, *op. cit.*, p. 118.
[23]Augustine, *Trinity*, 5.9.
[24]O'Carroll, *op. cit.*, p. 43.

analogy took the place of the divine relational dynamic among the three Persons, that was so implicit to the theology of the Greek Fathers. All that Augustine could do was, therefore, to elaborate on the human analogies of being, knowing, and loving as reflective of this. Memory, knowledge and will, as human attributes, were vaguely assumed to reflect on man being made in the image of God. In this analagous way, Augustine tried to get trinitarian language to 'work'. He ended up in discerning the complexity of the human soul, and so of the great divide between consciousness and unconsciousness, which has been a profound insight for western philosophy ever since. But it left the West with an impassible Trinity, whose immanence could not be connected with the divine trinitarian economy.[25]

Could it be then that, compounded with the scholasticism of the later Middle Ages, the cult of Mary filled a void in later medieval devotion that 'worked' more effectively in personal piety than ever Augustinian trinitarianism really could? Certainly, the Augustinian model was static in comparison with the inexhaustible experiencing of the Triune God found in the teachings of the Cappadocian Fathers. For them, instead of a modal trinitarianism, the mystery of the three Persons in the Godhead prompted the intense longing and desire of following after God within his own divine fellowship and love, that they came to call *epektasis*. Such desire for God is inexhaustible for the satisfaction of the desire of One Person of the Trinity only leads to further and deeper desires with the Others. Unlike, then, the stagnation implicit in a platonic deity, there is no ultimacy of contemplation, but instead an ever deepening penetration into the Three-Personed God. Simeon, the New Theologian, (949-1022) in tenth century Constantinople, is an important spokesman for this ardour of soul that such a doctrine inspired. So he tells us: 'when the three-personed deity draws within the saints, and is known and felt to be present, it is not the fulfilment of desire, but the cause and beginning of a much greater and fervent desire. Because from

---

[25] Jenson, *op. cit.*, thus concludes, 'the danger of the West's abstract trinitarian analysis is not only that it is false but also that it likely to reflect negatively upon the fundamental liturgical and proclamatory levels of discourse ... The doctrine in its Western form has not easily been seen as functional within religious life', p. 131.

this time on, the man who enjoys the Presence [of God] finds that it gives him no rest. It drives him on toward the flames of an ever deepening desire for the Godhead, as if he were being consumed and devoured by fire. The mind can find no limit in the One it yearns for. It cannot grasp him, and it cannot set limits on its own desire and love. Yet as it strives to grasp and hold on to the endless goal, it feeds within itself a longing that knows no bounds and a love that can never be satisfied'.[26]

Perhaps it is this arousal of the faculty of desire, in contrast to the over-emphasized faculty of reason in the West, that helps also to explain the deep sense of soulfulness within Eastern Orthodoxy, although we may also wonder today what has happened to the Greek Fathers' heritage of trinitarian faith.[27]

## IV Mysticism in Western Trinitarianism
What is significant for our argument is to see that where there was contact with the trinitarian insights of the Greek Fathers in the Middle Ages, a renewed mysticism of trinitarian faith was aroused. By mysticism, we mean the personal experience of the Presence of God. So that by trinitarian mysticism we are really referring to the ways in which the immanence and economy of the Trinity are conjointly experienced in the life of the believer. The directness of such an experience of union with God himself is the outcome of such an experience of God's presence. The presence of the Blessed Trinity gives one a realisation of one's own nothingness, and therefore the need to live a life of self-surrender and self-abandonment to God. But such mature mystical experience has nothing whatever to do with parapsychology. But it has everything to do with the contemplation of Three Persons in one Godhead, as the source and expression of love, communion and union. As we have seen, the economy of the Trinity in our

[26]Simeon the New Theologian, *The Practical and Theological Chapter*, P McGuckin (ET), (Kalamazoo, 1982), p. 34.
[27]Contemporary theologians such as Vladimir Lossky, *The Mystical Theology of the Eastern Church* (Cambridge and London, 1973) are rich in their trinitarian reflections, but do not trace the impact of this doctrine historically upon their churches.

salvation must be integrated with the 'theological trinity' or immanent trinity, that focusses upon the intra-trinitarian relations of Father, Son and Holy Spirit. Outstanding in this respect is the influence of William of St Thierry, the Victorines, and Jan van Ruysbroeck. But whereas the Victorines, such as Richard of St Victor, are still Augustinian in their sequence of emphasis, namely first the unity of the Trinity, then the explanation of the three Persons,[28] the others are much more directly influenced by the Greek Fathers in emphasizing the dynamic relationships of the Three Persons in one Godhead. So we shall focus upon these two exemplars.

William of St Thierry (1085-1148) was a Benedictine monk who only assumed the Cistercian habit during the last thirteen years of his life. He sought to repudiate the scholasticism of men like Peter Abelard, William of Conches and Gilbert of Porrée.[29] It was against these that he wrote a major treatise on the Trinity, *The Enigma of Faith*. On the other hand, Ruysbroeck (1294-1381) living through all the intense mysticism of the fourteenth century, writes from concern to deny the heresies of the 'Free Spirits' who denied the need for the structures of reason and morality in the Christian life, rather like those today who are seduced by post-modern consciousness.

William envisages the Trinity as a spring of water that wells up to eternal life, so it is a reality that is given to contemplate, not to reason about. For it springs up inexhaustibly from the fountain head of Scripture, God's Word. Prayer and thought intermingle richly in his treatise. William emphasizes seeking 'the face of God' as the essence of the spiritual life. He is convinced that this is what contemplation is about, so it is the contemplation of the mystery of the Trinity that energizes his experience of God. 'He can be seen in this world by the pure of heart, but he cannot be comprehended. But in this question of seeing God, it seems to me', he adds, 'that there is more value in

---

[28]WJ Hill, *The Three-Personed God: the Trinity as a mystery of salvation* (Washington, 1982), pp. 225-32.
[29]O Brooke, 'Studies on William of St Thierry' in *Studies in Monastic Theology* (Kalamazoo, 1980), pp. 1-218.

one's manner of living than in one's manner of speaking'.[30]
For it is in this 'seeing of God' that 'we become more like him
by knowing and loving him'. 'As in the Trinity, which is God,
the Father and the Son mutually see One another, and their mutual
vision consists in their being One, and in the fact that the One is
what the Other is, so those who have been predestined for this
and have been taken up into it, will see God as he is, and in
seeing him as he is, they will become like him. And there, as in
the Father and the Son, that which is vision is also unity; so in
God and man that which is vision will be the likeness that is to
come. The Holy Spirit, the unity of the Father and the Son, is
himself the love and likeness of God in man'.[31]

Immediately then, William would indicate that to affirm trinitarian
doctrine is also to be caught up in the ethical issues of a
transformed and spiritual life and likeness. For the intra-
trinitarian relations of the Holy Trinity also determine the same
relations and their consequences in the union between the believer
and the Triune God. Yet, William hastens to add, 'the manner is
different',[32] for still man sees only as in a mirror darkly. The
fulness of this still awaits the eternal state. Nor can man's
nature, as a creature, ever be confused with the Creator.
Consequently, William adds, 'whoever has in Christ been
awakened to God, is stirred by the warmth of the Holy Spirit, and
in his love for God has become small in his own eyes'.[33] He
now learns to prefer one form of knowledge for another; to know
his own weaknesses rather 'than to know the ramparts of the
world, the foundations of the earth and the heights of the
heavens'. In other words, he is no longer motivated by curiosity,
but rather by humility.

Knowledge of the Trinity is thus for William a transforming
knowledge. To know the Son of God in his humiliation is to act
like him and to live like him. This is what it is to be truly

---

[30]William of St Thierry, *The Enigma of Faith*, JD Anderson (ed.),
(Kalamazoo, 1974), p. 37.
[31]*Ibid.*, p. 39.
[32]*Ibid.*, p. 41.
[33]*Ibid.*

human. William sees three degrees of such knowledge of God. The first is that of faith, in submission to the authority of God's revelation of himself. The second is that of reason that is appropriate to faith, in agreement with the divine truth about the Trinity. The third is that of eliminating and beautifying grace, which transforms faith into love.[34] Such knowledge is summed up in the divine names of God, by which he is known as Father, Son and Holy Spirit. Just as Yahweh is God's proper name in the Old Testament, so Father, Son and Holy Spirit is his proper name now. This name is the basic discourse that we have about God, for which man, made in God's image and likeness, is given a longing to relate to. Since this is the personal name of God, his name does not describe genus and species as the pagan gods did in Hellenism, but God's proper character. For each name within the Trinity refers essentially to the others, as Father to Son, as Son to Father, and as Father and Son to the Holy Spirit, and he to them.

In warning against the use of analogies about the Trinity, William then states: 'when words are used to treat of God, the sense of the words must be fitted to the realities [of the Trinity], and not *vice versa*'.[35] Indeed, as the theologian seeks to penetrate into the mystery of the Trinity, 'whoever investigates any concept of the Trinity or of divine affairs through verbal images, enters into the labyrinth of divine relations'. These catch up the enquirer into a dynamic range of challenges that will be overwhelming because of his glory. Human modality can only be overwhelmed in its inadequacy, for he is inexpressible and unimaginable. It is therefore the Holy Trinity who causes us to fall prostrate before him and cry out, 'you cause us to pray and entreat that you do not permit us to err in any way in the contemplation of, or the belief in, that form to which we seek to be confirmed. Also, you instruct us in all the Scriptures which are about you that, just as you are three in One, so also we are to be made one in you, through the power of the faith by which we believe this.'[36]

---

[34]*Ibid.*, p. 79.
[35]*Ibid.*, p. 91.
[36]*Ibid.*, p. 116.

Thus the form of faith itself is trinitarian, shaping the believer appropriately to that faith. Consequently, there can be no valid concept of God that is that of the detached observer. For it is binding to the whole life of the believer to belong also to God. The fruit then of such trinitarian faith is unending contemplation of the Father, through the Son, by the Holy Spirit. The love then of the Triune God is an *effective* love, since before the ages he predestined us to be adopted sons and in the time of his good pleasure he poured out his love in our hearts through the Holy Spirit. Thus the Spirit teaches us to pray as we ought, and draws us into that inseparable union of the Father and the Son.

For William then, a transforming love, in communion and union, is the vocabulary and experience of those caught up within the realities of trinitarian faith. For those who have experienced this, never again can they see the doctrine of the Trinity as a biblical afterthought, or as a concept 'out there', about which we may speculate and write. Instead, trinitarian spirituality grabs us, changes us, and radically alters our perspective. Mysteriously we are caught up like the Apostle into the heavens, to sense inexpressible and inexhaustible realities, that, by contrast with our earthly condition, show up the unreality and falsity of our human lives. Like Bernard of Clairvaux, William uses the term *affectus*, to describe this impact that trinitarian relationships have upon the life of the believer. We are affected by him so radically that our souls undergo a change by the very fact that we now love the Father, the Son and the Holy Spirit.

In his treatise *On Contemplating God*, William also elaborates on the doctrine of the Trinity as the source, spirit and strengthening of this affective love. For the Holy Spirit is seen as the Love, Unity and Will of the Father and the Son, who dwells in us by grace, and who unites us to God through the goodwill he breeds within us. To love God is in turn the spirit of adoption, whereby our hearts cry receptively 'Abba Father!' This is how we learn to love God, or rather how God loves himself in us, for God demonstrates his love for us by making us lovers of God by the reception of his Spirit. This is the source of true happiness, and its measure reflects upon the measure of our experience of divine love. In this experience of trinitarian love, we are his workmanship, created unto good works, for he is our justifier and sanctifier. Thus prays William: 'we love you, or rather you love yourself in us, we affectively and you effectively, making us one in you, through your unity, through your Holy Spirit, who you have given us'. This transformation William attributes to the reality 'for the Father to know the Son is nothing else but to be what the Son is, and for the Son to know the Father, is simply then what the Father is' (see Matt. 11:27). So to love and to feel God 'is nothing other than to be of one spirit with him'.[37]

However, the mystery of the Holy Trinity that Origen and Gregory of Nyssa, and later Dionysius the Areopagite, had described, was apophatic. This insurmountable negative theology, that denied earthly categories of thought to express God, seemed inherent in the introspective methodology implicit in it. For the Creator surpasses all human categories of thought, so no further determinations are available. It is here where Jan van Ruysbroeck, the Flemish mystic, became so infuential in Germany in the latter Middle Ages. For he showed how this barrier could be overcome. For him, the Trinity is never at rest, hence never permanently withdrawn into its own darkness, silence, and waylessness. For as the soul's relation to God partakes in the movements *within* the Godhead, a dynamic interpersonal theology unfolds. Light bursts out of the darkness, deeper speech breaks forth from the silence, and the waylessness turns out to be the ingoing and outflowing of God's own life within the soul of man. There is a practicality about this 'common life' that hides the deepest interiority in the practice of everyday virtue.[38] So that at whatever level Christians may find themselves, they are caught up to a reality of divine attention.

Surely, argued Ruysbroeck, the message of the Trinity is none other than the central message of the Gospel. 'If anyone loves

---

[37] William of St Thierry, *On Contemplating God*, p. 58.

[38] L Dupré, *The Common Life, the origins of trinitarian mysticism and its development by Jan Ruusbroec* (New York, 1984), p. 63.

me he will obey my teaching. My Father will love him, and we will come to him and make our home with him' (John 14:23). The Apostle Paul affirms further: 'he who unites himself with the Lord is one with him in spirit' (1 Cor. 6:17). The good news of the Gospel stands or falls on this task of making the great gift of union become true. But without relating the immanent Trinity with the economic Trinity, this task involves intrinsically serious difficulties, as the history of Christian spirituality has clearly shown. Yet there are apparently irreconcilable objections in the interplay between God's triune character and man's own needs. To be uniquely ourselves, and yet genuinely human in a fallen world, as well as to be both entirely in God and entirely in ourselves, defies the control and management of logical, objective reasoning. Yet Ruysbroeck came to see these apparently irreconcilable objects to be complementary aspects of one single organic unity. So he came to see how we are both rich and poor, hungry and satisfied, active and passive at the same time, when we live out the trinitarian faith.[39] For God is, at one and the same time, repose and activity, essence and persons. This same simultaneous interplay between repose and activity, rest and work, being and doing, likewise characterizes those that he has made in his own image and likeness. Just as subordination of any of the persons of the Trinity is a heresy of this dogma, so in the union between God and man there can never be absorption of one in the Other, such as we find in pantheism.[40]

As a contemplative, Ruysbroeck claims that the life shared within the Triune God, is also the model of our relationship and union with God. It is a faith that enables us to appreciate definitively the nature of the divine love that should characterize human persons also. First, he notes that the divine Person is a distinctive reality that yet exists only in self-surrender. It is a living paradox that being consists in losing one's self. 'The Father loves the Son and has placed everything in his hands' (John 3:35). The Son has 'come in my Father's name' (John

---

[39] J van Ruysbroeck, 'The Perfection of the Sons of God' III, p. 26, quoted by P Mommaers, *The Land Within* (Chicago, 1975), p. 53.
[40] *Ibid.*, p. 57.

6:43), 'and by myself I can do nothing ... for I seek not to please myself but him who sent me' (John 5:30). The Spirit is identified as making the Father and the Son real in the life of the believer (Rom. 8:14-17; Gal. 4:6; 1 Cor. 12:3). So the Person is not a simple reality, sharply delineated by possessive traits, but a complexity of reality orientated from and to the Other. This is not a view of the Triune God that we can accept meaningfully, if 'God' is firmly held in the grid of philosophical categories. But as three Persons, each for the Other, God's nature, says Ruysbroeck, 'is eternally active insofar as it is a single Being'.[41] Both Beings, the personal Being that is for the Other, and the essential Being, always exist together.

When Father and Son who love us, make their abode with us (John 14:23), the conversion experience leaves us still with our essential humanity. Yet we become profoundly transformed, the more there is the experience of self-surrender and self-abandonment. Ruysbroeck is clearly convinced from his own experience, that man becomes even more human and a richer personality, by becoming more indwelt by the Triune God.[42] Moreover, our seeking of God will grow in intensity, not now from desire and acquisition, but as a consequence or reflection of being one with the Other. For increasingly he will live the Other's fellowship.

Another insight from Ruysbroeck is that the community of love that exists in the Trinity is a continuous reception from the Other, which is possible because of the unending abandonment. The Son is Son as he goes on relating from and to the Father. It is precisely his issuing from the Father and moving back to the Father, that makes his Sonship distinguishable. In this, muses Ruysbroeck, there is unceasing newness, in an endless dynamism of everlasting satisfaction and inexhaustible seeking of each Other. Is this then what Jesus prayed we might have, 'that they may be one as we are' (John 17:11, cf. 25-6)?

---

[41] J Ruusbroec, *The Spiritual Espousals and other works*, JA Wiseman (ET), (New York, 1985), p. 247.
[42] Mommaers, *op. cit.*, p. 105.

In reply Ruysbroeck comments: 'He did not mean one in every aspect, for he is one with his Father in nature, since he is God, and also one with us in our nature, since he is a human being. He lives in us and we in him through his grace, but are not one with him in nature. For the Father loves us and we love him in return, and in this loving and being loved we always feel a difference and a duality; this is the nature of eternal love. But when we are embraced and enveloped by the Father and the Son in the unity of the Holy Spirit above all exercises of love, then we are all one, just as Christ, both God and a human being, is one with the Father in their fathomless mutual love'. This experience of divine love is lived in a state of emptiness, just as Christ 'did not consider equality with God something to be grasped, but made himself nothing' (Phil. 2:6,7). Nevertheless, Ruysbroeck warns us 'whenever I write that we are one with God, this is to be understood as a oneness in love and not in being or nature. For God's Being is uncreated and ours is created, so that God and creature are immeasurably different. They may therefore unite, but they cannot become one'. He describes our natural being as like a wild and barren desert in which we wander lost, since we cannot transcend our own being Yet God loves us and so blesses our desert, while when we 'die in God' we enter more deeply into the enjoyment of who he is. This becomes an inexhaustible experience that makes the whole theme of 'enjoyment' one of the key thoughts of the mystic.

It is when we contrast these writings of William of St Thierry and Jan van Ruysbroeck with the later writers of the Reformation that we realise that we have lost a richness and insight into the dynamic character of the Trinity that they possessed. For example compare the Collect of the Prayer Book for Trinity Sunday with one of the prayers of William. The Collect says: 'Almighty and everlasting God, who has given unto us Thy servants grace, by the confession of a true faith, to acknowledge the glory of the eternal Trinity, and in the power of the Divine Majesty to worship the Unity: we beseech You, that You would keep us steadfast in this faith, and evermore defend us from all adversities, who lives and reigns, one God, world without end'.

I think we must admit that this really tells us very little, if anything, to inspire us to live in relationship with the Triune God. In contrast, William of St Thierry gives us this closing prayer in his treatise *On Contemplating God*:

'You, therefore, God the Father,
By whom as Creator we live,
You, wisdom of the Father,
By whom we have been made anew and taught to live wisely,
You, Holy Spirit, whom and in whom we love, and
So live happily, and are to live yet more so,
You, who are Three in one Substance, the one God,
From whom we are,
By whom we are,
In whom we are,
You, from whom we departed by sinning,
To whom we were made unlike,
But away from whom we have not been allowed to perish,
You, the Beginning to whom we are returning,
The pattern we are following,
The Grace by which we are reconciled'.

The Reformers in general remained wary of what they conceived to be trinitarian speculation, or what Calvin called 'the high articles of the Majesty of God', about which 'one must philosophize soberly and with great moderation'.[43] Indeed, we must still do so. But to exclude all such trinitarian investigation, as Melancthon did from his systematic theology, is going too far. We are only reaping the consequences in contemporary Protestant theology.

## V Conclusion: Trinitarian Theology is inevitably relational
The historical split between spiritual theology and dogmatics is the consequence of a low trinitarian emphasis in our heritage. It maintains the artificial distinction between the direct

---

[43]Quoted by GH Tavard, *The Vision of the Trinity* (Washington, 1981), p. 78.

apprehension of God's presence, to which we can only respond in prayer and worship, from the theoretical apprehension of a God that is objectively defined and speculated about. Spiritual theology and dogmatics must remain correlative approaches, since spirituality is essentially the active knowing of God, in the same broad sense in which friendship and marriage are essentially the active knowing of real people. While the cognitive aspect of knowing presupposes the opening and giving of one's self to the person who 'knows', it must be based on actual, personal experience. Thus authentic knowledge of God is essentially relational, by knowledge of both acquaintance and involvement. It cannot be part of that modern tendency to be the detached observer, who tends to reify everything. Thus, for the early Fathers, *theologia* was the specific personal knowledge of the Triune God, who was contemplated as he is in himself. *Theologia* was thus the realm of prayer and adoration. To do theology, says Evagrius Ponticus, is to pray, and to pray is to be a theologian. It is not the sphere or interest of merely scholarly disputation. For this knowledge of the three-personed God, is itself known as the love-gift of the three active divine Persons, calling for, calling forth, a love-life of response to all three, as modelled on and actually sharing in that divine fellowship of the Son to the Father, in the Holy Spirit.

Five consequences may be seen to result from this relational experience with the Triune God.

A Real knowledge of God can only be participatory knowledge. An objectified stance makes all our claims of 'theology' to be merely our 'anthropologies' *de facto*, whether we do so consciously or not. Since God exhausts all our definitions of himself, and indeed overturns them when we try to put him within them, we can only seek by his Spirit to 'know him' as the Reality and Substance that *is*. As Jesus declares, only the Father knows the Son, only the Son knows the Father (Matt. 1:27). Likewise, Jesus admonished Thomas: 'If you really knew me, you would know my Father as well' (John 14:10). So 'just as the

Father knows me and I know the Father' ... 'I know my sheep and my sheep know me'. Indeed, says Jesus, 'I have called you friends, for everything that I learned from my Father I have made known to you' (John 15:15). Again, in our Lord's prayer of John 17, Jesus actually prays that we may have this participatory life of the Holy Trinity, 'that they may be one, Father, even as we are One' (John 17: 22), a profound and mysterious participation indeed.

B    Appropriately then, prayer and worship can only be the activities of knowing God in this participatory manner. The verbalized 'knowledge of God' as we may awkwardly call it, will therefore only be authentic if it is the fruit of these devotional activities. This then, is the criterion Christian theology can have that excludes secular thinking about God from the authentic discipline. For if theological knowledge is not the fruit of these activities and relationships to the Father, through the Son, by the Holy Spirit, then it is not Christian theology at all.

C    Knowing God then as an activity of prayer and worship, centres upon and radiates from the awareness of one's own self and of all other believers, as in the hands of a Holy God, who through the cross actively forbears judgment, forgives our sins, and justifies our persons (in the sense of prolonging a once-for-all forgiveness and justification that is ours already). It is thus necessarily an activity of grateful communion and adoring fellowship.

D    Thus divine revelation should be defined as God's work of bringing us into, and sustaining us in our activity of thus knowing him, in love. For it is not a speculative and theoretical knowledge of God as philosophers debate about, but the personal experience of divine love, from the Father, through the Son, by the Holy Spirit, that gives Christian theology its distinctive form of knowing. For there has been revealed to us God's personal name of Father-Son-Holy Spirit, just as Yahweh was given to Israel. In the Old Testament theophanies, the immediate experience of God's presence was too overwhelming to accept as the actual confrontation with the transcendence of God. Instead, the mediating presence of 'the angel of the Lord', or divine messenger seemed appropriate. Nevertheless, the consequent ethical changes in the recipient were dramatic enough to accept that God himself had visited him. Likewise, in Christ we appreciate a personal communion, although in retrospect we may theologize about the fuller awareness of Father-Son-Holy Spirit as operative in our lives.

For theologians like Barth, the great gulf that separates man from God is overcome by 'revelation', rather than as viewing man made in the image and likeness of God, separated by sin, and needing forgiveness, as we have seen. It is this triune emphasis of God, as his distinctive character, that keeps justification instead at the very centre of the relationship between God and man.

E    Spiritual life and growth then, for the Christian, consists in ultimate terms of sharing in the multidimensional process whereby life goes out from the Father in, to, and through, the Son, returning to the Father, in, and through the Spirit whom the Son guides. The Father gives, the Son receives, the Spirit inexhaustibly supplies. We live then 'by the faith of the Son of God' (Gal. 2:20), so that we depend, believe, accept, obey, in the merits of the Triune Fellowship. We are introduced into what Ruysbroeck termed 'the Common Life', that is so different from that 'impassible God' of the philosophers, that is so static and indifferent to the human needs of personal relationships. Instead it is an introduction into the divine *perichoresis*, of inter-communion with the Father, Son and Holy Spirit, who God is. The implications are inexhaustible, yet every time the Church has faced a pagan world, it has had to return to proclaiming the ways in which the Father-Son-Holy Spirit has no identity with the gods of the classical world, then or now.

# Kenosis and Kerygma : The Realism and the Risk of Preaching

ALAN E LEWIS

## I  The Puzzle

Towards the denouement of *The Heart of the Matter*, occurs a scene which is quintessentially Graham Greene.  Scobie is unwilling to renounce his adultery; yet for the love of his wife he has come reluctantly to Mass.  By communicating in his state of mortal sin he will damn himself, and do so doubly thereafter through suicide.  He reflects that his self-destruction for the sake of love is only possible because of God's own loving self-destruction.  Scobie will damn himself by recrucifying Christ, but only because God in Christ allows himself to be crucified and recrucified: 'It seemed to him for a moment cruelly unfair of God to have exposed himself in this way, a man, a wafer of bread, first in the Palestinian villages and now here in the hot port, there, everywhere, allowing man to have his will of Him ... *to put Himself at the mercy of men who hardly knew the meaning of the word.  How desperately God must love*, he thought with shame'.[1]

That stunningly encapsulates the sheer, dangerous riskiness of the love which Christians conceive to be reality's creative energy: the God of mercy at the mercy of those who scarcely know what mercy means.  The fictional context for so grasping an insight into divine recklessness and peril may be transubstantiation; but Scobie's thought contains the intuition that God is self-hazarded to damage less in Christ's form as eucharisitic Body than as ecclesial, and ultimately incarnational.  Not only in her sacrament, but in the Church herself, with her capacity for mercy's merciless betrayal and love's loveless contradiction, does

---

[1] G Greene, *The Heart of the Matter* (Harmondsworth, 1962), p. 213 (italics added).

God allow humanity to have our will of him. Which jeopardy in and from the mystical body of his still-sinning saints is grounded in the perils of Christ's own mortal flesh. There God was defenceless against the pain and hunger of nature's deprivations, against the weakness of the will and the cunning of the devil, against religion's hypocrisies and imperial insecurity, against rebellion and repudiation, the violent agonies of sin and the deadliness of death. *This* divine risk, of incarnation and of cross, self-emptied and obedient unto death, is the *analogia analogans* which determines and interprets the 'desperate love' whereby the Church is chosen, called and sent, entrusted with the ministry of reconciliation and commissioned to baptize and preach.

At the beginning of salvation history, Yahweh, for the sake of all the nations, graciously and powerfully delivered a chosen people, who by ingratitude, idolatry and apathy proved unfaithful partners and unprofitable missionary servants. Israel's infidelities and failures only confirmed God's loving patience with the unreliable, and the saving, redemptiveness of his anger and his justice. Yet that did not cancel the uncoercive riskiness of his commitment. Even, or precisely, in election and commission, his people had the freedom and capacity to conceal from the Gentiles God's creative light, to flout his righteous Torah, to silence or distort his prophetic word.

This ecclesiological conundrum is repeated and intensified at the Pentecostal turning of the ages. In the aftermath of betrayal, denial, crucifixion, God's reliance on his own resisters and destroyers is ratified and absolutized. The outpouring of the Spirit of the Son falls upon the city that has rejected God's own Son (Acts 2:22f.), and the missionary call goes precisely to the crucifiers: the Gospel for the circumcised deputed to the Galilean denier of Christ, that for the uncircumcision of his persecutor from Tarsus (Gal. 2:7). Our cherished cachet 'apostolicity' signifies, therefore, not sanctity and soundness, but incorporation, across the generations, into the calling and commissioning of traitors and enemies. Then and now, in his choice of witnesses and servants, God's own reconciling cause is surrendered to hands that have proved hostile and unstable, his *euangelion* placed on lips fearful to acknowledge truth, or once sworn to destroy it.

Perhaps this latter risk especially - the susceptibility of his dependence upon the Church's *words* - impresses with shame upon a specifically Reformed mind how desperately God must love. If for Graham Greene it is the Real Presence of the sacrament which shockingly clarifies love's self-abandonment to the mercy of the loveless, others feel driven by intuition and tradition, by scriptural imperative and christocentric logic, to wonder no less at the Real Presence of the Word.

The Eternal Word, by which all things were made, has become fleshly word, exposed to human sight and touch and hearing, exposed therefore also to humiliation, hurt and finally to hell. That Word speaks still, of course: a living *kerygma* which resonates with powerful, transfiguring effect. But it does so strictly as 'the word of the cross', a word of *kenosis*, of suffering and death, impotence and folly. The task of its proclaiming is, likewise, assigned to the weak and the foolish, to those who are empty of might and of importance, whose delivery is not in language of plausibility and wisdom but in the broken words of trembling and fear (1 Cor. 1:26-2:5).

To anyone who seeks to understand this puzzle of preaching, or simply to engage with it, by ear or mouth, it may well seem 'cruelly unfair of God to have exposed himself in this way': imperilling his gospel to unfaithful servants who may trip in any age upon the stumbling-block of their own message, and to the cultural despisers in our own age who mock at the inoffensiveness of the outmoded medium. Yet faith which comes by hearing (Rom. 10:17) continues to affirm that in the church's precarious proclamations, the living Lord himself is truly present, the Word of the Crucified audible and resurrecting. Therefore, returning below to the mystery thus previewed, we must certainly ask the question 'how?': 'how is preaching *ever* possible?'; and also the question 'why?': 'why is preaching still necessary *today*?' But the ultimate question for a theology of preaching, as of all else, is 'who?'.[2] 'Who is this Preacher who proclaims the truth about himself amid the falsehoods of social antagonism and ecclesial fallibility? Who is this active Word of God, incarnate and crucified, whose living self-articulation is mediated by men (and women) who hardly know the meaning of the Word?'.

## II The Preacher

One of the several theological themes which his students, colleagues and friends automatically associate with the name of James B Torrance, and for whose clarification the church in Scotland and far beyond is especially in his debt, is that of Jesus Christ as the one true Worshipper. Who has done more in recent times to help us rediscover the christological foundation of worship: the biblical, patristic and reformed axiom that the sacrifice of praise which is humanity's true response to the grace of God is itself the gift of God, vicariously offered on our behalf by Christ in *his* humanity?[3] Doxology is the supreme, and supremely concrete, expression of that obedient communion with God for which humanity was created, and to which we have been restored in Christ. Worship, therefore, in its very humanness is a divine gift rather than a human capability. True prayer and praise are possibilities of grace: participations in the prayer and praise of God's own Son. It is not that in the church we offer worship to Christ in grateful response to his salvation, but that he himself made once, and continues to make, the full, perfect response of human faith, as our sole Saviour, Priest and Representative, empowering us by his Spirit to share in movements of adoration, confession and intercession toward the Father which are uniquely his.

Clearly the christological background of that response to God

[2] See especially, D Bonhoeffer, *Christology*, E Robertson (ET), (London, 1978), pp. 27ff.
[3] See especially JB Torrance, 'The Place of Jesus Christ in Worship', *Church Service Society Annual*, (1970), pp. 41-62; reprinted in RS Anderson (ed.), *Theological Foundations for Ministry* (Grand Rapids, 1979), pp. 348-69. Also, JB Torrance, 'The Vicarious Humanity of Christ', in TF Torrance (ed.), *The Incarnation* (Edinburgh, 1981), pp. 127-47.

which finds voice and visibility in worship as a whole, applies
no less to one central doxological event: that in which the Good
News of Jesus Christ is audibly proclaimed in words. He who is
the Subject of worship as well as its Object, is *a fortiori* not
only the one preached and proclaimed at the centre of worship,
but the sole Preacher, who proclaims himself. It is artificial and
superfluous, of course, to define the centrality of preaching
relative to the many loci, modes and elements of Christian
worship, still more to regulate its position and proportion in
liturgical practice. That would be to postulate some competition
between the formal, verbal exposition of the Word, in a given
context, and the variety of accompanying events by which the
same truth may be expressed and heard. Prayers and psalms,
readings and responses, dialogue and diagrams, sacraments and
even silence, all may constitute the proclamation of the gospel's
living Word. So too may the infinity of shapes and sounds,
words and happenings, deeds and gestures, by which the faith of
Christians is publicly or privately portrayed far from any
sanctuary or pulpit. Only in this broader sense is proclamation
'central'; yet central it is. For the church cannot be herself unless
in all her forms of worship and of life she speaks and hears
repeatedly the Word that creates her reality, identity and goal.[4]
That variously takes the form of a creative, reassuring word that
promises forgiveness; a disturbing word that criticizes and
demands repentance; a holy, missionary word that separates her
from the world and sends her to the world; or a profane,
humanizing word which unites her with the world and seals her in
solidarity and mutuality with every neighbour in the world.

Preaching in the narrow sense is naturally only one small medium
of the multiplex renditions and auditions of the Word by which
the church lives. And it is not unnatural if contrasts of culture
and changing trends within them mean that in some times and
places the formal preaching of the Word will dominate the
structure even of Reformed worship less than in others. Even so,
the liturgical and practical accompaniments to preaching

[4] See my article '*Ecclesia Ex Auditu*: A Reformed View of the Church as the
Community of the Word of God', *SJT*, 35 (1982), pp. 13-31.

constitute a wider 'proclamation' just because they do bear analogy to that preaching. This dramatic, quasi-theatrical verbal declaration of the truth can never wholly lose its normativeness, to which the rest *only* bear analogy. For, as it will be argued, there is an intrinsic link between the matter of the Gospel itself, and the language of human speech, communication and address. No cultural or liturgical marginalizing of the sermon should or can domesticate the scandal of the identity between the Word of God and the words of humankind, those ordinary yet so extraordinary verbal tools by means of which human persons relate and interact.

All of this is secondary, though, to the question of the identity of preaching and of the preacher. Like so much else in worship, preaching appears to belong most naturally to the category of 'response'. Does the church not preach the Gospel in response to her great dominical commission? And does the content of that preaching, whether as comfort or as challenge, as teaching or an exhortation, not cry out unavoidably for a response, demanding that we go forth, to be and think and act in ways appropriate to that which we have heard? It is indisputable that preaching happens under the apostolic imperative, and in turn creates and articulates the demand for costly, obedient discipleship in response to the indicatives of grace. Yet the correctness of that statement should not conceal its pitfalls: the danger that in preaching, especially, the church manifests her incorrigible penchant for self-sufficiency and self-expression. Effective, 'successful' proclamation of the gospel too easily becomes our own ecclesiastical responsibility, and its function and goal the stimulation of our appropriate individual responses. In the first case the efficacy of preaching may depend upon the oratory, scholarship or personal charisma of the preacher. In the latter, the effect of preaching may be Christian lives reduced to complacent moralism or self-gratifying activism.

To both of these distortions, these expressions of churchly self-confidence whose terminus is often failure and the loss of confidence, if not cynicism and despair, the dogmatic and pragmatic antidote is once again the vicarious humanity of Jesus

75

Christ. In his own essay on christocentric worship, James Torrance indicates and indicts the false inferences sometimes drawn from a Reformed 'theology of the Word'. These are, that the preaching of the Gospel, albeit as the Word of God itself, leaves its hearers by themselves anxiously to endure its spiritual rebuke and meet its ethical demands; or proudly by their own decision and commitment to effect the crucial act and final moment in their own salvation.[5]

By contrast, what the Reformers actually emphasized was the saving decision and obedience of Christ himself. The decision and response of believers is no supplement to his, but the work of the Spirit, who by grace incorporates them into Christ's own perfect 'yes' to God. Indeed the substance of that 'yes' is precisely Christ's willingness to live and die not for himself but *for us*, as our representative, identified in his sinlessness with our own fallenness and sinfulness. This obedience, the total and active alignment of his own will with the will of the Father who has sent him, constitutes and verifies Christ's Sonship, his oneness with the Father, his identity as the one who embodies and reveals the truth of God, who speaks and is God's Word. Which in turn means that the Word and Son of God is the one true Man, who hears and obeys the Word of God, faithfully announces and enacts God's truth. The Lord who in his Father's name sends out disciples and apostles to proclaim the Word, is also himself the Apostle and Evangelist, who obeys the sending Father and fulfils the divine commission. If therefore, as McLeod Campbell so vigorously showed, Christ in his vicarious humanity is the one true Priest, who repents, confesses, intercedes on behalf of the world he represents, he is equally the one true Prophet, who preaches, teaches and performs the truth, on behalf of those with whom he shares his mission to that world. In every response to the command and word of God, we participate by the Spirit in the response of Christ himself, who in all the church's proclamations is the Proclaimer as well as the Proclaimed.[6]

[5] 'The Place of Jesus Christ in Worship', in Anderson, *op. cit.*, p. 367.
[6] See especially D Ritschl, *A Theology of Proclamation* (Richmond, Virginia, 1960), pp. 33ff.; cf. TF Torrance, 'The Word of God and the Response of Man' in *God and Rationality* (Oxford, 1971), pp. 137-64.

## III  The Preaching

Something breathtaking, perhaps rather shocking, but in any case archetypally Reformed, was taking place when Bullinger declared in the *Second Helvetic Confession*: 'The Preaching of the Word of God is the Word of God. Wherefore when this Word of God is now preached in the church by preachers lawfully called, we believe that the very Word of God is proclaimed and received by the faithful ... The Word itself which is preached is to be regarded, not the minister that preaches; for even if he be evil and a sinner nevertheless the Word of God remains still true and good'.[7] That encapsulates both the realism and the riskiness of preaching, in the tradition of Calvin - and also that of Luther, who said that no preacher should feel guilty for saying of his own words, '*haec dixit Dominus*'.[8] That outrageous identification - outrageous just because it may be made with no guilt of arrogance, though never without humility - is a strictly *trinitarian* presumption. Through her pneumatologically-determined union with the Son, the preaching church is gathered, powerfully but riskily, into the very activity of God, as a mode of the *mission Dei* itself. The word proclaimed in and to and by the church is God's own Word. In its very creatureliness it is the Creator who speaks thereby. 'The Word of God preached means ... man's talk about God in which and through which God speaks about Himself'.[9]

Thanks supremely to Karl Barth, contemporary Reformed dogmatics has perceived an analogy between the Triune God himself and the three-fold Word of God which in its triple differentiation remains one single Word.[10]  Indeed Barth, yielding nothing to Bullinger in his audacity, identifies preaching as the *first* form of the Word of God.  For in the event of preaching the Word comes alive in its dynamic, critical, vivifying power.  Without that living voice to interpret Scripture, the

---

[7] *The Second Helvetic Confession*, ch. 1; in *The Book of Confessions*, United Presbyterian Church in the USA, 2nd edn. (Philadelphia, 1970), 5.004.
[8] M Luther, *Wider Hans Worst*, 1541, WA, 51,517.
[9] K Barth, *CD* I/1, GW Bromiley (ET), (Edinburgh, 1971), p. 95.
[10] See *ibid.*, pp. 88-124; cf. Ritschl, *op. cit.*, pp. 29ff, 41ff.

writings of the second form of the Word of God would be dead letters (2 Cor. 3:1-6), tablets of revelation positivistically engraved.[11]   And without both scripture and preaching, the Incarnate Word, crucified and risen but now ascended and thus in a sense absent, would not still be present, by his Spirit, wherever the community of faith gathers in his name and hears his Word.

Granted, it is the incarnate and resurrected Lord who gives his authority to Scripture as truthful attestation of himself; and it is Scripture which authorizes, guides and judges the witness of the church.   Nevertheless, in the order of hearing, the Word of preaching has the priority.   For how but through proclamation, and through the Bible thus illuminated, could we recognize Christ's Lordship and know his existence as the Word made flesh?

Still, this very circularity simply expresses and confirms the oneness of the three-fold Word, in analogy with the unity of God. Within that oneness is contained the identity between the preaching of the church and the person of the church's Lord, between the *kerygma* which is Christ himself, and the *kerygma* we proclaim about him.   Which identity in turn exhibits the realism of the Reformed claim that the Word of God itself is truly present in our preaching; as well as the risk by which God chooses the frail words of an even frailer speaker - that minister who may be 'evil and a sinner' - as the means by which the incarnate and ascended Lord is present to us as his people. We shall see that if the former is a function of preaching's participation in the oneness of Christ's personhood, the latter reflects an analogy between this preaching and the duality of the one Christ's human - and divine - relatedness.   But these both turn upon the *absence* of this incarnate Christ, and the events in which he who had to go away (cf. John 14-16) continually comes again to his people and the world, through his Spirits's power and vulnerability.

---

[11] See JKS Reid, *The Authority of Scripture* (London, 1957), especially ch. vii; also O Weber, *Foundations of Dogmatics*, vol. 1, DL Guder (ET), (Grand Rapids, 1981), pp. 189ff., and G Ebeling, 'Word of God and Hermeneutics', in *Word and Faith*, JW Leitch (ET), (London, 1963), ch. xi.

**IV  The Presence**
Clearly the Lord's Supper is one such primary event of the
ascended Christ's presence-in-absence.  It is the controlling
promise of Calvin's understanding of communion, for example,
that Christ is, bodily, now altogether absent from the finite
world, glorified instead in heaven, that 'kingdom neither bounded
by location in space nor circumscribed by any limits'.[12]  The
worldly absence of the Lord is not to be violated by crudely
dragging down his flesh back into space and time, as in Luther's
consubstantiation, which localized Christ's eucharistic presence.
Yet neither, for Calvin, are the promises of the absent Christ,
*still* to be present, and *already* to return while the parousia is
awaited, to be dismissed.  God is made a liar by a purely
nominalist interpretation of the bread and wine, as empty signs
quite disconnected from the body and blood of Christ to which
they point.[13]  Not carnally, but by the Spirit, yet not nominally
but really, Christ makes himself present to the community of
believers.  Wherever they set forth, interpret and receive the signs
and symbols of his crucified flesh, there, we need not doubt and
dare not dispute, is Christ himself, in all the mediated immediacy
of Spiritual Presence.

Since, however, on this view, the sacraments are graphic
appendices to the Word itself, which need in turn to be verbally
explained,[14] it is *a fortiori* true that preaching too effects the
Real Presence, by the Spirit, of Christ himself.  He promised to
proclaim God's name precisely when he had 'ceased to be in the
world'.[15]  By mundane words, no less than earthly, earthy
elements, God 'bears us up as if in chariots to his heavenly

[12]Calvin, *Inst.*, IV.xvii. esp. sections 18, 26 & 27.  Cf. TF Torrance,
*Space Time and Incarnation* (Oxford, 1969), pp. 31ff; also JB Torrance, 'The
Place of Jesus Christ in Worship', *loc cit.*, p. 357.
[13]See *Inst.*, IV.xvii.10.
[14]See *Inst.*, IV.xiv.3,4.  Cf. G MacGregor, *Corpus Christi* (Philadelphia,
1958), pp. 52f.
[15]Calvin, *Commentary on the Epistle to the Hebrews and I & II Peter*, WB
Johnston (ET), (Edinburgh, 1963), p. 27 (on Heb. 2,11).  Cf. RS Wallace,
*Calvin's Doctrine of the Word and Sacrament* (Edinburgh, 1953), ch. vii; also
WP Stephens, *The Theology of Huldrych Zwingli* (Oxford, 1986), ch. 8.

glory', there to enjoy the presence of the Absent One.[16] Of course, neither preachers nor the words they speak may any more be confused with Christ himself than may bread and wine; yet neither may they any more be separated. Christ so consecrates the language of his human servants that through it he communicates himself. As the sacramental signs themselves are not impotent and empty, but effect the reality they signify, so by the ministry of words and the words of ministers, the truth of God himself sounds forth, and finds its goal. The preacher speaks: the voice of God is heard; the world is judged and justified, divided and united; God's people are summoned, healed, rebuked and led.[17] *This* is the impossible possibility of preaching, its absolute but so abusable authority in our own or any age: the promise of God's Word, which does not fail, that he will unfailingly but freely empower creaturely words to be the instrument and mode of his creative and disturbing self-expression.

The divine freedom in this self-accommodation to our language is never to be compromised. Trinitarian realism authorizes the church audaciously to identify her preaching as the Word of God, and liberates her humbly to submit to that authority herself, not balking at the sin and imperfection of those who speak and of what they say.[18] Calvin was scrupulous to distinguish his own sacramental doctrine from the medieval and tridentine dogmas which infused the sacred signs themselves with their own capacity

---

[16]*Inst.*, IV.i.5; cf. IV.xvii.15,16.

[17]On the divisive, deadly effect of the Word, in Calvin, see Wallace, *op. cit.*, pp. 92ff., and more generally Colin Morris, *The Word and the Words* (London, 1975), pp. 53ff. For the Reformed tradition, criticism and judgment are properties of the gospel itself, whose grace contains its own demands. This corresponds to, while differing from, the Lutheran instinct that the Word has a negative effect strictly in the form of Law; only when justifying is the Word gospel. See, e.g., Ebeling, *Word and Faith*, pp. 312ff., and *Luther: An Introduction to his Thought*, RA Wilson (ET), (London, 1972), ch. 7; and G Wingren, *The Living Word*, V Pogue (ET), (Philadelphia, 1960), *passim*. On the judgment which preaching of the Word exercises upon the very Church which preaches that Word, see Barth, *CD* I/1, p. 92f.

[18]See Ritschl, *op. cit.*, pp. 75ff.

to convey and effect the saving grace of God.[19]   So too, the power of words to be the Word of God is never an intrinsic, natural potentiality; nor even is a power sacramentally transferred from the Spirit himself to the words he utilizes.   Only in the sovereignty of his own freedom, and the daring, loving choice of his own condescension, does God elect to speak to us in the finite forms of human understanding and communication.   Therein, as we shall see, lies God's great risk.

Nevertheless, however perilous and self-handicapping, God's free choice and use of words is neither arbitrary nor irrational.   Words do have a fittingness, a divinely-given aptness to be the sacramental signs and vehicles of God's self-articulation.   The physical nourishment of bread and the enlivening of wine, make the eucharistic elements appropriate symbols and analogies of the strengthened soul and gladdened heart effected by the Spirit in communion; though the analogy, says Calvin, only applies when we eat in faith, not simply with the mouth.[20]   So too, faith can perceive through the dimness of transcendent mystery, some reason for Scripture's use of 'word', that fleeting, fallible, futile human utterance, as an analogy for the eternal truth and purpose of the personal Creator.   And the church can understand in part why it is supremely to her language that the 'eternal Word made flesh' entrusts his missionary cause, and through her words that the Spirit makes her absent Lord be present.   She sees a correspondence 'from above' between who God is and what he does, and the events that happen by means of human words.   Not that God is in our image when he 'speaks', but that we are in his image when we speak.[21]

In the events of speech, women and men express themselves, expose their inner truth and personhood.[22]   Our bodies we have

---

[19] E.g. *Inst.*, IV.xiv.9.

[20] *Inst.*, IV.xvii. e.g. sections 3,10.

[21] Cf. Ebeling, *Word and Faith*, p. 327.

[22] See Ebeling, *Introduction to a Theological Theory of Language*, RA Wilson (ET), (London, 1973), *passim*; and *The Nature of Faith*, R Gregor Smith (ET), (London, 1961), esp. pp. 182-91. Cf. Ellul, *The Humiliation of the Word*, JM Hanks (ET), (Grand Rapids, 1985), *passim*; and Weber, *op.*

given to us; our language is our own. By what we utter and fashion with our words we declare - so often unaware - the truth about ourselves. That truth differs for each self-revealing person; yet one truth is the same for all: that while every speaker is unique, each can find wholeness and authentic individuality not in isolation but in togetherness and mutual dependence. This separateness and this relatedness are equally sustained by words; for words both create distance and foster dialogue.[23] Words make an address to others, creating contact and inviting their response: communication and relationship result. Yet the words that form these conversations are those of separate partners, so that no matter how close the union they create, spoken words confirm the uniqueness of each partner, and their irreducible mystery to one another. And because address cannot compel union, understanding and reciprocation, every such word runs the risk of repudiation and rejection in response.

Mercifully, it is that very vulnerability which allows words to create new possibilities, to offer love and to open up the future.[24] When I express myself in speech, I bestow upon the other, give freely to my hearer, recognition that he or she is not an object but another Subject, an equal and equally personal co-respondent. Just so, the previously silent Man, dissatisfied with the company of beasts, burst out at last in speech when he encountered Woman, impressed not by her difference but by her likeness to him in their identity of bone and flesh (Gen. 2:23).[25] Likewise, the address which honours and confirms the personhood of others, yields up to them the gift of our own humanness. We who confront them with our speech are not objects either, for them to analyse, comprehend, exhaust and tire of. We are living mysteries ourselves - more veiled than disclosed despite our words; and our language carries with it the promise of unfathomable personal potentiality, a future with much more to be explored, and waited for, and wondered at.

---

*cit.*, pp. 178ff. See too, Morris, *op. cit.*, especially chs. 2,3.
[23] Ellul, *op. cit.*, p. 17.
[24] Cf. Ebeling, *Word and Faith*, p. 327, and *Theory of Language*, pp. 54ff.
[25] See P Trible, *God and the Rhetoric of Sexuality* (Philadelphia, 1978), pp. 95ff.

In all such ways, and many more, is it not possible to see how words do correspond to the reality of God, to glimpse how 'word' bears analogy to his own being as personal, self-giving love and his creative, self-revealing act?[26] He establishes that analogy when he chooses freely to address us in our own personhood, engages us eventfully, historically, in the joys and perils of reciprocal relations. He empowers our words so to participate in his transcendence that they facilitate our own self-transcending dialogue both with others and with him. Above all, he has become 'oral' himself, has embodied his love in a speaker of words, and entrusted his news to other human speakers, promising that when their words are uttered and received, the forgiveness of which they speak becomes reality. In that speaking and hearing, communication is restored, distance bridged, estrangement reconciled, a new creation born. So that in created words, God's tomorrow, still unveiled, mysterious, inexhaustible, breaks unexpectedly into the present, amid his absence and our waiting, making preaching itself the peculiar prolepsis of God's final rule,[27] wherein the creativity of love and grace shall powerfully abound beyond the negativity of sin and death.

## V  The Peril

Just here, however, postponable no longer, lies the surd riskiness of preaching! The exultant promise of the power of words compels us to confront repentantly their scandalous impotence, and return finally to that desperate love of God who puts himself at the mercy of those who hardly know the meaning of the Word. For the eschatological event of preaching realises now, through words, God's last triumph not least over the negativity, sinfulness and deadliness of words themselves. Where grace abounds much more, space is yielded to the magnitude of sin (Rom. 5, 12-21); and in particular, the Spirit only maximizes the creativity and

---

[26]On the creativity of language see e.g., Ebeling, *Theory of Language*, pp. 58ff.; Ritschl, *op. cit.*, pp. 72, 143ff.; Ellul, *op. cit.*, pp. 63ff.; Morris, *op. cit.*, pp. 26ff.; also REC Browne, *The Ministry of the Word* (London, 1958), especially p. 27.
[27]See W Pannenberg, *Anthropology in Theological Perspective*, MJ O'Connell (ET), (Edinburgh, 1985), p. 396.

redemptiveness of language by allowing, intensifying and exceeding its unredeemed destructiveness. The more realistic our account of preaching as the Word of God, the riskier God's accommodation, thus implied, to the words of humankind. Those words, though greatly similar, in the analogy of faith, to God's own act and being, are *only* analogies, dissimilar enough in their finitude, fallibility and fallenness.[28] So that when our words effect reconciliation and tell the truth, they overcome the estrangement and the falsity in which words themselves are deeply mired. If God, by the proclamation of the Church, recreates and humanizes us through speech, he does so only by healing and humanizing speech itself, and thus by first hazarding himself to the brokenness of words and their demonic, dehumanizing harm.

That, we saw, was the Pentecostal humiliation of the Word, where God in Christ self-woundingly surrendered up his ministry of reconciliation and the mission of his love to preachers and apostles with a track-record of unfaithfulness and failure. To be sure, unstoppered utterance gushed forth then in the loquacity of the Spirit's *parrhesia* (e.g., Acts 2:29; 28:31). But these tongues and prophecies and sermons were the speech of liars, cowards, foes; and they confirmed that the Ascended Lord, made present-in-absence through the power of words, remained the powerless crucified Lord, still exposed as in his flesh to words of disobedience and betrayal, of repudiation and utter, deadly silencing.

The power and glory of Resurrection and Ascension are always wholly misinterpreted if they appear to cancel out the death of the Messiah. The Lord is glorified with his suppurating wounds, bearing humanity's brokenness and suffering into God's own heart, in the communion of his groaning, sighing Spirit (Rom. 8:18-27). It is the Crucified who proclaims himself in the church's preaching; and her *kerygma* can only be 'the word of the cross'. Our participation in Christ, the one true Preacher, thus bears analogy, the greatest similarity of all, to his scandalous

---

[28]On analogy here, see E Jüngel, *God as the Mystery of the World*, DL Guder (ET), (Edinburgh, 1983), especially pp. 261-98.

cruciform identity: the eternal Word born in the likeness of our sinful flesh, self-emptied unto death, susceptible to every human weakness, despised, rejected, terminated.

Can we abide the offensiveness of incarnation, and see that Christ's filial obedience which perfectly revealed the Father's heart and will comprised an unshielded struggle, from within its actual condition, against the sinfulness of human nature, and in full exposure to its consequential suffering, forsakenness and separation?[29] This life, from womb to tomb, was God's own act and self-expression, its lowliness the substance of his majesty, its *kenosis* the accomplishment, not the antithesis, of his *plerosis*. But here was *God's* humanity, obediently perfected, only because it was *our* humanity, wherein God's purposes were jeopardized to the possibilities of adamic disobedience and satanic opposition.

This is the human existence and condition to which we are referred when Reformed custom posits a correspondence between preaching as the Word of God, and the classical conception of christology: the one incarnate person of the Word, in whom fully human nature is assumed into union with divine. If the preaching of the Word perpetuates that union's saving power and presence, it does nothing to foreclose its contingency and peril. Our proclamations may realistically participate in resurrection, and anticipate the *eschaton*: healing, transforming, recreating. But they also re-enact the wilderness, Gethsemane and Calvary: God's hazard to the weakness of the human will, the arrogance of sin, the corruptibility of language. God's continuing risk with preaching and with preachers corresponds to Christ's own wavering temptation to speak an easy 'no' to the Father's costly will; to Satan's mastery of Scripture to invert seductively the meaning of the kingdom; to Peter's brazen mendacity and

---

[29] See Jüngel, *op. cit.*, p. 191. Cf. too D MacKinnon, 'Absolute and Relative in History', *Explorations on Theology*, vol. 5, (London, 1979), pp. 64ff. On the question whether even John McLeod Campbell - whose abiding significance James Torrance has done so much to clarify - came fully to terms with the humanity of Christ with regard to suffering and forsakeness, see GM Tuttle, *So Rich a Soil, John McLeod Campbell on Christian Atonement* (Edinburgh, 1986), pp. 119-25.

cowardly perjury; to Pilate's hypocritical connivance in the violent sacrifice of Truth to injustice, prejudice and fear. The humiliation of the Proclaimed Word, at the mercy of an all-too-human church, imitates the threat to the Creator Word from the unprotected humanness of Jesus and the self-protecting inhumanity of his enemies and friends.[30]

## VI The Present
Preaching, then, participates in the Word of God, strictly in its form as the surrendered, suffering, sacrificed Christ. This ruthless confession echoes both the timeless truth about words, and their contemporary cultural reality; it presumes the generic ambivalence of human language, while posing a specifically ecclesial dilemma, between the verbal and the visual.

The very ambiguity of words, we saw, fits them as analogues of God, in their capacity to separate as much as to unite, their lowly invitation to rejection and extermination no less than their soaring mediations of therapy and transcendence. 'What else is simultaneously as perishable and as creative as the word? ... In the word, man interacts with man as man, which is the reason that language reveals human inhumanity in the most sensitive fashion'.[31] With the clarity and creativity of language must be juxtaposed opacity and ruination - a defencelessness against abuse in the cause of infidelity, falsehood and fanaticism. Yet that serves not to relativize but to confirm the verbal analogy for 'the God of the cross', who is revealed in hiddenness, uniting himself with his mortal, fragile opposite, and yielding to violent, faithless opposition.

Likewise the *kerygma* of the Risen, self-proclaimed Lord, was ventured from the start on a medium that bore unmistakable resemblance to the message. Preachers who had spoken with

---

[30]See Barth's early, but still apposite, pitiless critique of the church, which makes her preaching a *peril*, and requires that the theology of preaching be strictly a *theologia crucis*: 'The Need of Christian Preaching', in *The Word of God and the Word of Man*, D Horton (ET), (London, 1928), pp. 97-135.
[31]Jüngel, *op. cit.*, p. 190.

duplicity and hate announced the truth and love of a crucified Messiah, himself the victorious victim of falsehood and of anger. And their implausible, trembling words verified the scandal of a God who shamed the wise with folly and the strong with impotence.

This added ambiguity of proclamation, wherein the foolishness of what and who is preached is mirrored in the foolishness of preaching and of preachers,[32] is grounded in the once-for-all commission, and enacted in every generation, of the kerygmatic church. Between hermeneutical integrity and shameless eisegesis, with clerical laziness and vigour, in cathedrals and the open-air, by polished rhetoric and cheap anecdote, through sacrificial friars and sleek televangelists, the perilous history of preaching has crookedly unfolded: the Word at the mercy of the best and worst of words. But our own generation has greatly intensified the foolishness of preaching in the eyes of culture, and magnified the question-marks that culture always puts to preaching. Pentecost loosened the tongue of faith, for praise and prayer, prophecy and preaching; and the Reformation was a 'word-event' which gave new birth to the vernacular: a turning-point for learning and linguistics.[33] But our contemporaries, and often we ourselves, are bored and disillusioned now with language - the medium for so much data and so little listening - and are disgusted with the poison and the wickedness of words.[34]

Concerning Hitler, it has been said: 'When He made the Word, God made possible also its contrary ... He created on the night-side of language a speech for hell. Whose words mean hatred and

---

[32] See I Pitt-Watson, *A Kind of Folly* (Edinburgh, 1976), pp. 1ff.

[33] See Ebeling, 'Luther's Linguistic Innovation', in *Luther*, ch. 1; J Pelikan, *The Christian Intellectual* (London, 1966); and EH Harbison, *The Christian Scholar in the Age of the Reformation* (New York, 1956).

[34] See Ebeling, *Theory of Language*, especially ch. 1; Ellul, *op. cit.*, especially ch. IV; J Macquarrie, *In Search of Humanity*, (London, 1982), especially p. 106; SW McWilliam, *Called to Preach*, (Edinburgh, 1969), pp. 32f.; JB Metz and J-P Jossua (eds.), *The Crisis in the Language of Faith* (*Concilium*, vol. 5, no. 9), (Edinburgh, 1973); J Stott, *I Believe in Preaching*, (London, 1982), ch. 2; and H Thielicke, *The Trouble with the Church*, JW Doberstein (ET), (London, 1966).

vomit of life'.[35]  Our own verbal history of manipulation, propaganda, and above all of genocidal mass-hysteria, leaves us as anxious to gag demonic speech, as to undam its charismatic energy, to connive in the idolatry of images as to persevere with speech amid our cultural dyslexia and muteness.  Of course, an imaginative, missionary church will adopt every means and medium available to communicate and authenticate the Gospel in its cultural milieu.  It would be unthinkable in ours not to exploit the visual - or to perpetuate the verbal unself-critically, as if the stumbling-block of Christ crucified required or justified a wilful outmodedness and ineffectiveness among his followers.

On the other hand, the 'word of the cross' itself liberates the community of faith from compulsive, worldly models of success, effectiveness and power; and her conviction that preaching is the Word of God itself, though anything but antinomian, lifts from the church the crushing burdens of 'relevance' and popularity.[36] Preaching *may* continue in a culture which humiliates the word, because the riskiness which lays an offensive message on unfashionable messengers reposes firstly and finally in God's own accommodation and commission.  Preaching *must* continue - responsibly, skilfully, critically - because the message itself is so concerned with words: the promise of forgiveness; the reconciling of estrangement including the divorce of sight and hearing;[37] and above all the restoration of broken men and women to the wholeness of personhood, in mutual togetherness and communion by adoption with the Triune family of God.  Because word is essential to personhood, both human and divine, since verbal address and reciprocity are the stuff of all relationship, it is speech supremely that effects the unity and community of Christ, his tumbling of every barrier within us, between us and around us. However risky, impotent and culturally inept, the preached word enacts God's personal, personalizing truth, and affords his humanizing, healing grace some hidden, cross-like leverage against the mighty social forces of depersonalization and

---

[35]G Steiner, *The Portage to San Cristobal of A.H.*, (London, 1981), p. 33.

[36]See Ritschl, *op. cit.*, pp. 47ff.; cf. K Runia, *The Sermon Under Attack*, (Exeter, 1983), ch. 5.

[37]See Ellul, *op. cit.*, especially ch. vii.

division.

Far from anachronistic, then, the verbal presentation of the
gospel may appear more pertinent and urgent than ever.
Christologically conceived, preaching makes God present in the
midst of an absence to which both faith and unfaith bear their
different testimony; and the church's words today of affirmation
and reconciliation surreptitiously invade a world rendered
increasingly speechless at the absence of reason, righteousness,
hope, and thus of God.[38] When the language of faith confronts
the collapse both of language and of faith in our generation, does
God himself not penetrate the godlessness and godforsakenness of
his own world? The church's speech may thus substantiate the
reality and love of God, for a generation haunted by silent
memories of an inhuman, loveless yesterday, and may promise
hope to a globe fearing an unspeakable tomorrow.

All of which not only discloses the possibility, necessity and
identity of Christian preaching, but also indicates an outline of
its contents for the present moment.[39] By his 'word of the
cross' God justifies the godless and selects the foolish, feeds the
hungry and befriends the outcast. That demands from those who
preach today a bold, iconoclastic word, dangerously critical of our
world's injustices, delusions and idolatries. By her prophetic
'no', the Church identifies her strangeness of tempo and of
vision, her commitment to the doing of a different will on earth,
her subversive protests against every status quo (ecclesiastical, no
less than social or political), her expectant allegiance to a new
and coming rule.

Yet that hope itself locates the gospel's 'no' strictly within its

---

[38]See my article, 'The Burial of God: Rupture and Resumption as the Story of
Salvation', *SJT*, 40 (1987), pp. 335-62.
[39]I have suggested more fully the themes for contemporary preaching,
especially in the European context, in 'Humanity Between the Cross and the
Resurrection', Occasional Paper no 2, Church of Scotland Board of World
Mission & Unity, Edinburgh, 1986. Cf., from a very different setting, J de
Gruchy, *Theology and Ministry in Context and Crisis: A South African
Perspective* (London, 1987).

'yes': the promise that the Crucified One is a risen and returning Lord, who holds out healing to those for whom his flesh was broken, forgiveness to those for whom he vicariously endured sin's guilt and judgment, life to those with whom he has been dead and buried. Words, we have said, themselves powerfully perform the new creation of which they speak. Therefore, this affirmative, triumphant theme of hope and radical renewal will dominate the church's conversation with the many victims of futureless despair, while she protests against the narcissism of the flourishing, optimistic few.

But should or can the church, however vocal with resurrection hope, fill up the silences of contemporary doubt, despair and fear, or deny the human shakiness of her own grasp on faith and understanding? The 'word of the cross' is the gospel of the Risen Lord who was crucified and buried, silenced by the enemies of life and love and speech. As surpassing grace protects rather than diminishes the space of that to which it is opposed, so resurrection hope acknowledges the human hopelessness which held even the Saviour of the world in its tomb-like grasp. His fellowship with the forsaken and the wicked in the grave requires that preaching in his name and by his power express faith's solidarity with unfaith, bewilderment and doubt. Here the preaching of the Word becomes itself a form of silence, the honest confession by the Church of her frailties and misapprehensions, and her oneness, in the interceding Spirit, with the wordless and the weeping among her neighbours. Such must be the humility and sensitivity of modern preaching: our open acknowledgment that we who speak the Word of God ourselves ask questions to which we have no answers, and know with our neighbours the unspoken inner pangs of failure, guilt and rage.

Yet once again, the human brokenness of the Church and of her preachers - intellectual, moral and emotional - only highlights the mystery of proclamation. For it encapsulates the risk which entrusts the Word of God to the implausible and the impotent, and assigns solely to the reality of that Word's presence, any persuasiveness and creativity in the words of the church.

# 5

# Participation and Atonement

ROGER NEWELL

How does the victory of Christ over sin and death impinge on my life nearly two thousand years later, so that, as Professor Torrance has described it, his death becomes my death and his resurrection my resurrection?[1] I will respond to this question by briefly discussing two 'subject-centred appropriation' models and concluding with an 'object-centred participation' model. The meaning of these phrases will be unpacked as the discussion progresses. However, at the outset it is important to note that the object-centred model is based on a more radical understanding of the incarnation which has been advocated by Professor Torrance and which has ancient roots in certain Greek Fathers, that is, understanding Christ's incarnation as a putting on of our fallen, sinful humanity. This understanding of the humanity of God in Christ will reinforce our decision to replace an appropriation-centred model with an object-centred participation in the life and death of Christ.

If it is true that this radical understanding of the depths of the divine descent into humanity deepens our insight into how our humanity is redeemed, I think it is also true that a knowledge of the human person gathered from the science of psychology deepens our understanding of the fallen humanity our Lord assumed, and thus both reshapes and enriches our understanding of Christ and the Christian's victory over evil. TF Torrance has shown that empirical science has much to teach theology when theology relates its faith to the historical-empirical world God has created and redeemed.[2] Similarly, I believe empirical

---

[1] JB Torrance, 'The Priesthood of Jesus', in *Essays in Christology for Karl Barth*, THL Parker (ed.), (London, 1956) p. 151.

[2] TF Torrance, *Christian Theology and Scientific Culture* (Belfast, 1980), pp. 7-9.

psychology's insights into our humanity deepen our understanding of the humanity which our Lord has worn and recovered. I will use certain analyses of William James and the Swiss psychiatrist, Carl Jung, not as an alternative to proper atonement theology, but as an exercise in integrative theological thinking enriched by a deeper knowledge of our creatureliness.

The first appropriation-centred response to Christ's victory over evil we shall look at is its use as a moral inspiration for our own ethical struggle. This response can be observed in times and thinkers as diverse as Thomas A Kempis in the fourteenth century, and Charles Finney, the American evangelist in the nineteenth century. A Kempis, to whom *The Imitation of Christ* is traditionally ascribed, gave classic expression to the piety which sprang from the movement known as the Brethren of the Common Life, and which had a profound influence on medieval Christendom. In *The Imitation of Christ* it is Christ's noble life of love which inspires and arouses our desire to be Christ-like and loving.[3] Christ is the inspiring banner under whom we follow. Our task is to love as Christ loves. And A Kempis promises, 'if thou couldst empty thyself perfectly of all created things, Jesus would willingly dwell with thee'.[4] This leaves us with one anxious, lingering question: how do I know I have emptied myself enough for Christ to dwell with me and share his victory?

Four centuries later, Pilgrims and Puritans from Europe arrived penniless on America's shores to build God's kingdom on earth. Through obedience, prayer and sheer hard work, many were convinced that America would be transformed into God's millenial kingdom. In Finney's thought, Jesus was the model of perfect, self-sacrificing love who inspires and stimulates reasonable people, endowed with freedom, to sacrifice their own interests for the good of their fellows. Therefore our task is to make ourselves new hearts or suffer the consequences of eternal pain.[5] The nagging question remains, have I, after all, managed to change

---

[3] Thomas A Kempis, *The Imitation of Christ*, 3:5.

[4] *Ibid.*, 2:7.

[5] DW Frank, *Less Than Conquerors* (Grand Rapids, 1986), p. 17. Finney quoted in p. 22.

my heart? This question became increasingly awkward, especially as, by the end of post civil war reconstruction, the anticipated moral transformation had run aground. Finney's postmillenial confidence in man's co-operation in building the kingdom of God was soon followed by his successor's premillenial pessimism.

Nonetheless for those optimistic spirits not dampened by rigorous introspection (William James's 'healthy minded'[6]), appropriating Christ's victory grants an opportunity for a modest consolation upon surveying one's own moral advance. This gentle inflation elevates the convert who successfully slays clearly identifiable dragons such as alcohol for the fundamentalist or big business for the social gospeller. However, our dilemma is larger than a struggle against a proscriptive list of sins which one (fortunately) rather adroitly avoids. The optimism of appropriating Christ's moral victory resolves too easily the recalcitrance of human sin, which the Reformers had perceived as a radical disobedience pervading all our faculties including reason, common sense and even the noblest aspirations of human love. The very nature of man is corrupt.

If the moral optimist's easy struggle fails to hear Isaiah's judgment that all our righteousness is filthy rags, the anguished pessimist's failed quest for moral victory engenders a damaging deflation for those whose introspective conscience is that which James describes as the 'sick soul'. The fiercely self-critical makes an appalling discovery: every good act conceals a selfish motive and a further good deed left undone. When can one have assurance that every last evil has been confessed and confessed with sufficient contrition?

The inherent frustration of the struggle to appropriate Christ's victory by worthy inner and outer acts prepares us for the other recurrent appropriation-centred response, namely, the utter passivity of absolute dependence whereby the inner moral struggle is abandoned and one surrenders fully to God's victory on my

[6]W James, *The Varieties of Religious Experience* (New York, 1958 (1901)), p. 137.

behalf. William James describes the surrender of the medieval mystic as the feeling that one's will has been emptied and one has been 'grasped and held by a superior power'. Thus St Theresa described her experience or vision of union with God as a being 'wholly asleep' regarding the things of the world and herself, 'deprived of every feeling', her understanding 'so stricken with inactivity that she neither knows what she loves, nor in what manner she loves, nor what she wills ... Thus does God, when he raises a soul to union with himself suspend the natural action of all her faculties. She neither sees, hears, nor understands, so long as she is united to God'.[7]

Nineteenth (and twentieth) century American evangelicals put this appropriation model more simply and marketably: 'let go and let God'. If you do both, you cannot fail to appropriate Christ's victory for your life. In their literature and preaching, there would follow very attractive success stories of those who have surrendered.[8] Judging by the testimonies public and published, this model appears to work for some. But others have with increasing weariness struggled to surrender and to claim the victory by faith, only to fail again and again to maintain the 'letting go'. Just to add condemnation to failure, there would always be someone nearby ready to heap guilt upon you by suggesting that (your) lack of victory is due to (your) hidden unbelief. Either way, in victory or defeat, the appropriating subject is given centre stage. The believer's failure, like his successes, too easily becomes the focus of faith detached from the faithfulness of God. Ironically, when the height of our human response is described as a sleeplike relaxation whereby God

---

[7]Quoted in James, *op. cit.*, pp. 313-4.

[8]Franks, *op. cit.*, p. 149. Franks has documented how this surrender and passivity before God became the dominant model of evangelical Christianity, following the loss of cultural leadership in the later nineteenth century. It was advocated by the leaders of the Keswick movement in England and by Americans such as Moody and Turnbull. James and Franks have documented the striking resemblance of the mind-healing techniques of passive relaxation and concentration in such overtly divergent groups as Christian Science, medieval mysticism and the positive mental attitude school. Cf. James, *op. cit.*, pp. 87-8, 96-7 and Frank, *op. cit.*, p. 149.

energizes our lives, we have a focus which is simultaneously a serious devaluation and denigration of our human response. The same devaluation occurs when one describes our faith or our love as merely a particle or stream of the divine love. If our faith was an actual part of the divine ocean, as Barth remarked, the quality of our Christian living and loving 'could not and would not be so weak and puny'.[9]

In both appropriation-centred models, the subject is 'thrown back upon himself' as James Torrance would say, in the former to achieve tangible fruits of repentance worthy of the Gospel, in the latter to attain an inner state of faith or serenity. In addition, failure or emotional pain is a sign, never of a pilgrim taking up one's cross and stretching atrophied spiritual muscles, but of unbelief, which one must eliminate. Whether by appropriation through imitation or inner surrender, the agent becomes burdened with the demands of law: to surrender or to work. Both models inadvertently precipitate humanity's twin dilemmas of the inflation of pride as we triumph or the deflation of despair should we fail to appropriate.

The Gospel, however, is larger than a necessary means to my beatitude. It is by replacing the subject-centred model of appropriation with an object-centred participation in Christ, that we can revalue our *de facto* narcissistic focus on 'my conversion', 'my victory', as the goal and Christ's death *pro nobis* as the essential means. Paul's summons to be baptized into Christ's death is a summons for the subject to give priority to God's activity in Christ, to understand our life as hid with God in Christ (Col. 3:3). In other words, participation in Christ rather than appropriation of Christ for my benefit repentantly redirects our focus to knowing and loving God for his sake, thereby reflecting the quality of God's own love for us. A theology of participation integrates our faith and our works as a grateful response to the initiating faithfulness of God and makes discipleship an ongoing and natural development of faith. Thus one can both take seriously the warfare of the Christian against

[9]K Barth, *CD* IV/2, p. 785.

the powers and principalities (Eph. 6) and the hopeful mood of
the Gospels, without tumbling into one of pride's twin errors.
But this possibility is contingent upon centring our subjectivity
and spirituality in christology, particularly a christology which
reckons Jesus Christ as the place where my sinful humanity, now
inflated, now deflated, is encountered by God, judged and
reconciled.

Here Jung's psychological insights into the healing of neurosis
enrich our appreciation of an object-centred participation, leading
up beyond the impasse of serenity or struggle. Jung's inquiry
into the human psyche convinced him that there were struggles
larger than those exposed by Freud through the analysis of our
personal childhood. Using the symbols given to him through his
own exploration, he charted this unmapped territory with the help
of datum points which he described as the archetypes of the
collective unconscious (shadow, anima, animus, etc.). Jung's
empirical investigations into the human psyche convinced him
that Jesus Christ functioned in Western society as the numinous
paradigm of wholeness (the integrated Self), who releases moral
energy in those who respond to his self-giving love. Curiously,
Jung insisted that the humanity of Jesus was irrelevant for
analytical psychology, since as a perfect being, he himself had
no inner conflict between good and evil.[10] Hence for Jung we
participate in a psychic archetype of the true Self (Christ), not a
person in whom our inner cosmic history and the activity of
world history intersect. Similarly, Jung rejected the Christian
doctrine of the trinity as incomplete because a trinity lacks
conflict with the shadow (the inferior self) and hence is immature.
Jung preferred a quaternity to the trinity for the sake of
psychological wholeness.[11]

It is significant that both of Jung's psychological criticisms of
Christian doctrine disappear when one defines perfection in the
wake of the incarnate Son's embrace and healing of our sinful

[10]C Jung, *Collected Works*, vol. 9, pt. II, 'Christ, a Symbol of the Self',
(London, 1951), pp. 36ff., 71 and vol. 11, 'A Psychological Approach to the
Dogma of the Trinity', pp. 125-6.
[11]*Collected Works*, vol. 18, p. 1475.

humanity. Then we see in Christ a place of divine warfare whereby our moral agony is lifted up and engaged as God's atoning activity in Christ. Though his death on the cross is the culminating conflict, his entire life is atoning, for throughout he has grappled, from womb to tomb, with ancient and primordial conscious and unconscious conflicts endemic to our humanity. In Christ, God gathers up humanity's groaning and travail within his own flesh and makes it part of God's history, which culminates in the resurrection triumph out of failure.

Here then is a response to Christ's victory which is not cast in terms of our appropriating the benefits of Christ's victory through moral effort or our cessation of effort. Here is rather an interior portrait of our participation through the *koinonia* of the Spirit in the one true man who has experienced the agonizing conflict between sin and love. This conflict will lead us also to our daily little crosses, whose design weaves a healing tapestry across our divergent experiences of joy and sorrow, serenity and struggle, culminating in death and resurrection. When our life's conflicts, failures and triumphs are intersected by the atoning journey of the Son into the far country, our life becomes a pilgrimage of relational union with the One who was made perfect through what he suffered (Heb. 5:8). We participate by the Spirit in the Son who bent back our twisted humanity as he 'grew in wisdom, stature and favour with God and man' (Luke 2:52). The word 'grew' (*prokopto*) is literally a nautical expression meaning 'to beat one's way forward blow by blow'. [12] Participation in the *prokope* of God sheds light on certain Pauline themes. For example, Paul uses the same word to tell anxious Philippians that his very imprisonment is advancing the Gospel (Phil. 1:12). Similarly, Paul at once accepts the prophecy of Acts 21 that he will be jailed if he proceeds to Jerusalem and yet feels compelled to continue, knowing that God had advanced the Gospel by lifting up his Son high on a cross and thereby had drawn all men unto him (John 12:32). [13]

---

[12] 'Prokope', O Stahlin, *Theological Dictionary of the New Testament*, vol. VI, G Kittel and G Friedrich (eds.), (Grand Rapids, 1968, (1975)), p. 704. I am grateful to Professor Torrance for making this point in one of his seminars.

[13] Phil. 3:10-11. Cf. also Acts 14:22, Eph. 4:12-16, 2 Cor. 4:8-10, 16.

What precisely does our participation in Christ look and feel like when our sinful humanity responds to the Gospel? It is the merit of Jung's analysis to provide a picture of the process whereby narcissism is transformed into wholeness. (It is a picture we shall recognize). Whenever the movement from narcissism to love occurs, the psychological consequences are epitomized by the symbol of the cross. Jung categorically states that all personal development leads to an ever menacing awareness of the conflict between good and evil which involves nothing less than a crucifixion of the ego, its agonizing suspension between two irreconcilable opposites.[14] Participation in Christ or being buried in Christ's death (Paul), cannot be reduced to a mystical relaxation technique of surrender, for it describes a profound inner conflict whereby the subject begins to make unconscious struggles conscious. Jung describes the terrain the neurotic or schizophrenic must traverse in order to experience the healing process whereby one ceases projecting inner conflict (or repressing), takes responsibility for them, and then voluntarily participates in the crucifixion of the narcissistic ego.[15] Unless I take up my little cross daily and daily lose my life to find it, I will project my inner conflicts and fight a legion of external battles and opponents who become not adversaries to agree with quickly or enemies to love, but rivals to defeat. And who after observing would doubt that many theological debates with external opponents are compensatory jousts fought in order to avoid inner battles and a radical repentance within our inner selves?

I believe our pilgrimage of participation in the Gospel, when seen in a dimension of psychological depth, reveals a baptism of the self into the death and resurrection of Christ which is both more costly than a selective and self-congratulating imitation, and is a more profound description of our encounter with God's activity of grace on my behalf than a mental-emotional technique of

[14]*Collected Works*, vol. 9, pt. II, p. 44.

[15]This is corroborated by Alfred Adler's description of mental illness as the refusal to die daily. Quoted in Ernest Becker, *The Denial of Death* (New York, 1973), p. 265.

relaxation and surrender. For as we participate in the Gospel, we come to realize that God uses man not only when he is a passive instrument, but as we share in the life of Christ, we truly experience our human capacity to create, explore, repent and serve. It is important to understand that the creative love of the Father never seeks self-denial or self-sacrifice as an end in itself or as inherently virtuous. The narcissistic ego is not to be crushed, but judged, forgiven and healed by its baptism into Christ's life and death. As CS Lewis's Screwtape reminds us, God desires to put to death our self-preferential love in order to replace it with a new kind of self-love, 'a charity and gratitude for all selves, including (sic) their own ... for he always gives back with his right hand what he has taken away with his left'.[16]

All the models we have discussed grasp the importance of getting beyond detached conceptual contemplation of ideas about the atonement. It is never adequate to merely analyse the atonement intellectually. However, the two appropriation models we have discussed are cast in such a way as to isolate us within a self-preoccupied, narcissistic model, which severely minimizes the power of Christ's atonement to burst away our old wineskins of anthropocentric strategies. The twin movements of Christ's participation in our fallen creatureliness and our 'blow by blow' participation in his life, death and resurrection cast us loose upon the gracious sea of the Trinity. I thereby allow myself to be caught up in the form of death and resurrection.

We may describe the form of dying and rising chronologically, but in daily living it is rarely a succession of events. Death and resurrection interpenetrate all the time.[17] It is by this pilgrimage that the entire person, both intellectually and emotionally, receives and stands under the imprint of the crucified and risen Word of God. My human, noetic response, like the ontic gift of grace, involves me in risking myself in an active, participatory way.

---

[16]CS Lewis, *The Screwtape Letters* (London, 1971, (1942)), pp. 73-4.

[17]See Maria Boulding, *Marked for Life, Prayer in the Easter Christ* (London, 1979), pp. 7-10 for a helpful discussion.

I have tried to describe a way of union and communion with Christ in which I come to know him both in the fellowship of his sufferings and the power of his resurrection. This is a communion where my failures and weaknesses are not necessarily signs of an inadequate surrender and failure to appropriate Christ's victory, but which may become by the Spirit, moments of depth encounter with my own evil and the love of God which has descended to touch me in the very hell of my sinful humanity. This grants us a revelation of our successes and our failures. Our weaknesses may become the avenues of God's strength. Our victories and moral advantages may become the repentant womb of a grace which reveals that, like Paul, my consciously cultivated virtues conceal an unconscious chaos of greed and pride. Both triumphs and failures become a place of meeting with the God who transfigures them into dwellings of surprising forgiveness. And this engenders a gracious spirit in me towards others who are similarly undeserving but forgiven. For I too have been touched by the judge whose righteousness does not condemn, but bears my condemnation for me in sacrificial love. Jesus Christ becomes for me not only the truth, but the way and the life.

# 6

# The Church : a Communion of Persons

ROLAND WALLS

In 1964, at the Second Vatican Council, the Roman Catholic
Church in the Dogmatic Constitution *Lumen Gentium* forsook its
age-long emphasis on the church as a *societas perfecta* and
returned to the rich biblical and patristic descriptions of the
church as the pilgrim people, the people of God, the Body of
Christ, and as the community who participate and share in the life
of God through Christ in the Holy Spirit.   Already, in his
encyclical *Mystici Corporis* in 1943, Pope Pius XII had gathered
up some of the results of scriptural and patristic research of the
previous fifty years.  So ended a long reign of what was in fact an
exercise in Platonic sociology, and so began the possibility of
dialogue and understanding between Orthodox, Catholic and
Reformed ecclesiologies.   In 1985 the Extraordinary Synod of
Bishops underlined the need to unpack the meaning of the church
as Communion, as community in Christ.

*Lumen Gentium* declared that the nature and mission of the church
could only adequately be understood in the context of the mystery
of God's saving, liberating work.  God's gracious will and
purpose, hidden from all eternity has now been revealed and
realized in Christ through the church: to share with men and
women the riches of his own divine life in an ineffable
communion of love through Christ in the sanctification of the
Holy Spirit.  'The Eternal Father in accordance with the utterly
gratuitous and mysterious design of his wisdom and goodness ...
chose to raise up human beings to share in his own divine life ...
Hence the universal church is seen to be a people brought into
unity from the Unity of the Father, the Son and the Holy
Spirit'.[1]

---

[1]*Lumen Gentium* I, 2.4.

The church then as communion is the product, the image and reflection of the very life of God the Blessed Trinity - of the communion of the persons of Father, Son and Holy Spirit. It is brought into existence by the love of God, the grace of our Lord Jesus Christ through the participation the sharing of the Holy Spirit (2 Cor. 13:14), to be a reflection of Persons in Community.

The orthodox bishop and theologian John Zizioulas has devoted a complete study to this fundamental aspect of the church.[2] 'The church', he says, 'is not simply an institution. She is a mode of existence, a way of being. She herself is an image of the way in which God himself exists'. How then does God exist? He exists in three substantial relationships, as Father, Son and Holy Spirit - substantial because these relations constitute the being of God. They are not accidental but essential. They are the relations of the one love of the Father, Son and the co-beloved Spirit who completes this shared love, for love desires to share what it receives and multiply what it offers. The life of the Trinity is a constant reciprocity in mutual selfgiving.[3] God then is Being as communion, where existence and life are identical with a shared eternal love. Zizioulas believes that Christian belief in the Trinity originated as much in the experience of the church community as in its reflection. 'God could only be known through the relations of Persons in a personal love'.[4] It is the communion experienced by and in the church which prompted reflection on the God revealed by Jesus Christ. What God has done by creating the church reveals who He is. He is the God whose very life is to be at once open to receive from another and to give oneself to the other - to live for, and in the other by the gift of himself in an eternal bond which is the Holy Spirit, and thus to be himself.

It is that eternal selfgiving of God that has been in the Holy Spirit poured out at Pentecost. That outpouring itself is the fruit

---

[2]See JD Zizioulas, *Being as Communion* (London, 1985).

[3]L Bouyer, *Meaning of Monastic Life* (London, 1955).

[4]Zizioulas, *op. cit.*, p. 16.

of the self-giving death and resurrection of the Son fulfilling the will of the love of the Father. Through the Holy Spirit the innermost mystery of the life of God the Holy Trinity is opened in sheer unmerited gift to us. We become the adopted sons in the Son of God. We become this not by mere imitation but by sharing in this new form of being - being as communion, being constituted by selfgiving. So in our created way we reflect and share in the divine nature (2 Pet. 1:4). This is eternal life, this is salvation: to be brought within the unbroken circle of God's being in communion. Just as God's being is a consummated distinction in a union of mutual love, so this too is the work of the Holy Spirit in the church as communion of persons. 'He is the gift of the Father's love by which we love him in the Son, by which we fully become ourselves in becoming his sons and daughters in a return to our source even the Father. The blessedness of the Kingdom of God when the church realizes what she really is, is a participation in the divine life of the Trinity. It is the deified state of co-heirs of the divine nature, who possess what the Holy Trinity possesses by nature'.[5]

To believe in the church as communion of persons reflecting in created human society the life of the Blessed Trinity means to move from the Aristotelian idea of an individual as a self-enclosed centre of a unit of existence, to open outward-going relational existence of persons. Persons exist only in relationship. They are constituted by relationship with other persons. It was Christian reflection on the Trinity that revealed this categorical distinction between individuals and persons. St. John of Damascus wrote, 'the persons are made one, not so as to commingle, but so as to cleave to each other and have their being in each other'.[6] The human being was created to be in the image of such a God and human society was made to be a communion of persons - not a collectivity of individuals. Salvation is therefore an escape from isolated, divided, selfcentred, individual existence into a new creation of outward going, relational community of persons. St Thomas Aquinas

[5]V Lossky, *Mystical Theology of the Eastern Church* (London, 1957), p. 65.

[6]St John of Damascus, *De Fide Orthodoxa*, 1.8.

identified person and relationship in his laconic sentence, *persona est relatio*.[7]

If the church takes its origin from the gracious work of God in constituting persons in community to be a reflection of his own life then it is clear that all merely sociological and anthropological accounts of the church are utterly irrelevant in discussing what she really is. The nature of the church is rooted in the nature of the God who created it.

What are some of the consequences which flow from this? Beatrice Bruteau in her article *Trinitarian Personhood*[8] argues that we as members of the Holy Community are not separate inert substances. On the contrary it is our relational activity which is the basic reality on which all else depends. I exist, I am, when I give myself gratuitously to another. For us as in the Trinity 'plurality of real persons is a plurality that is necessarily a unity'. No more in my ecclesial-being-in-relation do I exist by reacting to people and situations by what Bruteau calls a determined Karma which imprisons me. I am free in the act of loving self-giving to share the grace that made me free - without any prejudicial thought of how deserving the other is. Love is its own reason and it does not arise out of nature - the old Adam, but out of the grace found in and from the new Adam. Therefore as I act as a free, grace receiving, grace giving person I am realizing in my own existence the being of the church and reflecting in my being the image of the Trinity. Indeed, I am sharing in the ecstatic being in a gracious act of self-giving and in the enstasy of finding my life in the other. We thus fulfil the prayer of Christ that we may make our home in him as He finds his home in us. We extend in ourselves the mutual indwelling and coinherence of the Father and the Son. So it is that God has loved the church and us into existence not as single 'saved' individuals but as a community of persons. 'There is no such thing as one person - that is metaphysically impossible'.

---

[7] St Thomas Aquinas, *Summa Theologica*, 1a q.29 a24.

[8] B Bruteau, 'Trinitarian Personhood', *Cistercian Studies*, XXII (1987), p. 3.

The nature of the church is further revealed when we reflect that she takes her origin from God through the Paschal Mystery of the death and resurrection of Jesus Christ. There would never have been a revelation of God as Trinity without this death and resurrection. The movement of New Testament reflection on the Cross is the same as the mystical movement in the first revelation of Divine Love to Julian Norwich. On May 8th 1373, from 4 o'clock in the morning on her apparent death bed, she was granted a vision of the thorn-crowned head of the God-man 'and at the same moment my soul was filled with joy at the thought of the Holy Trinity: for wherever Christ is spoken of there the Trinity is meant'.[9]

The movement is from the sight of one who by giving himself to me gave himself in love to the Father. He revealed himself as a person whose existence is rooted in his relation to the Father. Christ who offered himself in an eternal spirit in a love which is rooted in his Father's love, and who in that love finds us in a death and misery which is ours. The resurrection is the testimony that the Father accepts and returns such love - giving him as the God-man the glory he had as the eternal Son. The cross and resurrection - the Paschal Mystery reveals the Triune God and is also the climax of his loving activity in bringing the old individual Adam to judgment and death, and renewing him, recreating him, bringing him back to life with and in the second Adam, the new man who renews our human nature so that it really reflects the God who made us. We are liberated from the old self-preoccupied, self-imprisoned individualism by a Person to be persons. That Person was the Son of the Father who was given and who gave himself to created a new community. In being the willing victim of our self regard he came to the loneliness of crucifixion to create a company of persons. Only such a costly opening from the side of Christ could give birth by water, by blood, by the Spirit to the new Eve, indivisibly flesh of his flesh, bone of his bone, his Bride and companion in a communion of love.

---

[9]Julian of Norwich, *Revelations of Divine Love* (London, 1966), ch. 4.

Fr John McDade SJ, in his contribution to the *Catholic Theological Association Proceedings*, 1986, spells out the intimate epistemological and theological relation of the Trinity to the Paschal Mystery. He writes, 'God's openness and movement towards the human realm which is exemplified most fully in the Spirit-filled exchange between the Father and the Son in the Paschal Mystery of the death and resurrection of Jesus is nothing other than the mystery which is at the heart of God's being. In this humiliation God is supremely God'.

Therefore the Paschal Mystery is inseparable from the gift of the Spirit - through the breathing of the crucified, risen Christ on the apostles and the tongues of Pentecostal fire on those assembled with one accord in one place. The church has been constituted by the death and resurrection of Christ as a community of persons born from a death which revealed the life of God as Creator and Redeemer.

If such is the origin and nature of the church then its sacraments, structures, discipline, pastoral care and mission must be brought into accord. In baptism we are by faith admitted to the very life of the Trinity of Persons. We are baptized not only in the name of the Trinity but into his name, i.e., into the life of the unity of persons, and our only entry into this life is by being baptized into, and taking upon ourselves, the death and resurrection of the Beloved who gives us the new life as persons in community. This once for all gracious gift is maintained corporately and personally by the Eucharist which constantly constitutes the church as an event as well as a continuous corporation until he come. The circle of the Trinity in the icon of the *Philoxenia* by Andrei Rublev is opened up to us by the proffered gifts on the table whereby we are invited to share in the gracious self-giving of the Son of God. We are offered a share in his death and life so that we may be the adopted sons and daughters in one Spirit of the Father.

In a real sense then the local eucharistic assembly - the local parish community has the fulness, the catholicity, of the community of persons. Here in the one Spirit united to the one Son we worship the Father. The problem of division among Christians is most acute here, for the local assemblies should reflect the same communion of the whole church. It should reflect from the eucharistic centre of each assembly a common care, a common faith and love undivided in space or time - a realized catholicity prolonging and implementing our baptismal unity. The president of the eucharist is more than the president of the local assembly. Such a ministry should be the sign of unity not only of the local body but of the whole body of Christ - past, present, future, regional and global. We need to see our ecumenical problems about ministry in terms of the eucharistic focus. We need to move away from administrative and merely juridical aspects at the local level and spell out the consequences of how it relates to the whole church and to the overcoming of our separation we shall begin from the centre and not from the circumference of our manifestation of our life in Christ. In Scotland this is particularly important. Here a reformed local parish episcopacy operates in the Church of Scotland over against a regional personal episcopacy and a global presidency of Roman Catholic ministry. Visible unity round one table in each place is demanded by the very nature of the sacrament. How do we move towards this and towards a universally accepted ministry? We need one another. We need to listen attentively to each other's experience of unity albeit incomplete and ravaged by our separations. No amount of ecclesiastical diplomacy and committee-compromise can take the place of this sharing of our experience of sacramental unity as we know it even in our separation. We need to explore the place of the ordained minister as the servant of unity and his present function in each of our church assemblies as the unifier of the manifold ministries of the body of believers. [10]

The visible sign of communion has been blurred and defaced by our arrogance, impatience, infidelity, intolerance and self-sufficiency. We have ceased to be conscious that we need one

---

[10] See P McFarlen, 'Eucharistic Ecclesiology', in *One in Christ*, 4 (1986), p. 314.

another. We have allowed the people of God to become almost indistinguishable from clubs and human associations for the promotion of religion and good works. We look like competitive multi-nationals in a free enterprise market. The world has not been able to know that the Father has sent the Son by our visible unity which is to be as unbreakable as the Son's unity with the Father.

Perhaps this is the place to make a plea for the right understanding (though not necessarily agreement) of the eucharistic discipline of the Orthodox and Roman Catholics. For these, the Eucharist is the sign and effective source of the visible unity round one table. The question then is not so much where we have come from to the table, but what we are going to do after communion. To go back into separation after the sacrament is to miss the point of the sacrament according to this view. Such discipline looks like, and in practice can be, exclusivism but is really meant to avoid the use of the Sacrament to paper over cracks that need attention, or to prevent the supermarket 'shopping around' attitude of those who see in the sacrament nothing more than help to the individual. The fact that both Orthodox and Catholics observe this traditional discipline in separation is a sign of the absurdity of separation. Catholics and Orthodox alike need to come to understand the evangelical attitude of those who believe the Sacrament is also the sign of gracious forgiving fidelity to this new covenant in Christ, which remains in spite of our perfidious betrayal of his gift of unity and peace. Underlying our continuing divisions is the question of ministry - what its nature is and how it should be exercised. Here again, we all need to examine how the exercise of ministry, presbyterial, episcopal and papal, really is the ministry of, and for persons in communion, who are intended by God to be not only a unity of believers, but also a sign of the predestined unity of the human family. God created the human race to be a communion of persons 'in his image' so that they might reflect the glory of the Three in One.

Part Two

# Christ in the History of Christian Thought

# 7

# Creation, Christ, and Culture in Dutch Neo-Calvinism

JEREMY BEGBIE

From the middle of the sixteenth century, it was the Calvinist wing of the Reformation which exercised the most decisive influence in the Netherlands, and the anti-Arminian Synod of Dort (1618-1619) which provided the Dutch Reformed Church with its most important doctrinal standard.[1] The movement with which we are concerned has its roots in that period towards the end of the nineteenth century when a number of Dutch churchmen reacted against what they saw as a drift in some circles away from historic orthodoxy. Out of this 'awakening' in the Reformed Church came a secession and the formation of the *Christelijke Gereformeerde Kerk*. The breakaway group eventually assisted in the founding of the Free University of Amsterdam in 1880. Largely under the inspiration of Abraham Kuyper, 'Neo-Calvinism' began to transform the political and cultural life of the Netherlands, and was soon carried to the New World with far-reaching consequences. Today, its force can still be felt in many parts of the globe, particularly in the United States, Canada and South Africa.[2]

---

[1] The five main sections of the Articles of the Synod of Dort became the basis of the 'five points' of Calvinism: (1) unconditional election, (2) limited atonement, (3) the total depravity of man, (4) irresistible grace, and (5) the final perseverance of the saints. These truths were thought to be in line with both the Belgic Confession (1561) and the Heidelberg Catechism (1562), and spread far beyond the Netherlands.

[2] Cf. JD Bratt, 'The Dutch Schools' and CT McIntyre, 'Herman Dooyeweerd in North America', both in DF Wells, (ed.), *Reformed Theology in America* (Grand Rapids, 1985), pp. 135-52 and 172-85 respectively; JD Bratt, *Dutch Calvinism in Modern America* (Grand Rapids, 1984) especially pt. vi; T Dunbar Moodie, *The Rise of Afrikanerdom* (Berkeley, Los Angeles and London, 1975), pp. 52-72; JW de Gruchy, *The Church Struggle in South Africa* (Grand Rapids, 1986), pp. 5-10, 21, 32, 81, 90, 201.

Ever since it emerged, Dutch Neo-Calvinism has had its share of internal debate, much of it generating more heat than light. Nevertheless, it is not hard to discern a number of common theological themes which give the movement its own distinctive character, and it is these, especially as they apply to the theology of culture, which I shall try to highlight and evaluate in what follows. As I hope will become apparent, a study of this tradition raises vital questions about the relation between Christ and culture which are still with us today and are in urgent need of tackling. To keep the discussion within manageable limits, I shall restrict myself mainly to the three most influential Neo-Calvinists: namely Kuyper, Herman Bavinck and Herman Dooyeweerd.

### God's Sovereignty and Sphere Sovereignty: Abraham Kuyper and Herman Bavinck

There is no doubt that Abraham Kuyper (1837-1920), statesman, church reformer, theologian, journalist, champion of Calvinism and co-founder of the Free University, should be considered the father of Dutch Neo-Calvinism.[3] Kuyper's dominant message was that only a full engagement by Christians in every area of culture was consistent with a biblical view of the world, and that only Calvinism could provide an adequate theoretical backing to such engagement. Calvinism supplies us with an all-embracing, comprehensive view of man's place in creation under God.[4] Undergirding this was Kuyper's passionate belief in the sovereignty of God: 'First stands the confession of the absolute Sovereignty of the Triune God; ... This is the fundamental conception of religion as maintained by Calvinism, and hitherto, no one has ever found a higher conception. For no higher conception *can* be found'.[5]

God's sovereignty is the 'authority that contains all right within

---

[3]For an excellent summary of Kuyper's life, see JM Van der Kroef, 'Abraham Kuyper and the Rise of Neo-Calvinism in the Netherlands', *Church History*, 17 (1948), pp. 316-34. Cf. also Frank Vanden Berg, *Abraham Kuyper* (St Catherine's, Ontario, 1978); and D Jellema, 'Abraham Kuyper's Attack on Liberalism', *Review of Politics*, 19 (Oct 1957), pp. 472-85.

[4]A Kuyper, *Calvinism* (London , 1932), pp. 27-42.

[5]*Ibid.*, p. 81.

itself ... and exercises power to ... destroy every resistance to [his] will'. [6]  As the sovereign ruler, God orders and regulates all things according to certain fixed principles: 'There are ordinances of God for our bodies, for the blood that courses through our arteries and veins, and for our lungs as organs of respiration. And even so there are ordinances of God, in logic, to regulate our thoughts; ordinances of God for our imagination, in the domain of aesthetics; and so, also, strict ordinances of God for the whole of human life in the domain of morals'.[7]

On this basis, Kuyper built his famous theory of 'sphere sovereignty'. In his Stone lectures, he argues that three 'spheres' of sovereignty govern human life: sovereignty in the state, sovereignty in society, and sovereignty in the Church.[8] Moreover, within each of these there are many further spheres. There can be no trespass of one sphere on another, for all the spheres of life have their own innate laws.[9]  'Human life', Kuyper argues, 'appears to be neither simple nor uniform but represents an infinitely complex composite organism.  It is so constituted that ... there are all kinds of spheres in life, as many as the starry hosts in the firmament, whose boundaries are drawn with firm lines, each having its own principle as a focal point ... And because each has its own domain, within the boundaries of that domain each has its own sovereignty'.[10]

---

[6]As quoted and translated by GC Berkouwer in *A Half Century of Theology* (Grand Rapids, 1977), p. 90.

[7]Kuyper, *op. cit.*, p. 114.

[8]*Ibid.*, p. 126.  It was the statesman, historian and writer Groen Van Prinsterer (1801-1876) who first used the concept of 'sovereignty within its own sphere (*souvereiniteit in eigen sfeer*)'. (Cf. H Dooyeweerd, *Roots of Western Culture* (Toronto, 1979), p. 53.)  Groen Van Prinsterer's life and work had a powerful impact on Kuyper.

[9]One of the primary motivating forces behind Kuyper's doctrine of sphere sovereignty was his deeply engrained suspicion of the state exercising too strong a hold on human society.  Cf. C Veenhof, *Souvereiniteit in Eigen Kring* (Goes, 1939), pp. 91ff.

[10]'Souvereiniteit in Eigen Kring', as quoted and translated by G Spykman in 'Sphere-sovereignty in Calvin and the Calvinist Tradition', in *Exploring the Heritage of John Calvin*, DE Holwerda (ed.), (Grand Rapids, 1976), pp. 182ff.

Kuyper's successor at Amsterdam, Herman Bavinck (1854-1921),
proposed a theology of creation which follows very much the
same contours as his mentor. 'Everything', Bavinck writes, 'was
created with its own nature and is based upon ordinances
appointed by God for it'.[11] 'As the moral law was created into
Adam's heart as the rule of his life, so all creatures carried in their
own nature the principles and laws of their own development ...
The whole creation is a system of divine ordinances ... God gave
to all creatures a certain order, a law which they do not
violate'.[12] Yet in the diversity of creation, 'there is also a
supreme unity ... It is [God] who created all things according to
his incomparable wisdom, who continually sustains them in their
distinct natures, who guides and governs them according to the
potentials and laws created in them ... Here is a unity which does
not destroy, but maintains diversity, and a diversity which does
not depreciate unity, but unfolds it in its richness'.[13]

In order to elucidate further the way in which God exercised his
rule over creation, particularly when that rule is not explicitly
acknowledged or known, Kuyper introduced the notion of
'common grace'.[14] Common grace is rooted in Christ as the
Mediator of creation[15] and ultimately in the eternal decrees of
God.[16] Although operative immediately after the fall, it found its
'solid historical starting-point (*vaste geschiedkundige
uitsgangspunt*)' in God's covenant with Noah.[17] Negatively,
common grace restrains the destructive effects of sin in man and
nature (the 'constant' operation of common grace[18]); positively,

---

[11]As quoted and translated by G Spykman, *ibid.*, p. 180.

[12]*Ibid.*

[13]*Ibid.*

[14]For a discussion of this topic and a brief survey of the proponents of the
doctrine prior to Kuyper, see H Kuiper, *Calvin on Common Grace* (Grand
Rapids, 1928). For many years Kuyper wrote on the subject in the journal
*Heraut*, and expanded his insights in a mammoth work entitled *De Gemeene
Gratie [DGG]*, 3 Vols., 4th ed., (Kampen, no date).

[15]*DGG* II, p. 645.

[16]*Ibid.*, pp. 609, 611.

[17]*DGG* I, p. 11.

[18]Kuyper's treatment of this negative aspect predominates in volume I of

it 'equips human life ever more thoroughly against suffering, and internally brings it to richer and fuller development'[19] (the 'progressive' operation).[20] Common grace thus provides the possibility of, and the impetus for, human culture. In cultural activity, the powers latent in creation are developed and brought to fruition to the glory of God.[21]

Among Kuyper's followers, this doctrine of common grace found its strongest supporter in Bavinck. Before the fall, according to Bavinck, God was related to man as the law-giver, the One who commands and demands. Man stood before God as to a judge, a relationship conditional on man's obedience. After the fall, God relates to man through grace (whether common or special).[22] Through common grace, which was formally established in the Noaic covenant (a 'covenant of nature'),[23] the pernicious effects of sin are curbed in mankind and the natural world.[24] God's common grace does not annul his 'cultural mandate' (Gen. 1:28; 2:15). Indeed, common grace preserves and promotes culture.[25] It is still man's inescapable duty to cultivate and subdue the earth, bringing its inherent potential to fulfilment.[26]

The doctrine of common grace, therefore, was designed to direct Christians to a sustained involvement in cultural life. In James

---

*DGG*.

[19]*DGG* II, p. 606.

[20]Kuyper's treatment of this positive aspect predominates in vol. II of *DGG*.

[21]*DGG* II, p. 118; III, p. 435.

[22]*Our Reasonable Faith* [*RF*] (Grand Rapids, 1956), pp. 271ff. and ch. XIV *passim*. Note Bavinck's forceful way of stating man's pre-lapsarian condition: 'The first man ... was given something, indeed, was given much to *do*; he was also given something, though this was little, which he was *not* to do'. *Ibid.*, p. 218.

[23]*De Algemeene Genade*, (Grand Rapids, no date), pp. 4ff.; *Handleiding Nij Het Onderwijs in den Christelijken Godsdienst*, (Kampen, 1913), p. 109; *RF*, pp. 48ff.

[24]*Beginselen der Psychologie*, (Kampen, 1897), p. 200; *Gereformeerde Dogmatiek* [*GD*] 4 vols., 2nd edn., (Kampen, 1908) III, p. 224.

[25]*GD* III, pp. 226ff., 661.

[26]*Ibid.*, p. 204; *RF*, pp. 187, 206ff.; 'Het Rijk Gods Het Hoogste Goed', in *Kennis en Leven*, (Kampen, 1922), pp. 49ff.

Bratt's words, it 'encouraged the redeemed to respect the good remaining in the world and to strive to augment it. Even more, it made many elements of human culture ... not just products but *means* of grace, instruments whereby God restrained sin and enabled men to develop creation as he had originally designed. Finally, it legitimized a certain amount of co-operation between the redeemed and unbelievers on the grounds that to some extent they shared a sense of the good and therefore a common purpose.[27]

Nevertheless, we are frequently told that we must not over-estimate the value of common grace. For the Neo-Calvinist, common grace must never be confused with 'special' or 'saving' grace; the former cannot bring a person to saving faith. It is Kuyper in particular who urges that there is a radical 'antithesis' between believer and non-believer. The focus of the Christian's personality (his 'heart') is fundamentally different from the non-Christian: only the former has been touched by special grace. The focus of a man's heart (his 'faith') is thus either on God or on some aspect of the created world. Kuyper ruthlessly presses this point home, applying it to virtually every realm of human activity, not least to the sciences.[28] This does not mean, however, that we can speak of a dichotomy between common and special grace as we see them at work in human history: 'They are not each enclosed within the walls of its own terrain. They work together in the same terrain. They, therefore, come in touch with each other. They meet each other in every plain of life'.[29] Moreover, there is a certain 'middle ground' between believer and unbeliever which is not affected by the antithesis - e.g., our sense of touch, seeing and hearing.[30]

## 'Christian Philosophy': Herman Dooyeweerd

In our own day, the broad lines of Kuyper's system have been

---

[27]*Op. cit.*, p. 20.

[28]The theme is expounded trenchantly in *Ijzer en Leem* (Amsterdam, 1885), and *Tweeërlei Vaderland* (Amsterdam, 1887). Cf. also *Encyclopaedia of Sacred Theology*, II de Vries (ET) (London, 1899), pp. 142ff.

[29]*DGG* II, p. 634.

[30]*Encyclopaedia of Sacred Theology*, pp. 157ff.

given formidable elaboration in the influential work of Herman Dooyeweerd (1894-1977), above all in his monumental *De Wijsbegeerte der Wetsidee* (1935-6) (*A New Critique of Theoretical Thought* (1953-8)).[31] Dooyeweerd, Professor of legal philosophy, encyclopaedia of law and medieval Dutch law at the Free University until 1965, unashamedly acknowledged the impact of Kuyper on his own thought and saw himself as standing squarely in the Kuyperian tradition.[32] But he was not uncritical of his theological forefather. Above all, in Dooyeweerd's eyes, Kuyper had failed to provide a biblically-grounded 'Christian philosophy' which would meet the challenges of modern Western civilisation.[33] To this end, Dooyeweerd begins by proposing that philosophy is the most fundamental systematic discipline of theoretical thought.[34] It is concerned with created reality as a whole in contrast to the special sciences which are concerned with only one aspect of creation.[35] The starting-point of philosophy (its 'Archimedean point') is the 'heart' of man, the religious root of man's life.[36] Following Kuyper, Dooyeweerd is convinced that the human heart is either turned towards God, or towards some form of the finite world.[37] Thus Dooyeweerd writes disparagingly of what he calls the 'pretended autonomy of philosophical thought'.[38] Rather, every philosophy works with an all-inclusive concept of reality - a 'cosmonomic Idea

---

[31]H Dooyeweerd, *De Wijsbegeerte der Wetsidee* (*A New Critique of Theoretical Thought*) [*NCTT*] 3 vols., DH Freeman and WS Young (ET), (Philadelphia, 1969).

[32]*NCTT* I, pp. 523ff.

[33]Dooyeweerd's evaluation of Kuyper can best be seen in 'Kuyper's Wetenschapsleer', *Philosophia Reformata* IV (1939), pp. 193-232.

[34]*NCTT* I, pp. 4ff. Cf. pp. 86ff.

[35]*Ibid.*, pp. 4, 85; cf. pp. 545-66.

[36]*Ibid.*, pp. v, 8, 12, 16. *Transcendental Problems of Philo-sophical Thought* (Grand Rapids, 1948), p. 67. *In the Twilight of Western Thought* (Nutley, New Jersey, 1960), pp. 173-95.

[37]*NCTT* I, p. 524. However, Dooyeweerd is keen to point out that recognition of this antithesis should not be used as a means of making a personal classification between specific groups of people. See *ibid.*, p. viii.; and L Kalsbeek, *Contours of a Christian Philosophy. An Introduction to Herman Dooyeweerd's Thought* (Toronto, 1975), p. 46.

[38]*In the Twilight of Western Thought*, pp. 1-60.

(*Wetsidee*)'.[39]   As far as Christian philosophy is concerned, it is founded on the notion of 'sphere sovereignty' in creation, the belief that the Archimedean point for all synthetic acts of thought is the regenerated heart of the believer, and that the Origin of the meaning inherent in the cosmos is the sovereign holy will of God who has revealed himself in Christ.[40]

Christian philosophy reveals to us that all creation is under 'law' - that is, as a finite unity, it is subject to the ordinances and norms which God has given to it. Law, in this sense, constitutes the 'boundary' between God and the cosmos: God is 'above' law, creation is 'under' law. [41]   The multiplicity of divine laws in creation can be distinguished and arranged as a list of 'modal law-spheres'.   Dooyeweerd distinguishes fifteen such spheres: the sphere of faith, the moral, juridical, aesthetic, economic, social, lingual, historical, logical, psychic (or 'sensitive), biotic, physical, kinematic, spatial, and numerical spheres.[42]   In line with Kuyper, Dooyeweerd believes that each modality has its own particular character, guaranteed by its 'nucleus' or 'nuclear moment' - the distinguishing and qualifying characteristic of that sphere.[43]   No modal aspect can be wholly explained or understood by reference to another modal aspect - each is irreducible.   Moreover, a contradiction of laws within the law-order is *a priori* impossible.[44]   We need not consider in detail Dooyeweerd's complex schematisation of the relationship between these spheres; the important point to note is that his labyrinthian

---

[39]*NCTT* I, pp. 94ff.

[40]*Ibid.*, p. 101.

[41]*NCTT* I, pp. 99ff.   This 'boundary', according to Dooyeweerd, is not to be construed as a spatial or physical boundary.   Still less should it be seen as a boundary for God.   Rather, it is an ontological boundary which limits *us* and which we are unable to cross.   Cf. *ibid.*, pp. 99 n. 1, 100.

[42]See e.g. *ibid.*, pp. 3, 24.   In the first (Dutch) edition of *De Wijsbegeerte der Wetsidee*, Dooyeweerd held that there were fourteen spheres.   In *NCTT*, he designates 'energy' as the meaning-nucleus of the physical sphere, and distinguishes a kinematic sphere with 'motion' as its nucleus, thus bringing the total to fifteen.

[43]*NCTT* II, pp. 74ff.

[44]*Ibid.*, pp. 36ff., 47ff.

system is in essence no more than an extension of Kuyper's theory of a universal law pervading the created order.[45]

Dooyeweerd's approach to human culture also follows the familiar Kuyperian pattern. All temporal reality displays a process whereby spheres are 'opened' or actualized, and insofar as man can influence this, he is called to develop creation in answer to God's 'cultural mandate' to subdue the earth and have dominion over it.[46] Picking up one of Kuyper's favourite emphases, Dooyeweerd, in his later works, deepens his concept of the 'cosmonomic Idea' by stressing that all human culture is shaped by 'religious ground-motives'. Religious ground-motives are the deep, 'supra-theoretical' directing forces at work in the very core of human existence.[47] Four such motives can be discerned in Western thought: the 'form-matter' motive - the driving force behind ancient Greek philosophy; the Christian 'biblical' motive - 'creation, fall, and redemption through Jesus Christ in communion with the Holy Spirit'; the 'scholastic' motive of 'nature and grace'; and the 'humanistic' motive, with its twin poles of 'nature' and 'freedom'.[48]

It is worth pausing to consider the theological assumptions behind Dooyeweerd's biblical ground-motive. Dooyeweerd speaks of the will of God as the origin of all things.[49] Man was created and called to bring the latent possibilities of creation to fulfilment, but this was only feasible insofar as he acted in obedience to the prime divine command - to love God and his neighbour.[50] With his fall into sin, man's heart turned away from God to the created world, so that his relationship with God, with others and with creation was corrupted.[51] However, as far as the divine structural principles governing reality are concerned,

---

[45]For Dooyeweerd's understanding of Kuyper on 'sphere sovereignty', see his *Roots of Western Culture*, pp. 54ff.

[46]*NCTT* II, ch. III *passim*; *Roots of Western Culture*, pp. 64ff.

[47]*NCTT* I, pp. 156ff; *Roots of Western Culture*, pp. 8ff.

[48]*Roots of Western Culture*, pp. 15-39, 115-74.

[49]*Ibid.*, pp. 28ff.; *NCTT* I, pp. 101, 107.

[50]*NCTT* I, p. 60.

[51]*Roots of Western Culture*, pp. 33ff.; *NCTT* I, p. 175.

these remained (and still remain) valid.[52]

What then of common grace? According to Dooyeweerd, first, common grace preserves the structural laws of creation.[53] Second, it is seen in God's gifts to specific people to maintain orderly human life.[54] Third, common grace is 'meaningless without Christ as the root and the head of the regenerated human race'.[55] Dooyeweerd is here correcting what he sees as a failing in Kuyper. Outside Christ, Dooyeweerd writes, 'there is no Divine grace, no "common grace" ... but only the manifestation of God's wrath on account of sin'.[56] 'Apart from Christ [common grace] does not become a blessing, but a judgment on humanity. Consequently every dualism in the conception of the relation between *gratia communis* and *gratia specialis*, in the sense that the former has an independent meaning with respect to the latter, is essentially a relapse into the scholastic schema of nature and grace. It is even a greater set-back than the Thomistic-Aristotelian conception, which at least conceived of 'nature' as a *praeambula gratiae*'.[57]

On the other hand, common and special grace are distinct for Dooyeweerd in that 'particular grace directly concerns the supra-temporal root of mankind, whereas common grace remains restricted to temporal life'.[58] Further, special grace affects only reborn mankind, whereas common grace 'embraces the "evil and the good together"'.[59] Further still, common grace does not undermine the 'antithesis', for even though the temporal order is maintained through common grace, all theoretical insight into this order is determined by the presuppositions of philosophical thought, and these are either regenerate or unregenerate.

---

[52]Kalsbeek, *op. cit.*, p. 65.
[53]*NCTT* II, pp. 33ff.
[54]*Roots of Western Culture*, p. 38
[55]*NCTT* I, p. 523.
[56]*NCTT* III, p. 525.
[57]*NCTT* II, p. 309. Cf. *Roots of Western Culture*, p. 38.
[58]*NCTT* III, p. 523.
[59]*Ibid.*, p. 506.

For their consistency, thoroughness and concern for fidelity to Scripture, the Dutch Neo-Calvinists deserve considerable respect and much wider appreciation in the English-speaking world than they have received to date. Few have offered a theology so comprehensive in scope, and when it comes to applying this theology to specific fields of culture (something which space does not allow us to consider here in any depth), few have been so courageous in venturing into areas frequently disregarded by other theologians. Their summons to cultural participation, their plea that no human activity can be considered value-free, their insistence that every social group works according to and in the interests of an ideology, all need to be heard again in an age when such views are repeatedly ignored. Nevertheless, in spite of these strengths, I believe some serious weaknesses are evident, and it is to these we now turn.

### God's Law, Creation and Redemption

We begin with the Neo-Calvinist doctrine of God. Two closely interwoven strands need to be highlighted: first, a pronounced emphasis on the inviolable *will* of God; and second, an inclination to conceive God first and foremost as the *law-giver*. These come together most forcibly in the oft-repeated affirmation of God's sovereignty. We should be clear that divine 'sovereignty', as the Neo-Calvinist sees it, is essentially the absolute power of God's will enacted in the establishment and enforcement of law. We are not allowed to speak of love at the heart of God. In line with the Synod of Dort, election is logically prior to grace; there was no pre-lapsarian grace. The Father's love for his creatures tends to be seen as little more than a potential quality or attitude shown only to the chosen few. The traditional federal Calvinist distinction between the 'covenant of works' (made with all mankind) and the 'covenant of grace' (made with the elect) is assumed without question, notably by Kuyper and Bavinck. [60] The logical consequence of this, spelt out very

---

[60]Cf. Kuyper, *DGG* I, p. 163. (In at least one passage Kuyper describes the covenant of works as an eternal relation between God and man: see e.g. *Dictaten Dogmatiek* IV, 2nd edn. (Kampen, 1910), pp. 38ff.) Cf. Bavinck, *RF*, pp. 272, 410. *Foederaltheologie* was first enunciated in the Netherlands

clearly in Bavinck, is that all are related to God as recipients of his judgment, but only some as objects of his love.

The substantial difficulties of this typically scholastic Calvinist model of God's character have been well set out by Professor Torrance and others and need not be rehearsed here.[61] What does require comment however, and what gives the Kuyperian theology its characteristic hue, is the way in which this doctrine of God is wedded to a thoroughly legalistic theology of creation. We have seen that through his theory of sphere sovereignty, Kuyper invites us to view the created world in terms of unchanging structures which express God's will. Bavinck follows a very similar route, and Dooyeweerd expounds a philosophy pervaded from beginning to end by what Vincent Brümmer has called a 'nomological ontology'.[62] Indeed, surely it is this, whatever Dooyeweerd may claim, which *de facto* forms the core of his 'biblical ground-motive'.[63]

by Gomarus, Trelcatius, Ravens-perger and Cloppenburg, but above all by Johannes Cocceius (1603-1669). Cf. DA Weir, 'Foedus Naturalae: The Origins of Federal Theology in Sixteenth Century Reformation Thought', (MPhil Thesis, St. Andrew's University, 1983), pp. 75-160.

[61]Cf. JB Torrance, 'Covenant or Contract?' *SJT*, 23 (1970), pp. 51-76; 'The Incarnation and Limited Atonement', *Scottish Bulletin of Evangelical Theology*, 2 (1984), pp. 32-40. Colin Gunton is surely right to claim that 'the tendency to see God as primarily power and only secondarily as love or self-giving is very deep-seated in our tradition' (*Enlightenment and Alienation*, (Basingstoke, 1985), p. 65.) The penetrating analysis by Eberhard Jüngel of the growth of the false view of God's power and omnipotence is particularly relevant in this connection.

[62]V Brümmer, *Transcendental Criticism and Christian Philosophy*, (Franeker, 1961) p. 247.

[63]Part of the problem here is Dooyeweerd's subordination of theology to philosophy. He insists that the ground-motive of Holy Scripture - creation, fall into sin, redemption through Christ in the communion of the Holy Spirit - must not be viewed as the result or end-product of theoretical theological reflection. Rather it is the 'supra-theological' starting-point of all truly biblical Christian thought. But *on what basis* is he defining this motive if not on theological grounds? There is good reason to believe that a very particular kind of theology is assumed in Dooyeweerd's description of the biblical ground-motive, one which diverges significantly from biblical thought. He too easily assumes that the 'biblical ground-motive' has been correctly discerned. (Brümmer has shown that Dooyeweerd's biblical ground-

There is little wrong with the recognition of a pervasive order in the world, but to use this as the dominant presupposition of theological reflection and to explain salvation from within this framework is highly questionable. Dooyeweerd, for example, writes: 'In Christ the heart bows under the lex (in its central religious unity and in its temporal diversity, which originates in the Creator's holy will), as the *universal boundary (which cannot be transgressed)* between the *being* of God and the *meaning* of his creation'. [64] Kuyper tells us that 'while that Royal Child of Bethlehem protected sphere-sovereignty with his shield, He did not create it. It was there from of old. It was embedded in the creation order, in the plan for human life'.[65] And Bavinck echoes Kuyper when he claims: 'Grace is something other and higher than nature, but it nevertheless joins up with nature, does not destroy it but restores it rather. *Grace ... [flows] on in the river-bed which has been dug out in the natural relationships of the human race'*.[66] But, as WJ Aalders reminds us, we cannot read the 'law of God *for* the cosmos (his purpose) simply by examining the law *of* the cosmos'.[67] There is an acute danger that unless the meaning of creation itself is sought in Jesus Christ the Creator Word, a theology of redemption will all too easily sanction a sub-Christian theology of creation. Certainly, we are often told by the Kuyperians that grace and redemption fulfil the purposes of creation, but invariably 'creation' has been defined in advance outside Christ according to some theory of universal law. From this perspective, it is not hard to see how Kuyperianism has been used to fuel the South African apartheid system. John de Gruchy, writing from within that political

motive in fact only operates in his system as a *noetic* (as opposed to ontic) theme. *Ibid.,* pp. 237-48).

[64] *NCTT* I, p. 99.

[65] As quoted and translated by Spykman, *loc. cit.*, p. 183.

[66] *RF*, p. 277, my italics.

[67] 'Calvinisme en Wijsbegeerte', *Nieuwe Theologische Stüdien,* XVI (1933), p. 246. See also Douglas Bax's comments about the tendency of the Dutch Reformed Church in South Africa to argue from what *is* to what *ought to be,* in 'The Bible and Apartheid', in *Apartheid is a Heresy,* J de Gruchy and C Villa-Vicencio (eds.), (Guildford, 1983), p. 116.

context, observes: 'The fundamental theological problem with Kuyper's doctrine is that it assumes a relationship between nature and grace, derived from the Synod of Dort and not Calvin, in which nature and creation, not grace and reconciliation, are determinant'.[68] We should not be surprised to find that Karl Barth attacked the Kuyperians during the rise of Nazism in Germany because of what he saw as their incipient but dominant 'natural theology'.[69] It is also interesting to find a pupil of Dooyeweerd criticising his master for leaving no room for the notion of creation through the Logos of God: 'Since [Dooyeweerd] starts from the law but fails to account for its execution through the creative Logos ... [he] fails to recognize the reality of creation as something different from legislation'.[70] Later, Brümmer adds: 'Dooyeweerd does not realize that if the basic theme of the Christian faith were really to determine the content of his cosmonomic Idea, it would force him to reject the 'nomological' ontology implied in this cosmonomic Idea'.[71] Few comments on Dooyeweerd have been so perceptive.

## Christ and Common Grace
The end result of working with such a legislative and determinative theology of creation is that a damaging gulf opens up between the orders of creation and redemption, ironically the very rift which the Neo-Calvinists are so anxious to heal. The notion of common grace only deepens the split, for it is usually rendered in impersonal and abstract terms as an expression and enactment of God's will in the world at large, in contrast to special grace which reveals God's unmerited love in saving his chosen people. But how can we speak convincingly of a 'grace' dissociated from God's election in Christ without destroying the unity of God's acts and being? To his credit, Kuyper attempts to root common grace in Christ, but one suspects that more crucial for him is its grounding in God's 'eternal decrees', and his description of common grace as an earthly and temporary

---

[68]*Bonhoeffer and South Africa*, (Grand Rapids, 1984), p. 109. Cf. also *The Church Struggle in South Africa*, especially pp. 201ff.
[69]*CD* II/1, (Edinburgh, 1957), pp. 173ff.
[70]Brümmer, *op. cit.*, p. 184.
[71]*Ibid.*, p. 247.

phenomenon, and special grace as supernatural and eternal, does nothing to help his case.[72] In the same way, although Dooyeweerd is quick to rebuke Kuyper on this issue and goes to great lengths to interpret common grace christologically, in his system as a whole there is little to show that he has taken his own point to heart, and he weakens his position considerably by arguing that common grace is restricted to the temporal world and special grace to the 'supra-temporal root' of man.

What is missing here is a thorough integration of creation and redemption by means of the *headship of Christ as man*. The fact that this nettle is never grasped is due, I believe, to a curious type of Nestorianism in Neo-Calvinist christology. Kuyper can write eloquently of Christ's universal lordship - indeed it is one of his major themes, but he distinguishes carefully between Christ as Mediator of creation as the second Person of the Trinity, and Christ as Mediator of our salvation as Son of God and *man*.[73] Christ is not Lord over the created world in his humanity. For Bavinck also, Christ exercises his reign over the world as the divine King but not as the crucified and risen Man in whom the created order is reconciled to its Maker.[74] Dooyeweerd veers away from this christology,[75] but has not followed through the methodological implications of his own line of thinking. In short, Neo-Calvinism tends to limit the significance of the human nature of Christ to the salvation of the elect, and the import of the incarnation and the manhood of Christ for apprehending God's purposes in creation as a whole is virtually ignored.

### Culture, Common Grace and the Cultural Mandate
All these difficulties become even more evident in the Neo-Calvinists' theology of culture. Kuyper wants to maintain at one and the same time that there is a hiatus between regenerate and

[72]*DGG* I, pp. 220, 497; II, pp. 277, 679.
[73]*DGG* III, pp. 646-53.
[74]*RF*, p. 384.
[75]'As regards his human nature, Christ is the root of reborn creation, and as such the fullness of meaning, the creaturely Ground of the meaning of all temporal reality'. *NCTT* II, p. 32.

unregenerate *and* that even in the absence of true religion God restrains sin and encourages righteousness. The former theory was designed to allay fears that encouraging cultural activity on the part of Christians might play down the radical change of heart which faith in Christ brings, the latter to explain how God could be at work for his own glory outside the confines of the Church. But it is very hard to hold these two convictions together without discarding the common/special grace distinction as traditionally formulated.[76] Furthermore, Kuyper argues that common grace is of enormous benefit to the Christian in restraining evil, allowing him to develop culturally etc., and yet he also affirms that all good works performed by a believer are due to the special grace of God. From this it is hard to avoid the conclusion that the Christian functions in two realms: the one which includes his earthly cultural pursuits, and the other which concerns his salvation. Once again, only a recovery of the oneness of God's grace focussed in Christ will lead to a resolution of this dilemma.

There is another feature of the Neo-Calvinist theology of culture which we must address, namely the way in which the Neo-Calvinists conceive our standing before God and relate this to the 'cultural mandate'. It is quite consistent with what we have found already that the Neo-Calvinists expound man's destiny primarily in terms of *duty* and *obedience* to God. Man's state before the fall casts a shadow over all that follows.[77] Whether elect or reprobate, all stand under the law (and laws) of God. Bavinck declares that 'man is ... always and everywhere bound by laws not invented by man, but set forth by God as the rule for life ... there are norms which stand above man. They form a unity among themselves and find their origin and continuation in the Creator and Lawgiver of the universe. To live in conformity to those norms in mind and heart, in thought and action, this is what it means most basically to become conformed to the image of God's

---

[76]Significantly, in the United States, this unresolved tension in Kuyper has led to the spawning of two sharply divergent schools of thought within Neo-Calvinism. See Bratt, *loc. cit.*, pp. 145ff.

[77]See the comment on Kuyper, *supra*, n. 59.

Son.   And this is the ideal and goal of man'.[78]

The upshot of this doctrine of man is that culture, which for the Neo-Calvinists has its origin in the so-called 'cultural mandate' of Gen. 1:28, delivered to man before the fall,[79] is construed first and foremost as a legal requirement imposed on us by a law-giving God.   Neither common grace nor special grace abrogates this mandate: on the contrary, God's grace supports it and enables the command to be obeyed.   This prompts a number of closely related comments.

First, the Dutchmen approach the early chapters of Genesis through the framework of the dual-covenant system, reinforced by a legalistic doctrine of God.   Consequently, their anthropology displays a legalistic twist from the start.[80]  Even if we examine Genesis 1-3 on its own ground, there seems good reason to believe that we are given a vision of man created not primarily for obedience but to be God's counterpart - to 'share in the personhood of God',[81] and a christological account of man's

---

[78]As quoted and translated by Spykman, *loc. cit.*, pp. 181ff., my italics.

[79]Sometimes Gen. 2:15 and 9:1 are also added, and although the last of these is subsequent to the fall, the mandate's first two occurrences are pre-lapsarian and are determinative for the Neo-Calvinists.

[80]It is fascinating to observe Nicholas Wolterstorff's theological argument in his attempt to construct a Christian philosophy of art along Neo-Calvinists lines in *Art in Action*, (Grand Rapids, 1980).   Man's uniqueness consists in his being responsible (p. 73) because God holds us responsible (p. 74). Wolterstorff believes that 'unique to man among earthlings is that God is his sovereign.   As a sovereign is lord of his subjects, so God is lord of man; God has the right to ask obedience, man the responsibility to obey'. (p. 75.)  (He does speak of God pledging himself to his people, but no mention is made here of God's filial intentions (p. 74)).   Having laid this basis, Wolterstorff goes on to speak of man's cultural responsibility to God to subdue the earth, to love his neighbour and to acknowledge God as Lord.   Only much later (pp. 83ff.) does he speak of redemption and its consequences.

[81]W Eichrodt, *Theology of the Old Testament* II (London, 1967), p. 126. Cf. TC Vriezen, *An Outline of Old Testament Theology* (Oxford, 1958), p. 200: 'God is known as the God who concerns himself with the human world and has communion with man'.   For a thorough discussion of this in relation to the decisive concept of the 'image of God', see C Westermann, *Genesis 1-11*, JJ Scullon (ET) (London, 1984), pp. 157ff.

destiny certainly means that God's loving desire to 'bring many sons to glory' must be brought back into the centre of the picture. Therefore, properly speaking, our cultural responsibilities should be exercised out of a sense of being adopted as sons and daughters rather than of being under some universal edict.[82]

Second, to put so much weight on capitulating to creation's inherent laws runs the risk of forgetting that the orders of creation are there for us to enjoy; they are channels through which we can delight in the gracious creativity of God and glimpse his goodness.[83]  In creating all things out of nothing, and in conferring upon the world its own appropriate rationality and order, God is the same God of unconditional mercy which He has shown himself to be in Christ.  This surely is part of what it means to take seriously the claim that all things were made 'through' or 'in' Christ.[84]

Third, further exposition of the theme of Christ as the agent of creation reminds us that not only does God sustain the created world and hold it in being through the Son,[85] but that through him, God is actively carrying it forward towards its goal.[86] God is at work 'developing the earth', bringing to fruition its implicit possibilities, forging order out of disorder and chaos, summoning all things to a destiny not given 'in the beginning'.  It is our calling to participate in this divine activity in union with the Son of God, in whom all things find their meaning and coherence, and in whom, by virtue of his incarnation, passion and resurrection, every evil in creation has been defeated.  It is here we need to appreciate the pivotal importance of the headship of the man

---

[82]See Professor Torrance's remarks about the difference between worship offered to a 'covenant' God and worship offered to a 'contract' God, in 'Covenant or Contract?', pp. 56ff.  The same applies to culture.

[83]Hans Rookmaaker, the art historian, is a notable exception among the Neo-Calvinists in this respect.  He has spotted clearly a danger in his tradition, and his own discussion of the 'norms' of creation is excellent.  Cf. e.g. *The Creative Gift*, (Leicester, 1981) pp. 57ff.

[84]Col. 1:16; Heb. 1:2, John 1:3.

[85]Cf. e.g. Col. 1:17.

[86]See FF Bruce's comments on Heb. 1:3 in *The Epistle to the Hebrews* (Grand Rapids, 1977), p. 6.

Jesus Christ, crucified and exalted, which, as we have already remarked, eludes the Neo-Calvinists and leads to so many unfortunate dichotomies in their theology. If it is in Christ that our humanity has been assumed and renewed, and if in that humanity the whole of created existence is included respresentatively, then our 'developing the earth' can only mean accepting, affirming and above all sharing in Christ's continuing ministry as Lord of creation.

Fourth, extending this last point, it is clear that the Neo-Calvinist concept of 'obedience' in culture needs to be revised. As we have tried to argue, to be involved as a Christian in culture entails not only *receiving* the renewing grace of God in Christ, but also *sharing* in Christ's risen life. It is the latter aspect which is absent in the Neo-Calvinists but which must be maintained if we are not to see culture as simply our own response to some external divine directive. A monistic and authoritarian doctrine of God usually issues in a denial of the autonomy and the authenticity of man, and to a notion of obedience as purely passive. But the Father of Jesus Christ only requires obedience of us in the sense that He comes alongside us, taking responsibility for our own condition, giving what He demands. This is his very nature. We are thus at our most obedient, not when we conform to some law imposed from without, but when we are conformed through the Spirit to the likeness of Christ our brother.[87] Significantly, a faithful exegesis of the 'mandate' of Gen. 1:28, 2:15 and 9:1 suggests that culture is more of a blessing than a bare command: the imperative carries with it the power of fulfilment.[88]

---

[87]See the perceptive remarks of Colin Gunton on this, *op. cit.*, pp. 90-101. This concept of the 'vicarious humanity of Christ', far from threatening human freedom, in fact firmly establishes it. As AE Lewis rightly asserts: 'The ontological determination of humanity in Christ's *manhood* is ... itself the foundation of human freedom, and of our engagement *qua* human in autonomous reciprocity with God', review of JB Webster's *Eberhard Jüngel*, in *SJT*, 40 (1986), p. 137.

[88]C Westermann, *Genesis 1-11*, p. 138; *Creation* (London, 1974), pp. 50ff. We should note that 1:28 begins: 'And God blessed them, and God said to them ...'. Moreover, the words 'be fruitful and multiply' frequently occur elsewhere

I have endeavoured to suggest that Dutch Neo-Calvinism is plagued by certain critical weaknesses which at root concern the fundamental doctrines of God, Jesus Christ and the created order. However, in conclusion, it needs to be said that in spite of the drawbacks of the Neo-Calvinist system, the very fact that we have been drawn so deeply into these issues is itself a tribute to the profundity of the theology of culture which Neo-Calvinism offers. That we should choose to diverge from this tradition and take a different path does not detract from the wealth of insight to be gained from its highly developed and rigorous concern for a Christian approach to cultural life. Any theologian working today in this area who seeks encouragement and stimulation from these writers will certainly not be disappointed: he or she will be richly rewarded.

---

in the Old Testament in the context of blessing. Cf. A Murtonen, 'The Use and Meaning of the Words l$^e$ bare k and b$^e$ rakah in the Old Testament', *Vetus Testamentum,* 9 (1959), p. 166; H Mowvley, 'The Concept and Content of 'Blessing' in the Old Testament', *The Bible Translator,* 26 (1965), p. 78.

# 8

# Theology as Service in Karl Barth

GEOFFREY W BROMILEY

## I  Background

In the crucial years of Barth's pastorate in Safenwil, four factors in particular combined to force him to rethink the role of theology. First came the demonstrable failure of the type of theology that he had learned in Germany when it came up against the harsh reality of World War I and its demands. As Barth perceived it, the almost unanimous endorsement that German theologians gave to their country's war aims brought to light the need for a new beginning on a new basis. Barth deduced from this experience, not the general futility of theology, but the calamitous consequences of a mistaken theological concept and content.

The simultaneous failure of German Socialism formed a second decisive factor. Barth might still believe that Socialism could have beneficial political and social results. Indeed, it was at this very time (1915) that rather paradoxically he joined the Swiss Social Democrats in order to improve conditions for workers in the small factories of Safenwil.[1] Nevertheless, he ceased to look to Religious Socialism for theological guidance, concluding that it did not provide the solid theological foundation that the church needed to fulfil its ministry to the world.

The problem of the pulpit served as a third and particularly significant factor in bringing about Barth's theological reorientation. In his address 'The Word of God and the Task of the Ministry' (1920) he himself expressed the difficulty that faced him as he prepared and delivered his weekly sermons: 'As ministers we ought to speak of God. We are human, however, and so cannot

---

[1] E Busch, *Karl Barth* (Philadelphia, 1976), p. 82.

133

speak of God ... This is our perplexity'.[2] It was a perplexity which by its very nature involved a theological question and demanded a theological answer. Wrestling with the task of being a minister of God's Word, and the almost intolerable responsibility that this task imposed, Barth came to see that he needed the service of theology to be able to fulfil it.

The final factor impelling Barth on his new course was his friendship with Eduard Thurneysen, then pastor of the neighbouring parish of Leutwil. During the difficult years of questioning and groping, Barth and Thurneysen met regularly for discussion, passing from one parish to the other 'like two strange wanderers between two worlds',[3] as Thurneysen put it in a letter on 6th October 1921. At one of these meetings the two made the momentous decision to read the New Testament a little differently. They also determined to listen to the Blumhardts and admitted that they had lost confidence in Schleiermacher and Kutter.[4] They slowly realized that they had now to do theology in a new way. As Barth would say later, 'it was Thurneysen who whispered the key phrase to me, half aloud: "What we need for preaching, instruction and pastoral care, is a wholly new theological foundation!"'.[5]

At this stage, of course, Barth did not fully grasp precisely what form this theology would take. Nevertheless, its general character soon became clear to him, and it would not change in essentials during the long and varied years of its material development. The underlying principle was simply that theology is a ministry no less than preaching, teaching or pastorate. It is a service that those who undertake it must refer to and for the church in God's name and in the power of the same Spirit who equips the church as a whole for the task of presenting Christ to the world.

---

[2]*The Word of God and the Word of Man* [*WGWM*] (New York, 1957), p. 186.

[3]*Revolutionary Theology in the Making* [*RTM*], (Richmond, 1964), p. 74.

[4]*RTM*, p. 75.

[5]'Nachwort', *Schleiermacher Auswahl* (1968), p. 294.

## II Themes

### A *Theology as Service*

Barth did not specifically describe theology as service in the early addresses collected under the title *The Word of God and the Word of Man*. The concept was implicit, however, in his criticism of existing theology in the address 'The Need and Promise of Christian Preaching' (1922).[6] It also lay behind his attack on the common idea that doctrine is less worthy and less important than life ('The Doctrinal Task of the Reformed Churches', 1923).[7] With special reference to his own increasing sphere of interest, he then gave the concept explicit expression in his first dogmatic series begun at Göttingen in 1924, *Unterricht in der christlichen Religion*. Thus in §2,3 he deliberately characterized dogmatics as 'a modest service'.[8]  Later in §13,2, asking whether one should call dogmatics a science or an art, he accepted the aptness of both descriptions, but argued that neither really takes us to the heart of the matter, for dogmatics is essentially 'a service ..., the ministry of God's Word to the second degree'.[9] In this regard, of course, we recall that for Barth theology was more than dogmatics.  It included expository and practical theology, with historical theology as a necessary auxiliary discipline.  If he focussed on dogmatics as the reflection that mediates between exposition and application, he recognized that what applies to dogmatics applies to theology as a whole.  It is all service.

After a first revision in *Christian Dogmatics*, Barth gave this understanding mature and expanded development in the relevant sections of *Church Dogmatics* I/1 and I/2.  He introduced the concept of theology as service in the opening discussion of I/1.[10]  Theology, he stated, must not pretend to be an end in itself or set itself up as lord or judge.  Academically we may no doubt see in it a branch of the humanities,[11] yet this does not affect its inherent status as a ministry of the church.  Pursuing the

---

[6]*WGWM*, pp. 97ff.

[7]*Ibid.*, pp. 218ff.

[8]*Das Unterricht in der christlichen Religion* [U] (Zurich, 1985), p. 47.

[9]*Ibid.*, p. 378.

[10]*CD* I/1 (Edinburgh, 1975), p. 83.

[11]*Ibid.*, pp. 84ff.

thought in I/2, Barth perceived the servant role of theology in the fact that it may not simply claim the role of a teaching office. It must recognize that it belongs to the hearing church if it is properly to do its work of teaching.[12]

In the *Open Letters* published in 1984, Barth saw a close link between the integrity of theology and its acceptance of a servant function: 'Christian theology is good, then, when it is not an end in itself but service, service in which one learns constantly John 3:30 ("he must increase and I must decrease").'[13] Later in life, taking up the general theme of Christian ministry in CD IV/3.2, he listed theology as the sixth and last of the ministries of the Word which form a series of twelve with six ministries of act. No less firmly than when he first took up theology again at Safenwil, he still contended that except in the context of the ministry of the Word all theological problems 'are irrelevant or lose their theological character'. As service, of course, theology had vital tasks in relation to all other ministries, e.g., to praise, preaching, evangelism and mission. Nevertheless, Barth reminds his hearers and readers that theology is 'a modest undertaking which can only aim to serve rather than to dominate'.[14] In the special lectures with which he ended his official teaching at Basel, he devoted a whole section to this basic theme of theology as service.[15] He began with the simplest statement that 'theological work is service, *ministerium*, or a servant's attendance'. He recalled that Calvin had included the *doctor* among the church's ministers and pointed out that although the *doctor* comes at the head of the list, he 'must speedily become the servant, waiter and deacon for all the others'. Theology, he argued, is an indispensable service. Practical ministry is not possible 'without a minimum of theological work'.[16] He had learned this by experience at Safenwil. Yet one must undertake

[12]*CD* I/2 (Edinburgh, 1956), p. 797.

[13]*Offene Briefe* 1945-1968, (Zurich, 1984), pp. 553ff. in *Karl Barth Reader* [*KBR*] (Grand Rapids, 1986), p. 16.

[14]*CD* IV/3.2 (Edinburgh, 1962), p. 881.

[15]*Evangelical Theology* [*E Th*] (Grand Rapids, 1979), pp. 184ff.

[16]*Loc. cit.*

this work as both a general and special service, not as a speculative or historico-critical *gnosis* which either becomes an end in itself or merely promotes personal gratification or advancement.[17]

## B *Theology as Church Service*

For Barth, of course, viewing theology as service meant setting it solidly in the context of the church. Theology was not just service in general. It was service in the special sense of Christian ministry entrusted to the church and undertaken both i) for it and ii) by it.

i) Although Barth saw that theology may be validly studied and taught in a university setting, he clung tenaciously to the conviction that it must be done as a service to or for the church. Already in 'The Doctrinal Task of the Reformed Churches' he was describing theology as 'the straight and rigorous way that leads from thought to action'.[18] In 'The Need and Promise of Christian Preaching' he stressed the necessary connection between theology and pulpit.[19] In *Unterricht*, developing the latter point, he immediately forged a link between dogmatics and proclamation in the thesis of §1.[20] In §2,4 he then described it as the task of dogmatics to prevent the church from losing its true point, to arouse it from its undogmatic slumbers.[21] A little later, in the address 'Church and Theology' (1925), he approvingly quoted Vilmar to the effect that 'if theology leaves the domain of the church it no longer serves beatitude but the intellectual variety of the individual ... We learn not for school but for life'. Theology is 'the place where the church answers for its action ... where ... there must be considered ... the very centre of its business, the ministry of the divine Word'.[22]

---

[17]*Ibid.*, p. 197.
[18]*WGWM*, p. 225.
[19]*Ibid.*, p. 101.
[20]*U*, p. 3.
[21]*Ibid.*, p. 50.
[22]*Theology and Church* [*TC*] (New York, 1962), p. 304.

By the time he embarked on his main dogmatic series, Barth had incorporated this insight into his title. He would now develop a *Church Dogmatics*, not presuming, of course, to think that he was expressing the mind of the whole church, but intending by way of his individual presentation to render theological service to the church. In *CD* I/1, therefore, he stated it as his primary thesis that theology bears responsibility for the testing of the church's proclamation.[23] We recall, too, that in I/2, emphasizing theology's need both to hear and to teach, he embedded it firmly in the hearing and teaching church. In order to teach, theology must identify itself with the hearing church, and even as it does so it discharges its servant function of helping the church better to fulfil its own primary ministry of preaching and teaching.[24] *Evangelical Theology* pointed yet again to the churchly function of theology with its statement that theology 'supports the church in its task of mirroring God's Word as exactly as possible'.[25]

ii)  As itself one of the church's ministries, theology was for Barth service *by* the church as well as *for* it. It did not lie outside the church as the work of an external agency or consultative body. The church itself bears responsibility for it. It cannot leave it to the university or to independent scholars or scholarly groups. Yet when Barth spoke of the church in this connection, he meant the whole church. Theology must not simply be put in the hands of experts within the church. Every member must have a part in this service. Nowhere did Barth state this more forcibly than in 'Church and Theology', where he argued that theology 'involves a special burden ... laid fundamentally upon the whole church'.[26]

Here was another reason why Barth chose the title *Church Dogmatics* for his own theological contribution. Dogmatics is a work of the church within the church, so that while the particular

---

[23]*CD* I/1, p. 250.
[24]*CD* I/2, pp. 797ff., 844ff.
[25]*ETh*, p. 191.
[26]*TC*, p. 304.

teaching might be Barth's own, he gave it in the context of the
church and as part of the church's common enterprise. Dogmatics
as Barth now described it is the church's self-examination face to
face with aberrations.[27] It is a question that is 'first put to the
church as a whole and only then to a specific group within it'.[28]

With reference to this common responsibility for theology, Barth
consistently stressed that all Christians are willy-nilly
theologians and must see themselves as such. As early as 'Church
and Theology' he had claimed that the thesis that all believers
'are theologians must be upheld as true'.[29] As late as *CD* IV/3.2
he thought it important that all 'indolent talk of non-theological
laymen' should be 'quietly refuted'. To him the statement 'I am a
mere layman and not a theologian' gave 'evidence of indolence
rather than humility'.[30] Christians do theology whether they
realize it or not. The real danger is that they will do it carelessly.
As Barth put it in *CD* I/1,: 'The freedom to 'theologize' quite
untheologically is the freedom to prattle heretically, and this is a
freedom for which there is no room in the church. All believers
must accept this ministry even though only some may have the
special gift [*Gabe*] and task [*Ausgabe*]'.[31]

C *Theology as Service of God's Word*
As a ministry of the church, theology had for Barth the primary
function of serving the ministry of God's Word. If practical
problems had turned him to theology at Safenwil, the problem
that occupied him most urgently, as we have seen, was that of the
pulpit. In some sense, this problem embraced all others, for
God's Word in the pulpit will be God's Word for the practical
matters of Christian life, work, witness and conduct, both
personal and social. Not surprisingly, then, Barth's concept of
theology as service placed theology in the service of the Word of

[27]*CD* I/1, p. 3.
[28]*Ibid.*, p. 77.
[29]*TC*, p. 304.
[30]*CD* IV/3.2, p. 881.
[31]*CD* I/1, p. 77.

God and those who are charged to proclaim it.

This appears at once in 'The Need and Promise of Christian Preaching', in which Barth asked whether it would not be good for theology 'if it attempted to be nothing other than knowledge of the quest and questioning of the Christian preacher'.[32] Then in 'The Doctrinal Task of the Reformed Churches' he defined doctrine as 'the human word in crisis with God's Word'.[33] Plunging into dogmatics at Göttingen, he began with the doctrine of the Word of God as indispensable *prolegomena*, and saw it as the task of dogmatic *prolegomena* to work out the proper relation of the proclaimed Word to the revealed Word according to the testimony of the written Word. Theology, then, is service of the threefold Word. Preaching provides the raw material for consideration, and dogmatics refers it back 'methodically to scripture and revelation'.[34] Because it has 'always been sick', 'preaching needs this ministry in order to do its own work'.[35] Without dogmatics, 'along with biblical and practical theology, the human words will not properly speak God's Word'.

Sermons ought to be 'a clear mirror of God's Word', but in fact 'they contain much obscurity and futility, limitation, confusion, and superficiality'. Dogmatics will not provide the actual material of preaching, but Barth believes strongly that if preachers will avail themselves of the ministry of theology, they will then know how to preach non-dogmatically on sound dogmatic themes.[36] Barth made much the same point in the important address 'Church and Theology', in which he stated that 'theology must be done expressly as ... guard duty over the guards'.[37] It was in *Church Dogmatics*, however, that he developed more expansively the thesis of his first dogmatic series. He now widened the concept of preaching. Proclamation gives dogmatics

---

[32] *WGWM*, p. 39.
[33] *Ibid.*, p. 241.
[34] *U*, p. 28.
[35] *Ibid.*, p. 47.
[36] *Ibid.*, pp. 336ff.
[37] *TC*, p. 303.

its material; the human word as ostensibly God's Word forms the question.[38]   Barth now saw, however, that the ministry of theology covers also the practice and worship of the church. Hence he could complain: 'It is a strange thing that when there are revisions of books of order and hymn books, every possible authority is usually consulted as a standard but not dogmatic science', adding wryly, 'the results naturally correspond'.[39]   The church's social work could also profit, he thought, from dogmatic scrutiny.   Nevertheless, he insisted that theology's main concern should be with the proclaimed Word, which on its human side is by nature 'a fallible human work'.[40]

## D *Theology as Service of Scripture*
From an early stage Barth had no doubt that the written Word constitutes the norm for theology, so that in this sense theology becomes service of holy scripture, i.e., an application of the primary apostolic and prophetic witness of the Bible to the ongoing proclamation of the Christian message.   Under the general rubric of the Word of God Barth perceived an integral link between word of proclamation on the one side and word of revelation and scripture on the other.   For him the Word of God embraced three ordered forms, the revealed Word as God himself in Christ, the written Word as authentic witness to it and the proclaimed Word as ongoing communication.   Theology itself in its own threefold form as exposition, reflection and application rested on this triunity in its essential *perichoresis*.   To do its work, however, it had to follow the order of the inner relationship, bringing the church's word into conformity with the revealed Word according to the primary testimony of the written Word.

Barth had this in view already in his first dogmatic venture when, posing the question of theological norm, he referred to revelation and scripture as 'the law by which dogmatics judges, the light in which it sets the *loci*'.[41]   Since God has raised up scripture as the authentic apostolic and prophetic witness, this meant testing,

---

[38]*CD* I/1, p. 59.
[39]*Ibid.*, p. 82.
[40]*Loc. cit.*
[41]*U*, p. 337.

correcting and directing the church's word and work by whether or not it conforms to scripture, though not apart from the Holy Spirit who both inspires and expounds it,[42] and always in relation to Christ as its content. Barth laid heavy stress on this point in *CD* I/1, where he stated that theology must examine the church's witness 'in respect of its agreement with the Word of God',[43] presented the Bible as an independent factor that we cannot finally evade or subjugate,[44] argued that, in practice, theology measures the human word of proclamation by the second form of God's Word,[45] and summed up his teaching in the thesis that dogmatics is 'criticism and correction of proclamation by revelation according to the biblical witness'.[46]

Barth changed his mind about many matters but he never changed it on this basic issue. As late as *CD* IV/3.2 he was still insisting that the theology of the community of a given time 'tests its whole action by the standard of its commission, and finally in the light of the Word of the Lord who gave it'.[47] This service first involves exegesis in an attempt to achieve a more exact hearing of scripture. It then involves historical theology as a study of the church's loyalty to the primary witness in its life and work in various cultures and settings. In dogmatics it then takes the form of reflection on the original witness in each new time and place. Finally, as practical theology it attempts normative direction for the church's ministry in the light of the three preceding investigations.[48] Because theology must serve holy scripture in this way, Barth regarded 'a fruitful relation to the Old Testament and New Testament witness' as essential if theology was to fulfil effectively its ministry in and to the church.

---

[42]*TC*, p. 303.

[43]*CD* I/1, p. 250.

[44]*Ibid.*, pp. 254ff.

[45]*Ibid.*, pp. 265ff.

[46]*Ibid.*, p. 280.

[47]*CD* IV/3.2, p. 879.

[48]*Ibid.*, p. 880.

## E  *Theology as Humble Service*

Already at Göttingen, Barth expressed himself clearly in *Unterricht*. He described theology as 'a modest service, not to be compared to the glory of service to the Word itself'.[49] He then introduced the metaphor of service at the base compared to the frontline service of the pastorate.[50]  He insisted similarly in 'Church and Theology' that we must do theology 'in great humility', referring to the constant distrust of theology as an 'unendurable domination', 'a papal authority of the scribes'.[51] Theologians no less than ecclesiastics love to rule, to lay down the law, to ascribe to themselves infallibility, to judge and command, in short to take up a role that finally belongs only to God himself in his self-revelation according to the biblical witness.  If theology is to do its proper work, it must learn the humility of service, serving the church by serving the Word, humbling itself before the church because it humbles itself before God and the Word of God.

In *CD* I/1 [52] Barth expanded his fundamental thesis.  Theology, he said, must not set itself up as an end in itself.  Proclamation, not theology, is the church's main job.  Again, theology must not regard itself as the lord and judge of its theme.  It has to learn this theme from God, bowing before God's revelation as we know it through scripture.  Again, theology must not think that its results have the same authority as revelation or scripture.  They are not 'a law as it were imposed on God'.  Always fallible, they are always reformable in appropriate subjection to their object.[53]

Barth returned to this theme in his discussion of theology as the sixth ministry of the Word in *CD* IV/3.2.[54]  He found in theology a 'dangerous undertaking, since it is menaced by every kind of human pride'.  Strictly 'its only purpose is to make itself

---

[49]*U*, p. 47.

[50]*Ibid.*, p. 333.

[51]*TC*, p. 304.

[52]*CD* I/1, pp. 84ff.

[53]*CD* I/2, p. 797.

[54]*CD* IV/3.2, pp. 881f.

superfluous'. Unfortunately it has a tendency 'to posit itself absolutely'. Exegetical theology, for example, far too easily supposes that it can master exegesis and church history, and 'thus do violence to them', constructing an 'arbitrarily conceived and unfounded system of thought'. Practical theology in turn readily passes itself off as a 'working doctrine' governed by 'every conceivable practical consideration but not by scripture, history and dogma'. In contrast, good theology as Barth saw it will be 'supremely positive and peaceable ... pursued ... without too much petty, self-opinionated bickering'. For Barth the root of theological pride lay in the Greek understanding of theology as intrinsically the human investigation of God and divine things. The path to the required humility begins with a purer concept of theology as 'the shaping of Christian thinking, speech, action and life in the light of its origin, theme and content'. Involving as it does a subjection to the object and an orientation to the ministry, such a concept entails and enforces a corresponding humility in the doing of theology and in the attitude adopted toward others who do theology and toward the church that it is designed to serve.

Barth felt so strongly on this matter that in his last years he took it up again in *Evangelical Theology*. Speaking first of the place of theology, he stated that 'because the Word of God is heard and answered by theology, it is a modest science'. It has to be modest, for 'its entire logic can only be a human ana-logy to that Word'. It cannot claim 'to control it', but only 'to co-respond with it'.[55] For Barth, it may be noted, humility was not just a human disposition that theologians must adopt and cultivate. He believed that it lies at the very heart of the theological enterprise. If science demands humility before any object, theological science especially demands humility before the divine Object.

Taking up the theme again in the concluding chapter on theological work he argued that service lies at the root of the modesty approach to theology. Modesty does not mean servility,

[55]*ETh*, pp. 16ff.

and therefore it does not rule out the assurance of which Barth himself gives ample evidence. Not being ashamed of the gospel, theology need not be ashamed of its own function. It does not have to justify itself apologetically or paedagogically. Nevertheless, it is no task for those who crave reward or status, nor for those who think they know everything, who can tell God about himself, and who despise the less informed and instructed. In particular, it is no task for those who arrogantly suppose that they can 'gain control over the Word and over the object of their science', for the whole endeavour 'would then lose its object and become, consequently, meaningless'. Theologians are not to be 'triumphal little popes, but those who take the lowest places and let God move them up', never losing sight of the fact that the Word 'disposes over them and that they do not dispose over it'.[56] Once again a scientific subjection to the object forms the ultimate basis for humility. Theology serves the Word itself in serving the ministry of the Word.

## F *Theology as Divine Service*
As ministry, theology must also be worship, for Christian service is primarily and predominantly service of God, or divine service. This means that good theology will necessarily contain, implicitly if not explicitly, the chief liturgical elements. It handles the Word of God, it is done in prayer, and it redounds to God's praise.

As regards prayer, Barth related it more specifically to the ministry of the Holy Spirit, in whom he discerned the subjective possibility of revelation. In 'The Need and Promise of Christian Preaching' he could say already: 'You have been introduced to "my theology" if you have heard this sigh', i.e., *Veni, Creator Spiritus*.[57] Then in *CD* I/2 he described theology as 'an action of the Holy Spirit in the church'.[58] Again in *CD* IV/3.2 he referred to the Holy Spirit as 'the true and proper *doctor ecclesiae*'.[59] He concluded, then, that 'theological work is

[56]*Ibid.*, pp. 188ff.
[57]*WGWM*, p. 134.
[58]*CD* I/2, p. 768.
[59]*CD* IV/3.2, p. 871.

surely inconceivable and impossible at any time without prayer.
All the gulfs and contradictions that occur in theological work are
in fact due to its not being done everywhere in the fellowship of
prayer'.[60] This tight binding of theology to prayer did not have
to mean that theology as such is prayer, but it did mean for Barth
that prayer is integral to theology. As he put it categorically in
*Evangelical Theology*, 'proper theology will have to be a
*Proslogion*, a *Suspirium*', 'theology must be an act of
prayer'.[61] He would recognize this basic need in *Church Dogmatics* by resorting from time to time to the direct prayer,
'Come, Creator Spirit'. He took care to introduce his lectures
with a similar appeal for the Spirit's divine aid and
enlightenment. He also stressed the need for a weekly turning
aside from work to engage in the public worship of God.[62]
'Theological work', he believed, 'lives by and in the petition for
his [the Spirit's] coming'.[63]

As regards praise, Barth had little to say about theology itself as
a ministry of praise. One of his most direct statements comes in
*Theologische Studien* 29, where he said that 'we have to realize
that fundamentaly theology is worship, thanksgiving and
petition, a liturgical action. The ancient saying that the law of
praying is the law of believing is not just a pious saw but one of
the cleverest things ever said about the method of theology'.[64]
Yet if Barth seldom referred expressly to this aspect of dogmatic
service, it surely dominated his whole enterprise. We remember
the magnificent section on the glory of God in *CD* II/1, and his
thesis that the beauty of God must find reflection in a
corresponding beauty of theology.[65] We remember his constant
sense of dealing, not with abstractions, but with the living God
of righteousness, wisdom and grace. We remember the many
passages in the *Church Dogmatics* in which his theology takes
on a devotional tone and almost imperceptibly and spontaneously

[60]*Ibid.*, p. 882.

[61]*EvTh*, pp. 165, 167.

[62]*Ibid.*, p. 162.

[63]*Ibid.*, p. 167.

[64]*Theologische Studien* 29, pp. 22ff. in *KBR*, pp. 12ff.

[65]*CD* II/1, pp. 654ff.

becomes doxology and impels us to doxology, lifting us up to a different level of contemplation of the high and holy theme. For Barth, as TF Torrance aptly commented in his Introduction to *Theology and Church*, 'theology is part of the church's humble worship of God', so that dogmatics, too, has 'a doxological task'.[66] The fact that this is largely implicit in Barth rather than explicit does not detract from its significance in Barth's understanding of theology as service. Ultimately theology is in its own way a liturgical ministry - divine service.

## III Comments

From one standpoint one might say that Barth's primary understanding of theology as service is a truism. As a function of the church theology can hardly avoid being a ministry. Its discussions have taken place in and for the church. Theological faculties were set up by the church to work for the constructive criticism of its message and the training of its ministers. Theological books were written and theological conferences held to help the church to render its various serices to its members and the world.

Nevertheless, the self-evident is often the unappreciated or even the disregarded. As Barth perceived, many people in the church regard theology as a dispensable luxury rather than a true ministry. Indeed, they even oppose it as detrimental to the church's proper work. Theologians, on the other hand, easily fall into an attitude of superiority nurtured by their status, their isolation from the church's main business, their intellectual concentration, or their arrogant substitution of subjective speculation for objective reflection. Whether it be directed to the church at large or to theologians in particular, Barth's insistent reminder that theology is service, that the church needs this service, and that theologians have a duty to perform it, is one which will always be apposite.

Not so self-evident is Barth's contention that theology is a service of the whole church. In a very general way one can hardly

---

[66]*TC*, pp. 30ff.

dispute the thesis, but now that theology has become technically so complex, and in many writers linguistically so obscure, ordinary church members find it hard to think that they, too, bear theological responsibility. Barth himself, for all his brave words about obscure parsons and little old ladies, tended to be impatient with the foibles and follies of theological novices. Church members cannot avoid making theological statements, but they may be excused for disclaiming any ministry of correction and direction, or in many cases for refusing to accept such a ministry from the theological experts. All the same, the principle of total theological responsibility is surely right.

Whether or not Barth was right to tie theology so closely to the Word may well be questioned. He himself seemed to have sensed at times that he was imposing an invalid restriction. Theology relates to what we do as well as to what we say. Even in what we say, words of prayer and praise need to be theologically informed as well as words of proclamation. Beginning with the problem of the pulpit, Barth naturally moved on at once to a theology of the Word, and since the Word is the Word of the self-revealed and self-revealing God, one can understand that for Barth theology should relate primarily to this central theme. The fact that the Word is indeed the Word of *God*, however, and not merely the word of preaching, opens the door to a wider concept of service of the Word such as Barth himself adopted in his discussion of the forms of ministry in *CD* IV/3.2. For the Word itself has to do with the whole life of the church, and therefore theology brings all that the church does and says under its scrutiny. As Barth found at Safenwil, the most practical problems have a theological root.

A controversial aspect of Barth's understanding is his establishment of the revealed and written Word as the norm that theology must use. Theology obviously has to have some norm, and even if this be primarily the subjective one of individual judgment, objective elements will be present in such forms as facts, consensus, tradition or simple rules of grammar and logic.

148

Of course, it may be argued that there is really no such thing as divine revelation. In Barth's view, however, this is theologically self-defeating, for it deprives theology of its theme and involves an abdication of its work and ministry. Another criticism might be that to stress the written Word in this manner plunges the church into a restrictive biblicism. Barth safeguarded himself in two ways. He related scripture strictly to the revealed Word as primary and authoritative testimony. He also set it under the lordship of the Spirit for authentic exposition and application. A third objection might be that Barth's view does not do justice to other norms like the church, tradition, the Fathers and the confessions. Barth's discussion of authority in *CD* I/2,[67] and his common practice throughout his work, demonstrate, however, an acceptance and use of secondary norms in the discharge of theological ministry. He saw that such norms help to prevent a subjective interpretation of the primary authority. But they, too, are subject to the primary norm of revelation that comes down to us in the given, objective and ongoing entity of the prophetic and apostolic witness enshrined in scripture.

On the positive side, one might say that Barth's concept of theology as service of scripture is wholly consistent with his presupposition - the presupposition of faith - that God's Word is God himself in his self-revelation: the Father who has spoken his own Word in the Son, and who by the Spirit speaks this Word through Scripture and scriptural proclamation.[68] The church proclaims God's Word, not because it says it does, but because God says what it says. If this is to be true, however, the church must know what God says. This explains and justifies its focus on the revealed Word as it knows this through scripture. Its theologians must help it so to apprehend this Word that its own witness to the world in every given place and time may be truly God's Word. Barth's understanding of theology and its role at this point stands or falls with his whole understanding of the Word. That is why he regarded a study of the Word as the first theological task. If his concept of the Word be rejected, then his

[67] *CD* I/2, pp. 585ff.
[68] *CD* I/1, pp. 295ff.

claim for the Word as norm obviously becomes one competing claim among many others. If it be accepted, in principle at least if not in detail, his position allows of little refutation, since the authority he proposes is the incomparable objective authority of God himself teaching his people about himself and what this involves for all they say and do. Barth's norm does not shut God out of the picture. It sees God himself as the ultimate norm, both as the object of the biblical testimony and as the subject of biblical exposition. In his discussion of the authority and freedom of the Word in *CD* I/2 [69] Barth added some persuasive supporting considerations in an eloquent depiction of the uniqueness, autonomy and astonishing efficacy of the Word. The question with which he confronts us is the searching one whether theology can in fact render its service to the church and the church's mission if it rejects this norm, either discarding it for one that seems to have greater appeal, or plunging into normless relativity and final futility.

Did Barth really need to put so much stress on humility as an integral part of the service of theology? Are not humility and service indissolubly related? Is not humility essential to Christian life and work? Is it not, then, a self-evident prerequisite of theology? No doubt this is all true, yet one can easily overlook the self-evident and a gap quickly opens up between precept and practice. Barth felt the pressures in his own life as honours came his way, and while talk about humility can never enforce it, a reminder that theologians too, and perhaps especially, must walk humbly with God and their fellows will never come amiss.

A final comment must be devoted to the comparatively slight attention that Barth paid explicitly to theology as service of God. Ought he to have said more along these lines? In answer, we must point out that theology will not itself be direct service to God as worship is. We must also recall that Barth's own theology increasingly tended to take on a liturgical character.

[69] *CD* I/2, pp. 538ff., 661ff.

Above all, however, we must bear in mind that for Barth, all
service, of whatever kind, is fundamentally service of God.
Faithfully undertaken and executed, theology serves God by
serving his church, which itself in all its members serves God in
the special service that it renders to the world. The ministry of
theology is God's in the twofold sense that he has given this
ministry and that first and last it is discharged on God's behalf.
'Good theologians', Barth said, 'do not serve themselves but the
Father of Jesus Christ'.[70] Like all of us, Barth has come under
criticism because he did not fulfil this ministry more successfully.
He himself can hardly be faulted however, for any failure to see in
the service of God the very basis and centre of the service of
theology. Theology is either service of God or it is neither
theology nor service.

---

[70]*KBR*, p. 16.

# 9

# Irenaeus, Recapitulation and Physical Redemption

## TREVOR A HART

Irenaeus of Lyons is known to us primarily for his major treatise the 'Refutation and Overthrow of *Gnosis* Falsely So-Called',[1] from which we gain much of our information concerning the various 'Gnostic' systems. In this polemical and apologetic work Irenaeus seeks to defend the integrity of the Gospel in relation to a view of the cosmos and of the relationship between God and man which is alien to it. Our concern in this paper will be to consider one particularly influential interpretation of his apologetic method and, more particularly, of its consequences for his understanding of salvation.

## I Irenaeus as an advocate of 'physical redemption'?

There has been no shortage of scholars willing to see Irenaeus as adopting a fundamentally similar method to that of his Alexandrian contemporaries Clement and Origen, and allowing a subtle syncretism to give his theology an essentially Greek (and thus unbiblical) flavour in its distinctive aspects. So, for example, Harnack begins his exposition of Irenaean theology with precisely this assumption. The theology of Irenaeus, he claims, remains a riddle to us if we do not discern those elements which it borrowed from the thought of Gnosticism.[2] Granted that Irenaeus' purpose was the utter refutation of the Gnostic systems, we must be aware that in order to achieve this end he was forced to adopt some of their most characteristic themes and presuppositions, dressing the Gospel up in new clothes. Harnack is not dissuaded from this assumption by the consideration that

---

[1]Otherwise *Adversus Haereses* [*Adv. H.*] in J Donaldson and A Roberts (eds.), *Ante Nicene Fathers: Translations of the writings of the Fathers down to AD 325* [*ANF*] (Buffalo, 1885), pp. 314-567; JP Migne, *Patrologia Graeca Latina* [*PGL*], vol. 7 (Paris, 1882), cols 431-1224.

[2]*History of Dogma*, vol. II, pp. 231ff.

Irenaeus nowhere affirms the apologetic value of any of the ideas put forward by Gnosticism, nor by the fact that he repeatedly affirms his intention to be utterly faithful to the Scriptures and the *Regula Fidei*, and criticizes those who seek to build their theology on any other basis.[3]  The idea that 'theology is interpreted faith'[4] is, Harnack tells us, simply 'the consequence of a happy blindness to the gulf which lay between the Christian tradition and the world of ideas prevailing at that time'.[5] Irenaeus, in his attempts to set forth and preserve the message of the New Testament and the *Regula Fidei* may have thought he was doing no more than this, but in fact he was guilty of a syncretistic fusion of biblical and Gnostic conceptuality.[6]

Harnack's interpretation of the theology of the eastern Fathers generally as the 'work of the Greek spirit upon the soil of the Gospel'[7] sees such a syncretistic approach as an *inevitable* consequence of the spread of the Gospel into a world where the dominant worldview was that of the Greeks.[8]  This assumption in itself, however, would hardly endue his interpretation with credibility, were there nothing in Irenaeus' writings to bear an essentially Hellenic or Gnostic interpretation.  In fact there is an abundance of language which may be so interpreted.  Significantly Irenaeus himself avoids using the provocative term 'deification' (*theopoiesis*), but he does speak of man as 'passing into God'[9] and as being 'promoted into God'[10] through the redemptive process, language which at first sight seems to amount to much the same thing.   When, therefore, he goes on to speak of salvation as the bestowal of immortality (*aphtharsia*) and

---

[3]See, e.g., *Adv. H.* I.viii.1 (*ANF* 326; *PGL* 7.520); I.viii.1 (*ANF* 326; *PGL* 7.521).
[4]Harnack, *op. cit.*, p. 234.
[5]*Ibid.*, p. 245.
[6]*Ibid.*, p. 246-7.
[7]See further *ibid.*, p. 17.
[8]'Theology is dependent ... above all on the spirit of the time; for it lies in the nature of theology that it desires to make its object intelligible', *History of Dogma*, vol. 1, preface to 1st edn., p. x.
[9]*Adv. H.*,IV.xxxiii.4. (*ANF* 507; *PGL* 7.1074).
[10]*Ibid.*, III.xix.1. (*ANF* 448; *PGL* 7.939).

incorruptibility (*athanasia*) upon man by Jesus Christ[11], and as a realization of the 'image of God' in man[12] such that he has real knowledge of God[13] and is united with him[14], Harnack has little hesitation in referring us to the influence of Gnostic and Hellenistic conceptuality.

The ensuing interpretation of Irenaean soteriology among Liberal Protestant scholars is that which has come to be referred to as the 'physical theory' of redemption. The essential idea is summed up conveniently by Loofs, who describes the physical theory as 'the understanding of redemption as the removal of *phthora* from human nature, completed through the union of manhood and Godhead in Christ'.[15] The point would seem to be that Irenaeus substitutes metaphysical categories for moral ones in his presentation of the Gospel, reflecting an essentially Greek interest in man's ontological standing with regard to the eternal realm (his 'being'), as opposed to a more biblical concern with his moral standing in relation to the categories of sin, judgment and guilt. Man's plight is understood primarily in terms of the physical conditions of mortality and death which are the *consequences* of sin, rather than that sinfulness itself.[16] Accordingly salvation is understood in terms of the administration of an antidote to this condition; namely the attribute of *aphtharsia*, rather than that forgiveness, atonement, and reconciliation secured by the cross of which the Bible speaks.

The way in which this transfusion of humanity with immortality is conceived as having been achieved is vaguely described as 'realistic' or 'physical'. Immortality and incorruptibility are, according to the Greek thought upon which Harnack and Loofs see

---

[11]See, e.g., *ibid.*, I.x.1; also II.xx.3.

[12]See *ibid.*, V.ii.1. (*ANF* 528; *PGL* 7.1124); also V.xvi.2 (*ANF* 544; *PGL* 7.1167-68).

[13]See *ibid.*, IV.xxxvi.7. (*ANF* 518; *PGL* 7.1098).

[14]See *ibid.*, III.iv.2. (*ANF* 417; *PGL* 856); also III.xviii.7. (*ANF* 448; *PGL* 7.937).

[15]F Loofs, *Leitfaden zur Studium der Dogmengeschichte*, 4th edn., (Halle, 1906), p. 203.

[16]See Harnack, *op. cit.*, vol. II, p. 292.

Irenaeus as having drawn, conditions proper to the divine nature.[17]  Nevertheless, through the physical joining of divine and human natures in the person of the God-man this condition is communicated to the human race, being infused into the humanity of Christ, and thereby passing in a 'naturalistic' or 'mechanical' manner to all men by virtue of a 'mystical union' with the Redeemer.  Thus the incarnate Word of God is in effect the metaphysical bridgehead through which this condition enters the race, the 'point of contact' through which humanity is given to share in the attributes of divine substance in a 'deifying' act. Redemption is consequently seen as *complete* in the very joining of manhood to Godhead in the person of Christ, the *acts* of Christ being obscured by a concentration upon his *nature*, and the incarnation usurping the place of the cross as the focal point of Christian soteriology.

The presence of Greek philosophico-religious terminology in the *Adversus Haereses* is hardly, in itself, however, a sufficient basis for seeking Irenaeus' meaning in the thought-world of Hellenistic Gnosticism, particularly in the light of his avowed intention to demonstrate the *falsity* of Gnostic thought.   It would be surprising not to find such language used.  Irenaeus was doing his theology in a particular cultural matrix, and in order to communicate with his fellows at all would have to employ familiar terms.  Thus far Harnack is beyond reproach.  Yet this must not preclude a consideration of the way in which he used language, and of the frame of reference within which that language is firmly set.  In its implication that for Irenaeus all that really matters for redemption is the 'bare event' of the incarnation, the physical linking of corruptible and incorruptible natures such that a transfusion of essence might take place, the Harnack-Loofs interpretation makes a nonsense of several aspects of his theology.

Thus, for example, Irenaeus' emphasis upon the need for human faith in order for salvation to be personally appropriated would seem to fly in the face of any suggestion that he understands

[17]See *ibid.* p. 241.

155

salvation primarily in essentially metaphysical categories, and as transmitted in some 'mysterious' and automatic manner. The name of Christ, he maintains, confers benefits upon and cures thoroughly and effectively 'all who anywhere *believe* on him'.[18] Likewise it is those who *believe* in the name of Jesus Christ our Lord who are made sons of God by him[19] and who, uniting themselves to God,[20] are made perfect by him because they acknowledge his advent. Those who, on the other hand, choose disbelief in the face of Christ's self-revelation will suffer the consequences of God's righteous judgment, being shut out into the darkness which they have chosen for themselves in preference to the light.[21] Thus, 'the righteous judgment of God (shall fall) upon *all* who, like others, have seen, but have not, like others, believed'.[22] God has indeed acted for man's salvation, 'thus making peace and friendship with those who *repent* and turn to him ... but preparing for the *impenitent*, those who shun the light, eternal fire and outer darkness, which are evils indeed to those persons who fall into them'.[23] Such language would seem to presuppose a rather different view of the nature of redemption to that sketched by Harnack. Far from any purely automatic or mechanistic endowing of the entire human race with immortality, Irenaeus clearly gives the fullest place to human response, and sees unbelief as precluding man's participation in the salvation which has been worked out for him.

Nor, secondly, is it the case that Irenaeus is preoccupied with a Hellenic interest in the 'physical' consequences of human sin to the virtual exclusion of a *theologia crucis* or any notion of redemption as involving an atonement between God and man. On the contrary his account is filled with the language of man's

---

[18]*Adv. H.*, II.xxxii.5. (*ANF* 409; *PGL* 7.830), my italics.

[19]*Ibid.*, III.vi.2. (*ANF* 419; *PGL* 7.861).

[20]*Ibid.*, II.xxii.2. (*ANF* 390; *PGL* 7.782). See further IV.xxviii.3. (*ANF* 502; *PGL* 7.1062), my italics.

[21]*Ibid.*, IV.vi.5. (*ANF* 468; *PGL* 7.989).

[22]*Ibid.*, my italics. See further IV.xxviii.2. (*ANF* 501; *PGL* 7.1062). Also IV.xxviii.3. (*ANF* 502; *PGL* 7.1062).

[23]*Ibid.*, IV.xl.1. (*ANF* 523; *PGL* 7.1112). See also IV.xxxix.3-4 (*ANF* 523; *PGL* 7.1111-2).

standing before God as a moral agent, and of the consequences of
sin for man's relationship with God. 'According to nature', he
writes, '... we are all sons of God, because we have all been
created by God. But with respect to obedience and doctrine we are
not all the sons of God: those only are so who believe in him
and do his will'.[24] In other words the question of our obedience
or sinfulness is one which is bound up with the question of our
relationship to God as Father. Sin and disobedience do not result
in merely 'physical' consequences, therefore, but serve to separate
man from that fellowship with God for which he was created.
Man is a creature placed under the obligations of life in the
presence of his Creator, and his failure to fulfil these same
obligations has led to his condemnation and guilt, and his slavery
to sin and the Devil, from which he now requires to be set free.
Thus we must give sufficient recognition to the fact that man's
plight is described by Irenaeus in relational language as well as
that which has been termed 'physical'.

Accordingly, in his exposition of how it is that man is redeemed,
Irenaeus has much to say about the restoration of man to a
relationship of *koinonia* with the Father through the mediation
of the Son. It is here that we find a wealth of language
concerning the suffering and death of Christ as God's way of
dealing with the existential breach which human sin has opened
up. 'The Lord', he maintains, 'has reconciled man to God the
Father, in reconciling us to himself by the body of his own flesh,
and redeeming us by his own blood'.[25] It was, in fact, for this
very reason that the Son of God 'became a man, subject to
stripes, and knowing what it is to bear infirmity'.[26] How,
Irenaeus asks, if Christ had not gone through that birth which
belongs to a human being, 'could he forgive us those sins for
which we are answerable to our Maker and God? And how, again,
supposing he was not flesh, but was a man merely in appearance,

[24]*Ibid.*, IV.xli.2. (*ANF* 524-5; *PGL* 7.1115-6).
[25]*Ibid.*, V.xiv.3. (*ANF* 542; *PGL* 7.1163). Cf also III.v.3. (*ANF* 418;
*PGL* 7.859-60).
[26]*Ibid.*, IV.xxxiii.1. (*ANF* 506; *PGL* 7.1072).

could he have been crucified, and could blood and water have issued from his pierced side?'[27]   There is, therefore, a soteriological concern behind Irenaeus' rejection of Gnostic docetism.  Only one who is fully human can be said to suffer and to die, and that Christ did precisely these things for us is a basic element of Irenaeus' understanding of redemption.

On the other hand he seeks to take with equal seriousness the fact that the one who suffers and dies is (in the terminology of later debates) *homoousios* with the one who is offended by human sinfulness.  'He was himself the Word of God made the Son of man, receiving from the Father the power of remission of sins, since he was a man, and since he was God, in order that since as man he suffered for us, so as God he might have compassion on us, and forgive us our debts, in which we were made debtors to God our Creator'.[28]   'Therefore', Irenaeus states, 'in the last times the Lord has restored us into friendship through his incarnation, having become "the Mediator between God and men"; propitiating indeed, for us, the Father against whom we had sinned, and cancelling our disobedience by his own obedience.'[29] In this way God himself puts his own words into deeds, and loves his enemies, praying even for those who crucify him.[30]  Thus whatever Irenaeus may have to say about the consequences of human sin for man's nature (in terms of death and corruptibility) he certainly gives full credence to the *relational* consequences in terms of guilt and condemnation, and to the interpretation of salvation as consisting essentially in an *atonement* or reconciliation between God and man, worked out in the life and death of Jesus Christ.  It is untrue, therefore, to suggest that he sees the incarnation in itself as the sum of Christian soteriology, beyond which nothing more needs to be said.

One scholar who has stressed the need to move beyond such an interpretation of Irenaeus is Gustaf Aulén in his book *Christus*

---

[27]*Ibid.*, IV.xxxiii.2. (*ANF* 507; *PGL* 7.1073).

[28]*Ibid.*, V.xvii.3. (*ANF* 545; *PGL* 7.1170).

[29]*Ibid.*, V.xvii.1. (*ANF* 544; *PGL* 7.1169).

[30]See *ibid.*, III.xviii.5. (*ANF* 447; *PGL* 7.936).

*Victor*.[31]    Rather than locating the dogmatic centre of Irenaeus' theology in the 'bare fact' of the incarnation, he argues, due recognition must be given to the vital significance of the whole life and ministry of Jesus in the theology of the *Adversus Haereses*.   The acts of Christ are charged with a salvific significance and are not obscured by any purely 'physical' communication of redemption in the joining of the divine and human natures of Christ.   Yet it is not simply the death of Christ on the cross to which Irenaeus points us, but rather the entire life of Jesus, culminating in his death and resurrection.   It is not sufficient, therefore, in interpreting Irenaeus, simply to shift the dogmatic centre from the womb of the virgin to the cross, from an essentially physical to an essentially ethical and forensic understanding.   There are elements of his theology which resist any reduction of his thought to either of these alternatives.

Thus Aulén notes the way in which Irenaeus attributes a saving significance to the obedience of Jesus throughout his life as well as in the events surrounding his death.   Indeed 'the earthly life of Christ as a whole is thus regarded as a continuous process of victorious conflict' over the powers of evil and death which hold humanity in their grip, his death being interpreted as 'the final and decisive battle'.[32]

Whilst Aulén's presentation (geared as it is towards his personal concern to discredit the 'Latin' model of the Atonement in favour of what he calls the 'classic' idea[33]) may well be thought to overstate its case, it succeeds at least in demonstrating the presence of the 'victor' motif in Irenaeus' theology, and in distinguishing this from an understanding of atonement in purely forensic or juridical categories.   Thus Irenaeus writes: 'Our Lord ... fought and conquered; for he was man contending for the fathers, and through obedience doing away with disobedience completely: for he bound the strong man, and set free the weak and endowed his own handiwork with salvation, by destroying sin'.[34]   Again

[31]G Aulén, *Christus Victor* (London, 1931).
[32]*Ibid.*, p. 30.
[33]See, e.g., *ibid.*, p. 6f.
[34]*Adv. H.*, III.xviii.6. (*ANF* 447-8; *PGL* 7.937).

this is a redemption which Irenaeus sees as requiring the incarnation: 'For it behoved him who was to destroy sin, and redeem man under the power of death, that he should himself be made that very same thing which he was, that is, man; who had been drawn by sin into bondage, but was held by death, so that sin should be destroyed by man, and man should go forth from death'.[35]

Thus Aulén's analysis conveniently draws to our attention the fact that in the theology of *Adversus Haereses* it is not merely the consequences of human sinfulness (whether those be physical or ethical) that are dealt with in the saving economy, but rather that sinfulness itself, as it is undone in the recapitulatory ministry of Jesus; obedience replacing disobedience; victory replacing defeat; freedom replacing bondage. In Christ God became man in order to secure for the human race victory over the powers of evil. Subsequently a new humanity emerges in the person of Christ to replace the old, a humanity characterized by the possession of freedom from the determinacy of evil. Sin, and not just guilt, is destroyed through the obedience of the Saviour. In short, human nature is transformed in the person of the Son, so that we too might share in a life set free from the bondage of the powers and principalities and possess the victory which is given by God through our Lord Jesus Christ.

There are two points in Aulén's exposition, however, which remain problematic. The first is the answer which he gives to the obvious question as to how it is that this victory benefits others. Granted that Christ lives a victorious life in the face of temptation and establishes a new humanity in his own flesh, in what sense is this actually 'for us'? How does his victory relate to ours? In response to this Aulén resorts to the language of pneumatology and eschatology respectively. For Irenaeus, he maintains, 'the Recapitulation does not end with the triumph of Christ over the enemies which had held man in bondage; it continues in the work of the Spirit in the Church ... The

---

[35]*Ibid.*, III.xviii.7. (*ANF* 448; *PGL* 7.938). See also V.xxi.3. (*ANF* 550; *PGL* 7.1182).

completeness of the Recapitulation is not realized in this life: Irenaeus' outlook is strongly eschatological ... It remains true, however, that in the process of the restoring and perfecting of creation ... the central and crucial point is the victory of Christ over the hostile powers'.[36] In other words the ministry of Christ sees the beginning of a process which continues in the Church, a process in which the Spirit empowers our humanity, enabling our personal victory over the powers of evil to what is in this life a limited extent. Whilst this may be true enough for Irenaeus in itself, it is, we believe, an inadequate exposition of his point of view, and one which, in due course, we must redress.

The second problematic element in Aulén's treatment is his understanding of the christological context within which Irenaeus perceives the redemption as taking place. He quite rightly notes that in *Adversus Haereses* 'incarnation and atoning work are ... set in the closest possible relation to one another'.[37] Redemption and atonement are the work of God himself who becomes man in order to refashion our humanity. Yet in the same instant that he affirms the importance of the victory and obedience of Christ as a reformation and recapitulation of human nature, he calls it into question again by his one-sided emphasis upon the God-manward dynamic. Irenaeus, he tells us, 'does not think of the Atonement as an offering made to God by Christ from man's side, or as it were from below; for God remains throughout the effective agent in the work of redemption ... When Irenaeus speaks in this connection of the "obedience" of Christ', therefore, 'he has no thought of a human offering made to God from man's side, but rather that the Divine will wholly dominated the human life of the Word of God, and found perfect expression in his work'.[38]

Aulén's concern here is to avoid what he realizes to be the dangers of any suggestion that Christ acts as Saviour in a purely human capacity over against God, who is the subsequently viewed

[36]Aulén, *op. cit.*, p. 22.
[37]*Ibid.*, p. 32.
[38]*Ibid.*, pp. 33-4.

as the object rather than the subject of atonement. This is a danger which he sees realized in the Latin view. In this, we believe, Irenaeus would concur wholeheartedly, yet his response to any such suggestion is a quite different one. It is God, certainly, who is the agent of atonement and salvation; but it is God *as man*. Aulén's response is one which fails to take the incarnation fully seriously, robbing Christ of any human obedience or victory in a way which Irenaeus certainly does not do. It is a docetic response, which fails to grasp the point of the patristic insistence that while Christ's humanity must be confessed to be *anypostatic* (i.e., as having no existence prior to or apart from the person of the Son), it must also be affirmed as *enypostatic* (i.e., as having full integrity within the hypostatic union). According to Aulén's presentation, the incarnation involves only a single dynamic, that from God to man; in fact, as we shall see, for Irenaeus it is crucial that we see in Christ a twofold dynamic, from God to man, and subsequently from *this* man to God on behalf of all other men.

Another scholar who sees the way in which for Irenaeus the entire ministry of Christ, culminating in the Cross and the empty tomb, has a salvific significance is Aulén's fellow Swede, Gustaf Wingren.[39] Drawing upon the same key themes of conflict and victory in Irenaeus' soteriology, however, he stresses the fact that it is as man that Christ is presented throughout the struggle, and that his obedience and ultimate victory are therefore essentially human.

For Irenaeus the problematic aspect of christology was precisely the humanity of the Saviour which he sought to establish over against the docetic tendencies of the Gnostics. Thus 'Jesus Christ is a man. He belongs to our race. As man he must confront both sin and death. In his temptation he takes sin upon him, and on the Cross death itself finally enfolds him. But neither of the two enemies of humanity can get this man into its power. Christ resists temptation and he rises from the dead. And when a man forces both evil and corruption to turn away from him, as Jesus

---

[39]G Wingren, *Man and the Incarnation* (Edinburgh, 1959).

does, the purpose for man is realized, for man was ordained to live
and to live in righteousness'.[40] We must avoid, therefore, any
interpretation of Irenaeus which suggests that the Son of God
simply put himself, in human guise, into the various situations of
human existence and triumphed over them due to his superior
power and knowledge. It is precisely Christ's real identity with
man in his weakness and sinfulness which gives his ultimate
victory its meaning and significance for others, for it is in this
very conflict with the forces of evil (both those within and those
without man) that human nature is recreated and redeemed.[41]
Thus there can be no victory without the anguish, suffering, and
temptation, no resurrection without the Cross. Indeed it is not
simply the *victory* of Christ which is salvific, but the whole
painful process through and in which this victory is wrought, for
it is in this process that man's reconciliation with the Father is
effected through the conforming of a human will and mind and
soul to that of God himself, a real atonement between God and
man in which man's sinful being is transformed and restored to
wholeness and life.

Wingren's interpretation, by definition, excludes the idea of Aulén
that Christ's obedience cannot be said to be a human obedience,
for in that case humanity has not been redeemed in the obedience
of Christ, but simply treated to the spectacle of divine power
manifested through the instrument of a human body. Yet in
affirming the full integrity of Jesus' humanity in Irenaean
theology Wingren is not forced into the opposite error of calling
his divinity into question, or of separating the two natures off
from one another in some Nestorian manner. Unlike Aulén he
perceives the fact that for Irenaeus there is no ontological dualism
between Creator and creature akin to the Greek Platonist dualism
between the divine and the human. On the contrary the fact of the
divine *becoming* in the figure of Jesus excludes any such
dualism, and points instead to the openness of the created order to
the working of God, and to his continual involvement in it.[42]

---

[40]*Ibid.*, pp. 113-4.
[41]*Ibid.*, pp. 117-8.
[42]See *ibid.*, p. 106.

Thus it is not the case that we must affirm the absence of divine action in order to preserve the presence of human action. Were this so, then the whole idea of an incarnation would be bound to collapse into docetism, ebionitism, Nestorianism, or meaninglessness.

For Irenaeus, on the other hand, Jesus is both the God who redeems and the man who is redeemed; both the God who pours out his Spirit, and the man who receives it and is transformed by it; both the God who judges and the man who is judged for others.[43] The relationship between Creator and creature is seen in dynamic and not in static terms. There is never any question that Jesus is God working out man's salvation; but nor is there any denying of the fact that Jesus is God *as man* in the midst of this process, with a human will and a human mind, suffering from the constraints imposed by these, and being subject to the assaults of temptation and worse. There is no need to deny this. The fact that his death is a human death, his obedience a human obedience, his righteousness a human righteousness, does not in itself exclude God unless a dualistic ontology and cosmology is adhered to in advance, and the relationship between the Creator and his creatures (as this is perceived by Irenaeus), broken through human sinfulness but restored in the person of Christ, is not of this dualistic sort. Whilst, therefore, we must be clear that Christ does what we cannot do, we must be equally clear that he does what he does *as* man, and that in his doing it the human situation is decisively altered. In Irenaeus' own words: 'The Word of the Father ... having become united with the ancient substance of Adam's formation, rendered man living and perfect, receptive of the perfect Father, in order that as in the natural [Adam] we all were dead, so in the spiritual we may all be made alive'.[44]

We have seen, therefore, that Irenaeus speaks of redemption in terms which refute any attempt to see his theology as concentrating on the bare fact of the Incarnation alone. Whatever he means when he speaks of salvation as the communication of

---

[43]See *Adv. H.*, V.xvii.3. (*ANF* 545; *PGL* 7.1170): 'As man he suffered for us, so as God he might have compassion on us, and forgive us our debts'.
[44]*Ibid.*, V.i.3. (*ANF* 527; *PGL* 7.1123)

immortality to man, and as the joining of man to God, therefore, he clearly does not intend to exclude the language of forgiveness and reconciliation, or the idea of the necessity for and provision of an atonement between God and man. In fact Harnack is too good a scholar to suggest that he does, and in maintaining his interpretation based upon the 'physical theory' he is forced to posit the existence of massive inconsistencies in the theology of Irenaeus.[45] It was only the latter's 'moralism' and his naïve eclecticism, Harnack tells us, that prevented him from moving to the logical conclusion of the 'realistic' or physical view, namely the automatic redemption of all individual men and women.[46]

It would seem equally likely, however, that these contradictions and inconsistencies in Irenaean theology arise only out of Harnack's own insistence upon interpreting *Adversus Haereses* out of the framework provided by an essentially Greek ontology and anthropology. Emil Brunner has made a spirited attack upon Harnack at this point, concentrating upon refuting the disjunction which Harnack assumes between the 'physical' and the ethical and moral, according to which Irenaeus emphasizes the former in a manner wholly inconsistent with, and at the expense of, the latter. A physical transformation of man's nature displaces the more biblical forgiveness of his sins. This, Brunner argues, is a distinction which does not exist for Irenaeus, and is simply a projection of Harnack's own Kantian presuppositions onto the second century writer.[47] There may well be much truth in this, but it should also be noted, given Harnack's hermeneutical procedure, that such an interpretation is entirely in accordance with the way in which Greek thought emphasized the priority of essence over existence. The state of man's 'being', therefore, is considered and defined prior to any consideration of his relationships with others or the dynamics of his life.

It is all the more important, therefore, to realize that for Irenaeus these two aspects of his theology are not contradictory at all, but

---

[45]See, e.g., Harnack, *op. cit.*, vol II., p. 245. See further pp. 272-5.
[46]*Op. cit.*, p. 275.
[47]See *The Mediator* (London, 1934), p. 249f.

absolutely inseparable.   He often links together the communication of immortality to man and the death of Christ. Thus, he argues, 'Our Lord ... *by his passion* destroyed death, and dispersed error, and put and end to corruption, and destroyed ignorance, while he manifested life and revealed truth, and bestowed the gift of incorruption'.[48]   Throughout *Adversus Haereses* the language of immortality and incorruptibility is inseparable from the language of atonement and reconciliation. To use Harnack's terms, the physical and the ethical fall together. For Irenaeus it would seem to be the case that what man *is* (his essence or nature) is not considered in a static manner, but is bound up with his relationships, and more particularly with his relationship to his Creator.   Man's *being* is changed, therefore, precisely because and insofar as his relationship with the Father is healed and renewed, and not in any mechanistic fashion.   Nature and person are frequently distinguished in patristic thought, but never separated.   The relationship between mortality and immortality is thus no longer that between two strata of the metaphysical hierarchy, but rather between the 'old man' in his entirety (as a person with a nature) and the 'new man' established in Christ.   The *imago Dei* is not a divine spark within man's nature as such which Christ fans into flame, but rather man's capacity for *koinonia* with God, which is renewed precisely in the reconciling and atoning work of the incarnate Son who makes those who believe in his name sons by adoption.

There are, then, many reasons for rejecting the analysis of Irenaeus provided by the liberal protestant school in terms of a theory of 'physical redemption'.   If the liberal protestant interpretation may be said to have one great strength, however, it is the way in which it highlights Irenaeus' apparent suggestion that in some sense the salvation of the human race is to be thought of as having been achieved and completed in the very event of the incarnation, such that 'the work of Christ is contained in the construction of his person as the God-man'.[49] For whatever Irenaeus *means* when he argues that 'Our Lord Jesus

---

[48]*Adv. H.*, II.xx.3. (*ANF* 388; *PGL* 7.778).

[49]Harnack, cited by Aulén, *op. cit.* , p. 18.

Christ ... did, through his transcendent love, become what we are, that he might bring us to be even what he is himself',[50] it is clear that he sees this 'becoming' on the part of man not only as absolutely inseparable from the corresponding 'becoming' on the part of the Son of God, but as a reality established in that very becoming. There is a sense in which both sides of this 'glorious exchange' are fulfilled in the person of the Saviour.

Thus, according to Irenaeus, it is through and in the very enfleshing of the divine Logos that the bestowing of man with incorruptibility and the divine image is brought about.[51] The humanity of Christ is the *Anknüpsfungspunkt* between God and man through which the human race is united to God, 'he himself uniting man *through himself* to God'[52] in his condescending to be born of the Virgin. Thus Irenaeus' answer to the question *ut quid enim descendebat?*[53] finds in the inhomination of the eternal Son not merely the efficient cause but the material cause of redemption (to borrow the language of a later age). In these last times, he maintains, our Lord Jesus Christ 'was made a man among men, that he might join ... man to God'.[54]

Thus we must affirm that in some sense for Irenaeus the person of Christ is his work, the incarnation is the atonement. The becoming man on the part of the Son is not merely a prerequisite of something else which is his work, but is in itself a redeeming of humanity, a uniting of mankind to God. The crucial question is, of course, in what sense is this the case?

Harnack, as we have seen, interprets this 'union' as a 'bare fact', a timeless metaphysical conjunction of humanity and divinity in the ontology of the God-man, which is itself of saving

---

[50]*Adv. H.*, V. Pref. (*ANF* 526; *PGL* 7.1120).
[51] See, e.g., *ibid.*, III.xix.1. (*ANF* 448; *PGL* 7.939). See further III.xviii.1. (*ANF* 446; *PGL* 7.932)
[52]*Ibid.*, III.iv.2. (*ANF* 417; *PGL* 7.856), my italics.
[53]*Ibid.*, II.xiv.7. (*PGL* 7.755).
[54]*Ibid.*, IV.xx.4. (*ANF* 488; *PGL* 7.1034).

significance. This we have rejected on the grounds that it fails to
take into consideration many aspects of Irenaean thought. Whilst
there certainly is a union or joining of two 'natures' in the
incarnation, Irenaeus never abstracts this from the personal
history of Jesus, as if it were salvific in some independent
manner. Indeed, if, as we have suggested, it is truer to Irenaeus to
see 'nature' as defined not in some absolute or static sense, but
rather in terms of man's existence as creature in relation to his
Creator and to other men, then we may say that for him the union
of 'natures' takes place in and through this entire history, from
the conception in the virgin's womb, through the ministry and
death upon the cross to the resurrection and ascension of Christ.
Throughout this historical sequence the Creator is 'united to his
own workmanship'[55] through the assumption of human nature,
by virtue of which 'he became a man'.[56] And it is precisely as *a
man* that he is united to God, and not as some abstract and static
'nature'. It is precisely in the dynamics of his human
relationship with God that this union is worked out and made
concrete, 'humanity sustaining, and receiving, and embracing the
Son of God'.[57] There can be no ontological union without a
corresponding 'union' of activity and existence; thus in the
humanity of Christ we see a man who is perfectly at one with the
divine will.

Thus the union of God and man in Christ is no 'bare fact' in the
Harnackian sense, but rather the interweaving of divine and human
existence in a life lived out as man for our sakes. This 'ὑπὲρ
ἡμῶν' applies, for Irenaeus, not just to the death of Christ but to
his entire human existence. By becoming man the divine Son
'caused human nature to cleave to and become one with God',[58]
defeating the enemy of man and fitting our nature for that
communion with his Father which was its intended destiny. 'For
in what way', Irenaeus asks, 'could we be partakers of the
adoption of sons, unless we had received from him through the

[55]*Ibid.*, III.xviii.1. (*ANF* 446; *PGL* 7.932).
[56]*Ibid.*
[57]*Ibid.*, III.xvi.3. (*ANF* 441; *PGL* 7.922)
[58]*Ibid.*, III.xviii.7. (*ANF* 448; *PGL* 7.937).

168

Son that fellowship which refers to himself, unless his Word, having been made flesh, had entered into communion with us'?[59] In assuming a nature like ours and becoming a man, the Son's purpose was to 'accustom man to receive God and God to dwell in man',[60] thus 'recapitulating in himself his own handiwork'.[61]

For Irenaeus, therefore, the union of humanity with divinity is achieved precisely in this vital co-existence in the person of the Son of God, wrought through his condescension in assuming our nature, and in that fulfilling of 'all the conditions of human nature'[62] which led him ultimately to the cross. In the dynamics of this one man's 'nature' the salvation of mankind was effected, 'attaching man to God *by his own incarnation*, and bestowing upon us at his coming immortality durably and truly, *by means of communion (communionem) with God*'.[63] It is in this establishing of man in his proper relationship of communion with God, therefore, that the communication of immortality consists, life itself being defined in terms of this fellowship,[64] and death or non-existence in terms of its absence.[65] Thus this 'union' is in itself a reconciliatory one, Christ having taken on our flesh in order to redeem it from its pitiful state, 'reconciling us to himself by the body of his own flesh',[66] and 'effecting by means of himself that communion which should be held with [humanity]'[67] such that we may say that he has saved it in his own person.[68]

In short, this one man 'leads man into fellowship and unity with God'[69] in such a way that Irenaeus can speak of this 'union' as an established reality. Through Christ's human life, death and

---

[59]*Ibid.*

[60]*Ibid.*, III.xx.2 (*ANF* 450; *PGL* 7.944).

[61]*Ibid.*, III.xxii.1. (*ANF* 454; *PGL* 7.956).

[62]*Ibid.*, III.xvii.4. (*ANF* 445; *PGL* 7.931).

[63]*Ibid.*, V.i.1. (*ANF* 527; *PGL* 7.1121), my italics.

[64]See, e.g., *ibid.*, IV.xx.5. (*ANF* 489; *PGL* 7.1036).

[65]*Ibid.*, IV. xx.7. (*ANF* 490; *PGL* 7.1037).

[66]*Ibid.*, V.xiv.3. (*ANF* 542; *PGL* 7.1163).

[67]*Ibid.*, V.xiv.2. (*ANF* 541; *PGL* 7.1162).

[68]See, e.g., *ibid.*, V.xiv.1. (*ANF* 541; *PGL* 7.1161).

[69]*Ibid.*, IV.xiii.1. (*ANF* 477; *PGL* 7.1007).

resurrection the reconciliation of man to God has taken place, he 'having been made himself the beginning of those that live'[70], recapitulating in himself his own handiwork and 'bearing salvation'[71] to it.

We have, perhaps, now reached a point where we can see the inadequacy of any interpretation of Irenaeus according to which all that matters for the salvation of mankind is the physical linking of two natures in the person of Christ. When Irenaeus speaks of salvation as consisting in the joining of man to God in Christ, this 'joining' is not to be thought of as occurring in some abstract or timeless manner, but rather as the taking up of human nature into the life of God through its assumption in the person of Christ, who as the human Son of God lives out a life of obedient sonship in which our nature is transformed and conformed to the divine will. Yet we have seen that Irenaeus can speak of salvation as accomplished precisely in this man's union with God, and this poses some immediate questions. How are we to think of this 'transforming and conforming' as taking place 'for us'? In what sense is this particular uniting of God and man salvific for others, insofar as it takes place in him and not in them? The answer to such questions is to be found in Irenaeus' use of the language of 'recapitulation' (*anakephalaiosis*) with reference to the humanity of Christ.

## II Redemption as the Recapitulation of humanity in Christ
Irenaeus speaks repeatedly of Christ having recapitulated or summed up the human race in himself, and thus having endowed it with salvation.[72] Whilst Loofs in particular has wanted to find here a dependence upon an earlier theological tradition already well established in Asia Minor,[73] many scholars have been content to see Irenaeus as consciously borrowing directly from the language of Paul in Ephesians 1:10, concerning the Father's intention 'to sum up (ἀνακεφαλαιόω) all things in Christ'.

[70]*Ibid.*, III.xxii.4. (*ANF* 455; *PGL* 7.959).

[71]*Ibid.*, III.xxii.2. (*ANF* 455; *PGL* 7.958).

[72]So, for example, see *ibid.*, III.xviii.7. (*ANF* 448; *PGL* 7.938). Also V.xiv.1-2. (*ANF* 541; *PGL* 7.1161-2).

[73]See Loofs, *op. cit.*, pp. 141-2.

Whilst Irenaeus' juxtaposition of this and other Pauline language (such as the Christ and Adam parallelism of Romans 5) may well reflect the influence of other early Christian writings, this ought not to detract from his own evident basic familiarity with the Apostle's thought. Nevertheless we must beware here of committing the fallacy of origins, and assuming any simple continuity of meaning between the biblical author and the second century bishop. Even if scholarly opinion were entirely clear about Paul's use of this term, this in itself would hardly be sufficient for our interpretation of Irenaeus. We must be careful to allow the writer's *own* use of the word to be just as determinative in our attempts to fathom his meaning.

When we turn to the text of *Adversus Haereses* there would seem, in fact, to be two main emphases behind Irenaeus' use of the language of *recapitulatio*.

A *Christ the New Man.*
The recapitulation effected in Christ involves a reiteration of the history of mankind's relationship with God. Christ is the New Man who fulfils the destiny of the original man. Yet in view of the oft expressed opinion that Irenaeus holds only to a token 'Fall' in man[74], we must emphasize that this reiteration is no mere perfecting of a thing essentially good in itself, no realization of a potential to which man has aspired and simply fallen short. Nature cannot, for Irenaeus, be said to presuppose grace in this sense. On the contrary, the recapitulation to which he bears witness calls man into account because it takes the form of a radical reversal of the essential direction of man's life before God, from disobedience to obedience, from sin to faith, from apostasy to fellowship, and hence from death to life; and it is in this very reversal that the salvation of man is achieved. In the history of the New Man the sinfulness of Adam is undone, and its horrific consequences eradicated.

In the person of Christ, therefore, God creates a new 'point of

[74]So, e.g., JT Nielsen, *Adam and Christ in the Theology of Irenaeus of Lyons*(Assen, 1968), p. 62.

171

contact' between himself and his fallen Creation. This theme of a new beginning in Christ, and Irenaeus' own concern to hold together the themes of Creation and Redemption in opposition to the Gnostics, lead him to make substantial use of the Pauline Christ-Adam parallel. Thus Christ's life of obedience is presented as restoring that which was lost through the sin of the first man. 'When he became incarnate, and was made man, he commenced afresh the long line of human beings, and furnished us ... with salvation; so that what we had lost in Adam - namely, to be according to the image and likeness of God - that we might recover in Christ Jesus'.[75] Unlike the first Adam, who was defeated by the devil, Christ, entering into the same situation in his recapitulatory ministry, emerges victorious from it, thus 'waging war against our enemy, and crushing him who had at the beginning led us away captives in Adam'.[76]

This parallel is developed, occasionally at length,[77] in order to affirm that Christ was 'himself made the beginning of those that live, as Adam became the beginning of those who die'.[78] In his victorious conflict with Satan, and his fulfilment of the righteous will of his Father, Christ remoulds human nature and establishes it on a new footing before God, 'through obedience doing away with disobedience completely',[79] since 'as by the disobedience of the one man who was originally moulded from virgin soil, the many were made sinners, and forfeited life; so was it necessary that, by the obedience of one man, who was originally born from a virgin, many should be justified and receive salvation'.[80]

This leads us on to a further reason for Irenaeus' extensive use of the parallel between Adam and Christ, namely the fact that he realizes the need to stress (again over against Gnosticism) the full

---

[75]*Adv. H.*, III.xviii.1. (*ANF* 446; *PGL* 7.932).

[76]*Ibid.*, V.xxi.1. (*ANF* 548; *PGL* 7.1179). See also V.xxi.2. (*ANF* 549; *PGL* 7.1180).

[77]See, for example, *ibid.*, III.xxi.10. (*ANF* 454; *PGL* 7.954-5). See further the parallels drawn between Eve and Mary in, e.g., III.xxii.4. (*ANF* 455; *PGL* 7.958-9), and V.xix.1 (*ANF* 547; *PGL* 7.1175).

[78]*Ibid.*, III.xxii.4. (*ANF* 455; *PGL* 7.959).

[79]*Ibid.*, III.xviii.6. (*ANF* 448; *PGL* 7.937).

[80]*Ibid.*, III.xviii.7. (*ANF* 448; *PGL* 7.938).

humanity of the Saviour. Thus he attacks the opinion of the followers of Valentinus who present a docetic Christ, and subsequently 'exclude the flesh from salvation';[81] in contradiction of their views Irenaeus maintains that Christ 'would not have been one truly possessing flesh and blood, by which he bought us back, unless he had summed up in himself the ancient formation of Adam'.[82] Not only does Christ possess human nature, therefore, but he possesses the very same human nature (generically speaking) that he himself created in the beginning, and not some other form of the same. Thus it is this Adamic nature that is the object of divine salvation.

In passing we may note the fact that the reiteration includes a retrospective, negative aspect. Christ assumed flesh and blood in order to suffer and to die, for it was this same flesh and blood which was under the divine judgment. Thus in his death Christ sums up ours. [83] The implication would seem to be that it would not have been 'fitting' or 'fair' for one who was not of Adam's race to make this 'redeeming' payment, and this is language which Irenaeus certainly uses elsewhere in connection with the victory of Christ over the powers of evil. Thus, he argues, 'the enemy would not have been fairly (*juste*) vanquished, unless it had been a man [born] of a woman who conquered him. For it was by means of a woman that he got the advantage over man at first ... And therefore does the Lord profess himself to be the Son of man, comprising in himself that original man out of whom the woman was fashioned'.[84] Again the point is that it is only fitting that the one who reiterates (and reverses) the disobedience of the first man should himself be of the same race.

Earlier we argued that for Irenaeus it is not just the physical and ethical consequences of human sinfulness that Christ deals with in his recapitulation of the human race, but rather that very sinfulness itself, expunging it from our nature by living out a life

---

[81]*Ibid.*, V.i.2. (*ANF* 527; *PGL* 7.1122).
[82]*Ibid.*
[83] See *ibid.*, V.xxiii.2. (*ANF* 551; *PGL* 7.1185).
[84]*Ibid.*, V.xxi.1. (*ANF* 549; *PGL* 7.1179).

of obedience from within that same nature. Thus he restores immortality to man, and endows him once again with that image and likeness of God which was twisted beyond recognition at the Fall. Christ's obedience, therefore, is not just an Anselmian *satisfactio* to the divine honour, or payment of a redemption price, but is in itself a positive gift bestowed upon human nature, a sanctifying of humanity in which it is lifted up from its fallen state to participate actively in the doing of the divine will. Yet clearly if this is to be the case, then that which Christ assumes in the incarnation cannot be anything less or other than the human nature which fell in Adam. 'He had himself, therefore, flesh and blood, recapitulating in himself not a certain other, but that original handiwork of the Father, seeking out the thing which had perished'.[85] 'Nor would the Lord have summed up these things in himself, unless he had himself been made flesh and blood after the way of the original formation [of man], saving in his own person at the end that which had in the beginning perished in Adam'.[86] Only thus can we really understand the force of Irenaeus' objections to Gnostic docetism; only thus can we see the theological force behind his insistence that in the incarnation Christ passed through every phase of human existence, sanctifying it in himself;[87] only when we have grasped the fact that for Irenaeus, just as truly as for the Cappadocians, that which has not been taken up into the recapitulation in Christ remains estranged and fallen, that 'the unassumed is the unredeemed', will we see the fundamental point of his insistence that '*flesh* is that which was of old formed for Adam by God out of the dust, and it is this that John has declared the Word of God became'.[88]

In the reiteration of the history of humanity's relationship with its Creator the complete refashioning of our broken and fallen nature is achieved; 'the Lord has restored us into friendship through his incarnation, having become "the Mediator between God and men"; propitiating indeed for us the Father against whom

---

[85]*Ibid.*, V.xiv.2. (*ANF* 541; *PGL* 7.1162).

[86]*Ibid.*, V.xiv.1. (*ANF* 541; *PGL* 7.1161).

[87]See, e.g., *ibid.*, II.xxii.4. (*ANF* 391; *PGL* 7.783-4).

[88]*Ibid.*, I.ix.3. (*ANF* 329; *PGL* 7.543-4)

we had sinned, and cancelling our disobedience by his own obedience; conferring also upon us the gift of communion with, and subjection to, our Maker'.[89]  The incarnation of the Logos sees the Old Man assumed and put to death, and the New Man raised up in its place.  All this takes place in the humanity which Christ assumed in order to redeem it; yet the question remains, in what sense is this effective 'for us'?  How is it that Irenaeus can refer to Christ 'saving in his own person' that which had originally perished in Adam, as if in this same event others too have been saved?  It is at this point that we must turn to the second nuance of the term *recapitulation* in Irenaean theology.

## B  *Christ in our Place*
In the person of the New Man the entire race is 'summed up'. Christ's humanity is not merely reiterative, but also *inclusive*, such that all men are implicated in his actions.  He is the 'firstfruits' of the new humanity, the part which represents the whole, and in which the whole is in some sense included.  Thus he came 'and gathered together all things in himself ... summing up all things in himself'.[90]  He who is the Creator of all things sums up his own handiwork[91] in himself by becoming a part of it, and reiterates its life before him precisely so that in this very reiteration and reversal 'all flesh', namely the whole race, may be raised up and renewed.[92]  The point is clearly that there is an ontological solidarity between this one man and all others whereby all that he does, and indeed all that he is, may be predicated of them too.  This is how Irenaeus understands the biblical affirmation that Christ is 'for us'.

Several points need to be noted, however, if we are not to risk serious misunderstanding here.  Firstly we must not ascribe this aspect of Irenaeus' theology to any mystical or primitive outlook whereby the individuality of the Saviour is compromised in his being presented as a 'corporate personality' or a 'concrete

[89]*Ibid.*, V.xvii.1. (*ANF* 544; *PGL* 7.1169).
[90]*Ibid.*, III.xvi.6. (*ANF* 442-3; *PGL* 7.924-5).
[91]*Ibid.*, IV.vi.2. (*ANF* 468; *PGL* 7.987).
[92]*Ibid.*, I.x.1. (*ANF* 330; *PGL* 7.549).

universal'. The technical distinctions between the categories of substitution and representation belong to a much later age in theology, but for convenience we must affirm that the substance of the former is vital to Irenaeus' understanding of redemption. The particularity of Christ's flesh is never called into question precisely because as the New Man he comes to do that which the rest of the race could never do for itself. He lives out a life of obedience instead of us; he fulfils the conditions of humanity instead of us; he dies on the Cross instead of us. This 'substitutionary' element is precisely the point of his coming at all. Thus there can be no confusion between him and us, between what he does and what we do. He is not to be thought of as one in whom the race is represented in the sense that he embodies better than any other its aspirations and potentialities. On the contrary, he comes in order to judge those aspirations and to put those potentialities to death, reversing the direction of human existence. As such he stands over against us as a unique instance of humanity, as the New Man over against the old.

Despite this careful distinguishing of the Saviour from the saved, however, Irenaeus perceives a real bond between them, a solidarity which goes deeper than the ordinary ties of nature and kinship, and which enables him to act in their place such that they themselves are implicated in his actions. Thus this 'substitution' is not so much exclusive as inclusive in significance, for in doing all that he does in our stead, Christ does it precisely for us. Only thus can we understand how it is that he is spoken of, for example, as 'sanctifying' his nature for us. Such a statement makes little sense if we seek to interpret it in terms of a purely external and transactional relation between Christ and others. Yet when we recognize that for Irenaeus this relationship is one of inclusive solidarity, we can see how Christ's obedience and righteousness can be said really to belong to others, as he gives his soul for their soul, his flesh for their flesh, attaching them to God by his incarnation.[93] In him all the divine promises to man find their fulfilment,[94] and thus it is only in our union with him

[93]*Ibid.*, V.i.1. (*ANF* 527; *PGL* 7.1121).
[94]*Ibid.*, III.xii.3. (*ANF* 431; *PGL* 7.896).

that we are given to share in the same.   In this sense he may be said to represent the whole race, but his representative status rests not in their having chosen him to do so, but rather upon his own decision as Creator to redeem his own handiwork, summing it up in himself.

A further point to note here is that Irenaeus nowhere suggests that this 'once for all' nature of Christ's humanity leads either to universalism or to an antinomian lessening of emphasis upon the imperatives of the Gospel.   As we have seen, he is quite clear about the need for a response of faith in order for salvation to be appropriated, and also about the need for obedience in the Christian's walk with God.   The fact that the new humanity has already been realized for us in the person of Christ does not, therefore, imply that there is no response to be made on the part of others, or that their own behaviour has become a matter of indifference.   On the contrary it has become all the more urgent a matter,  the whole logic of Irenaeus' thought according well here with the question posed by Paul in Romans 6:2 : 'how can we who died to sin still live in it'?   It is precisely what we are in Christ that makes our continuing sinfulness problematic.

Thus Irenaeus' challenge to mankind is, like that of Paul to the Roman Christians, one to *werden das was du bist*.   In the very same moment that we are set free from our guilt and feelings of alienation from God, therefore, knowing that our inadequacies and sin are obscured by the obedience and faithfulness of the Son in his life and death on the Cross for us, and that we consequently stand sanctified and righteous before God in him, we also find ourselves called to surrender our lives to God, and to allow Christ to reproduce the same new humanity in us through the work of the Spirit.   There is, therefore, a first order sanctification of our humanity in its assumption by the Son of God, in which we share by virtue of our union and communion with him;[95] but there is also a second order sanctification in which we are conformed to his likeness.[96]   We are reconciled to God in the person of the second Adam;[97] yet in ourselves we are still being reconciled to

[95]See *ibid.*, III.xviii.7. (*ANF* 448; *PGL* 7.937).
[96]*Ibid.*, V.xvi.2. (*ANF* 544; *PGL* 7.1167-8).
[97]*Ibid.*, V.xvi.3. (*ANF* 544; *PGL* 7.1168).

him, as our rebelliousness and disobedience is purged. Thus Irenaeus notes that even the angels 'are not able to search out the wisdom of God, by means of which his handiwork, incorporated (*corporatum*) with and conformed (*conformatum*) to his Son, is brought to perfection'.[98]

In stark contrast to some of the apologetic theologies of the early Alexandrian tradition in which the adoption of dualistic structures of thought made it difficult to do proper justice to the idea of an incarnation of the Son of God, Irenaeus insists upon maintaining the integrity of both the humanity and the deity of the Saviour in the history of the person of Christ,[99] for he realizes that it is precisely the *becoming* of God within this history that saves mankind. God *becomes* a man. This is what the Greek mind cannot tolerate, and what Irenaeus knows must be proclaimed, for it is in this *becoming* that the redemption is wrought.[100] Thus he rejects the dualism inherent within Greek thought as an appropriate conceptual tool for Christian theology, and attacks those who, operating within its strict confines, distort the apostolic message. Those who insist upon driving a wedge between the realms of impassible divinity on the one hand and humanity on the other *cannot* affirm a real becoming of the Eternal Son of God, and so empty the incarnation of its significance, ending up with either a non-human docetic Logos or a 'transfigured man', or else positing the separate existence of two sons, the human Jesus, and the divine Christ.[101] Irenaeus' response consists in an unequivocal affirmation of the identity of the one who suffers on the Cross and who lives among men with the eternal and uncreated Word of God,[102] thus distancing himself

---

[98]*Ibid.*, V.xxxvi.3. (*ANF* 567; *PGL* 7.1224). *ANF* reads '*confirmed* and incorporated with'.

[99]See *ibid.*, I.iii.6. (*ANF* 320; *PGL* 7.477-8); cf. *ibid.*, III.vi.2. (*ANF* 419; *PGL* 7.861), III.xvi. (*ANF* 440-4; *PGL* 7.919.

[100]Thus he accuses the Gnostics of borrowing their ideas from the Greeks, with the result that the God in whom they believe is unable to act in history, either in a creating or a redemptive capacity, being confined to the realm of divine impassibility. See *ibid.*, II.xiv.1-5. (*ANF* 376-7; *PGL* 7.749ff); also II.xi.1 (*ANF* 365; *PGL* 7.736-7).

[101]See, e.g., *ibid.*, III.xi.3 (*ANF* 427; *PGL* 7.882).

[102]See *ibid.*, II.xxv.3. (*ANF* 397; *PGL* 7.799). Cf I.ix.3. (*ANF* 329; *PGL* 7.541-2). Also I.x.3. (*ANF* 331; *PGL* 7.555-6); III.xii.9. (*ANF* 433; *PGL*

not only from Gnostic thought, but also from the ill-fated attempts of his contemporaries in the East to rescue the Gospel from Gnosticism while yet operating within its basic conceptual framework.

In making the person of the Incarnate Son his dogmatic starting point, rather than the dualistic framework provided by the categories of Greek thought, Irenaeus maintains that which he believes to be the very heart of the Christian Gospel, namely the fact that, in the man Jesus Christ, God has entered into this world of sin and suffering, and has taken human nature upon himself in order to redeem it for others. The Creator has, paradoxically, become a part of his own creation in order to recapitulate it in himself, restoring to it that which it once possessed but which had been lost.

It is the theme of the solidarity of mankind with the New Man, coupled with the realization of just who this New Man is, that provides the key to interpreting Irenaeus' use of the language of redemption as a union with God. We have noted already that he never speaks of man as being deified, perhaps because of the problematic use of this term in other theological traditions. Yet Irenaeus does refer to man as being joined to God, and even as promoted into God[103] in the incarnation of the Son, and it is here that so many scholars have found justification for categorizing him along with the Alexandrians as one who adheres to essentially Greek (and unbiblical) notions of redemption. Yet it is instructive to read further in the passage just cited, where it becomes quite clear that this 'promotion' into God is not some blending of divine and human οὐσίαι, but rather man's being taken up into the life of the Godhead, being adopted into the filial relationship enjoyed by the Son, and thus receiving life and immortality.

Furthermore it is essential that we recognize that for Irenaeus the becoming of the Son is the lynchpin of our adoption. In the

7.902).
[103]*Ibid.*, III.xix.1. (*ANF* 448; *PGL* 7.939).

incarnation the eternal Word of God (who is uncreated and co-existent with the Father, an assessment which seems to contain the intention of the later Nicene *homoousios* in excluding any dichotomy between the Logos and the Father) becomes man; thus in this particular human existence human nature is 'joined to' and reconciled with God. The humanity of Jesus is precisely the humanity of God, yet there is never any suggestion in Irenaeus that it becomes 'divine' as a result. It is taken up into the life of God because the divine Son becomes a human Son as well, living out his relationship with the Father from within our broken nature, and thus redeeming it. In solidarity with the man Jesus, therefore, we too are given to share in this relationship that falls within the very being of God himself; we are adopted into the sonship of Christ by virtue of that solidarity with him which is established in the incarnation,[104] this being in itself a joining to or union with God, albeit God as man. It is in this sense that Christ attaches men to God by his incarnation,[105] pouring out upon them that 'paternal grace' which belongs by nature to him alone in his relationship with the Father.[106]

In conclusion, therefore, we may say that Irenaeus' theology bears little real resemblance to the 'Greek' theology of Clement and Origen, even though he can and does use similar language to describe redemption on occasion. The fundamental difference in his exposition of the Gospel stems from a refusal to frame his message in terms of the dualistic framework provided by Greek thought. Thus even when his language coincides with theirs, his meaning is quite different. For Irenaeus the incarnation is the central thrust of the Gospel message, proclaiming as it does a real knowledge of God himself on the part of men, and also a real union with him, in the person of Jesus Christ. It is in this divine becoming that salvation is mediated to the fallen race, and thus it is for Irenaeus that the person of Christ is precisely a matter of salvific significance.

---

[104]See, eg, *ibid.*, III.xvi.3. (*ANF* 441; *PGL* 7.922).

[105]*Ibid.*, V.i.1. (*ANF* 527; *PGL* 7.1121).

[106]See *ibid.*, IV.xxxvi.4. (*ANF* 516; *PGL* 7.1094).

Man is redeemed through his solidarity with the New Man, in whom God establishes a new relationship with his Creation, a relationship which hitherto has existed only within the Godhead itself between the Father and the Son. Thus in the humanity of Jesus Christ there is mediated to us that fellowship with God which is 'life in all its fulness', because Jesus Christ is God himself who unites us to himself in order to redeem us. We are saved in union with the humanity of God, therefore, receiving in and through that humanity forgiveness for sins and newness of life as adopted sons and daughters of the Father.

# 10

# Christ in Our Place in the Theology of John McLeod Campbell

## DANIEL P THIMELL

Any preacher who has ever entered the pulpit with the awesome and yet joyful burden of proclaiming the Gospel of Christ will find something in the theological contribution of James Torrance which strikes a responsive chord. For his is a theology persuaded that the Word-made-flesh discloses to us the innermost heart of God, that Christ is God's gracious gift of himself to the world.

It is not surprising then, that this theologian-to-pastors has spearheaded the modern resurgence of interest in the theology of John McLeod Campbell. For the theology of his nineteenth century counterpart is, above all, preachable. His doctrine was 'hammered out on the anvil of the parish ministry'.[1] As he went about his pastoral visitation, he soon discovered a lack of joy and assurance among his people. That God had sent Christ as his provision for sinners, that the righteousness of Christ was imputed to those who believed, they had no doubt. *All their doubts were as to themselves*.[2]

They had been instructed in the tenets of Federal Calvinism, according to which God had made a Covenant, or contract, with Christ whereby he would be gracious toward certain ones on the conditions that Christ die for their sins. But how could one know whether he was one of the elect? In order to answer this question, the Practical Syllogism was developed: Major premiss: The truly penitent person is one of God's elect. Minor premiss: (based on self-examination) I have repented. Conclusion: Therefore I am

---

[1] JB Torrance, 'The contribution of McLeod Campbell to Scottish Theology', *SJT*, 26 (1973), pp. 295-311.

[2] J McLeod Campbell, *Reminiscences and Reflections*, (London, 1873), p. 132.

182

(probably) one of the elect.[3]  But such a conviction, warned the Westminster Confession, might only be reached after a lifetime of doubt and struggle.

And so this young minister, wanting to instruct his people in the Gospel of grace, was driven to re-examine the teaching of the Bible.  He was always an evangelist at heart, but he soon saw that he could not hold out the Gospel to everyone under the old Federal scheme.  He could not say with confidence that 'Christ died for *you*', because the high Calvinist orthodoxy of his day held that only God knows who are included in the atonement by his prior, secret election.  So McLeod Campbell saw clearly that such a doctrine, however consistent it might be given its own premises, was not preachable.

What is it about the writings of a nineteenth century theologian who was deposed from the ministry after only five years in a country pulpit,[4] who wrote in an awkward, obscure style, that is finding such a welcome response among many theologians and preachers today?

We find a clue in an 1857 letter from McLeod Campbell to his brother-in-law Neil Campbell, who was seriously ill at the time: '... what is nearest our hearts is, that you should be *prepared* ... for the great change that may be near ... To know the love of God as a love that reaches us in our sins, and presents to us the free forgiveness of our sins in the blood of Christ, is the ... path to peace in life, and in death ... Dear Neil, there is no other path. No other for you, no other for me, no other.  Unless the forgiveness that the death of Christ for my sins shows me to be in God for me, draws me to God, and gives me confidence to trust my soul to Him, I do not understand the Gospel ... let the love of

---

[3]For Campbell's critique, cf. *Nature of the Atonement*, 4th edn., (London, 1959) p. 223.

[4]He was deposed by the General Assembly for teaching the 'doctrine of universal atonement and pardon through the death of Christ' and that 'assurance is of the essence of faith and necessary for salvation', RB Lusk, *The Whole Proceedings in the Case of the Rev. John McLeod Campbell, Minister of Row* (Greenock, 1831), p. 1.

God draw your heart to Him with cords of love. Look steadfastly at the Cross of Christ, and freely; and yield your heart to all the comfort of it and all the hope ... Dear Neil ... [do] not be tempted to delay committing your soul to Him ... Fix your thoughts on *Christ dying for your sins*, and receive the teaching of the Spirit of God in your heart, enabling you to understand that blessed sight'.[5]

Here is a Godly man with a pastor's heart and an evangelical desire to fix our gaze on the self-sacrifice of God in Christ in such a way that the Gospel of grace comes home to us in all its unconditional freeness. He was convinced that good theology addresses the pastoral needs of the people. And this correlation between theology and pulpit was the hallmark of all his writings. True theological understanding begins with the fact that God has spoken to us in these last days, fully and finally, by a Son. For McLeod Campbell, the preacher's task is not to affirm modern humans in their lostness, nor is it to begin with their self-understanding, as Bultmann would have it, nor with one's own ultimate concern, as in Tillich, nor to promise worldly success, as today's health-and-wealth preachers are wont to convince us. For the only Gospel worth preaching is the one grounded in the person of the incarnate Son of God.

**The Self-interpretation of God**
The burden lying so heavily upon McLeod Campbell was the conviction that Calvinist theological systems with their abstract language had obscured the Person of God and constructed artificial barriers hindering the warm fellowship which God the Father had sought to re-establish with his orphaned children. To be sure, humankind needed saving, and the Cross was the crucial culmination of Christ's reconciling activity. But he was pleading for an atonement that really atones, and a reconciliation which really reconciles.

Campbell was convinced that in the life, death and resurrection of Jesus a true at-one-ment between estranged parties was

---

[5] J McLeod Campbell, *Memorials* vol. 1, (London, 1877), pp. 303-5.

accomplished. Therefore to see the Cross as the place where the 'transferred effects' of sin are somehow placed on Jesus, and then to consider justification as the action of God dealing with us 'as if' we are righteous, by virtue of the 'transferred merits' of Christ is to contruct a system so unreal as to be almost unbelievable.

All of this, while derived from a proper desire to do justice to the Biblical emphasis on demands of Law, results in the Gospel being preached primarily in judicial rather than filial categories. And so the vibrant personal relationship which Christians ought to have with God dies the death of a thousand legal qualifications. For there is something jarring to the spirit of sonship in being 'required to pause and say "I would cry to my Father, I see His heart towards me, - the Son reveals it: but I must remember that to be justified in drawing near with confidence I must think of myself as clothed by imputation with a perfect righteousness, because the Father of my spirit must see me as so clothed in order that He may be justified in receiving. me to His Fatherly heart"'.[6] What has happened here? Direct trust in the Father's heart has been supplanted by 'trust in the judicial grounds on which the title and place of sons is granted to us' (348).

While legal and commercial metaphors are employed in scripture, exclusive concentration on these obscure the fact that God is primarily a Father, and only consequently a lawgiver, for the Commandments, as McLeod Campbell reminds us in a sermon,[7] are the heart of the Father coming out in the form of Law. And while Christ dies in order to fulfil the righteous requirements of the law, God's primary concern is not that the law be satisfied but that his fatherly heart be satisfied. For his heart's desire is that many sons be brought to glory, being re-united with their Father.

In other words, McLeod Campbell became convinced that the fundamental issue is the *doctrine of God*. High Calvinists, he felt, had begun with an abstract conception of God and his

---

[6]*The Nature of the Atonement*, pp. 221-2. Henceforth references to this book will be included in parentheses in the text.

[7]*Responsibility for the Gift of Eternal Life*, (London, 1873), p. 106.

attributes. Some, like John Owen, even argued that God is not love in his innermost being. He only decides to be loving to certain ones. For justice is his essential attribute, while his love is arbitrary (163ff.).[8]

Such a conception of God fits well with a limited atonement, for it is then asserted that God is related to all people according to law and the dictates of justice, but only to some on the basis of love (63). But here Campbell finds the Achilles heel of the Calvinist doctrine of atonement: 'an arbitrary act cannot reveal character'. If the cross, as an act of love, is an arbitrary act, grounded not in the innermost being of God, then 'what He has done has left us ignorant of himself', and 'He is to us an unknown God' (64).

But as McLeod Campbell is fond of reminding us, the Son's mission was to declare the Father's Name. When Jesus came into the world, according to the record of the Hebrews, he confessed, 'Lo, I come to do thy will, O God'. And that Will was not for the Son to act out an arbitrarily assigned part, but to shine as the very Light of Life, thereby showing us the Father (129).[9]

Therefore we must say that God interprets *himself* to us. It is not for us to begin with prior speculations or conceptions regarding the divine nature and then seek to fit the Gospel account into these. Rather than start with the 'abstract question - "what is an atonement for sin?"' and allow our own preconceptions to determine the response, 'it is surely wise to seek its answer in the study of the atonement for sin actually made' (119). For our desperate sinfulness distorts our apprehension of God such that we could not have anticipated the course God's love would take in the history of the human race. 'God himself must make it known to us' (5).

And in these last days he has spoken to us by a Son. Therefore the incarnation must be seen as 'the highest fact' in which God's

[8]Cf. JB Torrance, 'The Incarnation and Limited Atonement', *EQ*, 55 (1983).
[9]Cf. Heb. 2:20ff.; 10:5ff.

interest in and purposes for all people may be seen (xxv). The significance of this is momentous. For McLeod Campbell is departing from the typical Calvinist approach of beginning with a doctrine of God as fundamentally self-determining Will and whose overriding concern is that Law be fulfilled.

The Federal Calvinist believed in the incarnation, of course, but did not allow it to be determinative. In the incarnation we are only given a manifestation of the will of God. The sonship of Christ has no bearing on our understanding of God's interest in us or in his innermost heart. What is important is that Christ is a subject, disclosing to us a Moral Governor or Lawgiver. Campbell saw that when Christ's life is no longer understood as at every point revealing the Father, this love is reduced to 'the fulfillment for man of the law under which man was ...'. The life of Christ becomes 'the working out of a legal righteousness for man to be his by imputation'. What has happened? We have been 'turned away from seeing God in Christ' (167-8).

But 'God is light, and in his light we are given to see light' (xxii). In knowing the Son we know the Father, 'not merely because of identity of will and character in the Father and the Son, but because a father as such is known only in his relation to a Son' (lii). Hence McLeod Campbell begins with what James Torrance has called a trinitarian-incarnational approach. The Calvinists affirmed the Trinity, but did not allow it shape their theology. It often remained an isolated doctrine, detached from its connection with the atonement. But the mystery of God's being as Father, Son and Holy Spirit is not a proper subject for speculative investigation as a thing in itself, independent of all finite existence. 'We can only be called to the study of it *in its manifestation in connection with man*' (378). For the Father has given himself to be known in his Son.

## The Fatherliness of God
So Campbell sought to allow the Father-Son relation to be the light in which he interpreted the whole of theology. God is not an abstract God, in essence a Lawgiver whose real concern is to

ensure conformity to Law and punish the guilty, but the God and Father of our Lord Jesus Christ who has unconditionally bound himself to his creatures in the humanity of his Son. That is to say, God, in his innermost being a fellowship of Father, Son and Holy Spirit, *is* love. He creates the world in love and for love. And when the human race turns away and goes off into the far country, the living God does not abandon his filial purposes. He assumes the nature and becomes the brother of those who have sinned.

But there can be no dilution of the holiness of God in the supposed interests of his love. In fact, the two are harmonious aspects of his being. God is both a Father and a Lawgiver. He is at once loving and righteous. On the one hand McLeod Campbell finds a 'real righteous severity' in God (187). For God *is* a moral being. He is goodness in his innermost being and he correspondingly gives human creatures goodness as the law of their being (xxxivf.). There is no moral weakness or laxity in God. He always demands that justice be rendered (185).

Indeed, 'it is just because [the awakened conscience realises that] he has sinned and deserves punishment ... that the wrath of God seems so terrible' (80-1). And this wrath against human unrighteousness 'was not a feeling that has passed, or could pass away: no revelation of the unchanging God could' (209).

We must never allow God's character as Lawgiver to 'sink' into his character as Father. But on the other hand, neither should we consider the notion of the Lawgiver as giving a more fundamental picture of God (72). For the Commandments, as we have already observed, are the heart of God coming out in the form of Law. 'What God is in that He is love is what God wills us to be' (xxxviii).

Therefore God is primarily the Father and only consequently, derivatively, the Lawgiver. From his manifestation in man, or, to be more precise, The Man, we come to know God as an eternal communion of love between Father, Son and Holy Spirit. The

Son comes right from the bosom of the Father to reveal the Father. Theology finds its proper starting point there in the self-interpretation of God.

Consequently we begin, not by grafting the gospel onto an abstract God who is primarily a sovereign, moral governor promulgating laws, enforcing them by rewards and punishments, dispensing mercy when and where he arbitrarily chooses, but with a Father God who longs for a personal relationship with each person he has made (188-9). There are laws and judgments to be dealt with, but *they are not so many conditions to grace*. God does not have to be conditioned into being gracious. He *is* gracious, and therefore he provides a means of atonement. 'We must forbid all *direct* dealing with wrath and judgment as though these might be *first* disposed of, and *then* attention be turned to other considerations. We have here to do with *persons*, - the Father of spirits and his offspring. *These are to each other more than all things and all circumstances*' (212).

God's overriding concern is to gather his offspring in his home again as his own dear children. Everything he does and has done for us and for our salvation is determined by his fatherly nature. The righteous demands of the law are satisfied, his wrath is dealt with, but not for the sake of Law, but for the sake of his fatherly longing.

And so McLeod Campbell declares in his *magnum opus*, 'the great and root-distinction of the view of the atonement presented in these pages is the relation in which our redemption is regarded as standing to the fatherliness of God. In that fatherliness has the atonement been now represented as originating. By that fatherliness has its end been represented to have been determined. To that fatherliness has the demand for the elements of expiation found in it been traced' (338).

Yet there is no tension between his fatherliness and his holiness. Neither the Cross nor his very being provide any battleground for his attributes, for he is one. His holiness, grounded in his fatherly heart, 'craves' our holiness.  Divine justice looks at the sinner, not simply as the proper subject of punishment, but with a desire that the sinner cease being unrighteous.  All the divine attributes are against a person insofar as he is a sinner, but they appear as 'intercessors for man, and crave his salvation' (29-30).

God's wrath against sin is to be understood in the passive sense as the 'distance' between God and alienated humans which ceases in their being reconciled to Him (213).  Seen in its active aspect, his wrath resembles the attitude of a 'judging doctor' eyeing a cancerous disease in us and wanting to root it out, that we might be saved.[10]

In the light of all that McLeod Campbell has expounded regarding the fatherliness of God, we would expect him to say that forgiveness is not an abitrary manifestation of the will of God, but is rather grounded in his nature.  And that is exactly what we find.  All profitable exploration of the atonement begins with the conviction that 'there is forgiveness with God'.  We must reject any doctrine which teaches that the atonement was necessary in order to change God's heart toward us and make him gracious.  The Scriptures are one in their testimony that the love of God is the cause and the atonement the effect.

But what exactly is forgiveness?  It is not a mere declaration of absolution by divine fiat, as the Socinians would have it.  Rather, it is 'love to an enemy surviving his enmity, and which, notwithstanding his enmity can act towards him for his good'.  To be more precise, the 'Father of the spirits of all flesh' is forgiving in his desire to free him from his evil condition in which he lives as an orphan, and bring him to sonship in the Father's home (18ff.).

---

[10]*Bible Readings*, (Edinburgh, 1864), p. 51.  This volume was bound with *Fragments of Truth*, (Edinburgh, 1898) most of which was written by McLeod Campbell.  Internal evidence strongly supports Campbell's authorship of *Bible Readings* as well.  Cf. *Fragments of Truth*, p. 276.

## The Headship of Christ

Before we discuss Campbell's exposition of the atonement proper, we need to consider his doctrine of the headship of Christ, or what has been called the 'vicarious humanity' of Christ.[11] For in keeping with his insistence on the self-interpretation of God, Campbell says that we can only understand the atonement in the light of the incarnation. The incarnation must be regarded as *the primary and highest fact* in the history of God's relation to man, in the light of which God's interest in man and *purposes for man may be truly seen*' (xxv). And so the life of Christ sheds light upon the work of Christ, and what he has done is to be interpreted in terms of who he is. And who he is, says Campbell, is the One who includes all people in his humanity.

This may be viewed from two different perspectives. In a very real sense, 'we have a common life which knots all generations together, and binds us to one another, making us members of one body, children of one family, the father of which is God'.[12] McLeod Campbell seems to take this as axiomatic, although acknowledging that it may rub against the grain of 'modern individualism' (401ff.). This helps account for the effect one generation's errors have on a later one, and even for the impact individuals have upon each other: 'We are all mysteriously bound together, we cannot sin, neither can we suffer alone; the sins of the fathers are upon their children to the third and fourth generation ... We are all bound together, and yet each has an individual responsibility...'.[13] This last qualification is important, because it indicates that we must always steer a course between a radical individualism on the one hand and a thoroughgoing 'realism' on the other (401f.).

From this perspective we can see how God, in the *assumptio carnis* joined himself with *all* humanity, for only so could he be human. But something more than Jonah is here. This Man is

---

[11]See JB Torrance, 'The Vicarious Humanity of Christ' in TF Torrance, *The Incarnation* (Edinburgh, 1981), pp. 127-47.

[12]*Bible Readings*, p. 131.

[13]*Ibid.*, p. 128.

also fully God. And so there subsists between Christ and humankind what McLeod Campbell calls a 'double relation'. On the one hand, there is a relation 'according to the flesh', for he partakes of our common humanity. He becomes the Brother and assumes the nature of all people. Christ has a relation with them as man, but he also possesses a relation with them *as God*, as 'Lord of their spirits' (416, 160). It is the Creator, the one in whom all humans live and move and have their being, and who therefore already has a universal relation to all people, who assumes the nature of the creature (379). That is to say, He is not only a man, but the 'head of every man'. As the head, he can impart life - eternal life - to the entire body of humankind.

Indeed, we can say that Christ is already the head of a renewed human race which is his body. The second Adam has reversed the disobedience of the first Adam and brought life where death had reigned.[14] As a result, humankind is 'raised to a level higher than at first' (xxxi).

This notion of the universal Headship of Christ is foundational to McLeod Campbell's interpretation of the atonement, because it provides an ontological basis for a real at-one-ment between God and humankind. In this way the air of unreality, of a legal fiction, that attaches to purely forensic models is replaced by the 'depth and reality of the bonds which connect the Saviour and the saved' (161). It is no longer a matter of God 'imputing' Christ's righteousness to us and our sins to him. This One Who has taken the nature of those who had sinned works out a real reconciliation 'from the flesh'.[15]

**Christ in Our Place**
We have at some length explored Campbell's understanding of the self-interpretation of God, the fatherliness of God, and the Headship of Christ, because all these are crucial for an adequate grasp of his model of the atonement. A proper interpretation of this great salvation wrought by God in the flesh of his Son

---

[14]See *Nature of the Atonement*, p. 160.

[15]*Fragments of Truth*, p. 248.

cannot begin with our own 'sense of need' or with our prior concerns about sin and guilt. These 'How questions' presuppose a certain understanding of 'Who' God is. If we bring to the Gospel the notion that its main agenda is to deal with our sin, our lawbreaking, we are thereby assuming that God is primarily a Lawgiver who wants to ensure conformity to Law.

But only God can reveal God. He has disclosed himself fully and finally in his Son, whom he has appointed heir of all things. Therefore we understand the atonement in the light of the incarnation, the 'How' in terms of the 'Who'. McLeod Campbell beckons us to assume the 'attitude of reverently learning' from the actual course God's grace *has* taken in the history of the incarnation for our redemption (xxix).

When it is asked, Who has come and taken our place for our salvation, we can only answer, the One by Whom and for Whom all people were created for sonship. Jesus Christ comes out of the bosom of the Father to fulfil his Father's 'yearnings' for us. And he comes in a reconciling movement of love to draw all people into the eternal communion of love within the Being of God himself as Father, Son and Holy Spirit (172f.).[16] He knows well our 'orphan spirits', lost in their alienation from the Father's heart. And so he unites himself to our humanity, and as the Head of every man constitutes in himself the 'living way' back to the Father (100f.).

The man Jesus fulfils both tables of the law as we were unable to do, living a life of 'perfect sonship towards God and brotherhood towards men' (xxv). But such obedience could not be seen as earning a reward - sonship - which is separate and external to his obedience. That would be the very kind of legal fiction Campbell is so anxious to avoid. Rather, God accepts it as a 'perfect righteousness in humanity'. For that is what it *is*. And that acceptance constitutes a 'justification of humanity in the person of Christ'. Thus for McLeod Campbell justification is being accepted for what we *are* in the person of Christ. It is on the

---

[16]Cf. *Thoughts on Revelation* (London, 1862), pp. 119, 135ff.

ground of his vicarious humanity that we humans are given a life of sonship. This is 'a work of infinite excellence performed by Christ as the representative of men' (70).

By virtue of his double relation with humankind, as the Lord of their spirits and yet bone of their bone and flesh of their flesh, he is the only one who can act on behalf of all of them and save them. When he joined himself to our human nature, and offered himself up for us, he acted on our behalf. Thus his acts are truly representative and all-inclusive in scope.

This is not to say that the incarnation is the whole of the Gospel. That would be 'stopping short' (xxviii). The Apostles declare that 'God commendeth His love toward us, in that, while we were yet sinners, Christ died for us', and 'herein is love, not that we loved God, but that He loved us, and sent His Son to be the propitiation for our sins'. Clearly, both St Paul and St John 'see the love of God, not in the incarnation simply, but in the incarnation as developed in the atonement' (xxx).

Between the evil condition of humankind and the joyous life of sonship lies a vast gulf. On the human side we see spiritual darkness, sin, guilt, inward disorder, toward which is directed the condemnation and wrath of God. But on the other side we see the divine intentions for us: 'eternal life partaken in, righteousness and holiness, the acceptance and favour of God, inward harmony' (15f.). Christ comes to span that gulf.

Doubtless due to Campbell's great stress on the Fatherly love of God, and on the Son's confession of his love and our sinfulness, all with the prospect of winning us to an answering love and repentance, some have characterized his 'vicarious penitence' model as Abelardian.[17] For those accustomed to finding in the

---

[17]See, for example, RS Paul, *The Atonement and the Sacraments* (London, 1961) pp. 140-9 and George Carey, *The Gate of Glory* (London, 1986) pp. 128-30. John Stott's otherwise illuminating book, *The Cross of Christ* (Leicester, 1986) goes even further to make the surprising suggestion that Campbell's book 'stands in the same general tradition' as Socinus (pp. 141-2). Apart from the fact that Campbell explicitly rejects the notion that God could

atonement a legal relation only between Christ and the sinner, this is understandable, because he rules out forensic notions of 'transferred merit' and the like. But we must bear in mind what Campbell replaces such concepts with. This is where his emphasis on the headship of Christ enters. For he embraces us in his all-inclusive humanity in a real way, so that we have a part in his dying and rising and even in his confessing.

It is not as if, argues McLeod Campbell, we are each to go our individualistic way and try to duplicate the work of Christ such that the real atonement happens not in him but in us. Rather, our relation to the atonement is more like that of a branch or twig to the tree. Far from being solitary, self-reliant plants, they draw their life from the tree. So it is in our relation to Christ, for he is the vine of which we are only so many branches (329f.).

Campbell also questions whether the Cross accomplished much if it only served as a great proof of love. No one should lay down his life unless it is 'necessary in order to save the life for which he yields up his own'. But it *was* necessary for Christ to die for us (26f.). For the 'way opened into the holiest by the blood of Christ' was 'the only way'. This is the meaning of Jesus' declaration that he is the way, the truth and the life. The way to the Father must be the way of his Cross (294f.).

'Vicarious penitence' is easily misunderstood if it is considered in isolation from the death of Christ or from his vicarious humanity. Then we are left with the problem of 'how Christ's repentance avails for others'.[18] We cannot simply turn to his famous statement about Jesus making 'a perfect Amen in humanity to the judgment of God on the sin of man', as if it were an adequate summary of his teaching (136).

---

forgive sins by fiat (*Nature of the Atonement*, pp. xxx, 19-21), he has too much to say regarding the necessity of Christ in our humanity fulfilling the righteous requirements of the law, even to reach the point of death on the Cross, to reconcile sinful humans to God, to warrant such an interpretation.

[18]Cf. I Hamilton's article on Campbell in *New Dictionary of Theology*, S Ferguson *et al.* (eds.), (Leicester, 1988) pp. 136-7.

McLeod Campbell interprets the atonement in terms of the Priesthood of Christ, which itself presupposes the vicarious humanity of Christ. For Christ, the One by Whom and for Whom all are created for that true worship which is sonship, assumes our humanity into union with himself and in our name and on our behalf becomes both Priest and Victim that by his blood he might fit us to partake in the worship (180ff.).[19]

Now, 'partake' or 'participate' is a favourite term of his, because it underscores the personal dimension in the saving life and death of Christ. 'It is to our personal relation to God as the Father of our spirits that the atonement belongs; out of disorder in that relation has the need for it arisen, to bring that relation into harmony with its divine ideal is the end which it has contemplated' (lii). And it is precisely this 'relational' notion which underlies his understanding of the atonement as 'spiritual'. For he often says that the atonement was 'moral and spiritual' rather than penal.

By this terminology he is not seeking to dilute the seriousness of our plight or of the divine remedy. The kind of penal atonement he was rejecting was one which in its extreme form represents the Son as by the cross 'exercising an influence over the Father to make Him gracious toward us' (229). This of course contradicts the essential Fatherliness and graciousness of God, making his grace conditional upon sin being punished. But God is love and grace in his innermost being, and this determines the character of all his actions toward us.

Of course most Calvinists would disclaim such an interpretation. But even then there remains an attempt to find in the atonement 'a ground of confidence towards God distinct from what it has revealed as the mind of God towards man' (230). That is to say, our confidence in approaching God is not grounded in his nature,

---

[19]The most comprehensive treatment of the Priesthood of Christ along the lines enviseaged by Campbell while itself making an important contribution is JB Torrance's article, 'The Vicarious Humanity of Christ', in TF Torrance, *The Incarnation*.

but in a work done on the cross. Hence we are not given a sense of sonship, but of legal access, and we find ourselves 'pleading the merits' of Christ's atoning work, rather than confidently approaching the loving heart of the Father disclosed in the Cross.

But this error is exposed in the light of the Son's mission: 'Lo, I come to do thy will, O God'. And that will, is to declare his Father's Names, to disclose his heart. Our faith is therefore directed by Christ in all his works and ways to the one whose will he came to fulfil. We can receive 'true knowledge of eternal realities from the atonement'. When Christ suffered, he was not receiving the wrath of God as a personal object of divine displeasure. God was never angry with him. The cup of suffering which was Christ's was received from his loving Father's hand, and throughout he was sustained by his love. Our sins were never in some mysterious way transferred to Jesus.[20] But he did feel the divine wrath, as the wrath of judging doctor who hates the disease while loving the patient. And he acknowedged that wrath in his confession, as we shall see presently.

This is not to disclaim a fulfilling of the law in the atonement. The atonement is 'moral' as well as spiritual, and as such is grounded in the very being of God who *is* moral. While there is no conflict between the spiritual and the moral, since God's law is grounded in his love, neither is there any diminution by that fact. We must recognize 'the fixedness of that moral constitution of things of which the law is the expression', and that the 'root of that constitution of things is the Fatherliness of the Father of our spirits' (205).

So Christ came not only to deal with a broken relationship, but with a relationship that had been broken in the violation of law. Law must be dealt with. Jesus did not simply come to reveal that God is forgiving, that he has never been angry, and therefore we all ought to return to his arms. He came to work out a costly at-one-ment in his life and in his death. And that meant among other things addressing this broken law. And this could only

---

[20]*Fragments of Truth*, p. 249.

mean that Jesus must die. 'Death having come as the wages of sin, it was not simply sin that had to be dealt with, but an existing law *with its penalty of death*, and that death as already incurred ... This honouring of the law ... has, indeed, been followed out to its fullest measure [in] that our Lord not only tasted death, but that that death was the death of the cross' (302f.).[21] The centrality of the death of Christ in Campbell's theology of the atonement could be substantiated by a long string of citations. But suffice it to say that the moral dimension is fully recognized.

What did McLeod Campbell mean by saying that the atonement was also 'spiritual'? He certainly was not intending to *spiritualize* the sober realities addressed and dealt with in Christ's atoning work. There is nothing ethereal or symbolic or otherworldly in his use of the term. In fact, by spiritual, McLeod Campbell is referring to the *relations between personal beings inhering in reality*. As such it is a fundamentally trinitarian notion, for God, who within his being comprises an eternal relation of love as Father, Son and Spirit, creates us for sonship. That is, he draws us within the embrace of his eternal communion of love. We are not so many detached monads; rather we are, to use a memorable phrase coined years later by John Macmurray, 'persons in relation'.

When humankind becomes 'alienated from his Life',[22] God takes human nature into union with himself in order to effect a reconciliation. He comes to be the 'Head and High Priest of redeemed humanity'.[23] But this will require a spiritual atonement, because man's sinfulness consists in 'his spiritual distance from God'. He is at enmity with the Father of the spirits and with his fellow man, and therefore his salvation will consist in 'spiritual nearness' to God and others. In this connexion Christ is said to be peace, for he constitutes in his humanity a healing of the double spiritual breach. This peace is 'a spiritual

---

[21]Italics mine.

[22]*Ibid.*, p. 199.

[23]*Ibid.*, p. 181.

reality', for he is a living way to the Father and to one's fellow humans (202f.).

The precise way in which Christ constitutes this way back to union and fellowship with God is expounded by McLeod Campbell in terms of the Priesthood of Christ. And within his priestly activity we can distinguish two movements: 'Christ's dealing with men on the part of God', and 'His dealing with God on behalf of men'. For, as James Torrance has said, 'the coming of Jesus Christ is at once the coming of *God as God* and at the same time, the coming of *God as Man* in our humanity'.[24]

But each of these movements of divine grace presents to us both a 'retrospective' and a 'prospective' aspect, the former 'referring to the evil from which that grace brings deliverance', and the latter 'referring to the good which it bestows' (4). Already we have a corrective for those interpretations of Campbell which question the substance of an atonement grounded in vicarious penitence. For McLeod Campbell does not reduce the atonement to repentance for others. That is but one aspect. And as we shall see, the retrospective dimension fully addresses our guilty past.

He begins by setting forth the God-manward movement, in its retrospective aspect. This is a movement of revelation. On the one hand Christ discloses the Father, as one who remains living and trustworthy and whose righteous will for us is surpassingly excellent. This he does not only by his words, but by a life of 'perfection in humanity'. For he walks with his fellow humans in brotherly love and forbearance while continuing to love and trust his Father. Such a life constituted a condemnation of sin by its contrast. But he also suffers a deep sorrow from their rejection and refusal to trust in the Father (129ff.).

Because he shares our common humanity, the pressure of our sins bear heavily upon his spirit. The dishonour, the hatred, the refusal to believe which he meets, and the consequent misery which we have brought upon ourselves bring him an intense

---

[24]*The Contribution of McLeod Campbell to Scottish Theology*, p. 306.

suffering. In this way he bears our sins. But this suffering is certainly not penal. It is rather the pain of holy sorrow, endured in sympathy with God. In this way he manifested in humanity what our sins are to God.

But there is also the retrospective aspect, a man-Godward movement. Here, if anywhere, observes Campbell, we ought to meet up with penal suffering (134). But pain endured for the sake of pain in meeting a demand of divine justice does not disclose the heart of God; it only reveals a Lawgiver. It may be objected that such suffering shows us the love of God in that he was willing to undergo such an affliction. But even that would not constitute a full revelation of God. McLeod Campbell argues that the actual revelation we are here given is that divine love suffers according to its own nature, and not by some arbitrary decree.

What do we find in this retrospective aspect of the man-Godward movement? If Christ's oneness of mind with the Father towards man constituted a condemnation of sin, it would, in his dealings with God on behalf of man take the form of a 'perfect confession of our sins ... a perfect Amen in humanity to the judgment of God on the sin of man ... For that response has all the elements of a perfect repentance in humanity for all the sin of man, - a perfect sorrow - a perfect contrition - all the elements ... excepting the personal consciousness of sin; and by that perfect response in Amen to the mind of God in relation to sin is the wrath of God rightly met, and that is accorded to divine justice which is its due, and could alone satisfy it' (135-6).

We must bear in mind that Campbell does not envisage a mere verbal transaction between Father and Son. He is telling us that Christ's entire incarnate life and supremely his death constituted this 'Amen in humanity to the judgment of God'. That his life was a life of prayer, that he actually did on countless occasions intercede verbally for sinners is one thing. But for McLeod Campbell, the Cross was uniquely the place where Christ offered that confession of our sin which we were unable to make.

One of his favourite expressions in his interpretation of the cross is 'the voice in the blood'. By this phrase he underscores the oneness of mind between Father and Son which continued unbroken on Calvary. But he also means to draw our attention to *Christ dying for our sins as itself a confession, an acceptance of the verdict of guilty*. For if we desire to find the way into the holiest, into the presence of the Father of our Spirits, we must recognize the 'separation from God which sin causes'. But Christ, our great High Priest, has taken the burden of our sins upon his heart and gone into the Holy of Holies and there offered his own blood as his confession on our behalf.

Our 'amen' of faith is but a little amen to the great Amen spoken in our humanity when Christ died for us. Therefore we are always directed away from our own feeble faith to the '*voice that is in the blood of Christ, viz. Christ's confession of our sins* (182).[25] For Christ did not simply come to reveal the fatherliness in the heart of God. In order to fulfil the filial purposes of God, something more than revelation was required. There must be a condemnation of our life as rebellious children in order for us to enter into a life of true sonship. This was accomplished in 'that expiatory confession of our sin which was perfected in the death of Christ' (307f.).

Campbell's use of the term 'perfected' here may seem to some a blurring of the distinction between incarnation and atonement. And it is true that he sees the latter as a development of the former. Nevertheless he can and does distinguish between the two. Even though throughout his life Jesus offered up his life as a daily sacrifice to the Father, this was not sufficient. In Gethsemane we learn that the atonement would of 'necessity' be perfected by his death on the cross. 'Something further had to come to pass ... something which ... the incarnation, simply as such, had not accomplished'. His time on the cross was a 'trial peculiar and extreme' (299f.).

Due to his oneness of mind with the Father, Christ alone fully

---

[25] Cf. *Nature of the Atonement*, pp. 224ff.

realized the meaning of death as the wages of sin. It was therefore natural for him to confess the righteousness of the divine condemnation of sin. And his dying was itself an acceptance of the verdict of guilty. 'For thus, in Christ's honouring of the righteous law of God, the sentence of the *law* was included, as well as *the mind of God* which that sentence expressed. In this light are we to see the death of Christ, as redeeming those who were under the law, that they might receive the adoption of sons ... It was not simply sin that had to be dealt with, but an existing law with its penalty of death, and that death as already incurred. So it was not only the divine mind that had to be responded to, but also that expression of the divine mind which as contained in God's making death the wages of sin. This honouring of the law ... has indeed been followed out to its fullest measure, [in] that our Lord not only tasted death, but that that death was the death of the cross' (303).

We should mark his use of the term 'oneness of mind' in relation to Father and Son, for it sheds light on McLeod Campbell's understanding of the nature of the atonement. It is out of this oneness that Christ says Amen to the righteous judgments of God on our sin. It is out of this oneness that he dies for us. It is also in oneness that he lays hold of the life of sonship that is there in the Father's heart for us. For oneness is not a unity of purpose only, but an ontological unity. It is a oneness grounded in the hypostatic union, in Christ as the God who is there for man and the Man who is there for God.[26]

But this oneness of being *does* mean a oneness of mind. In this way McLeod Campbell is able to discard notions of conditionaal grace in the Son's self-offering to the Father, and restore a window into the very heart of the Father in that atoning work. This oneness also explains his avoidance of the term 'penal' in the atonement, because he is convinced that the Father was never angry with Jesus, was never separated from him, and never stood

---

[26]I owe these phrases, 'the God who is there for man' and 'the Man who is there for God' to Ray Anderson's book, *Historical Transcendence and the Reality of God* (Grand Rapids, 1975), ch. 5.

over against him in an adminstration of punishment.

In the way McLeod Campbell reminds us of Anselm's work *Cur Deus Homo?*, to which he refers in passing (xxv). Trevor Hart points out[27] that Anselm considered the work of Christ to be a 'satisfaction' rather than a 'punishment', since Christ offered it up willingly in loving obedience to the will of the Father. Similarly Campbell tells us that when Phinehas, *in sympathy with God's judgment on sin*, slew those who committed apostasy in Moab, he thereby shed a 'ray of light ... on the distinction between making an atonement for sin and bearing the punishment of sin (119ff.). For when Jesus came into the world he declared that he had come to do the Father's will. 'The will of God which the Son of God came to do and did, this was the essence and substance of the atonement, being that in the offering of the body of Christ once and for all which ... made it acceptable to Him ...'.

In addition to the retrospective, we are also given within the priestly work of Christ, a prospective aspect. For he comes both to deal with our guilty past and to bring us to sonship. It was the absence of the latter aspect as a light for understanding the nature of the atonement that Campbell lamented. If the nature of the atonement is determined solely by retrospective concerns, we are left with a God who is primarily a Lawgiver whose concern is that Law be satisfied. And those who have a part in its efficacy are only granted legal access into the divine courtroom, rather than a place near the Father's heart. But McLeod Campbell said 'no', we were created in love for love. God the Father has brought us into being for sonship. And when we rebelled and became orphans, God came into our flesh and underwrote our lost cause, in order to attain the filial ends of Creation. Therefore these filial ends must have, along with our guilty plight, determined the nature of the atonement (152ff.).

Mirroring the two movements within the retrospectve aspect, there are within the prospective aspect, both Christ's dealing with

---

[27]In an unpublished paper, *Anselm and McLeod Campbell: Where Opposites Meet?* read to the Aberdeenshire Theological Club on 16 January 1989.

men on behalf of God and his dealing with God on behalf of men. The first describes the Son's witnessing for the Father, revealing his loving heart and desire for our sonship. By a life of faithful sonship, Christ testified to the joy of a life lived in union and communion with the Father. Although they did not know the Father, *he* knew him and 'enjoyed the Father as the Father'. In this way he declared the Father's name both in his life and in his death (162ff.).

But there is also a man-Godward movement, for Christ followed God 'as a dear child walking in love'. His was a life of true sonship, for he found peace and joy in fellowship with the Father. McLeod Campbell interprets the man-Godward movement in terms of the Priesthood of Christ. His life was a continual offering of prayer , love and trust. And in his trusting, Christ was prospectively laying hold of the hope of sonship for humankind that was in God. As part of his self-offering on our behalf we see Jesus 'bearing us and our sins and miseries on his heart before the Father' (167ff.).

His confession contemplates our own confession as a participation in his. This is a central point for McLeod Campbell. Already in his own day, there was no shortage of those who questioned the validity of a confession for sinners offered by a perfect Man. But he emphasized that Christ's confession was made entirely with the prospect of its being reproduced in us (177f.).[28] He added that his use of the term 'repentance' in this connexion was 'guarded', for by it he meant Christ's perfect condemnation of our sins, in his holy sorrow and contrition and acceptance of the verdict of guilty. But 'that word will have its full meaning in the personal experience of every one who accepts in faith the atonement ... for every such individual sinner still *adds* the '*excepted*' element of '*personal consciousness of sin*' (397ff.).

Campbell's point was that only Christ was so united to us that he felt the full impact of our sins and misery and yet 'sufficiently

---

[28]Cf. *Nature of the Atonement*, pp. 151ff.

separated from our sins to feel in his humanity' a 'Godly condemnation of [our sins] and sorrow for them' (149). James Torrance has shown that McLeod Campbell was concerned to call the sinner to *evangelical* as opposed to *legal repentance*, so that repentance is seen as a response to grace, participating in the humanity of Christ, rather than a legalistic condition of grace, which would cast a person back on his own efforts to mend his ways and thereby place himself into grace.[29]

Participation is therefore crucial to McLeod Campbell's theology. Christ's fellowship with the Father in our nature and as our brother anticipated our participation in it as what would be our salvation. And now as the High Priest and Head of a new humanity, Christ draws us into his life of worship, of union and communion with the Father through the Spirit (183). The Spirit plays an important part in this. For we have no power to join personally in the Son's confession of our sins apart from partaking in the Spirit (178). Although we have already been given eternal life in Christ, and Christ himself is 'present in our inner being ... where the sap of the vine passes into the branch', we are still summoned to respond. This life of Christ can be welcomed or rejected (363).

The Holy Spirit is always near us, inviting us to receive the life-giving word, but we can resist Him.[30] And yet we must say that our salvation is not a matter of our will. Even our faith is 'wrought by the operation of His Holy Spirit'.[31] The atonement does contemplate prospectively our participation in the dying and rising of Christ. To this end the example of Christ is held out to us. But this is 'entirely different' from any 'outside imitation of Him'. The only way we can fulfil God's purposes is through a 'living oneness with Him'. Indeed, 'we can only follow His steps by being filled with His Spirit'.[32]

---

[29]*Op. cit.*
[30]*Fragments of Truth*, pp. 266ff.
[31]*Ibid.*, p. 271.
[32]*Ibid.*, pp. 231ff.

But the work of the Spirit is grounded in the vicarious humanity of Christ. Because Jesus has taken our humanity upon himself and become our brother, he can represent us to God and God to us. Thus he can and does act for us and on our behalf. Under our burden and in our stead he offers up that righteousness which humanity could not of itself present and makes that confession which humanity could not have originated. And in that confession, 'Thou art righteous, O Lord, who judgest so', he dies for us. In this way, says McLeod Campbell, Christ stands forever, not as our substitute, but our representative. But that can only mean that Christ is not detached from us, that he presents us in himself and in all his saving acts. 'Christ is not *a* man merely; His death and His resurrection are not the acts of an individual member of the human race; that is what makes them atoning acts ... I am the *root* and the *offspring* of David. He is the root in whom the whole race has life, even as Adam is the root through whom death has passed upon all ... In that *He* died unto sin once, *we* died unto sin; in that *He* liveth unto God forever more, *we* have eternal life in Him. From Him as the root, life passes into each individual branch, that it may bear fruit ... Christ makes Himself one with the transgressors; He dies for us, He rises for us, He ascends for us to the right hand of God. Most truly He dies *in our place - for us*, and not *for Himself*; but He does not die *instead of* us, *that we may not die*, any more than He rises instead of us, or ascends instead of us. He dies that we may die - that in faith and hope we may also say, "If this cup may not pass from us except we drink it, thy will be done" - even as He rises and ascends, that we may also rise and ascend with Him'.[33]

---

[33]*Bible Readings*, pp. 149-50.

# 11

# Christology and Reconciliation in the Theology of Karl Barth

JOHN THOMPSON

The theology of Karl Barth has often been characterized by the term 'christological concentration'. H Hartwell states concisely what this means. 'The *Church Dogmatics* is wholly christ-ological in the sense that in it, generally speaking, every theological proposition has as its point of departure Jesus Christ, the Son of God and the Son of Man, in the unity of his person and work. This christological concentration of the *Church Dogmatics* and indeed of Barth's theology as a whole, is "unparalleled in the history of christian thought"'.[1] This statement implies that the knowledge of God is a knowledge given *exclusively* in God's revelation and reconciliation in Jesus Christ and that he is known to us as true God and true man in the unity of his being and action.

## Christology and Reconciliation

Traditional theology treated the person and work of Christ separately. The person of Jesus Christ as the God-man was related to the incarnation and the work of Christ was seen in the three offices of prophet, priest and king with particular emphasis on his priestly role and his death on the cross. To these were added the two states of humiliation and exaltation corresponding respectively to the human history of Jesus and his risen life. While Barth finds these distinctions in many ways clear, illuminating and helpful, at the same time he is dissatisfied with them, for they tend to separate what the New Testament sees as one, namely, the person and work of Jesus Christ.[2] Barth sees

---

[1] H Hartwell, *The Theology of Karl Barth : An Introduction* (London, 1964), pp. 15-6. The enclosed quotation is from E Gollwitzer, *Karl Barth : Church Dogmatics, a Selection with Introduction* (ET 1961), pp. 19-20.

[2] *CD* IV/1, pp. 122ff, where Barth discusses the merits and demerits of the traditional schemata.

the reality of Christ and his work centred in God's act of reconciliation and it is in the light of this comprehensive unity that he restructures and restates the traditional doctrines.

The mature centre of Barth's christological perspective is in his massive doctrine of reconciliation.[3]   This has two bases - election and covenant.  God has from all eternity chosen to be the God of man and to have him in fellowship with himself.  This will both precedes man's sin and has the power to overcome it. Its effect in time is manifest in a covenant of grace broken by man but reconstituted by God's act of reconciliation in Jesus Christ.  God is one who moves toward man, makes man's cause his own, submits himself in his Son to the enmity and opposition of sin, evil and the powers of darkness.  The being of God is seen and known in this act which reveals his original will and at the same time reconciles man and the universe to himself. In this innovative way Barth sees the person and work of Christ as one.  Jesus Christ is both the reconciling God and reconciled man in unity in the whole of his being and action.  Barth writes, 'He [Jesus Christ] exists as the Mediator between God and man in the sense that in him God's reconciling of man and man's reconciliation with God are event ... He exists in the totality of his being and work as the Mediator'.[4]   One can distinguish but not separate the person (two natures) and work (prophet, priest and king) of Christ nor can one treat his two states (humiliation and exaltation) as consecutive.  In Barth's view the being and the work of Christ are seen in dynamic inter-relationship and unity.

Using the parable of the prodigal son as a useful, interpretative model Barth sees God's act in Christ as the Son of God going into the far country of man's disobedience and rebellion and reconciling us to himself.[5]   At the same time man is exalted to unity with God.  There are thus two great movements in the one action.  Jesus Christ is the Lord (divine) who humbles himself

---

[3]*CD* IV/1-IV/3&4.
[4]*CD* IV/1, p. 123.
[5]*CD* IV/2, pp. 21ff.

(humiliation) and so atones (priestly work); at the same time he is
man reconciled (humanity) exalted (exaltation) to lordship (king).
Reconciliation is completed in this movement with its two
moments of coming down and lifting up.   There is, however, a
third aspect where Jesus Christ the reconciler risen from the dead
is mediator and declares his own reconciliation to man (prophetic
office).  Thus Barth combines yet distinguishes the different loci
in the older formulae, sees them in the unity of God and man in
reconciliation and centres this on the cross and resurrection as the
integrating factor in the being and work of Christ.   Berthold
Klappert is right to see the awakening of the crucified as the focus
of God's action and the centre from which the person and work of
Christ are to be interpreted.[6]  He is also right to query those
who see Barth's doctrine as simply starting with the incarnation
and giving it a new, dynamic character.  On the contrary what
Barth does is to integrate the older teaching in the total context
of God's reconciliation.

## The Doctrine of Reconciliation
### A *The Person and Work of Jesus Christ*
Barth can speak of the personal work and the working person of
Jesus Christ since the two are intimately interrelated.  We look
first at the working *person*.[7]  A distinctive feature of Barth's
doctrine of reconciliation is that the nature of the deity of Christ
is related to his humiliation.  It is precisely in his humiliation
manifested in his life and consummated on the cross that God
proves himself to be the high, exalted, holy one who inhabits
eternity.  Here God reveals himself as he really is, God with us
and for us and our salvation in the crucifed Lord Jesus Christ.  It
is in this depth that we see the height of deity, in making this
journey into the far country that he proves his deity.  It is in his
solidarity with man who has fallen prey to sin and death and the
powers of darkness, all comprehended as the *Nihil* (*das
Nichtige*), that we know him as divine and what the deity means.

---

[6]B Klappert, *Die Auferweckung des Gekreuzigten, Der Ansatz der
Christologie Karl Barths im Zusammenhang der Christologie der Gegenwart*
(Neukirchen, 1971), pp. 89ff.
[7]*CD* IV/1, pp. 157ff.

At the same time it is no Jesus in isolation but Jesus the Jewish Messiah, the One who fulfils the old covenant thereby creating a new.  He is the reconciler only as the man from Israel, bearing the burden of its promise but also of its guilt, shame and disobedience but bearing these away on the cross.  Jesus Christ is the revelation of God, his reconcilication of the world only as the fulfilment of Israel's history in which God proves himself and his faithfulness.  Here once for all he shows who he is by identifying with the humiliated Jesus of Nazareth.[8]

The second distinctive feature is the emphasis Barth puts on the obedience of the Son in relation to the Father.[9]  His obedience as man, even to the death on the cross, reflects the obedience of the eternal Son in relation to the Father.  In other words in the economy of salvation Jesus Christ proves himself to be the true God.  What he is and does as man points to and is an integer of his eternal deity.

This means that humiliation and obedience manifest in the life and death of Jesus Christ are not contrary to the nature of God but its true revelation.  They show the true deity of Christ and signify 'the humiliation and lowliness and supremely the obedience of Christ as the dominating moment in our conception of God'.[10]

Nor is there any division between God as he is in himself in his height and glory and God for us in humility.  The revelation of the one true God, of the deity of the Son of God, is in Jesus Christ the crucified.[11]

In itself, however, the life and death of Jesus is a riddle and would be closed off from us were it not for what follows.  What makes the cross and previous life of Jesus the act of reconciliation and shows Jesus Christ to be the reconciling God is the raising of

[8]*Ibid.*, pp. 166ff.
[9]*Ibid.*, pp. 192ff.
[10]*Ibid.*, p. 199.
[11]*Ibid.*, p. 185f.

Jesus from the dead.[12] This is the Father's positive verdict on all that Jesus was, said and did in his previous life and death. It is therefore the centre from which the totality of the being and action of Jesus is to be interpreted - the cross illumined by the power of the resurrection. Here the emphasis is on the working *person* giving it a christological priority.

The second aspect is the personal *work*.[13] In his coming he not only identifies with man in his sin but at the same time exposes that sin. Barth points out that Jesus Christ is *Deus pro nobis* - for us men and for our salvation - in four ways. First he comes as judge who not only shatters our pride but displaces us from acting as gods, being our own judges. He is *for us* as judge who comes to restore the right order. Secondly, he is for us as the judge who is judged in our place. In his vicarious humanity he bears the just judgment of God on our sin being made sin for us. He is for us, thirdly, by his suffering and death, his action and passion on the cross. Finally, he is for us by replacing the old man with the new, giving God his right, restoring righteousness where there had been only unrighteousness. He brings the new, true, reconciled man on the scene.[14] He is representative of all men, dying for all. It is in these ways, in their unity and variety, that he is *Deus pro nobis* and our salvation.

## B *The Royal Man*[15]
The reconciliation of God embraces at one and the same time the humiliation of the Son of God and the exaltation of the Son of Man. Jesus Christ is true God in self humiliation on the cross and so atoning; he is also and in consequence true and exalted man. This is the second moment of the one divine act. Here man lifted up to God is brought home in reconciliation. In this way he fulfils a kingly office, is the royal man. He is true man, indeed the only true man. He is both like us, sharing our humanity (including its sin), but unlike us in that he is from the

[12]*Ibid.*, pp. 299ff.
[13]*Ibid.*, pp. 211ff.
[14]*CD* IV/2, pp. 28ff.
[15]*Ibid.*, pp. 154ff.

beginning the victor over sin in a life of complete conformity to the will of the Father. If, in the first moment, Jesus is the grace of God in person and work here he is man obedient to God whose answer to grace is gratitude. The exaltation of Jesus occurs in its totality in the whole of his life, in his struggle with and overcoming evil. He is the royal man who manifests the true nature of man, what we are meant to be. In one sense he is unique since no other man bears the humanity of the Son of God. His humanity is enhypostatic in the Word. In another he is human as we are. This means no lessening of his humanity but its true expression.

In the whole of his life he acts in a royal way by his kingly rule, calling in question the lordships and authorities of this world while at the same time preserving and accepting authority and the powers that be. His whole royal way was both an affirmation of God's way with man and his good creation and at the same time a radical critique and judgment of all man's evil ways.

While all this is true of the history of Jesus it moves to a climax and fulfilment on the cross. The cross is 'his supreme exaltation, the triumphant coronation of Jesus the Son of Man'.[16] As Klappert puts it, he is *'homo exaltatus et regnans in cruce'*.[17] The cross is thus 'the dominating characteristic of his royal office'.[18] The life of Jesus is concealed in its opposite *sub contrario in cruce*. What happens to him and what he suffers in this way is the true expression of his royal lordship. His is a hidden rule with anticipations in the signs of the kingdom in his previous life.

Like his deity all this would have remained closed off from us were it not for the resurrection. Jesus appeared to his disciples, revealed himself to them in time and space as the crucified risen from the dead, as the victor alive, manifesting the meaning of his

[16]*Ibid.*, p. 141.

[17]Klappert, *op. cit.*, p. 315.

[18]*CD* IV/2, p. 292.

royal life.

It is in this total context that Jesus is royal man, true, new, reconciled, exalted man. This exaltation of man is the correspondence in Jesus of the Son's condescension. Barth can call it an exchange (similar to Luther's *fröliches Wechsel*) where the Son of God comes to where we are and in the same act lifts us up to where he is. By this act of God all are included; it is both an exclusive and inclusive christology. For this reason Barth never speaks of Jesus Christ in isolation from what he does in humanity and the church. He is both the universal lord, the cosmic Christ and the king and head of the Church. *De iure* all belong to Christ but not *de facto*. His is a corporate personality which in principle includes all yet awaits the work of the Holy Spirit to make people actually members of his community, called, gathered, built up and sent into the world.

## C *The Glory of the Mediator*[19]

Reconciliation in its material content is completed in these two aspects of the person and work of Christ. A third aspect is also involved. As the reconciler Jesus Christ is the one mediator between God and man. The reconciliation accomplished by Jesus Christ is revealed and active as he speaks his prophetic word, makes known his work as reconciler. In this Jesus Christ is the victor who moves on to conquer. Barth underlines two ways in which what has been achieved *realiter* in Christ is made ours *actualiter*, namely, by the resurrection and the Holy Spirit. The resurrection is the primal form of God's revelation reaching back to reveal the history of Jesus - and indeed Old Testament history - as an anticipatory revelation and reaching forward by the Holy Spirit to wage continuous warfare against all God's enemies and ours. It is a history of conflict reaching out to embrace mankind and down to overcome. It is carried out by the power of the already victorious work of Christ on the cross showing that Jesus, and not sin, evil and death, is victor. What he has done cannot be undone. Furthermore, it has not only the aspect of resurrection which is its constitutive form but is continued in the intervening

---

[19] *CD* IV/3.I, pp. 30ff.

period between the ages of the first and second coming by the power of the Holy Spirit. He is the presence of Christ in the here and now, making known the glory of the mediator until Christ comes again.

It is in this total sweep, integrating the various aspects of the working *person* and the personal *work* of Jesus Christ in differentiated unity, that Barth interprets the Christ event, the presence and action of God for us. Another aspect should also be mentioned. In doing all this God acts to manifest his glory, to justify himself and all his ways and works. We can sum this up by saying that God acts *pro se*, to disclose his nature; he acts *extra nos* in the objective act of reconciliation, an event which is none of our doing. He acts *contra nos*, against us, by judging and overcoming our sin. In all these ways he acts *pro nobis*. His 'no' is in the service of his greater 'yes'. At the same time, he acts *pro me*, for each individual person. It is in this way that God is active in Christ's reconciliation on the cross and by the resurrection.

## D *Reconciliation as History*

This total act of reconciliation Barth describes as history, not simply in the sense that it took place once upon a time but that in it God acts in a history between himself and man in a way that decisively changes the whole relationship between them. It is primal history as God's ways with man in his work *ad extra*; at the same time it is the basis of all other history and determines that of every individual. As a history of the relationship between God and man it reflects the inner relations of Father, Son and Holy Spirit. Who God is is fully manifest in the history and movement of the life and work of Jesus Christ. This is salvation history embracing all other history and (at a particular point in time) bringing it into union with the divine life. At the same time the New Testament has a biblical thought form which is shaped by what God has done for us in Jesus Christ; its particular character is that of narration.

**Interpretation and Evaluation**

A *Content and Method*

The most impressive aspect of this whole enterprise is the way in which Barth seeks to present Jesus Christ in his differentiated unity and wholeness. This is how he is depicted in the New Testament where person and work are one. This raises also the important question of where one should begin looking at the reality and work of Jesus Christ. Barth rightly begins with the unity of Jesus Christ in his being as God and man and in the relationship of this to what he does. Compared to his earlier christology which was dialectical, and his middle period which was primarily incarnational, his later more mature considered thought is *heilsgeschichtlich*, based on salvation history or the Christ event.[20]

This content determines also his method which is centred on the cross and resurrection as the focal points from which to interpret the whole significance of Jesus Christ. This is neither to deny the incarnation nor to minimize traditional teaching but to reinterpret both from this central biblical perspective. This in turn leads Barth back through tradition to the Patristics and through the Reformation to the New Testament. In other words he manifests a respectful freedom in relation to tradition. Two further things follow from this. More than in traditional teaching the deity of Christ is interpreted from what happens in the life of Jesus consummated on the cross and manifest in the resurrection. The humanity in turn is that of one who suffers and dies for us. His being is essentially co-humanity and is known in sacrifice and fellow suffering. Secondly, with such strong emphasis on the cross as the manifestation of Christ's deity, a new impetus has been given to theology to think through the doctrine of the Trinity from the economy of salvation. The significance of the Son's suffering in relation to the Father and his involvement by the Spirit in the death of Jesus has ultimate significance for the nature of God as triune. Barth can give a place to the participation of the Father in the Son's suffering since he wills

---

[20] A Nossol, 'Die Rezeption der Barthschen Christologie in der katholischen Kirche der Gegenwart', *Evangelische Theologie*, 4/5 (1986), p. 353.

for Christ the path of humiliation and obedience and accompanies him on it. To put it in Klappert's phrase, Barth draws the cross up into the being of God as the constitutive interpretation of the Trinity.[21]

The resurrection as essential revelation casts its light back over the whole preceding period and shows it as also participating in revelation. It is at the same time hermaneutically important as the key to our knowledge of God and his salvation history. The resurrection belongs not only to the order of being (*ordo essendi*) in showing who Jesus is but it also belongs to the order of knowledge (*ordo cognoscendi*) giving us true knowledge of God in Christ. To this needs to be added the Holy Spirit as Christ's own presence revealing his being and work to us and making us participants of his reconciliaition. Resurrection and Holy Spirit are the twin avenues God takes to impart his reconciliation, enabling us to know, love and serve him.

A further significant feature of Barth's methodology is that he overcomes the dichotomy in modern theology between a christology from above which tends towards docetism minimising the humanity of Jesus and a christology from below which tends to minimize or misinterpret the nature of the deity. By his union of above and below Barth combines in a unique way both aspects in the divine being and action for us beginning with the one whole Lord Jesus Christ in reconciliation.[22] At the same time he sees each aspect in its relationship to this unifying totality.

B *Ontological and Functional*
A further feature of much modern theology is the tendency to opt either for an ontological or functional conception of Jesus Christ. This is partly a result of repeating the old isolation Barth queries and seeks to replace. If the emphasis is on the ontological one is in danger of working with an ontology of being which to some extent predetermines the nature of the deity or emphasizes the person of Christ to the detriment of his work. A functional

---

[21]Klappert, *op. cit.*, p. 187.
[22]*Ibid.*, p. 4.

christology on the other hand emphasizes the work, the *beneficia Christi*, and fails to give due place to his person. Barth, however, sees each in a fruitful inter-relationship since the being of Jesus Christ and what he does is one and it is in this being and action that we meet with and know both the reconciling God and reconciled man.

Much has been written about the 'event' character of Barth's thought as if he too was in danger of seeing Christ in purely functional terms.[23] What he does rather is to interpret the nature of Christ in terms of dynamic acts without in any sense losing the ontological emphasis.[24] The whole of his doctrine of reconciliation is positive proof of this. In it he is dealing with the *being* of Jesus Christ in his *action* for us. Moreover, he does this in a way which combines the truths of the older orthodoxy and yet relates them to the total context of the New Testament witness to Jesus Christ. Two examples of his method may be given. He clearly affirms the truths of Chalcedon regarding the deity and humanity of Christ and the Virgin Birth. At the same time he believes that, taken by itself, Chalcedon is a kind of torso speaking in somewhat abstract terms of the being of Jesus Christ but requiring to be filled out in relation to what he does for us.[25] Ontological and dynamic or functional are thus not just complementary terms but embody twin aspects of the one, whole reality of the person and work of Christ. The restructuring of christology and soteriology in relation to reconciliation is eloquent testimony to this. Secondly, Barth affirms the old truths of the *unio personalis* of Jesus Christ, namely, that he is one person in two natures. He gives precedence to the union over the natures supporting the Reformed more than the Lutheran view in this regard. He agrees too with

---

[23]HR Mackintosh, *Types of Modern Theology* (London, 1937), pp. 314ff for the charge of 'actualism'. W Schlichting, *Biblische Denkform in der Dogmatik* (Zurich, 1971), pp. 162-76, gives a reply to the various critics on this point and shows how Barth combines both an element of movement and stability in his views.

[24]Hartwell, *op. cit.*, p. 36, cf. *CD* I/2, p. 170.

[25]*CD* IV/1, p. 133.

the *communicatio idiomatum*, that there is a union and communion between the divine and human in Jesus Christ. He sees these in no static way but in a living movement of inter-relationship, a *communicatio gratiarum*, a communication of grace given to the human from the divine and not vice versa. Typical of his uniting ontological and functional is his emphasis on the *communicatio operationum*. This indicates that in the union and communion of the divine and human natures there is a dynamic movement towards the common goal of reconciling the world with God.[26]

C *Reconciliation as History*

One of the points few commentators on Barth have noticed is that his is a narrative theology.[27] It tells a story, the particular history of God and man in union, relationship and fellowship in Jesus Christ. This history has very particular form, contours and content. It follows and is the movement of God to man and what he does in Christ as the God-man. It is a particular event in our space, time and history and as such is the exclusive place where reconciliation is to be found. It is as such an all-inclusive christology which reaches out to embrace all men and creation and is indeed the basis of created existence. In this way history is understood by Barth as God moving to man and in man in Jesus Christ. This primal history, as it might be called, has a transcendent character but with a particular historical manifestation. Our history is the predicate of revelation and not vice-versa. Since God has taken man and his history into union with himself in this particular form and place it has special significance for all times, places and people whether they know it or not. It is a history which, moreover, changes the whole relationship between God, man and the world. It is, in Barth's terminology, 'the revolution of God'.[28] Here is accomplished something once for all which is irrevocable and marches

---

[26]*CD* IV/2, pp. 73ff, 83ff, 113ff.

[27]DF Ford, 'Barth's Interpretation of the Bible', in *Karl Barth - Studies of His Theological Methods*, SW Sykes (ed.), (Oxford, 1979), pp. 55-87. Ford seeks to show how Barth's methodology, focussed on the history of Jesus Christ, has possible parallels in the literary genre of the realistic novel.

[28]*CD* IV/1, pp. 542-6; IV/2, pp. 171ff.

victoriously on.

This particular story is both simple and profound.  It is the story
of God's dealing with man, overcoming all the powers of death
and evil that hold him thrall and threaten the created order with
chaos.  It brings reconciliation and peace.  Its form as told is
realistic narrative because it deals with the world as it is *realiter*
in God's sight, presence and action.  We live now in a world
really reconciled but not yet redeemed.  This is what the scripture
narrates and theology repeats.  It happened once upon a time but
it is no myth, fairy-tale or unreality but that which undergirds and
sustains all life.  By this we live as creatures and as a new
creation in Christ Jesus.

As such this history corresponds in human life to the very being
of God, embodies his history of relationship, reflects the divine
trinity.  God is one in an above and a below as Father and Son
and yet equal in the unity of the Holy Spirit.  Just as he moves to
man and in man so he is in himself - life, love, fellowship,
movement.  This history is not atemporal but, as Barth says, in
the contemporaneity of past present and future, is highly
temporal.  Thus by his reconciliation at a particular point in time
God embraces all our life and history and at the same time
transcends it.

Barth sees the history of Jesus Christ as the content of God's
revealing action in a movement with a downward and an upward
aspect.  These two are contemporaneous and not successive.  This
is Barth's way of saying that in the light of the resurrection Jesus
was in all his ways and works the Son of God incarnate and the
royal man exalted on the cross.  This does not exclude but
includes normal natural time, space and history - movement in a
horizontal sphere from birth to death and beyond.  The downward
and upward movements at each point have also this quite normal,
historical sequence and nature.[29]

---

[29]W Kreck, *Grundfragen der Dogmatik, Einfuhrung in die evangelische
Theologie*, 3 (Munich, 1970), pp. 84ff, 86ff, 277-9.

D *The Humanity of God*
Barth's earlier theology concentrated on the Godness of God. His later thought did the same but interpreted this in a very distinctive way. God is God in his relation to man, namely, in the man Jesus in what has come to be called 'the humanity of God'.[30] Hence in the thought of Barth, seen in his doctrine of election and time, the humanity of Jesus plays an increasingly important role. In particular it modifies his conception of God and is central to reconciliation.

For Barth there is no God known to man except the God revealed in the humanity of Jesus. In the highest heights and the deepest depths he alone is the true God. In his glory and love God has from all eternity willed to be the God of man and to have man with and for himself. The proof and reality of this is seen and known in his reconciling act in Jesus Christ. At no time, therefore, should we or can we think of the Son of God without this man and our humanity. At no time can we conceive of the true God without the man Jesus. He is at the beginning of all God's ways and works *ad extra*. All God's activity in, with and for man and the world is done through him. Because of incarnation and atonement there is no deity *per se*, no *logos asarkos* but only a *logos ensarkos*. God and man are indissolubly one in Jesus Christ. This does not mean that the humanity of Jesus is divinized or becomes different from ours but is rather the organ of deity.

Another consequence of this is illuminated by E. Jüngel[31] when he states that while there is actual atheism, there is no absolute godlessness of man. In the representative humanity of Jesus all are ontologically related to God. Moreover there is no non-humanity (*keine menschenlosigkeit Gottes*) of God but only God in and with this man. In this way Jesus' vicarious humanity has a cosmic, representative character. What he is and does is for us men and for our salvation. No one is excluded.

---

[30]Karl Barth, *The Humanity of God* (ET) (London, 1971), pp. 33-64.

[31]E Jüngel, '... keine Menschenlosigkeit Gottes ...' *Ev. Th.*, 31.7 (July 1971), pp. 376-90.

Barth is right in seeing the humanity of Christ having this universal significance. This does not imply, as is sometimes stated, actual universalism. There is here, however, a question that remains to be answered as to why it is that some remain imprisoned in sin and disobedience when they are in reality liberated. Barth speaks of the impossible possibility of disobedience and unbelief actually happening - and so it does.[32] He points to the very nature of sin as an absurdity in that people refuse to accept their reconciliation and election, refuse to be converted by the one who in his own humanity has already accomplished their conversion to God. The thrust of Barth's doctrine is towards good news, emphasizing Jesus as Victor, the *reality* of the power of God in reconciliation, but he does not fail to state that *actually* there can be and is refusal as well as acknowledgment and faith.

## E *Critique of Barth's position*

As we have seen the charge of universalism has been made and answered. Other criticisms of Barth are that his strong emphasis on the objectivity of what God has done in Christ gives too little place to the humanity of Jesus and to faith as human response.[33] These can scarcely be sustained when one examines the place Barth gives to Jesus' humanity in a rich variety of contexts in the *Church Dogmatics*. The section on the royal man is itself testimony to the fact that he corrects the older Dogmatics and gives profound treatment of the Jesus of history as portrayed in the Synoptics.[34] Jüngel believes that Barth's strong emphasis on the objectivity of God's action did lead him to give an important place to human response and faith only in his later writings.[35] This again is questionable. The objective emphasis is so pronounced partly because of his debate with Bultmann but

[32]*CD* III/2, p. 146.

[33]C O'Grady, *The Church in Catholic Theology*, vol. 2, (London, 1969), pp. 79ff, pp. 288ff.

[34]*CD* IV/2, pp. 154-264.

[35]E Jüngel, 'Karl Barths Lehre von der Taufe. Ein Hinweis auf ihre Probleme', in *Barth Studien* (Benzinger Verlag, 1982), p. 270.

more particularly because it corresponds to the biblical testimony. But it is clear that in his teaching on baptism the human subject also acts within the action of Christ and provides a fruitful point of contact for dialogue with Roman Catholicism.[36]

TF Torrance has made a more acceptable criticism when he points out that in his doctrine of reconciliation Barth fails to give due place to the high-priestly, intercessory work of Christ as Hebrews for example indicates.[37] Since Jesus is God and man in one person forever his living presence as man at the right hand of God is scarcely mentioned and deserves more treatment than Barth offers. In other words his vicarious humanity continues to have significance within the veil in his presence with the Father.

Torrance also believes there is a dualism in Barth's doctrine of reconciliation which surfaces particularly in his views on baptism as two separate acts. The first is baptism by the Holy Spirit as a divine act; the second baptism with water as a purely human act and confession.[38] There is certainly a question mark to be put opposite Barth's views on baptism but whether this is due to a defect in his main doctrine of reconciliation is questionable. Torrance does not indicate where he thinks the source of the fault is to be found.

Barth's views on the relationship between the prophetic office of Jesus Christ and the sacraments can also be queried. It is Jesus Christ himself by the Holy Spirit who speaks his word of reconciliation to man. He is the *one sacrament* of divine grace; he alone has a right to this term. This means that Barth radically desacramentalizes baptism, the Lord's Supper and preaching. They are not to be regarded as means of grace but witnesses to it, human echoes of it, mirror images. What Barth is concerned to underline is the sole action of Jesus Christ in accomplishing

[36]*Ibid.*, p. 269.

[37]TF Torrance, 'My Interaction with Karl Barth', in *How Karl Barth Changed My Mind*, DK. McKimm (ed.), (Grand Rapids, 1986), p. 62.

[38]*Ibid.*, p. 63. See also Torrance, 'The One Baptism Common to Christ and His Church', in *Theology in Reconstruction*, (London, 1975), pp. 99-100.

reconciliation and making it effective in man. What he aims to counter is any sacramental view that endangers this or gives any semblance of a human activity that operates almost automatically. No human word or sign can ever represent Christ much less be a substitute for him.

Some believe this position of Barth's is a direct consequence of his christological concentration and is to be accepted.[39] Others do not see 'witness' and 'means of grace' as opposites. Helmut Gollwitzer states, 'I cannot see why Barth makes these exclusive - either witness or means of grace'.[40] While Barth's emphasis on the sole agency of Christ is to be accepted this does not exclude the use of means which can legitimately be given a sacramental character. Barth cannot fully avoid the conclusion that witnesses to grace can also be used by God as instruments of grace to the world. The chief agent, however, is Jesus Christ himself in dynamic action and victorious power making known his reconciliation to the world.

---

[39] Jüngel, *Barth Studien*, p. 277.

[40] B Klappert, 'Diskussion auf dem Leuenberg, 1973 (Auswahl)', in *Promissio und Bund, Gesetz und Evangelium bei Luther und Barth*, (Göttingen, 1976), p. 274.

## 12

# Luther's Attack on the Latin Heresy

GEORGE YULE

In his sermon on John 14:13-14 of 1537 Luther said 'for if this foundation stands and is ours by faith, that Christ is both God's Son and the Virgin's Son in one person, though of two different natures, of the divine nature from eternity through the Father, of the human nature through his birth from Mary, then I have all that is necessary, and it is superfluous to let my thoughts flit heavenward and explore God's will and plan. Then I am spared all the disputations of the Jews, Turks, heathen and all the world about God, how He is to be sought and encountered or how He is to be served and pleased. And I am relieved of all fear and anxiety of my own heart'.[1] That the significance of this statement has been rarely seen is another illustration of the correctness of the thesis put forward by Professor James Torrance and elaborated with such brilliance and clarity throughout his teaching career, that all the heresies of the Western Church stem from its failure to base the whole of the Gospel on the incarnation, whereby the nature of God was revealed as Father, Son and Holy Spirit and the whole of creation redeemed. From this James Torrance explored the implications of the fact of Christ being both of one substance with the Father, so that the revelation of Christ is the revelation of God Himself, and of one substance with us, so that this revelation took place in him who truly assumed our fallen humanity so that, in Athanasius' phrase, he ministered the things of God to men and as the true man, ministered the things of man to God. This great stress on the vicarious humanity of Christ, who for our sake received the Spirit, was baptized, and alone delighted to do the Father's will as the true man of prayer, and the true man of faith and who went the way of the cross out of love to God and man, was a constant theme of Torrance's teaching and

---

[1] *Luther's Works*, Weimar edition [W] (ET), 45.548, American edition [LW] 24.97.

reflects Luther's statement on John's gospel.

Although the Western Church has always given adherence to the Nicene Creed, it has failed in many ways to see its full implications and so has, often ostensibly in the interest of orthodoxy, departed from its true understanding. Like Arius it has sometimes thought that Christ revealed something other than God, as in liberal Protestantism where what is revealed is no more that our highest ideals from which religious deductions are then made, or as in scholasticism, both medieval and Protestant, where the church's formulation of the faith is equated with the faith itself, leading to a sterile orthodoxy.

Whereas Protestant heresies tend to follow Nestorian tendencies (there was a man Jesus into whom the Word of God came), Catholic heresies, and also those of Protestant scholasticism, have tended to play down the fact that Christ was truly human and assumed our fallen humanity. In practice they tend to be mirror images and both seriously impair the incarnation.

As Professor TF Torrance has recently pointed out in a most suggestive essay, the Western Church has often clouded the fact that the revelation in Christ was the revelation of God Himself and that in revealing himself in Christ as man He has reconciled the world. 'Reconciliation is not just a truth God has made known to us; it is what God has accomplished for us, the Truth of God who freely gives Himself to us in the Revelation'.[2]

At basis all heresies stem from a failure to comprehend the fullness of the incarnation. Pelagianism is obviously so. How can one add anything to the love of God, 'immense, unfathomed, unconfined', displayed in the gift of Christ? Pelagianism sprang partly out of legalism which is very much a Latin problem. Every language has its strengths and weaknesses in trying to describe reality. Latin, with its precision and limited vocabulary, has obvious stengths in law, engineering and certain types of logical

---

[2] TF Torrance, 'Karl Barth and the Latin Heresy', *SJT*, 39 (1986), pp. 461-82.

analysis but the Roman expertise in law meant inevitably that Christian ethics were given a legal twist which became deeply entrenched with Tertullian's strong moralism[3] and his doctrine, as Calvin saw it, of legal repentance,[4] that is that God only forgave if certain conditions were fulfilled. This made a Pelagian stance inevitable while the rather shallow view of Christian ethics which legalism entailed, blinded people to the impossibility of loving God from one's own recourses.

This Pelagianism came out also in the worship of the Church. As Joseph Jungman has shown, in the early days of the Church, prayers were addressed to the Holy Trinity 'through Jesus Christ our Lord', that is, Christ in his humanity was seen as our great high-priest who presents us to God. But with the Arian crisis fears of undermining the deity of Christ became so great that this mode of prayer dropped out of common usage and, confronted with the majesty of God without Christ as mediator, other human mediators were sought - Mary, the saints, the priesthood[5] and later in Protestantism one's own spiritual recourses.[6]

Luther's personal problems were a result of these theological inadequacies. He had been brought up in the deep piety that was widespread throughout the church in Germany and the Rhineland in the fifteenth century, but this piety flowed from the theological perceptions current in Western Europe given to it in the abstract forms of late medieval scholasticism for few were like Bonaventure who could 'enlighten the mind while stirring the emotions'.

The medieval preachers who helped mould this piety emphasized

---

[3] For the effect of Tertullian's moralism on medieval Christendom, W Ullmann, *A History of Political Thought, The Middle Ages* (London, 1965), pp. 20-2.

[4] Calvin, *Institute* III.3.20.

[5] J Jungman, The Place of Christ in Liturgical Prayer (Dublin, 1965), p. 225.

[6] This is a theme elaborated with great thoroughness by James Torrance. See for example, 'The Vicarious Humanity of Christ', in *The Incarnation*, TF Torrance (ed.), (Edinburgh, 1981), pp. 125-30.

the fear of death and hence the need for a worthy repentance, which involved the deepest contrition and scrupulous confession, and the making of an adequate satisfaction, to show one was truly penitent. So Luther entered the monastery under the constraint of 'when will you do enough that God will be gracious'.[7]  At first things went well for him in his new life but soon his anguish began and he was harassed 'not with women but with the really knotty problems'.[8]

There are many autobiographical references to his anguish.  'I myself was a monk; for twenty years I tortured myself with prayers, fastings, vigils, and freezing; the frost alone might have killed me.  It caused me pain such as I will never inflict on myself again even if I could.  What else did I seek by doing this than God, who was supposed to note my strict observance of the monastic order and my austere life.  I constantly walked in a dream and lived in real idolatry for I did not believe in Christ.  I regarded him only as a severe and terrible judge, portrayed as seated on a rainbow.  Therefore I cast about for other intercessors, Mary and various other saints, also my own works and the merits of my order.  And I did all this for the sake of God not for money or for goods.'[9]

This typical passage illustrates the thesis of Jungman that once the role of the humanity and priesthood of Christ in our salvation disappears then Christ is seen in his divinity alone primarily as judge, and one flees to other intercessors.  Many of these passages recalling his *Anfechtung* come from his discussion of the incarnation in his sermons on St John, and illustrate the force of the words of Luther at the beginning of this essay.  On John 1:14, he speaks of two groups who seek the law rather than grace. 'The sophists', (his term particularly for the Occamists), 'and the pope also taught that a man can love God above all things by virtue of his own strength ... Such people are twofold sinners; they are drowned and dead in sin, and at the same time they give

---

[7] W 37.661.22.
[8] TRI.240.12.
[9] W 45.482, LW 24. 23-4.

way to the illusion that they are righteous and can keep the law ... And once upon a time I was a fellow of that stripe. Then there are the other disciples of the law, toiling disciplining and tormenting themselves only to sense in their hearts that they are unable to keep the law with all its deeds. I too once belonged to that group ... Terrified by death and confronted by perils then one is prone to despair and to flee from God, as though He were the devil ... Instead this group is quick to call upon the saints, "Oh, holy Virgin Mary, Oh, St James, Oh, St Barbara help me"'.[10] Neither popular piety not scholasticism could alleviate his problem. The reference to Christ seated on the rainbow, the artistic image for Christ's judgment throne, was the commonest subject for the west doorways or west windows of medieval churches. As well it was the subject of great artists like Roger van de Weyden, and is frequently referred to by Luther.[11]

His fears came to him especially during the celebration of the mass.[12] 'I knew nothing', he wrote, 'about the promises and the use of the sacraments ... I shuddered at the name of our Saviour Jesus Christ'.[13] 'I was befuddled by all this for over thirty years'.[14] Indeed his anxieties reached their zenith after he came to Wittenburg.[15]

His anxiety increased as he more clearly realized the one does not do God's will till one delights to do it. This undermined any possibility of being truly contrite which was regarded as the prime requirement in the doctrine of merit. 'When I was a monk I tried to live according to the Rule with all diligence and I was

---

[10]W 46.660, LW 22.141-2.

[11]See for example, W 33..83, LW 23.57; W 41.197, LW 13.326; W 46.663, LW 22.145-6; W 47.99, LW 22.377.

[12]LW 54.19, LW 23.61, See B Hall, 'Hoc est meum Corpus', in G Yule (ed.), *Luther: Theologian for Catholics and Protestants* (Edinburgh, 1985), pp. 112-4.

[13]W 44.716, LW 8.188

[14]LW 22.145

[15]M Brecht, *Martin Luther His Road to Reformation* (ET) (Philadelphia, 1985), p. 80, n. 21, W 41.721.23-4.

used to be contrite, to confess and number off my sins, and often repeated by confession and sedulously performed my allotted penance.  And yet my conscience could never give me certainty but I always doubted and said, "you did not perform that correctly, you left that out of your confession, you were not contrite enough"'.[16] For he now realized that one had to love God for His own sake, not in order to be forgiven for that would be self love.[17]

This perception that we do not do God's will till we delight to do so was at the heart of Augustine's attack on Pelagius.  God's law, argued Pelagius, is clearly stated and would not have been given, if, in fact, it could not be fulfilled.  To help us we have the example of the saints and ultimately of Christ himself.  If these are insufficient there is the threat of hell fire.  To which Augustine replied 'a man who is afraid of sinning because of hell fire is afraid not of sinning but of burning'.[18]  Augustine knew that it was impossible to spur oneself to loving God.  It could only come when the love of God took control of one's affections.  This understanding of Christian ethics was often stressed in medieval theology but it was regarded for the Christian athlete, the perfect monk, not for the wayfaring man.  But Luther's biblical reflections led him to realize that this was enjoined on all Christians.  This formed the basis of his understanding of Christian ethics as the ethics of gratitude, the second kind of righteousness as he later called it, and which was an essential corollary to his understanding of justification *sola gratia, sola fide,* a theme to which we shall return.  But at this initial stage it seemed to Luther to be an impossible demand of the law and in fact made Christ into Moses.

Luther had entered the monastery to gain relief.  There he continued studying scholastic theology which he had begun when

---

[16]W 40.11.15, LW 27.13.

[17]He makes this point very clearly in *Commenting on Hebrews* 2:2. External observance of the law means one fulfils 'the law only out of fear of punishment or our of love of reqard. But to fulfil the law in this way is to practise hypocrisy'. W 57.3.113, LW 29.122.

[18]Augustine, *Epistles,* 145.4.

he entered the University of Erfurt in 1501, but on the whole these studies made him more despairing.

In an essay of great perception Oberman has shown that Luther was fully aware of the distinctive positions of the medieval schools.[19] In his preface to the second *Disputation against the Antinomians* of 1538, Luther wrote: 'In the name of the Church and of Christ the Medieval theologians themselves became Pelagians, not to mention Occam and his school who shortly afterwards became even worse' (Pelagians).[20] All medieval theologians had said that grace was necessary for salvation. The anti-Pelagians all stressed the fact that initially grace had to be given to sinners to enable them to receive and use the grace of Christ given in the sacraments by which alone they were enabled to do works that merited salvation. The Occamists, and some others to a lesser extent, said that it was possible for man unaided by grace to make an initial step by doing the best he was capable of doing, *facere quod in se est*, and actually to love God. For this a man would be rewarded with the grace of congruity and so 'he can go on a perform a work that merits eternal life'.[21]

Bradwardine had argued, two hundred years before Luther, that God's grace is always prevenient and that a sinner cannot acquire grace by his own powers, by doing *quod in se est*. This was not Luther's basic problem. As Oberman puts it 'his question is what does it mean when Paul says the justified man lives by faith'.[22] It is at this point that Luther's insistence, following Augustine, that we do not do God's will till we delight to do it, is of crucial significance for this was the way in which the New Testament

---

[19]HA Oberman, 'Iustitia Christi and Iustitia Dei; Luther and the Scholastic Doctrines of Justification', in *Harvard Theological Review*, 59 (1966), pp. 1-26, reprinted in HA Oberman, *The Dawn of the Reformation* (Edinburgh, 1987). Luther made the same point in his *Commentary on Galatians*, 1535, 2.16, LW 26.128, but see the whole discussion 124-36.

[20]W 39.149.17-9, quoted in Oberman, *op. cit.*, pp. 6-7. See also W 1.373.24ff., LW 31.67-8, The Heidelberg Disputation.

[21]W 40.219, LW 26.124.

[22]Oberman, *op. cit.*, p. 14.

went beyond the Old. The New Covenant of God, as Jeremiah had seen, would be written on men's hearts. What this involved was one of the great problems facing Scholastic theology and is behind Luther's problem in regard to the interpretation of Romans 1:17 'the righteousness of God is revealed in the Gospel'. Luther saw that the law written in men's hearts' was a part of the Gospel by interpreted righteousness, *iustitia*, as God's righteous demand. So how could this much higher demand, in Augustine's phrase, 'the law of men's hearts', be called good news? Little wonder he raged, 'I was angry with God and said, "as if indeed it is not enough that miserable sinners eternally lost through original sin are crushed by every kind of calamity by the law of the decalogue without having God add pain upon pain by the Gospel, and also the Gospel threatening us with his righteousness and wrath!" Thus I raged with a fierce and troubled conscience. Nevertheless, I beat importunately upon Paul at that place most ardently desiring to know what Paul wanted'.[23]

How was this resolved? Not by scholastic theology for its centre of gravity had shifted from the incarnation, and although he gained support for some aspects of his insights from the anti-Pelagian writings of Bradwardine and Rimini and of course a great deal from St Augustine,[24] yet in the presence of God, *coram Deo*, he always felt himself to be a sinner. The emphasis of the Occamists that man can actually love God from within his own resources, he came to see was totally misguided, and led him towards his views on the *Bondage of the Will*.[25]

---

[23]W 54.185, LW 34.337.

[24]The complexity of this question and the various shades of Pelagianism are shown in the case of Luther's Augustinian teacher, Usingen. He insisted that God's help precedes the sinner and aids him to dispose himself for grace but then he follows this with the picture of Revelation 3:30 of God standing at the door of man's heart and knocking with his spiritual help, while man opens the door through penance. HA Obermann, *The Harvest of Mediaeval Theology* (Yale, 1963), p. 180 n. 106. Luther himself seems to have held a variant of this view in the early part of his *Commentary on Romans*, W 56.202, LW 25.186. But see HJ McSorley, *Luther: Right of Wrong* (Augsburg, 1969), pp. 198ff.

[25]Commenting on Biel's statement that a man can love God above everything else by his natural unaided powers, Luther wrote: 'As a result the

During the Leipzig Disputation in 1519 he wrote: 'As for me I know and confess that I learnt nothing from Scholastic theology but ignorance of sin, righteousness, baptism and of the entire Christian life. I certainly did not learn from them what the power of God is, and the work of God, the grace of God and the righteousness of God, and what faith love and hope are ... Indeed I lost Christ there but I have found him in Paul'.[26]

The Bible was the basis of Luther's theological revolution. One of Luther's chief criticisms of scholasticism was its generally off-hand attitude to scripture, despite the continous tradition of biblical exegesis throughout the history of the church. In his first *Commentary on the Psalms* of 1513-1514 he attacked those 'who place the opinions of philosophers, and the fables of poets and the lawsuits of jurists above the holy Gospel of God which they disdain together with the entire study of the Scripture'.[27] 'They only regarded the Bible,' said Luther, 'as a source of information. "What have I to do with the Bible and the Gospel. I know these things". O vanity, one must meditate on this ...'.[28] By contrast Luther became steeped in the Bible. 'The Holy Scriptures are a vast and mighty forest', he wrote, 'but there is not a single tree that I have not shaken with my own hands'[29] but at first his reading brought deeper despair. 'What should I have given if anyone (had freed) me from the mass and horror of conscience and would have opened up for me the understanding of one Psalm or of one chapter of the Gospel'.[30]

---

will is neither sick nor does it need the grace of God. All of this is based on the stupid principle of free will - as if free will could by its own power, choose to follow opposite paths when it is prone only to evil'. L Grane, *Contra Gabrielem*, p. 359, quoted in AE McGrath, *Luther's Theology of the Cross* (Oxford, 1985), p. 129. See his informed discussion of this, pp. 128-36.

[26] W 2.414.22.
[27] W 3.575, LW 11.58.
[28] W 3.540, LW 11.23, see Brecht, *Luther*, pp. 82ff.
[29] W TR 1, No 674, LW 35.227 coming from the early 1530's.
[30] W 41.582, quoted Brecht, *Luther*, p. 87.

In his first lectures on the Psalms he naturally used the traditional fourfold interpretation but in a distinctive way. He insisted that the allegorical interpretation (relating to the Church), the tropological (the moral attitudes which the interpretation demanded) and the analogical (the way it pointed to the last things) had to be controlled by the literal which was 'the foundation of the rest'.[31] But he distinguished between the literal historical which related to the setting of the Psalm and the literal prophetic which referred to the coming of Christ, because from the beginning of his studies Luther maintained Christ was the *sensus principalis* of the Bible 'for all the Scriptures point to Christ alone'.[32]

This hermeneutical principle resolved his own problem and gave an amazing consistency to his whole theology and saved him both from errors of medieval and protestant literalism, which in effect make the Bible into a book of infallible religious lore like the Koran, and form the tendency to mere moralising of the humanists. To Luther, both approaches were concentrating 'on the letter that killeth'.[33] 'Christ is the Spirit in the letter, the soul in the body, the honey in the honey comb'.[34]

It was not merely an intellectual exercise. Deliberately he endeavoured 'to pray the Bible', that is to make its insights his own. 'Nobody is able to speak worthily or to hear any part of Scripture if his disposition of mind is not in conformity with it so he feels inwardly what he hears or speaks outwardly and says, "Ah this is true"'.[35] He made this comment in his exegesis of Psalm 77:20 in the *Dictata* where he also speaks of the conversion of St Augustine in Book 8 of his *Confessions*. 'There you will find an explicit and most felicitous practice of this psalm. Note there how he was disquieted and did not speak,

[31]W 4.305, LW 11.414.
[32]*Avoiding the Doctrines of Men*, 1522, LW 35.132. See McGrath, *op. cit.*, pp. 79-80.
[33]Letter to Spalatin, Oct. 1516, LW 48.23-26.
[34]W 4.306, LW 11.415-16.
[35]W 3.549, LW 11-37.

and how he thought and meditated on the divine plans and counsels for the salvation of mankind. Hence one who has not experienced this remorse cannot be taught this psalm with any words'.[36] Oberman makes two very important points regrding this. Luther treated Augustine's conversion as a kind of paradigm, 'the condition *sine qua non* of each real theological discovery as the necessary preamble to every true insight of the interpreter of Scripture'.[37] That is one's prayer must be in conformity with Scripture in order to be converted. Whereas Gabriel Biel had said *lectio, meditatio, oratio*, Luther reversed the process: *oratio, meditatio, tentatio.*[38] It was for this goal of *tentatio*, which at this stage he called *experientia*,[39] that Luther was longing.

Luther's discovery, as Oberman rightly says, was that at the heart of the Gospel the *iustitia Dei* and the *iustitia Christi* coincide and are granted simultaneously. The Occamists alone opposed the view that the grace of God was always prevenient. That was not Luther's discovery, for all the anti-Pelagians knew that. But it was believed by the whole medieval tradition and ratified by the Council of Trent that the *iustitia Dei* is the standard by which, at the last judgment, will be measured whether one has, with the aid of the grace of Christ (the *iustitia Christi*), performed works that merit salvation. And this had been the ultimate terror for the judge there was Jesus Christ himself, the Eternal Son of God 'seated upon the rainbow'. No wonder that Luther was perplexed by St Paul calling this 'Gospel' good news. No wonder he shuddered at hearing the name of Christ, no wonder he sought other mediators for 'I was always wondering, when will you do enough that God will be gracious'.

In history, said RG Collingwood, one does not really know what happened until one knows why it happened.[40] Luther's 'Tower Experience' is a perfect illustration of this for what one decides

[36]*Ibid.*
[37]Oberman, 'Iustitia Christi and Iustitia Dei', p. 10.
[38]*Ibid.*, p. 11.
[39]*Ibid.*, pp. 8-9.
[40]RG Collingwood, *The Idea of History* (Oxford, 1946), pp. 307-8.

about its dating depends very much on what was its meaning for
Luther.

It is here that Luther's statement in his sermon on John 14:13-14
is so significant. Following the section we have already quoted
Luther continued: 'He who teaches what it means that Christ is
both true God and true man ... can surely conclude and say: "I will
hear and know of no other God but I will look and listen solely to
this Christ. And if I hear him I already know on what terms I am
with God and I need no longer torment myself as I did before with
my anxiety about atonement and reconciliation with God ... Now I
can gain a real and genuine trust in God" ... For since Christ who
is one undivided person, God and man, speaks it is certain that
God the Father and the Holy Spirit, that is the whole Divine
Majesty is also present and speaking'.[41]   Oberman rightly
observes that now *fides Christo formata*, faith living in Christ
replaced the medieval *fides caritate formata*, faith 'active in love'
which was the unanimous tradition from Aquinas through Scotus
and Biel to the Council of Trent.[42] 'Just as the sophists say that
it is *caritas* which forms and trains faith we say that it is Christ
who forms and trains faith. Therefore the Christ who is grasped
in faith is the true Christian righteousness'.[43]

So the righteousness of God is the gift of 'Christ our righteousness'. This was what made Luther feel reborn because it
completely resolved the question: 'Am I contrite enough?' Luther
now saw the answer must always be 'no', but that was no longer
the question.

---

[41]W 45.549-50, LW 24.45.

[42]Oberman, *op. cit.*, p. 20.  Oberman calls attention to the classical
passages on this topic in Luther's *Galatians Commentary* of 1535. Notice
especially that Luther binds faith and Christ completely together. 'Faith', he
wrote, 'takes hold of Christ in such a way that Christ is the object of faith,
or rather not the object but the one who is present in faith itself.' 'Faith is
a kind of knowledge or darkness that nothing can see.  Yet Christ of whom
faith takes hold is sitting in this darkness as God sat in the midst of the
darkness on Sinai'. See also G Yule, *op. cit.*, pp. 15-6.

[43]W 40.229, LW 26.129-30.

*Luther and the Latin Heresy*

The first unambiguous passage where Luther links the themes of
'Christ our righteousness' and the righteousness of God of
Romans 1:17 is in his sermon on Palm Sunday of 1518/1519. He
starts off that this 'alien' righteousness 'is the righteousness of
Christ' and cites 1 Corinthians 1:30, that God 'has made Christ
our wisdom, our righteousness and sanctification and redemption'.
He then quotes a series of carefully selected christological texts
showing that all the promises of God are fulfilled in Christ. 'In
thy seed (that is in Christ) shall all the nations of the earth be
blessed; for unto us a child is born, unto us a Son is given. "To
us", it says because he is entirely ours with all his benefits ... He
who did not spare his own Son but gave him up for us all will he
not with him give us all things? Therefore everything Christ has
is ours graciously bestowed on us unworthy men out of God's
sheer mercy. ... Even Christ himself therefore who says he came
to do the most sacred will of the Father became obedient to Him,
whatever he did, he did it for us and desired it to be ours saying "I
came among you as one who serves". He also states, "this is my
body, which is given for you". Isaiah 43 says: "You have
burdened me with your sins and wearied me with your
iniquities"'.[44]

In this example of Luther's allusive thought which, as the late
Professor James Cargill Thompson perceptively pointed out,
'presupposes' a whole range of inter-related arguments[45] we have
the setting in this sermon for his interpretation of Romans 1:17,
'the righteousness of God is revealed ...; as it is written the
righteous shall live by faith'. 'Through faith, Christ's
righteousness becomes our righteousness, and all that he has
becomes ours'. This is an infinite righteousness and one that
swallows up sin in a moment for it is impossible that sin should
exist in Christ. 'On the contrary he who trusts in Christ exists in
Christ'. This righteousness replaces 'original righteousness lost
in Adam'. He then interprets the phrase in Psalm 31:1 'in thy
righteousness deliver me' as 'the righteousness of Christ my God

[44]W 2.146, LW 31.298.
[45]JC Thompson, *The Political Thought of Martin Luther* (1984), pp. 9-
10.

which becomes ours by faith and by the grace and mercy of God'. Faith for Luther was not one of a whole list of Christian virtues but that which, following from the love of God, was the basis of the whole Christian life.  So he continued: 'In many places in the Psalter faith is called "the work of the Lord", "Confession", "power of God", "mercy", "truth", "righteousness".  All these names are for faith in Christ'.[46]

Finally he showed that this alien righteousness was the basis of sanctification. 'Christ daily drives out the old Adam more and more in accordance with the extent to which faith and knowledge of God grow.  For alien righteousness is not instilled all at once but begins, makes progress and is finally perfected in the end through death'.[47]

I have set down what Luther has said in detail in order to show how this new insight became the basis of all his thought, how this depends entirely upon the classical understanding of the incarnation and how one now has a much sounder test for making a judgment as to what point in his career, this new understanding came so clearly into his mind so that he felt as though he 'had entered the very gates of heaven'.

Even so it is a very difficult issue to decide when this actually took place.  This is because this new understanding in fact embraces all the central issues of Luther's understanding of the Gospel, by reversing many of the aspects of the Western theology which had seriously misread the implications of the Nicene Creed.  Luther was like someone trying to piece together a large jigsaw from a distorted picture of what the final pattern in fact was.  The solution could not in fact come until many important sections were in place, but these could not cohere until the central section was clearly delineated.

---

[46]*Ibid.*, LW 31.299.  Similarly in his preface to the 1535 edition of *Galatians* he wrote, 'Paul wants to establish the doctrine of faith, grace, the forgiveness of sins or Christian righteousness'.  W 40.41, LW 26.4.
[47]W 2.147, LW 31.299.

There are stages in his thinking between 1512 and 1518 at which he seemed to have the solution in his grasp but then later wrote as if he had not done so, or certainly not seen its full significance. So one could logically deduce either he had in fact seen it but not worked out its full implications and so some of the older patterns of thought continued, or one could argue that, although he had major pieces of the solution in his hands, he had not grasped fully their crucial significance which did not come till later. Both approaches are logically possible and psychologically understandable, and it may not be of critical importance which is adopted provided the full christological importance and all its implications as worked out in the sermon *Two kinds of Righteousness* are given full weight. The *terminus a quo* can hardly be earlier than the very end of the First *Commentary on Psalms* and the beginnings of the *Commentary on Romans*, 1515 while the *terminus ad quem* cannot be later that this sermon on *Two kinds of Righteousness.*

But as he said in this sermon 'alien righteousness is not instilled all at once', so he recalled in a number of places that he already had some real insights but still was confused. 'For a long time (in the monastery) I went astray and didn't know what I was about until I came to the text in Romans 1: "He who through faith is righteous shall live". That text helped me. There I saw what Paul was talking about. I related the abstract', (the Righteousness of God?) 'to the concrete', (the one made righteous through faith?) 'and became sure of my cause'.[48]

Luther's discovery came from wrestling with the text of the Scripture. In his first major exegetical work *Dictata super Psalterium*, 1513-1515, Luther operated at first entirely within the framework of late medieval exegesis as exemplified in the school of the *via moderna*. What was new with this school was that God had made a *pactum,* a covenant or contract on the basis of which God promised to bestow grace provided the basic

---

[48]WATR, 5 No. 5 518, LW 54.442. See M Brecht, Iustitia Christi: Dei Entdeckung Martin Luthers', *Zeitschrift fur Theologie und Kirche*, 74 (1977), p. 192.

conditions of *'facere quod in se est'* were fulfilled.[49]

Luther initially operated with this scheme in these lectures.[50] 'In this covenant', he wrote, 'God is truthful and faithful and is bound by what he has promised',[51] but what for Luther was the *quod in se est* that man had to do for his part of the *pactum*? At first Luther saw God's righteous demands in a conventional way. On Psalm 9:4 he wrote of God as the righteous judge who gives to everyone his due in accordance with the Ciceronial legal adage, *redditio unicuique quod suum est.*[52]

But Luther now developed his view that the only thing possible for man to do confronted by the righteousness of God was to accuse himself. This comes out most notably in his comment on Psalm 51. 'Against Thee have I sinned that Thou mayest be justified'. 'He who justifies himself', said Luther, 'condemns God who throughout Scripture states that he is a sinner ... He who judges himself and confesses his sin justifies God and affirms his truthfulness ... And so he is now in agreement with God and truthful and righteous like God with whom he agrees'.[53] Luther linked this with his belief that 'the highest works of man are the praise of God. We cannot pay back anything but praise and confession'.[54] But no one blesses the Lord except the one who

---

[49]AE McGrath, *Luther's Theology of the Cross* (Oxford, 1985). Chs. 3 and 4 give a scholarly account of this medieval background. For the *via moderna* and the idea of the *pactum*, pp. 86-7 and n. 106. It is significant that the same confusion of thought existed in Medieval Scholasticism between covenant and contract as developed in Protestant Scholasticism - a theme so well explored by James Torrance in for example 'Covenant of Contract', *SJT*, 23 (1970), pp. 51-76. The distinction between covenant and contract is that which Calvin called evangelical and legal repentance and was in fact, though he did not use the words, what Luther discovered.

[50]McGrath, *op. cit.*, pp. 87-9.

[51]Psalm 51:4, W 3.289, LW 10.237.

[52]McGrath, *op. cit.*, pp. 105-10 for how the theologians of the *via moderna* and Luther on Psalm 9(10):9 worked this out in terms of the *pactum*.

[53]W 3.289, LW 10.238.

[54]W 3.262, LW 10.220.

is displeased with himself.[55]

Brecht in a very careful analysis of these lectures points out how often Luther is tentative in his judgments and confesses he inability to exegete the Psalms to his own satisfaction.[56] But this perception that 'what we are capable of doing' was to accuse oneself, and in so doing one can confront the *iustitia Dei*, though only a temporary solution, freed Luther from applying shallow ideas of human justice to God and firmly turned his mind to seeing that throughout the Bible the emphasis was on God's mercy and man's need.

Brecht clearly shows that Luther's exegesis of Psalms 71 and 72, which Vogelsang in a famous essay had suggested was the point at which Luther had resolved the meaning of the *iustitia Dei* being revealed in the Gospel, cannot be the case for Luther still saw the solution in terms of judging oneself. The man is saved who hears Christ's judgment in the Gospel and lets himself be judged thereby. Christ's humble actions are examples rather than redemptive.[57] But it is noticeable that Luther begins to discuss the later Psalms at a deeper christological level. In Psalm 85 for example he says that 'the righteousness of Christ must be placed before every meritorious work' and that it is 'faith in Christ by which we are justified and granted peace, and by that faith Christ reigns in us'.[58] On Psalm 116:12 he expounds the gracious character of 'God who returns good for evil'.[59] Attention is more and more being directed to the grace of God, but it is in an unsystematic manner.

---

[55]W 3.191, LW 10.162

[56]M Brecht, 'Iustitia Christi', pp. 179-223. I am much indebted to this perceptive work. He quotes in this connection a statement of Luther from 1542/3. 'I was for long confused ... I knew indeed something but did not know what it was'. WTR No. 5693. I am also much indebted to Professor David Cairns of Aberdeen for help in translation, and discussion of these issues.

[57]Brecht, *op. cit.*, pp. 194-8. McGrath comes to the same conclusion, *op. cit.*, pp. 119ff.

[58]W 4.19 & 20, LW 11.174.

[59]W 4.269.21-50, LW 11.403.

With his *Commentary on Romans*, 1515-1516, major parts of
the jigsaw fell into place. With greater clarity Luther showed that
it is just blindness to think that man can keep God's law unless
his heart was disposed to do so. This is a recurrent theme of the
Commentary. He attacked the Nominalists who said we could love
God without grace. 'For will-nilly they recognise the evil lusts in
themselves. For this reason I say, "Ha, get busy now I beg you.
Be men! Work with all your might, so that these lusts may no
longer be in you. Prove that it is possible by nature to love God
as you say 'with all your strength', and without any grace. But if
you live with and in these lusts you are not fulfilling the
Law"'.[60]

But delighting to do God's will is only possible from grace and
so Luther makes a scathing attack on the nominalist position. 'It
is insanity to say that man of his own powers can love God
above all things and can perform the works of the law according
to the substance of the act, even if not according to the intention
of Him who gave the commandment, because he is not in a state
of grace. O fools, o swinish theologians! By your line of
reasoning grace was not necessary except because of some new
demand above and beyond the law'.[61] The whole scholastic
approach was misleading. 'I owe to the Lord this duty of speaking
out against philosophy and of persuading men to heed Holy
Scripture ... For it is high time that we undertake new studies and
learn Jesus Christ "and him crucified"'.[62]

The more deeply Luther meditated on grace, the more deeply he
saw the nature of sin. Indebted to St Augustine, he went further.
Augustine had realised that preoccupation with the blessings of
life could become idolatry. Luther saw that our very religious
striving is also a form of idolatry for, 'it is even seeking God for
its own sake'.[63] When Paul used the terms 'flesh' and 'spirit',

[60]W 56.274, LW 25.262. See also W 56.502-503, LW 25.497.
[61]W 56.274, LW 25.261-2.
[62]W 56.372, LW 25.261.
[63]W 56.305, LW 25.291 see also W 56.355, LW 25.345. 'Man is so self

Luther insisted that he was not talking about higher and lower faculties in human nature. In the carnal man the whole man is flesh for the Spirit of God does not abide in him.[64]

Because one's spiritual life apart from grace was 'flesh', Pelagianism was completely ruled out. In the presence of God all one's works were spoiled by pride and self love although *coram hominibus,* before men, one had a genuine freedom. 'God did not create the kingdom of heaven for geese'.[65] 'I grant that free will can by its own endeavours move itself in some directions, we will say unto good works or unto the righteousness of a civil or moral kind, yet it is not moved unto the righteousness of God'.[66]

Luther tied election to Christ and attacked the idea that it was a blind fiat of God, for then 'there is no need to preach, pray, exhort, yea even for Christ to have died'.[67] 'The most pestilent preachers of today seek signs of election in good works',[68] but the only place for assurance was the mercy of God, 'the wounds of Jesus, "the cleft in the rock", are safe enough for us'.[69] For Staupitz, predestination was the starting point, whereas for Luther, who gained so much from him, it was, as for Calvin, the bulwark for justificaiton *sola gratia.*[70] The greatest assurance of election would come, said Luther, in a most daring insight, when, like Christ, one so trusted God that one was prepared to be damned for the sake of another.[71]

---

centered (*incurvatus in se*) that he uses ... even spirituality for his own purposes and in all things seeks only himself', also W 56.356, LW 25.346.

[64]W 56.343, LW 25.332. See also W 56.502-503, LW 25.497 and EG Rupp, *The Righteousness of God* (London, 1953), pp. 166-7, DC Steinmetz, *Luther and Staupitz* (Duke, 1980), p. 117.

[65]W 18.636, LW 33.67.

[66]W 18.767, LW 33.264.

[67]W 56.183, LW 25.163-4.

[68]W 56.503, LW 25.498.

[69]W 56.400, LW 25.389-90.

[70]DC Steinmetz, *op. cit.*, pp. 109-12. Calvin, *Commentary on Ephesians*, 1:4 where he said if people object to justification by grace 'election shuts their mouths'.

[71]W 56.691-92, LW 25.282.

In the Romans *Commentary*, Luther's view of faith greatly developed. He often used the word *credulitas*, and there is a great need for a thorough analysis of which word he used for faith in which context. But in his comment on 5:2 Luther wrote that 'the Apostle speaks against those presumptious persons who think they can come to God apart from Christ as though it were sufficient for them to have believed, and *sola fide*, not through Christ (*per Christum*) but alongside of Christ (*juxta Christum*) or beyond Christ, not needing him having once accepted the grace of justification. So there are nowadays many who fashion from the works of faith, works of the law and the letter, when for example, having received faith by baptism and penance they want to become acceptable to God, only in and with their own persons, without Christ'.[72]

But how did Luther link faith to the *iustitia Dei* in Romans 1:17? His discussion of 'The Righteousness of God is revealed in the Gospel' and the 'Just shall live by faith', is in stark contrast to the way he spoke of it in *Two kinds of Righteousness*.[73] There the *Iustitia Dei* was Christ our righteousness. The discussion was wholly centred in Christ and the benefit of his gifts for the whole Christian life. Here Christ is not mentioned. The nearest one gets to it is the phrase 'faith in the Gospel'. Where is his own injunction against 'those presumptuous persons who thought it was sufficient to have believed *sola fide* but not through Christ?' He quoted Augustine that 'the righteousness of God is that righteousness which He imparts in order to make men righteous', a commonplace in anti-Pelagian medieval thought. He attacked Aristotle's view that righteousness flows from righteous actions instead of preceeding them and ignores the phrase, 'the just shall live by faith'. It is entirely in line with his marginal gloss on verse one chapter one that 'the whole purpose and intention of the Epistle is to break down all righteousness and

---

[72]W 56.298, LW 25.286. See EG Rupp, *op. cit.*, pp. 170-1, and Lowell Green, 'Faith, Righteousness and Justification', *Sixteenth Century Journal*, iv.i. (1973), for enlightening remarks on this whole issue.

[73]See above pp. 10-1.

wisdom of our own'.[74]    That is it is still in line with his theology of the earlier commentary on Psalms.

It is that position which he himself later described as inadequate. Commenting on Psalm 143:12 in 1525 he wrote 'Christ is God's grace, mercy righteousness truth wisdom power comfort and salvation, given to us by God without any merit on our part. Christ I say, not as some express it *in blind words causally*, that He grants righteousness and remains absent himself for that would be dead.    Yes it is not given at all unless Christ himself is present'.[75]

'In blind words causally' sums up all the inadequacies of so much of medieval theology, the theology of *quod in se est*, and of all the other semi-Pelagian statements and the abstract language of even the anti-Pelagian statements which puts, as it were, a veil over the love of God and the cost of man's redemption wrought by Christ on the cross.    It inevitably, made faith, grace, and righteousness into abstract concepts and forgiveness into a legal transaction.

There is however a real problem here.    Many passages in the Romans commentary read as if Luther had reached his mature understanding that the *iustitia Dei* was the gift of 'Christ our righteousness', and hence only open to faith (*fiducia*) for any 'works' would deny this.[76]

Bizer in a famous essay pointed out that in Romans Luther continued to use *fides* and *humilitas* almost interchangeably

[74]W 56.3, LW 25.3

[75]W18.529, LW 14.204, 1517 revised 1525.  Notice how similar this is to his view of having faith without Christ, n. 76 above.

[76]Most notably on Romans 2:15, W 56.203-204, LW 25.188, 'Christ is my defence.  He has died for me.  He has made his righteousness mine righteousness and my sin his.  If he has made my sin to be his sin then I do not have it'.  If someone should argue that this was the point at which Luther's discovery came it would have to be taken very seriously.  The only argument against it, is why does he revert to his earlier positions in much of the rest of the commentary?

showing that he thought of humility being a necessary condition for being accounted righteousness by God, exactly as he had done in his *Dictata super Psalterium*. Brecht, who stresses the centrality of the incarnation, for Luther in a way in which Bizer did not, brings this out even more clearly. He shows that faith in this sense is handled almost like law in this commentary. Humility is needed to receive this righteousness which will then make us righteous and then, in line, with his very opening gloss on the Romans 1:1, will enable one to be righteous and then act righteously.[77] Without this, Luther would have been left with the view that he so strongly condemned, that doing righteous deeds makes one righteous.

Clearly Luther is moving very close to resolving how the *iustitia Dei*, Christ and faith are related but at this stage humility is still too much like the *contritio* of old which was the root of his problem. He has pared off all legalistic excesses that scholasticism, particularly Nominalism had given to repentance and especially that righteousness was a quality of the soul that had to be achieved, but for example, in his long exposition of Romans 3:7 where he contrasts the attributes of God with those of a sinner so that he can only come before Him in faith and humility, he concludes with *ergo fide et humilitate opus est.*[78]

This is a very difficult question and I have not the space to assess the contrary opinion (that Luther made his breakthrough in the *Commentary on Romans*) which is a strong one supported by most scholars. My only contention is that the solution must be controlled by the christological understanding that it brought to Luther so that he saw that once one had Jesus Christ as true God, showing the heart of the Father and true man, Son of Mary, our brother, one had all that was necessary, for then the 'righteousness of God' was the gift of 'Christ our righteousness'.

---

[77]Brecht, 'Iustitia Christi', p. 208.

[78]W 56.218, LW 25.204. The English translation: 'Therefore we need faith and humility' hardly brings out the causal importance of faith and humility.

The discovery that 'Christ our righteousness' was the righteousness of God given to mankind in love transformed Luther's theology and formed the basis of getting rid of many of the heretical views of the Western Church which blurred its understanding of the Gospel.

For Luther it clearly implied that revelation and reconciliation are one. Only by seeing what Christ has done for mankind can one see who he is and only by seeing who he is can one be assured that what he has done is totally effective. Luther's fiercely anti-Pelagian stance is based entirely on the incarnation. This is apparent in his early sermons from 1518, and indeed it became increasingly true in his Romans commentary. In his sermon, *On the Preparation for Death*, 1518, he wrote that Jesus Christ is the only saving image 'to counter the images of death, sin and damnation', for he is the mirror of the heart of God. The ruse of the devil is to lead one away from Christ. 'The devil leads persons beyond God so that they long for another god because they now imagine God's love to be extinguished by the storm, and his hate has grown'.[79]

It is further developed in his sermon on John. 'If he [the devil] were to persuade me to regard Christ as only man, I would be lost. But if my pride and joy is the fact that Christ, both true God and true man died for me, I find that this outweighs and eclipses all sin, death, hell and all misery and woe. For if I know that he who is true God suffered and died for me, and also this same true man rose from the dead, ascended into heaven etc., then I can conclude with certainty that my sin was erased and death was conquered by Him and that God no longer views me with anger and disfavour; for I see and hear nothing but tokens and works of mercy in this Person'.[80]

It is essential for Luther that in the incarnation God revealed

---

[79] W 2.688.1 in M Lienhard, *Luther's Witness to Jesus Christ* (ET), (Minneapolis, 1982), p. 107.

[80] W 45.559, LW 24.108. See also W 45.545-60, LW 24.94-110 and in his Galatians Commentary (1535) W 40.440, LW 26.282.

Himself. 'For if I hear the article that Christ is the one true God and no other I have hit upon "the one thing needful"'.[81] But this is because with equal emphasis he insisted that Christ truly became man. In this way revelation and reconciliation become one. 'But true Christian theology ... does not present God to us in His majesty as Moses and the other teachings do, but Christ born of the Virgin as our mediator and high priest'.[82]

Luther refocussed attention on the humanity of Christ. He did not see the priestly role of Christ as deeply as did Cyril of Alexandria or Calvin but few have so unerringly portrayed the vicarious identification of Christ with sinful men.

In 1537 he wrote: 'Formerly I myself was a doctor who excluded Christ's humanity, supposing it proper to separate his divinity and humanity. In the past the greatest theologians were wont to do this. They abandoned Christ's humanity and clung to his divinity on the assumption that it was unnecessary to give importance to the former. But one must approach and hold to the divinity of Christ without overlooking his humanity or acknowledging only the divine nature. Otherwise in the name of all the devils we tumble from the ladder that leads to Christ. Therefore beware of that! You must not know of any god or Son of God but him who was born of the Virgin Mary and became incarnate ... If you can humble yourself, adhere to the Word with your heart and hold to Christ's humanity, then indeed the divinity will become manifest. Then the Father, the Holy Spirit and the entire Godhead will draw you and hold you'.[83]

'What a very strange game they played', he wrote of the early Docetics who denied Christ's humanity.[84] Christ was a true man who ate and slept, showed emotions, was lonely, forsaken and

[81] W 45.549, LW 24.297.

[82] W 40.77, LW 26.28.

[83] W 33.155, LW 23.102. See also on Hebrews 1:3, W 57.3.99, LW 29.111.

[84] W 50.268.4, LW 34.208. I Siggins, *Luther's Doctrine of Christ* (Yale, 1970), p. 201. I am indebted to this book.

died.  Luther notes the sinful nature of Christ's ancestors in the genealogies in Matthew and Luke to indicate 'the stock from which he came was contaminated and horribly polluted'.  As the genealogy also contained Canaanites Luther commented 'Christ wanted to be born from the Canaanites, a heathen nation and in this way to begin working peace between Jews and Gentiles'.[85]

Luther's insistence that Christ took fallen flesh was of fundamental importance, for many in the Western Church were blind to the essential insight of Gregory of Nazianzus that 'the unassumed is the unredeemed'.  For it was fallen flesh which had to be redeemed and this was acheived by Our Lord taking our fallen humanity, and 'so being harassed by the law, death and hell'.  'He who was not under the law subjected himself voluntarily to it'.  Here his thought is again very close to Athanasius and Cyril of Alexandria.[86]

We were, said Luther, all captive to the law, so to save us Christ 'was born under the law.  The law did everything to him that it did to us.  It accused us and terrified us, it subjected us to sin, death and the wrath of God, and it condemned us with its judgment'.  It did this against us rightly, but not against Christ, for 'he committed no sin neither was guile found in his mouth.  Yet he permitted the law to terrify him, to subject him, to sin death and the wrath of God - none of which it had any right to do.  Therefore, I have conquered the law by a double claim, first as the Son of God as Lord of the law; secondly in your person which is tantamount to you having conquered the law yourselves'.[87]

Christ so identified himself with sinners said Luther that he took on the worst consequence of sin, hell, which Luther with great originality delineated as separation from God.  In a series of moving passages, particularly after 1518 in his interpretations of

---

[85]W 46.69, LW 24.375; W 46.102, LW 24.413; W 46.103, LW 24.413; W 44.311, LW 7.12 & 15.  See also Siggins, *op. cit.*, pp. 198-201, Lienhard, *op. cit.*, pp. 167-8, G Yule, *op. cit.*, pp. 98-101.

[86]Cyril, *Third Letter to Nestorius*, Ep X VII.  V. C., 'He [Christ] speaks of himself as subject under God with us.  So he also became under the law'.

[87]W 40.565.66, LW 26.369-70.

the Psalms he identifies Christ's descent into hell as his cry of dereliction on the cross, just as Hilary had done and Calvin later would do.[88]

But most of the Patristic tradition and almost all the medieval, limited Christ's suffering mainly to physical torment. His soul remained in possession of the beatific vision. But because in the great exchange Christ took to himself our sin, Luther said that on the cross our Lord experienced abandonment and damnation, and he criticized both the Scholastic theologians and the mystical writers for failing to see this.[89]

Luther in his *Anfechtung* had experienced something of this terror. About 1518 he wrote, 'I knew a man who said he had suffered these infernal torments in the shortest possible time, so great and infernal that "no tongue nor pen can show" nor can those believe who have not experienced, so that if they were completed or lasted half an hour or a tenth part of an hour he would utterly perish and his bones be reduced to ashes. Then God appears horrifyingly angry and with hm creation. There can be no flight, no consolation'.[90]

In his sermon on the preparation for death, Luther brought out this awful cost of our redemption as our greatest consolation. Christ the eternal Son of God feels abandoned by the Father, 'as one who is eternally damned'. It is that which explains the cry of dereliction, "My God, my God, why has thou forsaken me?" Between the Father and the Son lies the abyss of human sin.[91] Luther naturally interpreted Psalm 22 in this way. 'He felt in his conscience he was cursed by God' yet unlike us he took this judgment 'without blasphemy or cursing'. Although God was

---

[88]Hilary, *On the Trinity* IV. XIII, III.XV. Calvin, *Institute* II.16.10.

[89]W 5.497.22ff and 163.17-19. See Leinhard, *op. cit.*, pp. 116-20 particularly notes 54, 57 and 55 on these pages.

[90]W 1.158, translated EG Rupp, *Luther's Progress to the Diet of Worms* (London, 1949), p. 30. See also his comment on Jonah 2:2-6, (The German Text), W 19.221-31, LW 19.71-80.

[91]W 2.690.18 and 691.22. See Leinhard, *op. cit.*, p. 109.

present in this suffering man he was abandoned, not partially, but totally, because for our sake he bore our damnation. 'Christ loved the Father with all his strength; but his torments as they were above his human strength, forced his innocent nature to sigh, groan, cry, dread and shrink'.[92]

A mature reflection on this theme was his comment on Psalm 8:5 of 1537 where he equated this verse 'Thou wilt let Him be forsaken by God for a little while' with the cry of dereliction. Here is 'his real, sublime and spiritual suffering which no man can imagine or understand ... Thus the righteous and innocent Man must shiver and shake like a poor condemned sinner and fell God's wrath and judgment against sin in his tender innocent heart, taste eternal sin and damnation for us'.[93]

But he did not curse God or blaspheme and even in hell his faith in God remains for he cries out 'My God'. A man is no longer in hell said Luther when he can cry unto God.[94] Hell like sin and death has been defeated by Christ so that one in deepest hell 'can cry unto God', for in Christ's cry of dereliction one knows the heart and mind of the Father. 'For God cannot resist helping him who cries to God and implores Him'.[95]

This is the greatest example of the reversal of the sin of Adam by Christ. The Greek Fathers saw Christ's obedience reversing the disobedience of mankind since Adam. 'He became like us that we might become like him' was the theme which Athanasius and Cyril took up from Irenaeus and they worked this out in terms of Christ in his humanity, by his utter reliance on the Spirit, always obeying the Father and delighting to do His will. Here Luther is underscoring the cost of our redemption in terms of this complete obedience to the twin commandment of utter love to God and all

---

[92] Psalm 22, ET, H Cole, *Select Works of Martin Luther* (London, 1826), vol.4 pp. 354ff, especially 361-70, W 5.602-619. See Leinhard, *op. cit.*, pp. 116-9.

[93] Ps. 8. W 45.204-50, LW 12.126-7.

[94] German text W 19.221, LW 19.71.

[95] W 19.221, LW 19.71.

embracing love to one's neighbour. The cost of this obedience was the descent into hell. This became an illustration of a statement of Luther in his Romans Commentary that a man who completely loved God would even go to hell for love of God.[96] Luther saw that this, precisely, was what Christ had done.

By his fidelity to the fact that Christ is the *scopus* of Scripture, Luther had resolved the problem of how the *iustitia Dei* was Gospel, good news. In so doing he had, aligned himself with many of the great christological insights of Athanasius and Cyril of Alexandria, that God has revealed Himself in the frail humanity of Christ, and that any teaching akin either to Nestorius or Apollinarius would destroy this. Few since Cyril have so emphasized the importance of the unity of Christ, Son of God and Son of Mary. 'True Christian Theology ... does not present Christ to us in his naked majesty ... but Christ born of the Virgin, as our Mediator and high priest',[97] so that those who say 'the flesh profiteth nothing' divide 'the one indivisible person of Christ'.[98]

It is true that Luther did not as clearly recognize the role of the Spirit in Christ's obedience as a man as shown by Athanasius and Cyril and later worked out by Calvin and so sees less clearly the role of the active obedience of Christ and relates the two natures of Christ rather clumsily in the way he described the *communicatio idiomatum*. But then this is true of most of Western thinking since Chalcedon which preferred the crypto-Nestorian emphasis of Leo's Tome to the insights of Cyril.[99]

---

[96] W 56.391, LW 25.381-2.

[97] W 40.77, LW 26.28.

[98] Comment on John 17:6, ET in H Cole, *op. cit.*, 2.48. When Zwingli emphasized this text in the eucharistic controversy Luther recognized him as a Nestorian, *On the Councils of the Church*, LW 41.105.

[99] Cyril shows that one may use the language of the two Natures for Christ as a kind of psychological model. 'For the one and sole Christ is not twofold, although we *conceive* of him consisting of two distinct elements ...' *Third Letter to Nestorius*, Ep XVII. VIII a & b.

Despite this Luther broke the Western mould. In Jesus Christ God revealed Himself and in so doing reconciled mankind. Any Pelagian bias is ruled out for there can be no *quid pro quo*s in the love of God revealed in the cry of dereliction from the cross.

Part Three

# Christ and Salvation in Christian Theology

# 13

# The Struggle for God's Righteousness in the Psalter

## BREVARD S CHILDS

Some of the most significant theological work on the Bible during the last several decades has been done by church historians and systematic theologians who have studied the influence of the Old Testament on the Reformers.[1] Repeatedly the point has emerged that the Old Testament provided a major context from which to hammer out a fresh and powerful theology grounded in Scripture. The basic terminology of salvation, righteousness, election, covenant, and law was consistently rooted in the Old Testament. Far from being simply an historical background for the New Testament, the Reformers learned to recover the vertical dimension of the prophetic voice which continued to address the church as it had once confronted Israel.

In spite of the important theological and historical insights which have emerged from this research, the impact on the field of Old Testament itself has been far less than one might have hoped. Even in the area of Old Testament theology the recovery of the Reformers' approach to the Old Testament has played a minor role even in the robust theologies of von Rad and Zimmerli. Although no one would suggest that the Reformers' understanding of the Bible can be simply repristinated in the 20th century, the challenge remains to stimulate a profounder theological grasp of the Bible.

---

[1] Some representative works are the following: E Bizer, *Fides ex Auditu. Eine Untersuchung über die Entdeckung der Gerechtigkeit Gottes durch Martin Luther* (Neukirchen-Vluyn, 1966); H Bornkamm, *Luther and the Old Testament*, (ET) (London, 1969); JS Preus, *From Shadow to Promise. Old Testament Interpretation from Augustine to the Younger Luther* (Cambridge, Mass., 1969); G Ebeling, *Lutherstudien*, Band 1, (Tübingen, 1971); THL Parker, *Calvin's Old Testament Commentaries* (Edinburgh, 1986); W de Greef, *Calvijn en het Oude Testament* (Amsterdam, 1984).

I

I can think of no better place to seek aid from the Reformers than
when dealing with the subject of the Old Testament imprecatory
psalms which remain an insurmountable problem for many modern
Christians. Included in this genre is that group of psalms which
are dominated by a series of curses against enemies. Four psalms
stand out immediately (Pss. 35, 58, 69, 109), however, there are
numerous others which include elements of imprecation. Consider
the following words of Ps. 109.8ff:

*May his days be few;*
*may another seize his goods!*
*May his children be fatherless,*
*and his wife a widow ... May his posterity be cut off,*
*may his name be blotted out in the second generation.*

The theological problems arising from such an outburst are
manifest. How do you reconcile these sentiments with the
teaching of Jesus and the rest of the New Testament? What place
can such imprecations have with the words of one who said, 'love
your enemies, bless them that curse you, do good to them that
hate you'? Of course, the problems can be somewhat avoided by
following the example of many denominations which carefully
edit the Psalter for use in the Christian church. The *Hymnal* of
the Presbyterian Church, USA of 1933 omits completely from its
responsive readings Pss. 35, 69 and 109, and excises the
elements of imprecation from 139. Whatever one may think of
this device which may perhaps be justified in some ecclesiastical
contexts, it does not come to grips with the basic theological
problem. Clearly the issue at stake is far larger than how to use
or not to use a few Hebrew psalms, but rather involves the
relation of the two testaments as a truthful witness to Jesus
Christ.

II

A brief review of the history of exegesis since the 19th century
will illustrate some of the ways in which the Christian church has

sought to meet the problem.

A   Traditional, conservative interpreters such as Hengstenberg and Delitzsch have tried to understand the imprecations as simply an idiom for defending the justice of God.   Delitzsch formulated this position in a classic manner:   'all the imprecatory words in these psalms come from the pure spring of unself-seeking zeal for the honouring of God'.[2]   Even if one were to accept a measure of truth in this proposal, is not the problem too easily resolved? Are not there other elements involved beside the justice of God? Can one sustain an assumption of pure selflessness before the peculiar intensity of the psalmist?   An even less fortunate development is found in Hengstenberg who resorts to the apologetic tactic of justifying the Old Testament by pointing out the presence of curses also in the New Testament.

B   The other extreme within the theological spectrum is represented by the older German rationalists such as Hupfeld, or by theological liberals such as Oersterley.   They regarded the imprecatory psalms as belonging to an earlier, primitive stage of Israel's faith which has been totally replaced by the love commandment of the New Testament.   Not infrequently among these commentators one hears of the 'savage spirit' of the ancient Hebrews, and a contrast between the Old Testament and the higher spiritual ethic of the New Testament is suggested as part of a sequence of religious development.

C   The theory which has remained most widespread from the mid-19th century up to the present is a mediating position.   It was carefully worked out by Perowne[3] in his classic Anglican commentary, and further developed by SR Driver along with a host of others.   These commentators tried to discern the historical and psychological circumstances which called forth the curses, and, although never fully condoning the imprecations, attempted to soften the effect as an unfortunate, but understandable human reaction.   Perowne concluded finally that these psalms remained

---

[2] F Delitzsch, *Biblical Commentary on the Psalms*, vol. 1,   (ET) (Edinburgh, 1892), p. 418.
[3] JJS Perowne, *The Book of Psalms*, 2 vols., (London, 1890).

part of the old dispensation, but if carefully monitored, did contain some true lessons regarding religious zeal.

### III

Before I attempt to develop a different interpretation of the imprecatory psalms, it might be useful at the outset to contest the broad assumption shared by the last two positions that the theological problem is confined to the Old Testament. Confusion on this point greatly beclouds the theological issue.

First, when in the Sermon on the Mount, Jesus commands his disciples to love their enemies and to pray for those who despitefully use them, he does so, not in the manner of setting forth a new commandment at odds with their Jewish tradition, but he radicalizes the old with the purpose of rescuing the commandments of God from distortion.

Secondly, the Apostle Paul, when dissuading his readers from taking vengeance into their own hands in Romans 12, sends them back to the law of Moses in order to find there a warrant for his decisive argument: 'Vengeance is mine, I will repay, says the Lord' (Deut. 32.5; cf. Lev. 19.18).

Thirdly, to curse an enemy is just as severely forbidden in the Old Testament as in the New. Lev. 19.17ff.: 'you shall not hate your brother in your heart ... you shall not take vengeance or bear any grudge against the sons of your own people, but you shall love your neighbour as yourself'. To be sure, Leviticus has restricted the sanction to the members of the covenant, but there are also signs of a broadened context as well. Thus, Job defends his integrity by his refusal to curse his enemy. (31.29f.)

In sum, both Testaments stand or fall together, and the theological issues cannot be resolved by playing off the one against the other.

IV

The reformers took over many features from traditional exegesis, but put them with a new theological framework which gave their interpretation fresh power and remarkable illumination. In their handling of the imprecatory psalms Luther and Calvin share the same basic interpretive direction, but they place the emphasis of their exegesis quite differently. Several important themes continue to reappear and they form the common core of their exposition:

1  The chief function of these psalms is to witness to the righteousness of God and to the just claims of his rule against the wicked.

2  David's role is that of pointing to Christ, either as a prophet or as a type, and therefore his prayers are representative for the whole church.

3  The just wrath of God against his enemies fell on Jesus Christ through whose suffering, forgiveness was attained for the ungodly.

The great strength of Calvin's handling of the imprecatory psalms arises from his closeness to the biblical text coupled with a powerful theological rendering of its message. He never tires of emphasizing that David's prayers concern the vindication of God's name against false enemies. 'He is fighting in God's quarrel' (cf. on Ps. 69.9), and his zeal is inflamed by attacks on the glory of God and his church. Because David's confidence is grounded in God's objective righteousness and just rule, Calvin is completely free from all attempts psychologically to probe David's motivations. Rather, equipped with the 'testimony of a good conscience' (Ps. 109.26), the psalmist turns to God to vindicate him from his enemy. He flees to God who alone can vindicate his innocence against the false charges of the wicked (109.1). David appeals to God 'that as God is righteous, he would manifest his righteousness in defending his servant in a good cause' (Ps. 35.24). Calvin is much concerned to show that David did not act rashly in uttering curses against his enemies (Ps. 109.20). In fact, 'David does not pray God to curse his enemies' (109.30), but rather to destroy their evil designs and put them to shame (35.4).

Another important feature of Calvin's interpretation is his careful attention to hearing the psalmist's witness in its Old Testament context. Here Calvin differs markedly from Luther, especially from his earliest expositions of the Psalter which are still largely medieval in approach. At times Calvin is willing to suggest a connection between the enemy and a historical figure in David's life (cf. Ps. 58.1; 109.6), but almost immediately he draws back from historicizing the psalm beyond the explicit evidence of the text. He continues to observe biblical references to Old Testament institutions (58.1) and to Hebrew practises which he assumes are unfamiliar to his readers. Calvin's awareness of Old Testament literary conventions which may be accommodations to 'mistaken, though generally received opinion' (58.4), has a decidedly modern ring to it.

Calvin speaks of David frequently as a prophet (35.2; 109.26), but his role is primarily that of a type (69.36). 'David speaks in the name of the whole church', and whatever he says concerning himself 'behoved to be fulfilled in the supreme Head' (69.9). Calvin is much concerned to do justice to the historical details of the text which serve as a mirror for the larger theological reality. Also he allows much freedom in the manner by which the Old Testament text was subsequently appropriated, and he suggests that what was often a metaphorical usage in the Old Testament was rendered literally by the New Testament (69.21).

Ultimately for Calvin the issue of the imprecatory psalms is christological in nature and he sets his discussion within a broad trinitarian context. David's zeal for God's righteousness is only fully seen in the light of Jesus Christ. For Calvin the issue is not Christ's example of the forgiveness of his enemies, but rather what he achieved in vindicating God against the opposition to his just rule. David could endure the foul calumny of the enemy because he knew that Christ himself was not exempt from similar abuse (69.4). Likewise, the Christian church cannot shrink from exposing itself to reproach for the maintenance of the Father's glory (69.9).

It is interesting to note the sophistication with which Calvin handles the New Testament's use of these psalms. He observes, for example, that the mixing of gall or poison in the psalmist's food functions as a metaphor, whereas the New Testament applies the same imagery in a literal sense to the death of Jesus (69.21). Calvin interprets this move as a sign that cruelty to the people of God is also cruelty against Christ. One sees how strikingly different were Calvin's theological instincts from, say, Hengstenberg who immediately moved into a discussion of historicity and apologetics.

Finally, Calvin notes that David was able to raise shouts of victory even in the midst of the battle (109.28) because of his confidence in God's triumph over evil. He trusts that he shall be delivered from his sorrow (109.28) because he spoke in the person of Christ (109.6). Thus, Calvin concludes, 'the enduring possession of all good things depends upon Christ of whom David was a type' (69.36).

Luther's interpretation of the imprecatory psalms focusses also on the righteousness of God, but with an even greater emphasis on the prophetic identification of David and Christ: 'Through the Spirit David spoke this psalm [109] in reference to Christ'.[4] In addition, Luther approaches the psalm from a more anthropological perspective and is thus immediately concerned with the inability of sinful man to defend God's righteous cause. In a real sense, the strengths of Luther's interpretation have been developed most strongly in recent years by Bonhoeffer[5] whose interpretation forms an interesting complement to that of Calvin.

---

[4]M Luther, *Sämmtliche Schriften*, vol. V, Concordia edn. of Walch, (St Louis, 1896), p. 50.
[5]D Bonhoeffer, 'Bredigt über einen Rachepsalm', *Gesammelte Schriften*, Band 4, (Munich, 1965), pp. 413-22.

Bonhoeffer begins with the basic anthropological problem that no one in the church dare pray an imprecatory psalm. No one has only pure, selfless motives in seeking God's righteousness. To call for the wrath of God on the wicked is only to bring down judgment upon oneself. Yet the proper function of the imprecatory psalms remains to break the spell of sin and to bear witness to God's triumph over all the machinations of Satan.

Bonhoeffer, along with Luther, can emphasize that David breaks forth into joy in Ps. 58 because of his anticipation of Christ's victory. In David's prayer it is the guiltless Christ alone who can speak these words. Because the innocent Christ died the death of the godless saying, 'Father, forgive them', the church can now bear witness to God's righteous rule in these psalms. However, when the church prays the words of Christ, it also renounces its own rights and claims to find its only hope in God's salvation of the wicked.

In several respects these two classic Reformation interpretations complement each other. Calvin's emphasis falls on the objective righteousness of God's rule against the continuing forces of evil which rise to threaten it. He grounds his interpretation on the witness of both testaments to the selfsame divine reality. Luther and Bonhoeffer start from the human perspective and probe deeply into the burning issue of sinful man's inability to pray for God's cause without the personal involvement of private gain. Both Reformers make use of the New Testament's application of these psalms as a confirmation that God's enemies still call for battle against Christ's kingdom. Both are aware that the imprecatory psalms address the church with the fundamental question: *not,* is God on our side in the struggle for justice, but are we on God's?

## V

In conclusion, there are several hermeneutical issues raised by the history of interpretation which call for further reflection. Calvin's insistence that the Old Testament be heard in its own right rather than simply as an echo of the New, reflects his superiority to Luther on this issue, and has won the full support of modern biblical interpretation. Obviously the rigorous attention to Hebrew philology, historical context, and literary structures which modern critical study employs has brought the psalms into a sharp exegetical focus unknown to the Reformers. Yet Calvin led the way in taking seriously historical particularity as part of his theological interpretation. The hard question arises whether Calvin can still provide aid to modern biblical interpreters in holding together history and theology, particularly at a time when the threat of a permanent divorce arises from many different sides.

Calvin's awareness of the use of literary conventions in the psalms and his appeal to a theory of divine accommodation to human frailty (58.4) also lends itself to further reflection on the Bible's use of other cultural features. However, would it not have been more theologically consistent for him to have recognized also the elements of personal anger and frustration in the imprecatory psalms rather than to have pictured David, the psalmist, as an Old Testament saint with zeal only for God's kingdom? On this issue Luther's exegesis is more incisive. Unfortunately, this minor theme in Calvin's exposition subsequently became a major one in his conservative followers.

Then again, both Reformers offer important theological guidelines for the hermeneutical problem of how to move from the level of biblical witness to the subject matter itself to which both testaments point. Calvin spoke of the *substantia* or *res* of the witness. In fact, the great divide which separates the Reformers' exegesis from those of the modern period is not that the former were less concerned than the latter with the exact meaning of the text. Rather, the basic difference lies in whether one reads the Bible as an expression of merely human culture to be explained by appeals to historical, literary, and psychological forces, or whether the text bears truthful witness to a divine reality which continues to shape our lives and provides the foundation of our Christian faith.

In recent hermeneutical discussion much use has been made of the term 'construal' in order to serve a double purpose. On the one hand, it provides a means of treating the particular imaginative, yet time-conditioned rendering of a biblical text by its author or redactor. On the other hand, it allows the modern interpreter a way of regarding the biblical composition as the reflection of the personal ideology of its author rather than an authoritative testimony to divine reality. Nevertheless, it would seem apparent that this term functions in biblical exegesis in a way that is compatible with the hermeneutics of Schleiermacher rather than that of Calvin.

In sum, the difficult hermeneutical issues remain for modern biblical theologians of how to keep witness and reality firmly together without falling prey to 19th century theological liberalism, and yet without simply identifying the two in a system of 'right doctrine' which was the failing of post-Reformation orthodoxy. In this regard, the Reformers continue to offer helpful guidelines in showing how a form of *Sachkritik* - to use modern terminology - is possible, if the *Sache* is defined christologically and decisively shaped by the authoritative witness of both testaments.

# 14

# God, Grace and Salvation

TIMOTHY A DEARBORN

By way of preface, gratitude is expressed to Professor James Torrance to whom this author is deeply indebted. Professor Torrance continually stresses in his writings, lectures and life, that every Christian doctrine, and indeed, all of the Christian life must be approached from within the context of the trinitarian, incarnational Gospel. This article is but an attempt to develop some of the implications of this emphasis for the understanding of grace and salvation. Any inadequacies in the thoughts expressed in this article should be attributed solely to the author.

## I The Debate Over Salvation: Dualism versus Universalism

## 1 The Debate Over the Way to Salvation

Without hesitation, Christians will place the 'credit' for their salvation with God and with his initiation of their relationship with him. However, a chronic debate has raged within Christendom over the relative efficacy of God's sovereign grace and humanity's response of faith in the *ordo salutis*. Two positions have dominated the Church's reflection on this issue. Some would assert that no one comes to God unless drawn by God. All who are saved are saved because of God's sovereign, intrinsically efficacious predestination of them to salvation. Thus, they would tend to agree with Calvin's statement that humanity's faith is but an 'empty vessel'.[1] Others would assert that God creates the opportunity for people to be saved, but their salvation ultimately depends upon the free exercise of their will to choose to repent and believe in Christ. There is a synergistic relation between God's sovereign initiative and humanity's response such that humanity contributes faith to the gift of grace.[2]

---

[1] Calvin, *Institutes of the Christian Religion*, JT McNeill and FL Battles (ET and eds.), (London, 1960) III.xi.7, p. 733.

[2] 'Synergism' is used in this study as ' ... the view, namely, that whilst God

Traditionally, the Church has begun its reflection on this issue
with the observation that neither Scripture nor experience indicate
that all people will enter into relationship with Christ and be
saved.   Yet Scripture does proclaim that God wills the salvation
of all, and that eventually, God will be 'all in all' with every
tongue confessing Jesus as Lord.   How does one resolve this
apparent dualism (in Scripture and experience) and universalism
(in Scripture and one's eschatological hope)?   What can one
conclude about the interrelation of God's sovereign initiative and
humanity's response of faith?   The traditional conclusions can be
summarized in four positions:

1 *dualistic predestination*: God determines beforehand which
people will believe in him, consigning the rest to damnation;[3]

2 *universalistic predestination*: God determines beforehand that
all people will eventually, if not in this life then in the next,
believe in him;[4]

3 *dualistic synergism*: God has chosen to be make salvation
dependent on human choices, thus only those who choose to
believe, and to live obediently will be saved;[5]

truly acts upon the human will to incline it towards goodness, such action is
not so overwhelming that it cannot be resisted, and that man, even though
fallen, still retains liberty to co-operate or not to co-operate with the
assistance so vouchsafed to him. This, indeed, is the working faith of all who
intelligently value the Sacraments'.   (NP Williams, *The Grace of God*
(London, 1930), p. 6.).

[3] For Augustine's classic reflection of the issue from this perspective see,
*De Prædestinatione Sanctorum* 6-14. John Owen is one of many advocates of
this position.   JI Packer says in his introduction to a current edition of Owen's
work, that no one has ever, could ever, or need ever present this position more
adequately than Owen. (*The Death of Death in the Death of Christ*, reprint of
original edn., 1647, (London, 1959), p. 38).

[4] John Hick, JAT Robinson, and Nels Ferré are three contemporary advocates
of this view whose writings have had the widest influence.

[5] Among many other advocates of this traditionally  Arminian and Roman
Catholic view, Klyne Snodgrass goes so far as to write in a recent article,
'nowhere in the Biblical material does one find judgment according to grace or
faith ... Nor is judgment based on mercy.   Judgment is according to works
without respect of persons ... His wrath awaits those who reject him and do
evil, but life awaits those who respond in obedience ...' ('Justification by
Grace - to the Doers', *New Testament Studies*, 32 (1986), pp. 78-82).

266

4 *universalistic synergism*: God has chosen to make salvation
dependent on human choices, and ultimately all people will freely
believe in him.[6]

This controversy over the relation between divine sovereignty and
human freedom in salvation has been one of the most persistent
and divisive controversies in the history of the Church. Samuel
Mikolaski notes, 'the nature and function of grace in salvation is
probably the main point of division between the Catholic faith ...
and the evangelical-Protestant Christian faith'.[7] The doctrine of
God's sovereignty in grace is even more complex when one
applies it to the question of the salvation of people who are not
Christians. Is God's grace selective, limiting salvation to those
who have come to explicit faith in Christ? Or, is God's grace a
cosmically pervasive power which influences all people to seek
God within the context of whichever limited human religious
tradition they were born.

## 2  The Debate Over the Extent of Salvation

The question of Christians' and non-Christians' salvation leads
inevitably to the question of eternal destiny. Will all people be
saved, or is salvation limited to a portion of humanity? Dualists
assert that hell is an eternal reality for some people, and they
condemn the contemporary disregard of hell. Thus, Harry Buis
writes, 'there is no other doctrine that is clearly taught in
Scripture which is so generally denied or ignored in our modern
theological world'.[8] Nicholas Berdyaev refers to the disregard
of hell as 'the most striking evidence of human frivolity'.[9]

---

[6]In defence of this view, Hick writes, 'however long an individual may
reject his Maker, salvation will remain an open possibility to which God is
ever trying to draw him ... It seems morally (although still not logically)
impossible that the infinite resourcefulness of infinite love working in
unlimited time should be eternally frustrated, and the creature reject its own
good, presented to it in an endless range of ways ... We may confidently affirm
the ultimate salvation of all God's children'. (*Evil and the God of Love*
(London, 1966) pp. 379-81).

[7]SJ Mikolaski, *The Grace of God* (Grand Rapids, 1966) p. 6.

[8]H Buis, *The Doctrine of Eternal Punishment* (Philadelphia, 1957) p. ix.

[9]N Berdyaev, *The Destiny of Man*, N Doddington (ET), (London,1937) p.
338.

However, many Christians are increasingly hesitant to embrace the doctrine of hell, and especially the notion that God, in His sovereign initiative in grace, selects whom to save and whom to damn. An eternal hell is regarded by many as an indictment against God's sovereignty and his love, for surely if he would (being a God of love), and if he could (being sovereign), God would not consign any of his creatures to eternal separation from himself. Universalism has always been a strong minority view throughout the Church's history. Today, it increasingly sounds like the opinion of the majority. Nels Ferré asserts, 'the very conception of an eternal hell ... would make God a tyrant, where any human Hitler would be a third-degree saint, and the concentration camps of human torture, the King's picnic grounds. That such a doctrine could be conceived, not to mention believed, shows how far from any understanding of the love of God many people once were and, alas, still are'.[10] However, this assertion is seen as a grave danger by those who hold the traditional, orthodox dualistic view. 'The creeping paralysis of universalism ... is rapidly gaining ground throughout Christendom'.[11] Emil Brunner writes that universalism is 'in absolute opposition both to the Biblical understanding of God and to the Biblical understanding of man and of salvation'.[12]

3 The Debate Over the Nature of the God Who Saves

It must strike an observer of Christian dogmatics as ironic that the battle-lines over, of all things, the doctrine of *grace* should be so firmly established. Since it is the nature of *God's* grace about which the controversy rages, the root issue is not the nature of grace but the nature of God. John Hick boldly proclaims, 'either we reject the doctrine that any creatures are doomed to hell,

---

[10]N Ferré, *The Atonement and Missions* (London, 1960) p. 29. See also his *Evil and the Christian Faith* (New York, 1947) pp. 117-9. Bishop JAT Robinson asserts a similar idea: 'Whether He had to condemn to extinction one or millions, God would have failed and failed infinitely' (*In the End, God ... A Study of the Christian Doctrine of the Last Things* (London, 1950) p. 107).

[11]J Oswald Sanders, *What of the Unevangelized?* (London, 1966) p. 9 .

[12]Brunner, *Church Dogmatics*, vol. I, *The Christian Doctrine of God*, O Wyon (ET), (London, 1949) p. 363.

or we revise the doctrine of God'.[13]  However, according to what criteria does one 'revise' the doctrine of God?  John AT Robinson suggests that the Christian doctrine of God must be eschatologically based.  'That God will assuredly vindicate Himself in the face of His adversaries is the sheet-anchor of the Biblical faith'.  Therefore, the universalistic assertion 'that in the end He is Lord entirely of a world wanting His lordship, is consequently determinative of the whole Christian doctrine of God'.[14]

However, is an eschatological assumption the best criteria for formulating one's doctrine of God and thus of grace?  Are presuppositions about the nature of love, of sovereignty, or of human freedom appropriate either?  Within the assumptions about sovereignty, love, and freedom that each position adopts, the four dualistic and universalistic options are totally logical and consistent.  They can not be critiqued from within the context of their own assumptions.  It is the conviction of this article that presuppositions about love, sovereignty, freedom and human destiny are not the optimal starting points for theological reflection.  Is it possible that the conflict over the relationship between God's sovereignty and human freedom appears to be irresolvable because the issues have been inaccurately defined?  As Emil Brunner says, heresy may use the Bible for support, but it errs in its presuppositions.[15]  TF Torrance goes so far as to state that universalism and predestination are 'twin heresies'.[16]  The failure of dogmatic universalism and predestination to resolve adequately the issues of the relation of grace and faith in salvation stems from inadequate presuppositions.

Instead of beginning with human-centred questions pertaining to

[13]J Hick, *op. cit.*, p. 378.
[14]JAT Robinson, 'Universalism: Is It Heretical?', *SJT* 2, (1949) pp. 139-40.
[15]E Brunner, *The Divine-Human Encounter* AW Loos (ET), (Philadelphia, Penn., 1943) p. 18.
[16]Quotation without reference made by Jerry Walls in 'Can God Save Anyone He Will?', *SJT* 38, (1985), p. 156.

the extent and the means of salvation, this article is rooted in the conviction that one must begin with questions pertaining to God's self-disclosure. Insofar as theology is indeed 'the knowledge of God', the ultimate 'presupposition' for all theology is the doctrine of God. The study of the relation of God's grace and humanity's faith in the process of salvation inevitably depends upon one's conception of God. As Paul Jewett says, 'our doctrine of salvation must be grounded in our doctrine of God'.[17] Therefore, the question of the relation of God's grace and humanity's response of faith in the *ordo salutis* is not fundamentally an eschatological, or soteriological, or anthropological question. Rather, it is inherently centred in the doctrine of God.

## II The Centrality of the Doctrine of God for the Doctrine of Grace
### 1 The Nature of God: Christian Monotheism versus Trinitarianism
The truth or falsehood of one's doctrines of grace and salvation must be *determined by*, rather than *determinative of*, one's doctrine of God. In opposition to the claim of JAT Robinson quoted above, it is asserted in this article that no understanding of soteriology, eschatology, or even the nature of God's sovereign love can be 'the sheet anchor of the Biblical faith'. The unique contribution of the Gospel to human religious history is not discussions about the relative sovereignty of God's love *versus* human freedom.[18] Rather, the unique revelation of the Christian faith is the triune being and action of God disclosed in Jesus Christ. The doctrines of the Trinity, the Incarnation, the homoousion, the redemptive humanity of Christ in the hypostatic union of God and humanity, and the indwelling Holy Spirit as the Spirit of Truth in the Body of Christ are pivotal in formulating an adequate doctrine of grace and of salvation.

Confusion among Christians over the doctrine of grace has arisen primarily because of the failure to develop fully the soteriological implications of these doctrines. If one were to ask, what is the significance of these doctrines in the four positions which have

---

[17] P Jewett, *Election and Predestination* (Grand Rapids, 1985) p. 66.

[18] These debates are as deeply rooted in Islamic and Hindu theological debates as they are to Christian theological history.

dominated the debate, it appears that these positions have been
formed with little reference to the trinitarian nature of God. There
would be little in the four positions which would need to be
abandoned, if these central Christian doctrines were abandoned.
The trinitarian nature and being of God is determinative of all
theology, not merely the understanding of grace.[19] The thesis of
this article can be expanded to assert that controversy over the
doctrine of grace is not simply rooted in controversy in the
doctrine of God, but more specifically, in the doctrine of the
Trinity. An adequate understanding of the Trinity is central to an
adequate understanding of grace. Unfortunately, as Karl Rahner
says, 'despite their orthodox confession of the Trinity, Christians
are, in their practical life, almost mere "monotheists". We must
be willing to admit that, should the doctrine of the Trinity have
to be dropped as false, the major part of religious literature could
well remain virtually unchanged'.[20]

A 'monotheistic', rather than trinitarian doctrine of God leads to a
'monotheistic' doctrine of grace. As Rahner says, in such a view,
grace is reduced to something 'merited' by Christ, and is
'presented as the grace of the "God"-man, not as the grace of the
incarnate Word as Logos'.[21]  Either the divinity of Christ is
diminished and he becomes the prime human example of a life of
faith, love, and obedience, or his humanity is diminished and he
becomes a temporarily human vessel upon which God vented his
judgment and wrath.  A non-trinitarian understanding of grace
leads to definitions of grace as an attribute of God rather than as
God's essential being.  Thus, grace is defined as God's unmerited
favour, God's eternal decree, God's healing power, God's salvific
will, or God's cosmically present acceptance.  These are
impersonal notions of grace, because they stem from a

[19]Geervarghese Mar Osthathios writes, 'Trinity is the key that would unlock
many riddles that baffle thinkers of our day such as authority and freedom,
individuality and sociality, equality and distinction', (*Theology of a Classless
Society* (London, 1979), p. 12).
[20]Karl Rahner, *The Trinity*, J Donceel (ET), (New York, 1970), p. 10.
Jurgen Moltmann is in full agreement with this; see his *The Trinity and the
Kingdom of God*, M Kohl (ET), (London, 1981), ch. 1.
[21]Rahner, *op. cit.*, p. 13.

fundamentally 'impersonal' notion of God. God is a force or power more than he is the relationship of Persons in his innermost being. Brunner asserts that this loss of an awareness of the personal being of God, and the personal encounter of God with humanity 'is a disastrous misunderstanding which affects the entire content of Christian doctrine and also operates fatally in the practice of the Church'.[22] Even English language dictionaries are bound by impersonal definitions of grace as influence or power.[23]

When theology strays away from an understanding of God as the Triune Persons, grace becomes objectified and depersonalized. To illustrate this, it is pertinent first, to examine the Bible's definition of grace in relational terms; then briefly to observe the impact of non-trinitarian Christian theology on the understanding of grace; and finally, to develop some of the implications of a trinitarian doctrine of grace for the soteriological debates.

## 2 The Biblical Definition of Grace

To attempt in a few pages to summarize the Bible's definition of grace is a monumental, if not absurd undertaking. As JM Meyers rightly says, 'it can be said without equivocation that the whole Bible is a book of the grace of God'. This can be said in spite of the fact that there is not one specific Hebrew word for 'grace' and that as reported in the Gospels, the word 'grace' is never once used by Jesus. This article asserts that biblically, grace is revealed as the triune God's being-in-communion. Because of this love in his innermost being, grace is God's actions to incorporate

---

[22]Brunner, *op. cit.*, p. 21.

[23]*New English Dictionary*: 'The divine influence which operates in men to regenerate and sanctify, to inspire virtuous impulses, and to impart strength to endure trial and resist temptation'. *Webster's Seventh New Collegiate Dictionary*: 'unmerited divine assistance given man for his regeneration and sanctification'. NP Williams asserts that these definitions are rooted 'too deeply in popular use and acceptance ever to be dispossessed' and therefore theology must accommodate itself to these impersonal notions of grace (*op. cit.*, p. 42). Rather, theology must reassert the trinitarian, relational meaning of grace.

humanity into relation with himself (Deut. 7.7). Every aspect of God's dealings with humanity is an expression of his grace, for it is a manifestation of God's being-in-relationship, his call to humanity to enter into that relationship, and the disclosure of the consequences of humanity's refusal to live in communion with God and one another. The whole Bible is about grace. Creation, the Covenant, the Law, the priestly cultus, even God's acts of judgment are gifts of his grace. It is no wonder that no single word exists in Scripture to describe grace. Rather, grace is the sum total of all God's dealings with humanity. To clarify this, it is valuable to summarize briefly two words used in Scripture to describe God's grace.

### 1 *Hesed*

While no one word for grace exists in the Old Testament, there are a cluster of words describing God's relationship with Israel. Of these, *hesed* is certainly the most central word to describe God's grace in the Old Testament, best translated as God's covenant faithfulness or lovingkindness. Out of his great love, God chooses to enter into relationship with his people, binding himself to them and them to him. God's *hesed* not only creates people's communion with him, but with one another. Just as God shows *hesed* toward his people, so are they to show *hesed* toward him and one another. *Hesed* powerfully portrays the bi-lateral nature of relationships and thus of grace. The covenant exists because of God's initiation and his covenant faithfulness. This *hesed* calls people to live in *hesed* and respond with covenant faithfulness. *Hesed* conveys the truth that people's relationship with God is not based on their action but on his acts and faithfulness in drawing them into relationship with himself. In fact, Walther Zimmerli notes that *hesed* attains such a comprehensive meaning in the Old Testament that 'the *hesed* of Yahweh can then be spoken of almost as a person'. These very personal acts of God call forth a personal response of relational faithfulness from people. *Hesed* lacks the sense of condescension and stooping which is implied in *nhe*. Rather, it expresses the sense of mutual 'right conduct in free kindness within a given relation'. It is important to note that LXX translates *hesed* by ἔλεος not by χάρις thus preserving the traditional Greek understanding of grace as unmerited favour, rather than God's faithfulness in relationship.

## 2 Grace (Χάρις)

Grace (Χάρις) had to be redefined in the New Testament in order to express the distinctive Biblical meaning. In Greek though its prime meaning is to find or to give favour as in bestowing a gift on someone who does not deserve it. For example, Aristotle defined Χάρις as 'helpfulness towards some one in need, not in return for anything'. The dominant meaning for Χάρις in Greek thought was to find grace or favour in the eyes of a superior. This notion does not fully express the understanding of grace developed through the Old Testament of God's steadfast faithfulness and persistent commitment to draw people into relationship with himself. God in his steadfast love draws people into relationship with himself and one another. 'God has saved us ... not according to our own works, but according to his own purpose and grace (Χάριν) which was granted us in Christ Jesus from all eternity' (2 Tim 1.9; see also Eph. 2.9; Rom. 3.28, etc.). Through the incarnate life, death and resurrection of Jesus Christ, events have occured which radically altered people's understanding of grace, of God, and indeed of all of life. The basis of human life and of humanity's relationship with God and one another is no longer found in one's own effort, but in God's final act on humanity's behalf.

Some might question how such prime significance for grace can be ascribed to the life of Christ, when the word Χάρις is never attributed to him in any of his teaching in the Gospels. Is grace a theological construct inappropriately imposed upon the life of Jesus of Nazareth by his followers? Though Jesus did not use the term grace, his entire life and entire verbal teaching were expressions of it. Foremost in Jesus' portrayal of grace is his emphasis on his own life being a life of grace. He came not to be served but to serve and to give his life as a ransom for many (Mk. 10.45; Lk. 18.31-33; Mt. 20. 17-19, 28). Though Christ is

274

never recorded as having spoken of grace, it can rightly be asserted by John that he was full of grace. In fact, that which gripped the early Church's attention and provoked their understanding of grace was the self-giving life, death and resurrection of Christ. The fact that the Gospel writers rarely use Χάρις to describe the life and impact of Christ merely expresses the fact that the word, as commonly used, did not yet have its distinctive, biblical meaning. The death and resurrection of Christ is the turning point around which the biblical redefinition of grace rotates. As Moffatt says, 'grace is a meaningless term apart from the resurrection'. In Christ's passion, the essence of grace is disclosed - God's gift of himself to establish humanity in relationship with himself.

It was the Apostle Paul, who in reflecting on the life of Christ gave to Χάρις its distinctively Christian meaning. Paul was overwhelmed and set free by the wonder that out of his love for humanity, God should submit to the Incarnation and crucifixion. To express the meaning of this, Paul took the common word for grace and seized it for the Gospel, filling it with a distinctively new meaning. For Paul, grace always relates to the Cross and the Person of the Lord Jesus Christ (see Rom. 3.24-26; 5.1-21; I Cor. 1.14). In the majority of the New Testament uses of grace, Christ is the basis and even the content of its meaning. Thus, grace becomes understood as the very being of God, as well as God's act in response to humanity, and God's incarnate response as man to God on behalf of humanity. As TF Torrance says, 'Grace is in fact identical with Jesus Christ in person and word and deed'.

Grace is not just God'' favour, but is God himself acting to reconstitute the very life of humanity (I Cor. 15.8-10; 2 Cor. 4.6). The objective, historical intervention by God as a man on humanity's behalf has opened up for humanity a new way of being human. Grace is not simply the action of God in Christ, nor the power of God, nor the will of God manifested in Christ. It is neither merely God's attitude, attribute, nor presence. Those views depersonalize grace, making it something separable from Christ. Grace is a Person for grace is God's being in Three

275

Persons, and God's life as the divine/man, Jesus Christ. Thus, as Paul says, life is Christ.

This complete association of grace and Christ is the essence of the biblical redefinition of grace. Through this identification Χάρις was wrenched from its Hellenistic context and given new meaning. Yet, tragically, it is precisely this association which the Church has only marginally maintained throughout its history. As TF Torrance says, 'thus any attempt to detach grace in a transferred sense from the actual embodiment of God's grace in Jesus Christ is to misunderstand the meaning of the Pauline charis altogether'. Biblically, grace is inherently a relational term. It is not merely an objective action, though all relations imply objective action. Nor is it a subjective power, though all relations involve subjective power. First and foremost, grace is the encounter of Persons in communion. Grace is the triune God's life in communion, and grace is God's reconstitution of humanity's life into communion through the life of Jesus Christ and the indwelling of the Spirit. When the understanding of grace has been detached from its relational roots, and especially when it has been disassociated from the Person of Jesus Christ, there have been tragic consequences for the Christian faith and for the life of Christians.

C  Historical Misunderstandings of Grace

Tragically, grace has frequently been viewed as an attribute or attitude of God, or as a thing or power. Thus, grace could be analysed in (it)self, apart from complete association with God. Much of the terminology and the debates over grace which have dominated the Church's discussions throughout its history stem from this disassociation.  As a result, grace has been analysed and divided almost into different 'kinds' of grace.  Though parenthetical comments have been made affirming the oneness of grace, it has been divided into categories such as created and uncreated, prevenient and subsequent, healing and elevating, supernatural and natural, concomitant and consequent, habitual and actual. As Leonardo Boff says, though the doctrine of grace should help Christians discover more of the goodness and kindness of God, 'instead it became a storehouse of esoteric propositions that had been formulated more to condemn errors than to embody and vivify the experience of Christians'.[24]

Because one's theological presuppositions influence one's theological conclusions, instead of analyzing the aberrent development of the doctrine of grace itself, those aberrations can be traced to roots in inadequate conceptions of God. More specifically, inadequate developments in the doctrine of grace can be attributed (at least partially) to inadequate conceptions of the implications of God's triune being and action. The lapse from trinitarian conceptions of God in Christian theology can be summarized in two groups: placing primary emphasis either on God as the Supreme Substance or the Supreme Subject.

## 1 God as the Supreme Substance and Grace as a Thing

One of the most common deviations from personal trinitarian thinking stems from an effort to preserve the oneness of God. While trying to affirm the Trinity, God's oneness has frequently been attributed to the *ousia* or substance shared in common by the Father, Son and Spirit. Though the intent of this is to affirm the oneness of God, it leaves Christian theology vulnerable to a materialistic misunderstanding of God. Furthermore, it makes God's being in *una substantia* the foundational characteristic of God, rather than God's being one in communion.

If God is the Supreme Substance then he (It) can be misconstrued as a (The) Thing. He (It) can degenerate in human devotion into an object to be analysed and manipulated. Proper use of earthly matter such as ritual objects of devotion can influence the heavenly matter to exert a favourable force on human life. Further, God as the 'primal stuff' can be equated with the rest of creation as emanations or manifestations of the Supreme Substance and thus all matter can be regarded as divine. Salvation can be regarded as the restoration of divinity to humanity. The distinction between the Creator and creatures is thus dissolved.

[24]Boff, *Liberating Grace*, J Drury (ET), (Maryknoll, 1979), pp. 19-20.

*God, Grace and Salvation*

Using Aristotelian categories of primary and secondary substance, Aquinas attempted to rescue theology from this materialistic misconception. Aquinas asserted that substance can only be applied to God in the sense of 'self-grounded existence', but this subtle distinction was difficult to grasp and this stress on a substantive rather than relational being of God provided the foundation for a materialistic theology of grace.[25]

This conception of God can have profound implications for the understanding of grace. *First*, it can lead to the idea of grace as the sacramental impartation of the substance of God into the soul of humanity. This view dominated, and to an extent still dominates Roman Catholic sacramental theology. Grace is not a relational encounter with the Person of God as much as it is the gift of a 'portion' of God to people through baptism and the Eucharist. Grace almost becomes a commodity which the Church can/must dispense as the divinely appointed Custodian of Grace. Much of the medieval theological debates on the efficacy of grace stems from this view. This formed a foundation of the Roman Catholic notion of the sacraments as 'things' which impart the divine essence to humanity. Sacramental 'things' (bread, wine, oil, and water) are spiritually re-constituted earthly manifestations of the divine Substance.[26]

*Second*, it is only one step away from this view to assert that grace is cosmically present because: a) humanity is in God's image, already possessing a 'portion' of God, and b) God is over all, in all, and through all. Therefore, God's grace is universally

----

[25]Aquinas,*Summa Theologia*, Ia.29,3 ad 4, p. 55 (*existere per se*).

[26]This leads to the notion that the Sacraments, as containers of grace, have an efficacy in themselves, without regard to the faith of their administrator or recipient. Though initially, the intent of this notion was to glorify grace and not make grace dependent on human merit or faith, it led to the popular diminution of grace, for one's focus was placed on the Sacraments. Rather than focussing on God himself, the focus is placed on the actual Sacrament themselves for they become the focal point for one's reception of grace. This naturally led to a highly materialistic and mechanistic notion of the sacraments containing grace and causing grace in their recipients lives. Aquinas endorsed this view (*op. cit.*, II.1.109-4) and it is foundational to Catholic sacramental theology.

278

operative in all people, who may even be totally unaware of God's presence. Instead of God being a Triune Person, known relationally, God is a power or set of characteristics, in which humanity participates whenever people behave in a manner expressive of those attributes. Thus if people are acting lovingly, unselfishly, justly, etc., they are expressing God's grace. This view has a persuasive influence in much of contemporary liberation theology, and dogmatic universalism.[27]

## 2 God as the Supreme Subject and Grace as an Act of Will

Throughout the history of Western theology there has simultaneously existed the view of God as the Supreme Subject.[28] Whether defined in Greek monarchical theology of the Father as the Cosmic Ruler, or in the terms of post-Enlightenment subjectivist theology of God as the One in whom humanity is in the image, the first emphasis is on the One God, and only secondarily on God's Threeness. Greek theology was able to preserve God's ontological Threeness through its understanding of God's Fatherhood as the 'origin' of the Godhead, and its insistence on the begetting of the Son and the proceeding of the Spirit from God's Fatherhood. But as Karl Rahner has shown, beginning with Aquinas, Western theology emphasized God's Fatherhood as the common essence of the Godhead, rather than as the origin of divinity.[29]

The question of origin and relation within the Trinity is

---

[27]See e.g., Juan Luis Segundo, *Grace and the Human Condition*, vol. 2 of *A Theology for Artisans of a New Humanity*, John Drury (ET), (Maryknoll, 1973).

[28]The full development of the history of Subjectivism in theology is outside the scope of this study. For excellent reflections on it, and illustrations of extrinsicism in theology, see EL Mascall, *Recovery of Unity* (London, 1958), and L Bouyer, *The Spirit and Form of Protestantism* (London, 1956).

[29]Rahner, *op. cit.*, pp. 16-18. 'Here the first topic under study is not God the Father as the unoriginate origin of divinity and reality, but as the essence common to all three persons. Such is the method which has prevailed ever since. Thus the treatise of the Trinity locks itself in even more splendid isolation, with the ensuing danger that the religious mind finds it devoid of interest. It looks as if everything which matter for us in God has already been said in the treatise *On the One God*'.

obviously complex. In fact, as Barth says, it is '*the* divine mystery'.[30] Because of the mystery, many prefer to avoid the topic as irrelevant theological speculation. However, the nature of the relations within the Trinity is of fundamental significance for the doctrine of grace. Obviously, to speak of origin (as with speaking of substance) within God is hazardous. It immediately provokes temporal images, suggesting a time when the Son and Spirit were 'not'. Also the distinctions between the Persons might be imagined so clearly as to lead to tri-theistic connotations. Further, it suggests relations of superiority and supremacy. To overcome these misconceptions Aquinas referred to 'origin' within God as an act of God's nature in which he wills, knows, and loves himself. Origination must not be misunderstood as conveying change within God. For as Aquinas says, 'a mutable way of being is altogether foreign to God's nature'. [31]

However, this distinction has been a difficult one for the Church to comprehend, and the discussion of the origin of the Three Persons in the Trinity has lead (still leads?) to serious controversy and confusion.[32] The nature of the Father/Son relationship within the Trinity is of pivotal importance in understanding God's triunity and thus for understanding grace. As TF Torrance says, in referring to the Son as Son *of* the Father,

[30]Barth, *CD* I/1, p. 495. Aquinas writes, 'the basis for distinctness within the godhead is origin'. (*Summa Theologia*, TC O'Brien (ET), *Father, Son and Holy Ghost*. Ia. 33-43, vol. 7 (Oxford, 1976) Ia. 41, 1 *resp*., p. 159.

[31]Aquinas, *op. cit.*, Ia. 41, 2, ad 3, p. 165. Aquinas asserts that the begetting of the Son occured from the Father's nature by his will. Thus, Aquinas repeatedly stresses that to say 'begetting' and 'begotten' is the same thing as to say 'Father' and 'Son': 'in speaking of begetting and being born, says, "in other words being the Father and being the Son"' (Ia. 41, 1, ad 2 p. 161 - quoting Lombard, *I Sent*. 26,2; cf. Ia. 33, 2 ad 4 p. 11).

[32]For example, if the Father is the begetter, and the Son is the begotten one, then it is logical to conclude that the Father is the underived God and the Son is the derived God. The Father is supreme and prior, the Son is subordinant and secondary. Athanasius strenuously avoided granting the Father priority or superiority over the Son and Spirit. He insisted that the Son and Spirit are as much God as the Father, 'for each is whole and proper to the other, so that the same things are said of each except that one is called Father and the other Son', (*Contra Arianos*, 3.3-4; (cf. 2.33ff.; 3.1ff.; 4.1).

'he is not thought of as derived or caused, for he is Son *of* the Father as the Father is Father *of* the Son: thus the *of* belongs to the full mutuality of the Father and of the Son within the one unchangeable Being of the one God, without any kind of superiority or inferiority being implied'.[33]

Without some image for the origination of the Son and Spirit, 'relationship' might be imagined as a constraining ontological category within God - unless God is triune, God is not God. It was precisely to avoid this misunderstanding that the Cappadocians stressed the Father as the cause of the Godhead. However, rather than this notion leading to either subordinationist, modalist, or monotheistic conclusions, John Zizioulas offers the helpful insight that this stresses the meaning of God having his 'being in triune communion'. 'The fact that God owes His existence to the Father, that is to a person, means (a) that His "substance", His being, does not constrain Him (God does not exist because He cannot but exist), and (b) that communion is not a constraining structure of His existence (God is not communion, does not love, because He cannot but be in communion and love)'.[34] Reference to the Father as the begetter, and the Son as the begotten clarifies and affirms the centrality of freedom and the meaning of personhood within the very being of God. God's being is the consequence of his freely established communion as the triune God. This provides the basis for a new definition of freedom and personhood, for rather than freedom being the capacity of an individual to formulate independent choices, freedom is the expression of personal life in communion. God's freedom is in his communion, and his communion is the basis for his freedom.[35] This understanding of the relation between freedom, personhood and communion protects against the erroneous supposition that grace is merely an act of the Father's will. Rather, grace is the expression of the personal, free being

---

[33]TF Torrance, *Theology in Reconciliation* (Grand Rapids, 1965) p. 252.

[34]Zizioulas, *Being As Communion: Studies in Personhood and the Church* (London, 1985), p. 18.

[35]This obviously has profound implications for human freedom. Cf. Zizioulas, p.18.

of God in triune relationship.

However, if the above-mentioned cautions regarding reference to the Father as the 'source' of the Godhead are neglected, serious misunderstandings about the nature of God, and thus the nature of grace can emerge. The most critical misunderstanding is that one can posit God (the Father) as being something (one?) in himself different than he is towards humanity in Christ. There is a God behind the back and above his self-disclosure in Christ. This has profound, tragic implications for christology, and thus soteriology. *First*, the idea can emerge that God is gracious towards some people in Christ, but responds differently towards others outside of Christ. This notion is especially evident in scholastic Calvinism and is illustrated by the admonition of John Owen not to let the revelation of God's love disclosed in Christ 'swallow up' the dim figure of the Father who lurks behind the Son. 'Otherwise faith would lead us astray into a false security'. Owen argues that love is not God's nature but an act of his will; thus, he can as 'naturally' be wrathful toward some as he can be loving toward others.[36] With this view of God, grace can be conceived of as an act of God's will, his monarchical condescension granting favour and forgiveness to his undeserving human subjects. As an act of his will, rather than his nature, one is never sure if and to whom he is being gracious.[37] This could lead either of the opposite conclusions of dogmatic dualism or dogmatic universalism. In viewing grace as God's sovereign inscrutable will, one could develop the dualistic conclusion that God is free to will and establish the salvation of whomever he pleases. Or, one could reach the universalistic conclusion that the God of sovereign love must certainly efficaciously will and

---

[36] J Owen, *op. cit.*, pp. 282-3. Owen goes so far as to say, 'We deny that all mankind are the object of that love of God'. (p. 115). Similar ideas are given contemporary expression by JI Packer and even Emil Brunner. See JI Packer, *Evangelism and the Sovereignty of God* (Leicester, 1961); Packer, 'Introduction' to Owen, *op. cit.*; Brunner, *op. cit.*

[37] This notion is expressed by John Owen who says, 'everything that concerns us is an act of his free will and good pleasure, and not a natural, necessary act of his Deity' (*op. cit.*, p. 115). Thus, Owen elevates 'will' as the highest and determinative attribute of God's three faculties: 'reason', 'will' and 'emotion'.

establish the salvation of all.

*Second*, this can lead to the separation of grace from Christ. God can easily be gracious to people outside of Christ. Christ becomes almost a dispensable moment in salvation history. This idea is evident in Orthodox and Catholic notions of the Church as an extention of the Incarnation. It is also evident in contemporary notions of cosmic grace, omnipresent in the world because God is omnipresent. God is constrained by his love to save everyone. In fact, if he failed to save all, he would fail to be God.

## III The Trinitarian doctrine of God and the Trinitarian Nature of Grace
A The Distinctive Pattern of Trinitarian Grace
The pivotal point for the doctrine of grace is the doctrine of the Triune God. If in Jesus Christ the fullness of God in his grace and truth is revealed (Jn 1.14), then Christology provides the starting point and the foundation for the doctrine of the Trinity. As James Torrance says, "we must first look long and hard at Who Christ is, before we can adequately answer What he has done and How he has done it".[38] One's understanding of the incarnation of God as the man, Jesus of Nazareth, is the beginning point for a trinitarian approach to the relation of grace and faith in salvation. This provides an approach across the theological abyss which divides universalism and dualism, and brings clarity to the relationship of God's sovereignty and humanity's response of faith. As an alternative to the four predestinarian and syngergistic approaches described above, another option is proposed in this article: 5) *onto-relational participation*.[39] The stress of the Bible is neither on a sovereign God, nor on humanity's response of faith and obedience. Rather, the stress is on God taking the initiative to establish relationship with

---

[38]JB Torrance, 'The Vicarious Humanity of Christ' in *The Incarnation*, TF Torrance (ed.), (Edinburgh, 1981), p. 144.

[39]For a discussion of the concept of onto-relational personhood, see TF Torrance, *The Mediation of Christ* (Exeter, 1983) p. 57f.; and J Zizioulas, *op. cit.*

*God, Grace and Salvation*

humanity. In a trinitarian understanding of grace, one recognizes that grace has a threefold bi-polar movement: from the Father to the incarnate Son in the Spirit; from the Son on behalf of humanity in the Spirit to the Father; from humanity in the Spirit through the Son to the Father.

God not only offers himself to humanity. In the Spirit through the Son God offers humanity to himself. Salvation is not simply *by* Christ, as if he died to purchase blessings for humanity that can be received upon fulfilment of the conditions of repentance, faith, and obedience. Rather, salvation is *in* Christ, as one participates through the Spirit in his perfect life of repentance, faith, and obedience lived vicariously on humanity's behalf. God's sovereignty in grace is complete. He not only extends to humanity his 'unmerited favour', he also provides humanity's response to that favour. Grace is understood most adequately when it is viewed as God's gift of himself in relationship to humanity, and his gift of humanity in relationship to himself. In Christ one not only encounters the movement of grace from God to humanity: God coming to humanity for personal communion to which one must respond in faith. One also encounters the movement of grace from humanity to God: Christ responding on humanity's behalf in a life of perfect faith, obedience, and worship.

Humanity's being has been ontologically reconstituted within the triune communion through the Spirit in the Son. But this is not an automatic, impersonal reconstitution (rebirth). Rather, it is inherently relational, and relationships entail a bipolar response.[40] Christ has already responded to the Father on behalf of all humanity. However, to participate in this, one must in faith be adopted by the Spirit into the humanity of the Son. Thus, God's sovereign grace and humanity's responsibility in faith are not in opposition. There is a relationship between

[40]David Cline notes that what stands out in the biblical chronicle of God's relationship with humanity is its personal, relational character. 'Communion, fellowship, personal relationship is not a thing ... It may be initiated by one, but it must be sustained by two', 'Predestination in Biblical Thought', *TSF Bulletin* (Summer, 1973) p. 3.

284

God's being and human being established in Jesus Christ. This onto-relation is open to humanity, for through the Spirit people are adopted into it. People participate in this adoption through a response of faith, gratitude, worship and service. As Athanasius says, in the Incarnation, the divine Son took to himself human nature in order to offer to God on behalf of humanity the worship, faith and obedience which sinful humanity was incapable of offering, and to bear for humanity the wrath and judgment of God which sinful humanity deserved. As Athanasius says, the Incarnation demonstrates to us 'the distinctive pattern of grace'.[41]

The distinctive pattern of grace as revealed in the Incarnation provides an alternative to the stalemate between predestination and synergism in the debate over the sovereignty of grace in salvation. Several concepts which were developed by the early Church to understand the nature of the Son's relation with the Father, and of the Son's relationship with humanity in the man, Jesus Christ are foundational to a trinitarian, incarnational doctrine of grace.

## B The Perichoretic Nature of Trinitarian Grace

The early Church laboured over the formulation of appropriate words to describe the nature of the Trinity and the Incarnation. Applying the terms the Fathers developed in their effort to understand the christological and trinitarian issues to soteriology yields significant clarity into the relation of grace and faith in salvation. Though their acceptance theologically was (is) surrounded by controversy, the meaning and intent of the terms *homoousios, hypostasis,* and later, *perichoresis* were pivotal in constructing a trinitarian Christology and thus a trinitarian soteriology. These classical tools are integral to formulating a contemporary understanding of the relation between God's grace and human faith in the process of salvation. Rather than review the meanings of the homoousion and the hypostatic union, which have been ably explored by others, the remainder of this article will focus solely on the lesser studied concept of *perichoresis,*

---

[41]Athanasius, *op. cit.,* 1. 15-16; cf. 3.19.

God, Grace and Salvation

and develop some of its implications for the doctrine of grace.[42]

1 The Movement of Perichoretic Grace in the Incarnation
*Perichoresis* was first used in Christian theology to describe the
union of divine and human natures in Jesus Christ. The original
meaning of *perichoresis* was to encircle or encompass. It was
used in classical Greek theology to describe the permeation of
matter by God.[43] The Cappadocians applied this term to
Christology to describe the relation between the divine and human
natures in Christ. Gregory of Nazianzus wrote that the divine and
human names of Christ can not be ascribed to two different
persons. Rather, the two sets of names are to be regarded as
'being mingled like the natures and flowing (*pericôrêsôn*) into
one another, according to the law of their intimate union'.[44]
*Perichoresis* came to be defined as an intimate union through
which the divine nature enters into human nature, interpenetrating
it, and taking it into communion with God. This mutual 'in-
existence' or 'mingling' occurs without confusing or mixing the
divine and human natures into one divine-human nature, yet also
without separating them into two divided natures.

*Perichoresis* is another way of expressing 'the four adverbs of
Chalcedon'.[45] The two natures are united in an unconfused and

---

[42] For excellent reflections of the relation of the homoousion and hypostatic
union to the doctrine of grace see, Alasdair Heron, 'Homoousion with the
Father', and JB Torrance, 'The Vicarious Humanity of Christ' in TF Torrance
(ed.), *The Incarnation*, pp. 58-87, 127-47; JB Torrance, 'The Incarnation and
"Limited Atonement"', *EQ* 55, (1983) pp. 83-94.

[43] Etymologically, *perichoresis* means 'reciprocal containing'. It is probably
derived from the verb *chorein* which signifies the permeation of all things by
God. For background on the word see, GL Prestige, *God in Patristic Thought*,
2nd edn., (London, 1952) pp. 289-91.

[44] Gregory Nazianzen, *Ep. CI: To Cleodonus Against Apollinarius*, in
*Nicene and Post-Nicene Fathers*, VII, p. 440. (cf. Gregory of Nyssa, *Contra
Eunomius* Book 1, 95 (MPG 280B)). Prestige notes the use of
αηντιπεριχωρεὥ, 'interchangeable' in a gloss in Leontius of Byzantium, *c.
Nest. and Eut.* 2, (MPG 1320B). Leontius says we can speak of the two
natures of Christ interchangeably. (Prestige, *op. cit.*, p. 292).

[45] The pivotal affirmation of the Church Fathers at Chalcedon was belief in
'One and the same Christ, Son, Lord, only-begotten, confessed in two natures
(ἐν δύο φύσεσιν), without confusion (ἀουγχύτος), without conversion

286

unmixed, undivided and inseparable *perichoresis*. This is a one-sided process for the initiative is God's. God penetrates humanity taking it into himself. Humanity does not penetrate God. God in grace assumes sinful human nature into union with himself through the Divine/man Jesus Christ. In Christ, human nature is perfected, achieving its *telos*. In essence, *perichoresis* describes the movement of grace - God taking humanity into relationship with himself through the God/man Jesus. Salvation is possible not only because Jesus was fully divine, but precisely because Jesus was fully human. Jesus is not just the revealer of authentic humanity, he ontologically establishes it. His humanly divine life is not just the model for others' lives. His life is the basis for others' life. When people participate through the Spirit in Christ, they become authentic persons, sharing in the Son's personhood.

Symmetry (synergism) is impossible because sinful humans are incapable of making a personal response to God. Since their pursuit of an hypostasis independent from God cuts humanity off from personal being, God must make their response on their behalf. Through the perichoretic union of human and divine natures in Christ, God in Christ made the response of faith and love to God which humanity was unwilling and unable to make. Through this *perichoresis*, people become persons as they participate in Christ's humanity. Through the union of Christ's humanity with the Person of the Son of God, people vicariously (through the Incarnate Son) participate in the triune communion. Athanasius wrote, 'when the Lord, as man, was washed in the Jordan it was we who were washed in Him and by Him. And when He received the Spirit, it was we who by Him were made recipients of it'.[46]

## 2  The Movement of Perichoretic Grace within the Trinity

---

(ἀτρέπτως), without division (ἀδιαιρέτως), without separation (ἀχωρίστως)'. These adverbs are central for understanding the nature of grace, and *perichoresis* is a term which summarizes the hypostatic union which Chalcedon described through these adverbs.

[46]Athanasius, *op. cit.*, 1: 47,48.

The perichoretic movement of grace in not just within the divine/human natures in Christ. *Perichoresis* also characterizes the triune communion *ad intra*.[47] Communion is the mutual participation of persons in another's life and being. *Perichoresis* explains the meaning of passages such as Jn 10. 38: ' ... know and understand that the Father is in Me, and I in the Father'. Through reflecting on this passage, pseudo-Cyril developed the second dimension of *perichoresis* - within the Trinity. He states that 'I am in the Father and the Father is in me' expresses the *perichoresis* in one another of the *hypostasis* of the Father and the Son.[48] The relation of the Three Persons is perichoretic, such that their being and action interpenetrate one another. The Father is in the Son. The Son is in the Father. Both are in the Spirit and the Spirit is in both. They are one in essence and in love in such a way that their relations constitute their personhood.

The notion of *perichoresis* clarifies simultaneously the Oneness and the Threeness of the Trinity, avoiding the ever-present errors of tritheism and modalism. The distinctiveness of their personal characteristics as Father, Son and Spirit is not diminished by their communion but rather is secured and enhanced. As Moltmann says, 'the Persons themselves constitute both their differences and their unity'.[49] Viewed perichoretically, the Trinity is not composed of three individuals who enter into a relationship with one another. That would be tritheism. Nor is the Trinity three modes or repetitions of the being of the one God. That would be modalism. Instead, the threeness and the unity of God are linked together is such a way that the threeness is not dissolved into the

---

[47]The Council of Florence affirmed the doctrine of circuminsession, which is the Latin approximation of *perichoresis* (it is not exactly equivalent), saying 'because of this unity [of nature] the Father is completely in the Son and completely in the Holy Spirit; the Son completely in the Father, completely in the Holy Spirit; the Holy Spirit completely in the Father, completely in the Son'. (*DS* 1331). Hilary also gave early expression to this in *De Trinitate* IV, 40; VII, 31-2 (*MPL* 10,226). For a discussion of this see A Deneffe SJ, 'Perichoresis, Circumincessio, Circuminsessio', *ZKT* 47 (1923), p. 507f.

[48]Cyril, *de Sacrosancta Trin.* 23. See also John of Damascus, *De Fide Orthodoxa*, I, 8 (MPG 94, 829A).

[49]Moltmann, *op. cit.*, p. 175.

unity nor the unity divided by the threeness.  They are One God in
three Persons without confusion or separation.[50]

3  The Movement of Perichoretic Grace in Salvation
The perichoretic nature of the union of divine and human natures
in Christ, and of the triune communion of Father, Son and Spirit
has profound implications for the understanding of grace and of
salvation.  Clarity is brought to the debates over God's role and
humanity's role in salvation, and the extent of God's sovereignty
and of humanity's freedom.  Viewed perichoretically, the role of
God and of humanity in Christ can not be divided or separated,
confused or mingled.  They interpenetrate as God in Christ takes
humanity into the triune communion, and as people participate in
this adoption by responding in faith to and by the work of the
Holy Spirit.

a) Implications of Perichoresis for Grace
This has far-reaching consequences for the understanding of grace.
Grace is being-in-communion.  God is gracious in himself,
because he has his being in triune communion.  And, God is
gracious toward humanity because in Christ by the Spirit
humanity is adopted into the triune communion (grace). Grace is
inherently relational--onto-relational. This reveals fundamental
inadequacies in prevalent concepts of grace.  *First*, to perceive
grace as the sacramental infusion of the essence of God into the
souls of persons is to diminish grace into a substance rather than
a relationship.  *Second*, to perceive grace as God's cosmic
presence is inherently an impersonal notion of relationship.
Communion implies a bipolar response.  It cannot be either
something automatic, or something one-sidely imposed.  *Third*,
to assert that God must inevitably bring all creation to salvation
makes communion itself a constraining structure of God's
existence.  Communion becomes the Lord, rather than the Lord

---

[50]This is obviously a form of unity in difference and difference in unity
which does not fit with normal human conceptions of relationships.  As John
of Damascus says, understanding how the Father, Son and Holy Spirit are
'united without confusion and divided without separation indeed transcends
thought', *Exposition of the Orthodox Faith*, I.8.  SDF Salmond (ET), in
*Nicene and Post-Nicene Fathers* IX (Oxford, 1889), p. 6.

being the Father, Son and Spirit in triune communion. *Fourth*, to perceive salvation as the consequence of God's decree, an act of his will, makes 'will' the constraining structure of God's existence and denies the sovereignty of God as the Triune Persons.

b) Implications of Perichoresis for Soteriology
Thus, this also has far-reaching consequences for the understanding of salvation. Salvation is onto-relational. It is neither solely ontological, as if it were an automatic, impersonal intrinsic encounter with God either through his cosmic presence or through the sacramental impartation of the being of God into humanity with an *ex opere operato* efficacy. Nor is it solely relational, as if it were an extrinsic encounter through faith without any ontological change in people in Christ. Both the ontological and the relational dimensions must be affirmed for an adequate understanding of salvation. Humanity's being has been ontologically reconstituted in Christ's atoning life, death and resurrection. This ontological reconstitution is not impersonal but personal - it is onto-*relational*. To participate in this reconstitution, one must in faith be adopted by the Spirit into the incarnate Son's relationships within the Trinity. This onto-relational perspective contributes vital insight to the understanding of the *ordo salutis*.

*First*, salvation is complete in Christ. All parts of humanity's salvation are complete in the action of the Triune God in Jesus Christ. He is the Head and Representative of the New Humanity. He assumed fallen humanity to transform humanity's being-in-isolation into being-in-communion through his vicarious life of repentance, faith, and obedience. His sacrificial self-offering on the Cross was vindicated and fulfilled in his resurrection. Christ's vicarious, victorious life, death and resurrection is offered on behalf of all of humanity, not just a portion of humanity. God wills the salvation of everyone, and Christ represents all in his all-inclusive humanity.

*Second*, salvation is exclusively in Christ. There is no salvation outside of or apart from union with Christ, through being adopted by the Spirit into the perfect human response to God of the Incarnate Son. To be outside of communion with the Father through the Son in the Spirit is to persist in being-in-isolation which is to persist in being-unto-death. To reject adoption in Christ, who is the only way for the restoration of humanity to communion is actually to choose hell over heaven. Both are present realities, and the Final Judgment is the bringing to light of that darkness. It will expose what has been (partially) hidden in this life. The light of the Gospel exposes this darkness and deadness, but the message of the Gospel is inherently not about death but about life. The Gospel is light and not darkness, though the light inevitably exposes humanity's preference for the darkness.

*Third*, salvation calls for people's response of faith in Christ. The Gospel is the good news that humanity's personhood is ontologically constituted in Christ. One's faith or lack of faith does not alter this ontological fact. But, this personhood is relational. Unless one participates in this reconstitution by the Spirit in faith, one persists in being impersonal. Therefore, the proclamation of the Gospel to all people by the Church is an intensely urgent privilege. It is the urgent invitation to people to participate in the restoration of their personhood through the Spirit in the Son with the Father. As Zizioulas says, 'being means life and life means communion'.[51] Peter Fransen describes this correlation between personhood and fellowship as 'the fundamental law of the person'. If we neglect this law, we 'belittle' ourselves.[52] To be outside of relationship with Christ is to be less than a person. The Church enters the world with an urgent commission to beseech all people to be reconciled with God through the Spirit in the Son lest they perish.

The trinitarian, perichoretic nature of grace provides a basis for an alternate approach across the traditional theological impasse

---

[51]Zizioulas, *op. cit.*, p. 16.

[52]Peter (Piet) Fransen, *The New Life of Grace*, Georges Dupont (ET), (New York:, 1969), p. 60.

between the sovereignty of God and the freedom of humanity in salvation. The traditional categories of predestination and synergism are obviously not void of all truth.[53] They would not have occupied dominant roles in the Church's theological reflection if they did not express some truth and at least partially coincide with the Biblical witness. It is not claimed in this study that an alternate, trinitarian and perichoretic approach is *the* truth which should replace all other views. Rather, it is proposed as a way of overcoming the theological stalemate between the two sets of views, and of shedding more light on the nature of grace and salvation, as well as God's predestination and humanity's response. Viewed from a trinitarian, perichoretic perspective, both dualism and universalism are inadequate as Christian dogmas. It is impossible and inappropriate to formulate eschatological positions of either dogmatic dualism or dogmatic universalism which are biblically consistent, and expressive of the trinitarian, perichoretic nature of grace. Neither view fully coincides or is reconcilable with the biblical evidence or with trinitarian, incarnational theology.

God's salvation of all people is universally complete in Christ for all creation has been summed up and united in him (Col. 1.16-17). From the perspective of the triune God (which is the only true perspective), he has reconstituted the being of humanity from being-in-isolation to being-in-communion. That is biblical universalism. However, people can persist in denying this sovereign action of the triune God and pursue the impossible,

[53]Some might question why the doctrines of election and predestination have not been addressed in this article, when they are such pivotal doctrines in the traditional soteriological debates. They are not neglected because they are considered of secondary importance. An understanding of election is integral to understanding the relation of grace and faith in salvation. Rather, *perichoresis* is proposed as a doctrine which further clarifies the meaning of election and its relation to the response of faith and obedience from humanity. In fact, the great election passages, essentially express the perichoretic nature of grace: 'I will take you for My people, and I will be your God' (Ex. 6.7; Hos. 2.23; cf. Eph. 1.4-5). God takes the initiative in drawing people into relation with himself, and this initiative entails the response from among those whom he elects of being his faithful people. 'I will say "You are My people!" and they will say, "Thou art My God!"'

illusory assertion of self-defined being. That is biblical dualism. The eschatological outcome of human destiny is in Christ. He is both the Judge and the justifier of humanity's onto-relational personhood. The Church is not called to make judgments about the salvation of other people. The Church is first called to live with gratitude over the wonder of her adopted participation in the triune communion. The Church is also called to proclaim with urgent compassion the invitation and necessity of all people to enter into Christ through the Spirit to the glory and praise of the Triune God.

# 15

# What does it mean to say, 'God is Love'?

EBERHARD JÜNGEL

Everyone on earth knows love. But do they therefore *understand* what they know? Do they know what love is? And what does the word *love* mean, when we associate it with *God*? What is meant in the New Testament when God and love are unreservedly identified with one another? What, therefore, does it mean to say, 'God is love'?

In attempting to answer this question I want to deal first with the difficulty which nowadays generally confronts us when we use the word *God*. In the second part of the paper it will be asked what the word *love* means when we dare to join together with the first letter of John in the pithy affirmation that 'God is love'.

It is part of the very core of all religious experience that the holy God does not appear in the context of human reality without fundamentally shaking this same context. 'Woe is me, for I am lost!' confessed the prophet Isaiah when he caught sight of the threefold Yahweh. And two thousand years later Friedrich Schiller's poetical language of transcendental reflection expresses it thus:

> 'When in humanity's sad nakedness
> you stand before the law's greatness,
> when guilt neareth holiness' array,
> there fadeth 'fore truth's ray
> your virtue. Before the ideal
> fleeth cowardly the abashed deed.
> No creature hath this goal achieved,
> o'er this ghastly gorge doth lead
> neither skiff nor bridge's bow.
> Nowhere findeth an anchor ground.'

God as the abyss of being which rends all earthly contexts asunder - whoever knows nothing of this side of religious experience may confidently mark himself out as lacking any inkling of true religion.

In this case, however, the Christian faith also appears to be without an inkling of religion. Because talk of the *loving God* is characteristic of the Christian faith. 'God is love'; so we read in the first letter of John. Is the hard core of all religious experience thereby devitalized? I would like to demonstrate the contrary in this paper. In two steps I intend to show that the God who is love elementarily and radically interrupts our lives. In the first part we will reflect on the necessity to speak of God at all. In the second part we will then clarify what deserves to be called love, if God and love are indeed identical with one another.

## I

'How can you bring yourself to say "God" time after time? How can you expect that your readers will take the word in the sense in which you wish it to be taken? ... What word of human speech is so misused, so defiled, so desecrated as this! All the innocent blood that has been shed for it has robbed it of its radiance. All the injustice that it has been used to cover has effaced its features. When I hear the highest called "God", it sometimes seems almost blasphemous'.

The Jewish philospher of religion, Martin Buber, shares these sentences from a conversation with 'a noble old thinker'.[1] The questions of this old man belong to each earnest attempt to use the word 'God'. It is important that they accompany the word 'God' whenever and wherever it is used. For there is no worse blasphemy than a conscious or even thoughtless misuse of this word. On this point not only all earnest Christians but Christians together with Jews are in agreement with earnest atheists who, when pointing accusingly to the ruinous

---

[1] M Buber, *Eclipse of God. Studies in the Relation between Religion and Philosophy* (1977), pp. 15-18.

consequences of religious God-talk, say in their own atheistic manner: Thou shalt not take the name of the Lord, thy God, in vain. It would at all times do us good to recognize earnest and deliberative atheism as a *negative* reminder of the severity of the first and second commandments. We must likewise acknowledge the questions of that old man, when we nevertheless dare to use the word 'God' and speak of *him*.

It cannot, however, be the consequence of all those, ever so correct, references to the atrocious misuse of the word 'God' in human history and to the possible misuse of this word that we should simply be silent. It cannot in any case be the consequence for Jewish and for Christian faith in God that we should cease to speak of God and instead - be it because we are stifled, resigned or ever so pious - should be silent about him.

Indeed, there have been and there are impressive attempts in world religions and even in Christianity to be silent about God in a positive sense. In silence one calls him to mind and tries to conform one's mind to him. And it must in no way be a deceased, a dead God whom one silently calls to mind. Our human thoughts and words are indeed hardly suitable to bring the living God to expression in an undistorted way. What could be more obvious than to consider each and every use of the word 'God' as being at best a provisional use which as such must yield as readily as possible to the authentic attitude toward God? All of our talk about God would then only be 'one last word prior to being silent'.[2] It would at best be a silence which is more precisely expressed through speech. That is without a doubt an impressive view and a pious way of life. I once actually saw it being performed, when in a television discussion between representatives of the major world religions - in which, by the way, a Marxist strangely enough, or perhaps characteristically enough, took part - each participant at the end of the conversation was asked to state briefly what was really essential in his religion or confession. There were some stirring statements - for example, from the Catholic Karl Rahner and from

---

[2]Cf. K Rahner, *Grundkurs des Glaubens* (1976), p. 56, cf. pp. 32ff.

the Arch-Protestant Helmut Gollwitzer. And yet their words faded, when the Buddhist's turn came to state what was really essential. He said - *nothing*. Instead, he laid his finger on his lips. When you're dealing with God, lay your finger on your lips! Everything in us is silent! No doubt an extremely impressive gesture of Buddhistic - and not only of Buddhistic - piety. What could be more appropriate over and against the misuse of the word 'God' than this position? And yet, this can hardly be the position of the Christian faith. The apostle Paul expressed it pithily: 'necessity is laid upon me. Woe to me, if I do not preach the Gospel!'[3] Paul who otherwise gladly and pertinently referred to himself as a *free* man was apparently unfree in this regard. He did not have the freedom to be silent about God. He had to speak of him.

'I believed, and so I spoke'; so we read in 2 Cor. 4:13. This has to do with a quote from the Old Testament which Paul took from Psalm 116. New and Old Testament, Christians and Jews appear to be in total agreement, when it comes to this point: God may not - nay, God cannot be kept silent. Whoever would wish to be silent about God, would be neither a true Jew nor a true Christian; he would at best be guilty of self-misunderstanding.

Martin Buber also dared to contradict that critical man with whom he conversed. Yet he did not ignore his objections and go on to speak of God regardless; instead, he wrestled with these objections. He made them his own and, as a result, spoke of God in a manner which was not contrary to these objections but rather in agreement with them. And indeed, we can only speak of God in a credible manner when we do not ignore anything which appears to (and actually *does*) speak against him. Instead we must contend with these objections (which are always our own objections as well) so that our talk of God may verify itself in the face of these same objections. In this way Buber replied to the man: 'Yes, ... [the Word 'God'] is the most heavy-laden of all human words. None has become so soiled, so mutilated. Just for this reason I may not abandon it. Generations of men have laid

---

[3] 1 Cor. 9:16.

the burden of their anxious lives upon this word and weighed it to the ground; it lies in the dust and bears their whole burden. The races of man with their religious factions have torn the word to pieces; they have killed for it and died for it, and it bears their finger-marks and their blood ... Certainly, they draw caricatures and write "God" underneath; they murder one another and say "in God's name". But when all madness and delusion fall to dust, when they stand over against Him ... and no longer say, "He, He" but rather sigh "Thou", shout "Thou", all of them the one word, and when they then add "God", is it not the real God whom they all implore, the One Living God, the God of the children of man? Is it not He who *hears* them? And just for this reason is not the word "God", the word of appeal, the word which has become a *name*, consecrated in all human tongues for all times?"[4]

The word 'God' is indispensable, therefore, because man calls to God, because man can call upon God, because 'God' is a word of invocation, an interjection, because it has its *Sitz im Leben* in highly existential exclamatory statements before it appears in theological declaratory statements. For when we call upon God, the most remarkable thing in the world occurs: in such an *exclamation* - 'Oh God! My God!' - we interrupt our everyday life, we even interrupt ourselves. And we do this in order to come *forth from ourselves*. This word is therefore indispensable, since in and with this word 'God' a person can and should go forth from himself in joy and sorrow, since we can *elementarily interrupt* our life with this word of exclamation and salutation so that we are no longer solely and uninterruptedly by ourselves. Rather, being truly and elementarily interrupted in our egocentricity we are, from now on, close to God.

To be addressed always means to be interrupted in one's own life by another. Calling upon God presupposes exactly this: the state of having been addressed by God. When we call upon God and say 'You' to him, we realize in the most concrete manner the fact that we have always been people who have been addressed by God. And to this extent we actualize in such an invocation of

---

[4]*Ibid.*, p. 17f.

God the fact that we do not come to ourselves when we are by ourselves; rather, that we must be *outside of ourselves* in order to be able to come *to ourselves*. No interruptions of our life are more elementary or more consequential than those which we experience, when we allow ourselves to be addressed by God and to respond to this divine address by now addressing Him ourselves - in other words - by saying 'God' and 'You'. Whoever says 'God' and 'You', is being so interrupted that he is in a very acute sense *outside of himself* (Luther), whereby he at this point - outside of himself - is able to come to himself in a new way and is able to gain new strength - a stength which he does not by any means find on his own. When a human being is being interrupted in such an elementary way so that he is outside of himself, he then can become a *different*, a *new*, a free person.

This happens in faith, in love and in hope. Faith, love and hope are elementary interruptions of the context of human life which is normally determined by our being active, by our producing and earning, by our efforts toward self-fulfillment. The human being who is busy fulfilling himself wants to *have* - not only something, not only something more; rather, he wants himself: self-possession, self-control are his ideal. 'For when I possess myself, I am *free*', thinks the person who is busy fulfilling himself. 'I am. But we do not have ourselves. Therefore we must first of all become'.[5] Where however in faith, love or hope the word 'God' arises, a human life is being interrupted in such a manner that the ideal of self-possession becomes obsolete as a falsely oriented anthropological category. For in such an interruption a human being appears as a *person* beside his producing and earning. Yes, he can only receive himself when *outside of himself*. *Outside of himself* he is being given to himself. *Outside of himself* he does not have, he does not possess himself. Outside of himself he *is* totally by another - and in exactly this manner he is by himself.

To be outside of oneself, to be elementarily interrupted in one's search for self-fulfillment - that is however an ec-sistence which

[5] E Bloch.

is not only promising but also filled with danger. The human being *can* be utterly endangered by such an elementary interruption. Whoever is outside of himself, can be hurt easily and can definitely be misused. Even the least passionate human being knows this. He loses control over himself. A great deal depends upon where and with whom one actually is when one flits out of oneself. Whoever is outside of himself, we said, leaves himself. For precisely this reason, however, everything depends upon whether one can entrust oneself to something or someone, when one is outside of oneself. And that is, in turn, only the case when I find the way back again into that context of life within which I was elementarily interrupted, and when I can invest the *strength* which I have won outside of myself toward this context, within which I was so elementarily interrupted that I flitted *outside of myself*. When this does not occur and I am hindered in returning to the interrupted context of my life, then the ec-stasy of being-outside-of-oneself is shamelessly being misused.

One needn't think of the great demagogues in order to comprehend how greatly that which does a human being good can also be misused towards harming him. For example, we know how a whole people can be brought outside of itself in a diabolic manner so that it can no longer find a fruitful way back to itself and instead finds a frightful way back to itself or no way back at all. The same can certainly occur in an intimate circle and in the family. And religion is not in any way immune from such excesses.

Thus we will have once again to consider the frightening possibilities of misuse to which the word 'God' is submitted. One can indeed speak of God in such a way that a self-occupied life is perhaps elementarily interrupted and a human ego flits outside of itself, but the God who causes the human ego to leave itself and upon whom the human ego then has to rely can very easily be deformed (through the misuse of the word 'God') into an inhuman super-ego (*Über-Ich*). This super-ego then turns an elementarily interrupted human life into a broken existence. 'God-polluting' is perhaps a cruel but unfortunately all too often an appropriate word. Yet, forgetting about God does not help to prevent such God-pollution; rather, the only thing that helps here is proper, reponsible talk of God. This is what Paul is talking about, when he says that he must proclaim the Gospel - necessity rests upon him.

One could of course understand Paul's admission: 'Necessity is laid upon me. Woe to me, if I do not preach the Gospel', as if the apostle were subject to an overwhelming super-ego, a despot who in his divinity were all too human. The terminology of constraint is unmistakably at hand. And yet, that which constrains the apostle and gives him no other alternative than to speak of God is just about the exact opposite of what consitutes a tyrant. Paul himself says as much, when he defines his talk of God as the proclamation of the *Gospel*. Gospel means: gladdening news. And this news gladdens by making people free; the Gospel is liberating news. Thus the apostle - and not only he but also every Christian - must speak of God, because 'God' is a thoroughly gladsome word, a liberating word. Or, to be more exact: because *God himself* has made the often misused and ever again misusable word 'God' into a gladsome and liberating word.

God - a word which causes joy! God - a word that makes free! Wherever this is not the case, wherever 'God' is a word which instead of spreading freedom and joy causes fear and trembling or merely disperses boredom, then there is no proper talk of God himself; instead, it is talk of a substitute god, probably intended to replace an overwhelming super-ego which we sense to be missing. One could then become so unstable - yes, so frightened, by such a divine lord whose essence solely consists in a concept of abstract omnipotence that one then is only silent about him in powerless rage or in powerless contempt. A God whom one can only fear but cannot love cannot be endured by any half-way healthy human being. In the end such a God won't be worth one more word.

The Christian faith, however, knows 'God' to be a word which

makes people free and joyous. That is how the Christian people
have come to know God, when they came to know God as the God
of Jesus Christ. And in the very same way everyone can come to
know the God who reveals himself in the man Jesus. For in this
man God has defined himself, his divine being. The author of the
first letter of John translated this vibrant definition into human
expression and, for that matter, into a theological declaratory
statement. It is found in 1 John 4:8 and reads simply 'God is
love'.

An element of love is the *language* of love. Every great love
urgently seeks verbal expression. Indeed the expression of love
is no less essential to love than the act of love itself. And every
love story which is at all exciting demands to be *told*. One
doesn't infringe upon God's majesty when one tells of his being
like a love story. On the contrary, one infringes upon God's
majesty when one does not tell the love story about the Creator
of heaven and earth.

And yet, what does it mean to say, 'God is love?' What does the
word 'God' mean, when it is identified with the concept of love?
And what is this love which can be equated with God?

## II

The first answer to the question 'What does 'God is love' mean?'
must make reference to the mysterious character of this truth. For
in love God and man share a mystery, one and the same mystery.
One must speak of a *mystery*, when one begins to speak of God
and of love. For one has always to speak of a mystery when any
type of being opens itself up only *from inside out*. One cannot
penetrate into a mystery from outside or with force. No entrance
to a mystery can be opened from the outside. Its doors only
open-up themselves from the inside.

But when they have opened themselves up, the mystery not only
becomes experiencable, rather, it also becomes thoroughly
cognizable while yet remaining mysterious. Thus it is not the
case that we would be inferring an incognizability in God, in

referring to him as a mystery or the mystery of mysteries. And it is definitely not the case that God would cease to be mysterious once we have gained cognition of him. Rather, herein lies the difference between a mystery and a riddle. A mystery does not cease to be mysterious, even when it has been understood. On the contrary! Yet whoever knows the solution to a riddle, will find that for himself the riddle has lost its riddling character. Whoever, on the other hand, understands a mystery, will discover that the mystery has become even greater. It becomes more interesting and mysterious the more one understands it. This is well known to us from the event of human love. The more two lovers understand each other, and the more intensely they know one another, the more mysterious and interesting they find each other. When, however, one person doesn't find the other person mysterious any longer, then there is no longer any love between the two of them - and probably no longer any vibrant loyalty.

In this sense God also and above all deserves to be called a *mystery*. He becomes all the more mysterious the better one understands him. And the more deeply one enters cognitively into the divine mystery, the more interesting and mysterious it becomes. For God is love. In the event of love cognition and interest reciprocally potentiate one another. In the event of love the mystery of love calls for that understanding which makes this mystery even more mysterious.

The statement 'God is love' is formulated truth. So that it should not coagulate into a formula - and that is the great danger which confronts all formulated theological truth - it must ever again and ever anew be lived and thought about. This truth is being lived wherever people love one another. Therefore the first letter of John insists that we love one another. For 'if we love one another, God abides in us and his love is perfected in us'.[6]

Yet, Christian truth not only wants to be *lived*, it also wants to be *thought about*. This does not mean that this vital activity can only be irritated or even discontinued by abstract reflection;

[6]I Jn 4:12.

on the contrary, thinking maintains this act of life in its purity
and vitality and protects it from self-deception and deterioration.
The Christian faith knows that exactly where it is most vital it is
also at all times threatened by superstition. Just as someone in
our competitive society is more greatly threatened and more
corruptible through his success than through his lack of success,
so also faith is most threatened where it is successful, threatened,
that is to say, by the danger of superstition. And nowhere is this
danger greater than where that climactic statement of the Christian
faith, 'God is love', is so vibrant in the lives of people that they
come to consider themselves to be divine in their love. When I
say this, I am not thinking primarily of the more or less tasteful
array of divine predicates with which human sexuality is nowadays
being adorned. That is only the consequence of the fact that the
church for its part diabolized sexuality for so many centuries.
And diabolization is always the best route toward deification: at
some time or another a turnabout takes place. When considering
the danger of superstition in connection with the sentence 'God is
love', however, I am thinking above all of Ludwig Feuerbach's
famous thesis: In the statement 'God is love' God must be
sacrificed to love in the sense that neighbourly love be
acknowledged as being divine. 'Love conquers God ... for if we
do not sacrifice God to love, we sacrifice love to God'.[7]
According to this, the statement 'God is love' is not supposed to
express the humanity of the loving God but rather the divinity of
loving human beings. God is not love, therefore; rather, love is
divine.

Nowadays, Feuerbach's thesis persists mainly in the somewhat
trivial notion that 'God' is nothing other than the prospering of
love between human beings, whereby both the love between two
people as well as individual and societal works of love with which
people come to each other's aid are intended. Basically, however,
the word 'God' is in this context superfluous. The statement 'God
is love' has been reduced either to the tautology 'love is love' or
to the statement 'love is the best'. And the exhortation 'love one
another' steps into the place of *faith* in God. Love would

---

[7]*The Essence of Christianity*, G Eliot (ET), (New York, 1957), p. 53.

therefore be the death of faith.

Over and against this type of thinking the Christian confession 'God is love' *proceeds* from the conviction that *love* first receives its entire meaning in *faith in God*. Thus, when faith identifies God with love, it sacrifices neither God to love nor love to God. No, love is not to be sacrificed to God! For that too would be superstition, if, for fear that 'God would dissipate into a love for one's fellow man', one would now (despite the sentence 'God is love') so differentiate between the two that God comes to lurk behind love as a type of 'loveless monster'. Faith can afford to identify God and love with each other unreservedly. For faith implies the most strict differentiation between God and man that is possible. When differentiation occurs, when God comes so close to man that man in faith in him can definitively differentiate between himself and God, then God can be identified unreservedly with love. When, however, God truly is love, then 'love never ceases'. Contrary to Feuerbach and his somewhat trivial inheritors the Christian faith is of the conviction that it is to love's *benefit*, when we do not, in identifying God and love with one another, sacrifice God to love, and then go on instead to deify loving people.

No loving human being, of course, *is* love. Nor yet are two people who love one another love. They are loving people. But in the event of love they remain separate from love itself. Loving people themselves are often aware of this in a most tragic way. In a newspaper one could read about a young couple in love who during a vacation trip drove their car into the Adria after having experienced a consummate time of love. At the hotel there was a note upon whch both lovers had expressed their fear that they would never again experience such a *time filled with love*: 'It can never be the same again. Therefore we want to die'. This incident may cause us to shake our heads. Nevertheless, it shows how greatly aware loving people are, how greatly they experience in the event of love that they are *not* love but rather remain separate from love itself. God, he alone, *is* love.[8] We

[8]Regin Prenter.

*experience* love from which, however, we remain acutely distinct when having loving experiences.

Yet, what do we experience? What, that is to say, is love? And what is this God whom we identify with love?

In order to answer this question I must first of all refute a prejudice, a prejudice which frequently and primarily confronts us in Protestant theology. This prejudice goes like this: Self-love or a relationship to one's self (self-relationship) has nothing in any way to do with true love. Wherever self-love or a self-relationship is at hand, that is where we are 'only' (we are told) dealing with *eros* (need-love), with the satisfaction of an elementary desire, of an elementary human need. In contrast to this *eros*, true Christian love is supposedly needless, selfless, without any self-relationship. Such self-forgetting love is then called *agape* (gift-love) and is set up in blatant contradiction to *eros*.

I consider this crass contradiction to be a dangerous abstraction. One can indeed (and one must) *differentiate* between *eros* and *agape*. But this differentiation is only in order when it doesn't lead to a contradiction but instead leads to the proper *relationship* between *eros* and *agape*. In both cases we are definitely dealing with a specific type of self-interest and self-forgetfulness.

Each love is aimed toward a specific *thou*. The loving I looks with pleasure to the loved thou. Where love is, there is vision! - *Ubi amor, ibi oculus!*[9] Part of love is the gaze of love in which the loving I *desires* the loved thou. The I wants to *have* this thou. And in this sense an element of love is certainly always a very specific self-relationship, the self-relationship: I want to have you, and I don't want to have myself without you anymore. Love is something other than amiability. In love I am outside of myself.

[9]Richard of St Victor.

306

With this determination of love a second moment of its being has been expressed. Love's desire in which a loving I wants to *have* the loved thou includes the phenomenon that the loving person does not want himself anymore without this loved thou: without you I am nothing. The loving I treasures the loved thou more than itself. Without self-surrender the loving I cannot and *does not want* to have the loved thou. Love is reciprocal self-surrender, and love's desire, which is a part of love, is the most extreme enemy of rape. The irrefutable self-relationship in every love relationship is hence surpassed by an even greater selflessness. When this happens, one's self-relationship is not somehow annulled; rather, it is given gravity in a proper way, namely in such a way that I find myself foremost and anew by the loved thou. In selfless surrender the loving I forgets itself in such a way that it comes to itself by being close to the loved thou (and thus outside of itself). In this sense we can define the formal structure of every love. Love is - when considered formally - amid an ever so great (and rightfully ever so great) self-relationship an even greater selflessness of unconditional self-surrender.

And God is precisely this. The loving human being participates in this surrender, but it isn't this surrender. It *has* love, but it *is* not love. God *is* amid an ever so great self-relationship an even greater selflessness. God is, already in and of himself, a communion of reciprocal otherness and as such love. He is the selfless Self-surrenderer in the self-relationship of Father, Son and Spirit and the Self-sharer in the Holy Spirit. He is *over-flowing* love. God indeed comes from God, but God does not want to come to himself without having come to humankind.[10] Thus He *is* amid the ever so great Trinitarian self-relationship ever greater and forever greater selflessness. Within this formal definition there is however at the same time a hidden material definition of love which now must be exposed.

When I forget myself in love to such an extent that in order to have the loved thou I surrender myself totally and unconditionally

---

[10]The prologue of the Gospel of John.

to this same person, then love is in part a radical withdrawal from my self. To be sure, such a radical withdrawal from one's self occurs for the benefit of a totally new type of nearness, as we will soon show. But in love that word of Jesus proves to be true in a most profound way: 'Whoever seeks to gain his life will lose it, but whoever loses his life will preserve it'.[11] Our human language expresses this precisely, when we say of a lover: 'He has lost his heart'. The heart is the centre of life in man. It is in the heart that decisions are being made which concern my self. Whoever loses his heart, flits into death's proximity. That is the inexorable earnestness of every love which is inseparable from love's great delight. One doesn't have first to experience unrequited love and the self-despair which the loving I experiences thereafter in order to realize this. Rather, each experience of despair in a loving relationship shows at least indirectly how much loving persons are susceptible to destruction in a successful love relationship which, let it be noted, is much more serious than an unsuccessful love relationship! Because the loving I receives itself totally from the loved thou without which it *does not* want to *be*, therefore, every genuine love in a specific way has death behind it. By making people new, love causes death in a hidden way.

Augustine once said it soberly: *facit in nobis quamdam mortem* - in a certain sense love causes death in us. Love poetry from every generation could sing a song (and not just one!) of this phenomenon. 'For where love awakens, there dies the I, the dark despot'.[12] 'Who named love love? Its true name is death. For when love befalls man, death befalls him' - so we read in a Japanese poem.[13] To this extent both life and death occur in every love. Yes, love is actually the unity of life and death. But this unity does not imply an equal balance. Love disturbs the equilibrium of life and death by putting death in the service of a new life. An equal balance of life and death would also be an overbalance of death. For then death would have the *last* word over and against life. From out of the radical self-withdrawal of

[11]Lk 17:33.
[12]Fr Rückert.
[13]Around 900 BC, poet unknown.

the loving I proceeds, however, a new, a totally new type of nearness. In love the loved thou comes closer to me than I am able to come to myself. And loving people live from this nearness in which I myself am no longer my own nearest neighbour. Thus there emerges in love a unity of life and death. But this unity is a unity for the benefit of life, for the benefit of new, eternal life.

It is this unity of life and death for the benefit of life which is meant, when it is said that '*God* is love'. For this statement is the pertinent expression of the belief that the eternal, living God has in such a way identified himself with the crucified man Jesus that he no longer wants to be the living God without this dead man. And there is still more: God shared the death of the crucified Jesus, because he does not want to be the living God *without us*. 'God is love' means: God does not want to be God without an other, without us. Not without *us* - we who have always trespassed and ever again trespass against God and our neighbour and therefore deserve to be called *sinners*: 'Sinners', that means to be people who are corrupted, corrupted by self-corruption, people who destroy and reject the beauty of being images of God.

No-one loves like God, who turns without any reason not to man in his desirability and attractiveness but to the dead and repulsive man on the cross, whose death show us who we are. Here we see the difference between *eros* and *agape*, between erotic and charitable love. *Agape*, *caritas* loves not only what is already loveable; rather, it is love before there is anything loveable. That which is loveable *becomes* loveable through such love. Only in such a way is love victorious over lovelessness. And it is this victory in which Christians believe.

*Agape*, *caritas* loves the sinner who is totally unworthy of love, who ever again bungles his life and dangerously aids death in obtaining its victories. It is the human being who ever makes death stronger than it already is. Only God loves in such a way that he submits the omnipotence of his eternal life to the power

309

of death in order to conquer death by suffering death. Only God can begin to love where there is nothing worth loving, where he himself is not being loved first. No human being can begin to love on its own - just as no human being can begin to speak, believe or trust on its own. God is *He who loves on his own*, because he himself is *love*, overflowing love, which flow precisely to those places where lovelessness triumphs.

The deepest meaning contained in the sentence 'God is love' consists herein, that the lovelessness which causes one defeat after another in the world of human love and appears to damn our love to powerlessness is not given over to itself; rather, this lovelessness itself experiences love and is thus conquered. Consequently, in the history of humankind, love which according to the standards of the world is totally powerless will prove to be the only true power. Just as God revealed himself as the victor over death in Jesus's resurrection, so he also vouches for the victory of love. To believe in God means to believe in the victory of love *in view of* triumphs of lovelessness and hate and in trust in this divine victory of love (which we don't have to procure) to now oppose in a *human* way the lovelessness in this world with deeds of love. Out of faith in the God who is love there results with necessity - and *with desire*, as Luther rightly used to say - human works of love. For faith on its part becomes active in love.[14]

Such human deeds or works of love which are not directed toward that which is already worth loving but rather come to the aid of that which is totally unworthy of love, and in so doing make it worth loving and worthy of being loved, preserve the *personal relation* which is characteristic of love. (One can only speak of *love of things*, *objects*, etc. in a figurative sense: love is always directed from one person to persons.)[15] In that active human love which corresponds to the love of the cross (*amor crucis*), however, it becomes more obvious than in erotic love

[14]Gal. 5:6.

[15]It is on the other hand to be considered seriously whether the talk of the *love of truth* is a genuine reference or not, inasmuch as truth is at least ascribed an ontological state which is analogous to a person.

310

that love applies to a person in and with his world or, for that matter, to persons in and with their worlds. In such works of love precisely that is being elected which is foolish, weak, low and despised in the world - 'even things which are like nothing'.[16] As such, the personal structure of love always also implies a relationship to the world - be it in the sense that the world participates in the love which applies to loved persons and thus indirectly likewise becomes something like an object of love, or be it in the sense that loved persons are explicitly differentiated from their position in the world and the social worth or worthlessness which is connected with this position. The personalism of love thus transforms, along with loved persons, their being-in-the-world and in this sense also the being of the world. This is especially true for those human works of love which correspond to the love of the cross (*amor crucis*) that they observe extremely sensitively and critically the conditions of human existence so as to make them more humane, even though they cannot be made worthy of being loved.

In such works of human love which not only address themselves to that which is worth loving, but even more to that which is as nothing in the world, in such deeds of human love (which correspond to God's love) we will not confuse ourselves with God. The chance of this occurring is just about as remote as our confusing ourselves with love itself in the experience of erotic love directed towards a thou worthy of our love. In *love* we will not believe in ourselves, just as in *love* we will not despair of ourselves. In faith in the God who *is* and who therefore promises the victory of love, we will gladly be satisfied with the fact that we are precisely that - loving people. And that, as I said, in a double sense; as responsible doers in active love who nonetheless consider that to be worthy of our love which is in actual fact unworthy, and by doing so *make* it worthy of being loved, as well as people in unabashed passion who are not ashamed of their erotic love. One must never be ashamed of love. For in love we share one and the same mystery with God. What more could we ask for?

---

[16]Cf. 1 Cor. 1:27f.

Since we share this mystery with God, we can become that beyond which nothing greater can be said of us, for nothing greater can be said of us than that we are in no respect godly, but in every respect *human* people.

# 16

# Does The New Testament Teach Universal Salvation?[1]

## I HOWARD MARSHALL

'Lord, are only a few people going to be saved? (Lk. 13:23). Some would argue that, since Jesus himself refused to answer this question directly but rather said: 'Make every effort to enter through the narrow door', we cannot answer it and should not try to do so. We are free to assume that 'all' will be saved. Those who take this line, however, fail to note that Jesus goes on to say that 'many will try to enter and will not be able to', which effectively rules out the possibility that Jesus leaves open the universalist position in this particular saying. We cannot on the basis of this text adopt an optimistic agnosticism. The question that Jesus refuses to answer directly is not whether the saved are many or all, but whether they are many or few.

I propose to take up one aspect of the question as to whether all will be saved, namely the evidence provided in the writings of Paul, since it is here, if anywhere in the New Testament that the proponents of universalism find evidence for their view.[2]

---

[1] It is a pleasure to offer this discussion on an aspect of the biblical doctrine of salvation as a mark of esteem and good wishes to my friend and colleague, James Torrance. The lecture on which the essay is based was given under the auspices of The Drew Lecture Foundation at Spurgeon's College, London, on Thursday 19 November 1987, and my thanks are due to the Foundation for the invitation to give it.

[2] The only other discussion of the biblical basis for universalism in the Drew lecture series is CS Duthie, 'Ultimate Triumph', *SJT* 14, (1961), pp. 156-71. See further W Michaelis, *Versöhnung des Alls*, (Bern, 1950); H Schumacher, *Das biblische Zeugnis von der Versöhnung des Alls*, (Stuttgart, 1959); RJH Shutt, 'The New Testament Doctrine of the Hereafter: Universalism or Conditional Immortality', *Exp. T* 67, (1955-6), pp. 131-5; NT Wright, 'Towards a biblical view of universalism', *Themelios* 4:2, (1979), pp. 54-8; ME Boring, 'The Language of Universal Salvation in Paul', *JBL* 105, (1986), pp. 269-92. Other literature on the topic includes: JAT Robinson,

## I The Evidence of Paul

Discussion of the Pauline material has been placed in a new light by the work of ME Boring. His argument is that the evidence presented by Paul's letters gives the appearance of tension and conflict, and this arises from the fact that Paul uses two types of images in his writings. There is first of all the kind of language which talks of the saved and the lost as two groups and of an ultimate separation between them, But side by side with this we have a kind of monistic language which talks of the ultimate sovereignty of God and of the total subjugation of his enemies. So in Rom. 5 we have language which is universal in its reference to the parallel effects of Adam and Christ which affect everybody, and in its stress that the saving deed of Christ is greater than the condemning deed of Adam. These two strands exist side by side in Paul who can thus make 'logically inconsistent, but not incoherent, statements'.[3] Boring wants to claim that Paul makes both limited and universal statements with regard to salvation, but that he does not draw out the ultimate logical consequences of each in a way which would reveal them to be inconsistent with each other.

A  Boring is right in affirming that Paul uses a variety of images in discussing the nature of salvation. He expresses it positively in terms of inheriting the kingdom of God, being saved, being reconciled to God, being redeemed from sin, and being with the Lord. But this has its negative side. In nearly all of these images the picture is of people who are already lost and who need to be delivered. Paul is quite clear that people are on their way to destruction if they do not respond to the gospel. They are already perishing. In general, those who practise the works of the flesh will not inherit the kingdom of God (Gal. 5:21). Those who sow to the flesh will reap corruption (Gal. 6:8; 1 Cor. 6:9f.). Those

---

'Universalism - is it heretical?', *SJT* 2, (1949), pp. 139-55; TF Torrance, *SJT* 2, (1949), pp. 310-18; JAT Robinson, *SJT* 2, (1949), pp. 378-80; JD Bettis, 'A critique of the doctrine of universal salvation', *Religious Studies* 6, 1970, pp. 329-44; RJ Bauckham, 'Universalism: a historical survey', *Themelios* 4, (1979), pp. 48-54.

[3] *Op. cit.*, p. 288.

314

who are guilty of the body and blood of the Lord will be condemned by God (1 Cor. 11:32).

Paul also has a concept of sin against the Holy Spirit (cf. Eph. 4:30). The Lord will punish people guilty of sexual immorality, for they are rejecting not man but God who gives the Holy Spirit (1 Thes. 4:6, 8). This suggests that such people sin against the Spirit (cf. Rom. 12:19).

The final judgment is one of wrath and fury upon the wicked (Rom. 2:5, 8f.; 5:9; 9:22; cf. Phil. 1:28; 3:19; Col. 3:5f.; Eph. 2:3; 5:5f.), including those whose opposition to God is shown in opposition to the church, is doomed to destruction and will be destroyed (2 Thes. 2:3, 8). Only those who do not persist in unbelief will be saved, even out of the Jews (Rom. 11:23). Salvation includes deliverance from the wrath and from destruction (1 Thes. 1:10; 5:9), and it is offered provided that people do not move away from the hope of the gospel (Col. 1:23).

These points show that often Paul operates with a framework of two types of people and two ultimate destinies.

B   Within this particular type of imagery some scholars have found the possibility that judgment may not be final. A doctrine of purgatory has been detected in 1 Cor. 3:12-15 by E Stauffer.[4] However, this is a mistaken view of the passage, which is referring rather to the way in which people may be saved 'by the skin of their teeth', as we would say. In any case, Paul is here referring to people who are believers but whose works will be tested by fire, and in the next couple of verses he speaks of people who try to destroy God's temple and will themselves be destroyed by God. The doctrine of purgatory is irrelevant to the destiny of non-believers.

Appeal can also be made to 1 Cor. 5:5 where the incestuous offender is to be handed over to Satan for the destruction of his

---

[4]E Stauffer, *New Testament Theology* (London, 1955), p. 212.

flesh that his spirit may be saved in the day of Christ. But again the reference is to a believer, a member of the church, and Paul is dealing with the purpose, not with the guaranteed result of this mysterious process.

C  We must next look at the kind of material noted by Boring where a different imagery from that of the saved and the lost is used and the suggestion is of a universal lordship of Christ into whose realm all people are brought.

1  In 1 Cor. 15:22-28 we are told that, as in Adam all die, even so in Christ all will be made alive. But Paul's point is not to affirm that all die in Adam and all will certainly come to life in Christ, but rather that just as the death of each and all is due to Adam so the resurrection of each and all is due to Christ. He means simply that in every case where people receive life it is through their union with Christ. Against those who would dispute it Paul is arguing that it is upon the man Christ that the hope of resurrection is dependent, just as death is due to the man Adam. Wherever death and resurrection take place, they are due respectively to Adam and Christ. Death of course is universal, but this is not necessarily so of resurrection. Indeed, the next verses show that Paul thinks of the resurrection only of 'those who belong to Christ'. The resurrection is followed by the subjugation of his enemies. Boring recognizes all this, but argues that Paul is moving into the image of 'God-the-king who unites all in his kingly reign'.[5] But it must be noted that subjugation is not the same thing as unification and reconciliation. Paul teaches the destruction of the cosmic forces opposed to Christ, including death.

2  All this is relevant to the understanding of Rom. 5 where similar statements are made. Boring treats this passage in the same way as 1 Cor. 15:20-22, and he argues that to 'receive' grace and righteousness (Rom. 5:17) is a case of 'passive' reception rather than of 'active' taking; he claims that *lambano* normally has this sense. This seems to misinterpret the evidence.

[5] *Op. cit.*, p. 280.

316

There are places where Paul talks of receiving by faith (Gal. 3:2, 14) and where the verb appears to refer to the decision of the recipient (Phil. 2:7). Certainly Rom. 5:11 is in the context of justification by faith, and the rest of the passage must be surely be understood within its context in Romans and not treated as an isolated statement on its own.

Furthermore, we must ask what is the force of 'all' in this passage. I suggest that 'all' in Rom. 5 really has primarily in view 'both Jews and Gentiles and not just Jews': that is the point that Paul is concerned to make. He is of course referring to all mankind and not just saying 'some Jews and some Gentiles', but the thrust of the section is that Christ's action, like Adam's affects both Jews and Gentiles. The one/many contrast is used of both Adam and Christ to show that both affect the whole human race and not just the Jews. So Paul's aim is not necessarily to assert that all will be saved but that the work of Christ is for all, and that he alone is the Saviour in virtue of the one saving event of his death. Eternal life is the gracious gift of God in Christ, and it is received by faith. There is no question of all people automatically receiving life apart from faith in Christ.

3  In Rom. 9-11 we have the prophecy that all Israel will be saved and that the fulness of the Gentiles will come into the church. God has bound all men over to disobedience so that he may have mercy on them all. Here 'them all' must mean 'Jews and Gentiles alike' in the light of the earlier teaching in the letter. The problem is the identity of the full number of the Gentiles and all Israel. So far as Israel is concerned, the condition is quite plain: 'if they do not persist in unbelief' (Rom. 11:23). It is unimaginable that Paul would drop this condition. The question is then whether God can predestine 'all Israel' to believe. But here we must note: a) Paul is writing about events in this world and not in the next; b) there is no indication whatever that he is concerned with the destiny of those who have already died. He is thinking rather of the community of Israel in the last days. In fact there are obviously people who have died in a state of being 'hardened'.

4  In Phil. 2:10f. we are told that Christ will be exalted so that every knee will bow to him, and every tongue will confess that he is Lord. Boring[6] argues that this text is not to be understood in the framework of the saved and the lost; it is not concerned with salvation but with universal acknowledgment of Christ as Lord - and here Boring sides with E Best who states that 'for a man to stand on another's neck and compel him to confess he has been vanquished is not a victory compatible iwht the God of the cross'.[7]  Thus the text is in a way open to a universalistic understanding, but Boring would argue that it really belongs within 'the encompassing image of God-the-king and its one-group eschatology'.[8]

In assessing this argument we need to raise the question whether statements made within one encompassing image can overrule statements made in another.  Boring rightly refuses to allow this move, arguing that the logical inferences of each image are never drawn; thus Paul does not push himself into explicit inconsistency.  But it would be truer to say that in one set of images the question of salvation and loss is not directly in view. The question of the scope of salvation is not being raised.

Two points are important in the understanding of the passage. First, the text is making the point that all who confess God as Lord must also confess Jesus as Lord at his *parousia*.  The language is drawn from Is. 45:23, which is also quoted with reference to God the Father in Rom. 14:11.  Now in the passage in Romans the reference is to facing judgment and giving account of ourselves to God.  But in Phil. 2 Christ occupies this divine position as judge.  The passage is primarily a statement about his supreme position under the Father.  Whoever confesses God as Lord must give that same honour to Christ.  In other words the point is not that everybody *will* confess Christ as Lord but that

[6]*Op. cit.*, p. 282f.

[7] E Best, *The First and Second Epistles to the Thessalonians* (London, 1972), p. 368.

[8]*Op. cit.*, p. 283.

everybody who recognizes God as Lord *should* also recognize
Christ as Lord.

The second point is that vs. 10f. are concerned with the purpose
of God's exaltation of Christ. They do not constitute a statement
that everybody will in fact acknowledge Christ as Lord, but rather
a statement that the purpose of God in exalting Christ is to win
for him universal acknowledgment as Lord. As GF Hawthorne
notes, 'how these purposes will be fulfilled, or when they will be
fulfilled, or whether they will be fulfilled are not questions which
can be answered from the statements of the hymn itself'.[9]
Nevertheless, we should note that later in this same letter Paul
refers to people who are enemies of the cross and whose destiny
is destruction (Phil. 3:18f.).

D  We come finally in this section to two passages in Colossians
and Ephesians.

1  In Col. 1:20 God's purpose is 'to reconcile to himself all
things, whether things on earth or things in heaven, by making
peace through his blood, shed on the cross'. Here we have a
programme of reconciliation of cosmic scope.

The passage is basically about the place of the readers in the
kingdom of God's Son. Formerly they were under the power of
darkness, but now they have been rescued from it and transferred
to a new ruler. They have been redeemed or set free, and this took
place when their sins were forgiven. In vs. 21ff. they are said to
have been alienated and become enemies through their evil deeds,
but now they have been reconciled by the death of Christ so that
thay are seen as holy, blameless and irreproachable in the sight
of God. We have two descriptions of the same basic event
couched in different terminology. But the latter is introduced by
what is apparently disgression, a description of Jesus which
describes his role in creation and in reconciliation and which thus

[9]GF Hawthorne, *Philippians* (Waco, 1983), p. 94.

serves to place the readers in a cosmic context with the object of showing that they are no longer subject to any power other than Christ. There is a parallel between creation and reconciliation and in each case the effect is to stress the supremacy of Christ. The *everything* in v. 20 must be the same as in v. 16, namely things visible and invisible, thrones, rulers, principalities and powers. They are described in neutral terms here, but elsewhere they are uniformly negative as powers opposed to God. In 2:15 Christ strips the principalities and powers and makes them a public spectacle; he leads them in his triumphal procession as enemies destined for death. Although Paul daringly applies the same metaphor to himself in 2 Cor. 2:14, there is no reason to suppose that the evil powers are similarly redeemed by Christ.

a) The main point that Paul is making is that it is only through Christ that this reconciliation happens. Since it is for 'everything', there is no room for any other reconciler or act of reconciliation.

b) In 2 Cor. 5 reconciliation has to be accepted to become effective. This is implied here, for v. 23 goes on to speak of the necessity of remaining grounded in the faith and not moving away from it.

c) What is being described is what happened on the cross. It was the place where the powers were led in triumph. There is no future act of reconciliation here. A past event is described.[10]

d) According to Paul's earlier letters the creation is still in bondage to the powers of evil and groans to be released. Paul looks forward to the revelation of the sons of God and the redemption of their bodies: this is clearly the event described in 1 Cor. 15 which is linked to the *parousia*. Paul has no expectations of any saving event after the *parousia*. Everything is summed up in that event. So there is an already/not yet tension in this act of reconciliation. Reconciliation has been achieved in the death of Jesus, but the offer 'be reconciled to God' continues to be presented to the world.

The situation envisaged in Colossians appears to be the same. What is being described is an act of reconciliation of cosmic

---

[10]P O'Brien, *Colossians, Philemon* (Waco, 1982), p. 53.

scope which has taken place through the death of Christ. As a result of the proclamation of the gospel there has been a response by the readers of the letter, so that they are now reconciled and have come into submission to their Head, Jesus Christ. But the powers are still active. It is not said that they will all come under willing submission to Christ. Paul knows only the fate of judgment for rebellious mankind which refuses to accept the reconciliation. It is not clear whether there is reconciliation available for the hostile powers. The implication of 2:15 which describes the triumph of Christ over the powers at the cross is that they are under sentence of death. It may be best, therefore, to assume that whe Paul speaks of the reconciliation of all things in 1:20 he is thinking primarily of the human world and the possibility of its turning away from the powers to be reconciled to God. On the other hand, it is conceivable that he envisages the possibility that the powers who have been defeated at the cross may turn in repentance towards Christ and be reconciled to God; but if this is what he means, he certainly has not said so directly and clearly.

Moreover, all this applies to the powers. There is nothing to imply that mankind are treated in any other way than on the basis of faith in Christ. There is no hint of a future act of universal reconciliation other than that which has already taken place in the cross. No future event is prophesied or described. Paul is dealing with what Christ has done, and with what has happened as a result to the readers. And he warns against the fact of God's wrath directed against those who persist in sin (Col. 3:5f.).

2   Finally, in Eph. 1:10 God's purpose for the fulness of time is 'to bring all things in heaven and on earth together under one head, even Christ'. The fulness of time may well refer to the end-time which was inaugurated by the incarnation as in Galatians.[11] To sum up is to bring everything together or perhaps to make everything new, to unite under one head, namely Christ. So this

---

[11]Many commentators, however, apply the phrase to the end of time: FF Bruce, *The Epistles to the Colossians, to Philemon and to the Ephesians*, (Grand Rapids, 1984), p. 261f.

is the purpose of the coming of Christ, which has already begun to be put into operation. But there is no suggestion that this will include people who refuse to be included. The powers of evil are still active and hostile (2:2; 6:12) and they are under God's wrath (2:3). Wrath is coming on the disobedient (5:6). As in Colossians, there is no basis here for believing that all mankind and all the hostile powers will in fact be reconciled to God. Paul's aim is to stress that all God's plans come to fruition in Christ and that his sovereignty affects the whole universe.

The effect of our discussion is to show that, while Boring is right to draw attention to the variety of imagery used by Paul, the suggestion that, if pressed, the various images would present an inconsistent picture, is to be resisted. Nothing that we have discovered in the 'lordship' passages places a question mark agains Paul's use of the categories 'saved' and 'lost' or against his belief that there will be those who ultimately face the wrath of God.

## II The Significance of the Evidence
We have now surveyed the relevant material in Paul. In the rest of the New Testament there is certainly no explicit teaching in favour of universalism, and there is no implicit teaching either.[12] Those who look for it in the New Testament are clutching at insubstantial straws. But is that the end of the matter? CS Duthie concludes his examination of the Johannine material by admitting that the evidence is slight, but claims to find 'the beginning of a movement toward universalism'. He claims indeed that the notion is 'present in sufficient strength to generate [a] tension' between the doctrines of everlasting punishment and universal salvation'.[13]

On this there are two things to be said. The first is that this conclusion that the notion is present with what Duthie calls 'sufficient strength' is not justified by the evidence. Suppose for

---

[12]For a survey of the New Testament evidence see Appendix 1.

[13]*Op. cit.*, p. 161.

a moment that the case was the other way round and the clear evidence was in favour of universalism; if the evidence for everlasting punishment, as Duthie calls the alternative, were as palpably weak as the actual evidence for universalism is, no reputable scholar would treat it seriously. He would be laughed out of court for his prejudice and blindness.

If universalism were a New Testament doctrine, we should expect to find the following statements clearly made in the New Testament or, at the very least, made implicitly:
a) that what is presented as the final judgment is not final, and that people's lot can change after death (or after judgment);
b) that there will be some future offer of the gospel (since it will surely be agreed that salvation can only be through Christ and through personal response to him); or, alternatively, that in some way God will change the hearts of all mankind to respond in faith to him;
c) that everybody will in fact make this response.
None of these is to be found. All that can be found is the statement that God is not willing that any should perish but wants everyone to come to repentance (2 Pet. 3:9). But this is advanced as a reason why the Lord delays the end of the world and the judgment, not as a basis for belief that he will have mercy after the judgment.

But suppose, second, that Duthie is right and that there is a movement in the direction of universal restoration in the New Testament. What then? What is implied by a 'movement towards'?

We have surely to hold fast to the teaching of the New Testament that God loves sinners and yet that he judges them. This is in my view the major contribution of Aberdeen's greatest theological son, Peter Taylor Forsyth.[14] Against the liberalism of his day

---

[14]PT Forsyth, *The Work of Christ* (London, 1910). CS Duthie, *op. cit.*, p. 169, claims that Forsyth was nevertheless a crypto-universalist, on the basis of his statement: 'There are more conversions on the other side than on this'; but does 'more' imply 'all will be converted'?

he insisted repeatedly that the character of God was not merely love, for that could be reduced to mere sentiment, but holy love, and that the holiness and justice of God must be preached as much as the love of God; it was only thus that he could make sense of the atonement, by interpreting it in moral categories. To talk of the ultimate nature of God as loving without at the same time talking of this ultimate nature as being holy and righteous is to do injustice to Scripture where God's love and holiness are not opposed but are different expressions of the same eternal fact. There is no way that the holy wrath of God against sin can somehow be subsumed under his love so that it ceases to be real. It is incorrect to say that God's justice will give way to his love or that his wrath against sin is not the ultimate reality in his nature. Since holiness is his very nature, God is implacably opposed to the action of his creatures who freely choose to sin. And this resistance must surely continue throughout eternity; it is not something that God can put away at will. Yet because he loves his creatures in their sin, he wishes to save them from the consequences of their rebelliousness, and the only way in which he can do this is the way in which he has done it, by himself satisfying the holiness of his own nature in a vicarious sacrifice for sin.

Consequently, any doctrine of universal salvation must be based not on a denial of the reality of judgment but on the claim that God will somehow deliver sinners from it. It can now be argued that God is in fact revealed in the Bible as the God who forgives sinners. On the other hand, he provides a way of atonement, foreshadowed in the sacrificial system in the Old Testament and effected fully and finally in the sacrificial death of Jesus, thereby showing himself to be both just and the one who justifies sinners. On the other hand, he extends forgiveness to those who turn to him for mercy and put their faith in him through Jesus Christ. God is thus seen to make forgiveness possible and actual.

Granted, then, that this is how God is revealed in Scripture, can we on this basis go further and say that God will act again in the same kind of way at the End, making it somehow possible for those who died in their sins to be forgiven.  Would this not be of a piece with his revelation of himself as a Saviour in the death of Jesus?  Would this be a legitimate extrapolation from the doctrine of the atonement?

One theologian who finds hints of such a movement is E Stauffer who contrasts what Paul says in Galatians and Romans: 'Once Paul had written: "the scripture hath shut up all things under sin, that the promise by faith in Jesus Christ might be given *to them that believe*". (Gal. 3:22).  But now the last reservation has disappeared: "God hath shut up all into disobedience, that he might have mercy upon all" (Rom. 11:32).  The universalism of the divine creativity requires and guarantees the divine salvation'.[15]  Here Stauffer is arguing that Paul's thought undergoes a shift towards universalism between Galatians and Romans.  He seems to hold that despite the *earlier* expression of a different view of Galatians and the *parallel* or even *later* expression of a different view in John and Revelation, we go by what Romans says.  Now there is no question but that Stauffer is wrong in his exegesis of Romans; he can produce no reason why the exegesis of Galatians should not control the exegesis of Romans at this point, and above all why Rom. 11:32 should not be read in the context of Romans itself where the need for faith as the only way to salvation is hammered home as recently as nine verses previously; to suggest that one verse in Paul where faith is not mentioned upturns the entirety of what Paul wrote elsewhere is ludicrous.

Consequently, those who defend the movement towards universalism must admit that it is not presented explicitly in the New Testament.  The question would then be whether taking this step is the same kind of thing as happens when we make ethical extrapolations from the teaching of the New Testament.  For example, we can say that the New Testament shows a movement towards antislavery.  And we would agree that we can walk further along this path because it brings out the latent principles of the New Testament.  We can find a movement towards the emanci-

[15] *Op. cit.*, p. 224.

pation of women. Both are cases where the full significance of basic ethical insights had not yet been fully recognized. Is the salvation of all as opposed to some a similar fuller insight?

We are being asked to come to a new understanding of what God will do which goes beyond the finality of his revelation in the cross and which requires him to act differently towards sinners than he has done in the cross. The question is not really one of the extent of God's love; that he loves all and does not wish any to perish is clear biblical teaching; the question is rather whether his love leads him to act in different ways from those already revealed in Christ. It is there that the danger in universalism is found, for, if we adopt a doctrine of God which is not bound up with his self-revelation in Christ, we have departed from the Christian doctrine of God. If, then, we adopt universalism, we are moving away from the revelation given in Christ - and in Scripture - on no other basis than our own sense of what is fitting.

Some people are, in Duthie's term, 'crypto-universalists'. They would like to believe that universalism is true and that none will be finally condemned. Of course, the Lord takes no delight in the death of the sinner, and God forgive us if we take delight in it. But the danger is that the wish can become father of the belief that ultimately all will be saved. That is a step that we dare not take, that we cannot take, so long as we are biblical realists. What we are called to do is to proclaim the gospel of faith in Jesus Christ as the only sure hope for mankind.

Appendix 1:

The other New Testament evidence is briefly as follows:

A The teaching of Jesus. Over against the consistent picture in the Gospels of the reality of a final judgment leading to the exclusion of some from the kingdom of God it could be argued:

1 A good deal of the material may be due to the Evangelist (or the tradition) elaborating on the teaching of Jesus and giving it an emphasis or even a fresh direction that was not present in the original material. This would be especially characteristic of Matthew.

2 In the end of the day Jesus says that all sins are forgivable except one, the sin against the Holy Spirit. But have we any evidence that there will be people who will in the end sin against the Holy Spirit? And does 'never' really mean 'never'? Neither of these points is convincing.

1 This is not the place to enter into a detailed discussion of the authenticity and original wording of the various sayings of Jesus which we have cited. I would be prepared to affirm that the picture presented by the Evangelists is a uniform one, and that this picture represents the general impression of what Jesus taught.

2 Attempts to rid the saying about the unforgivable sin of its significance are quite artificial. The question is generally put in terms of the meaning of *aionios*, 'everlasting', and it is contended that this word expresses quality rather than temporal extent. However, this contention is baseless, since Luke's form of the saying simply has 'will not be forgiven', and Matthew has 'will not be forgiven in this age or the coming age'. Similarly Mark uses the expression in parallel to 'is never forgiven', literally 'not ... to the age'. The only possible way round this is to suggest that 'the coming age' or 'the age' is not the final age but a penultimate period followed (although Jesus does not mention it) by the final age itself in which (although Jesus does not mention it) sin will be forgiven. We must also remember that there is no teaching in the Gospels which suggests any change in the final destiny of people once it has been settled. There is no escape for the rich man from Gehanna (Lk. 16:26), and the door to the banqueting hall is firmly shut (Mt. 25:10 par. Lk. 13:25). It must also be remembered that when the saying teaches that all other sins can be forgiven, this is by no means the same thing as saying that they necessarily will be, and that the one sin which cannot be forgiven is rejection of the Spirit.

Are there, however, any implicit clues which suggest that universalism was a belief held by Jesus which he did not communicate directly to his friends? Can we find evidence that he himself held this belief which by its nature he could not share with anybody else? Obviously it would be difficult to provide such evidence, and this is why it is difficult to refute the convinced universalist who insists that Jesus could have held this belief despite the lack of open attestation. But in the total absence of positive evidence that Jesus believed that God willed the ultimate salvation of all, we have no justification for interpreting his statements about ultimate separation as being anything other than what they *prima facie* are and stating that they are merely warnings. When Duthie comments that despite every effort to find evidence for universalism in the Gospels 'the evidence on the other side has the stronger appearance', he is indulging in under-statement. It would be more to the point to say that, if we attribute to Jesus an underlying universalism, we make nonsense of the beliefs and attributes that we can certainly attribute to him.

B In the Gospel of John alongside expressions of the universal scope of the love of God we find that nonbelievers are condemned already (3:18). The resurrection will be to life or to condemnation (5:28f.). Jesus foreknew that there would be some who would not believe (6:64). It is possible to die in one's sins (8:24). Judas is doomed to destruction (17:12). Nothing suggests that this is anything other than the last word on sinners.

C Hebrews stresses the reality of judgment for those who turn their backs on the salvation offered to them by virtue of the sacrifice of Christ (6:7; 10:31). The Writer trusts that such a fate will not befall his readers, but that they will hear his warnings and respond to them, but it is to Christian believers that he says such things, and he never betrays any hint that those who do not believe in Christ now will be given a chance later (cf. 9:27).

D In 1 Peter 3:18-20 Christ went after his death and 'preached to the spirits in prison who disobeyed long ago'. In 4:6 it is affirmed that 'the gospel was preached even to those who are now dead, so that they might be judged according to men in regard to the body, but live according to God in regard to spirit'. The essential points of interpretation relevant to our problem concern the identity of those addressed by Christ, the nature of his message, and the nature of their response.

It seems reasonably certain to me that the language in 3:18-20 refers to supernatural powers and not to human beings. It also seems quite clear that the context demands that the reference is to Christ's proclamation of victory over the principalities and powers who are now in submission to him (3:20); only this message could act as encouragement to persecuted Christians who felt that they were opposed by powers stronger than themselves. And, if Christ proclaimed his victory, there is no indication that he was making an offer of salvation; on the contrary, the evil powers come into subjection to him.

It follows that 4:6 is about some different event, and much the most plausible is that Peter is commentating about the way the gospel was preached in their lifetime to Christians now dead; to the world they appear to be under judgment, but at God's bar they are vindicated and will live in his presence.

Even if this interpretation is open to question, the passage is certainly no proof of universalism. Nothing is said about all the dead responding positively to any such message and receiving a post mortem salvation. In fact, 4:5, with its comment on the way in which persecutors of the church will have to give an account of themselves to the judge of the living and the dead, points in the opposite direction. I suggest that 4:6 makes no sense in its context if it refers to such a post mortem preaching. And certainly it is no comfort to persecuted Christians who suffer for doing good and who try to bear witness in a malicious world to be told not to worry because Christ proclaimed forgiveness to the evil spirits and they accepted it: how does that help them to face persecution? If the point is to say that their witness to their persecutors will be as successful as Christ's to the evil spirits, then it must be replied that the most important element on this exegesis, the response of the spirits, is not mentioned at all. There is no support for universalism in 1 Peter. (For a fuller treatment see my forthcoming exposition of 1 Peter to be published by InterVarsity Press, Downers Grove, Ill.)

# 17

# Salvation, Culture and Science Fiction

STEPHEN MAY

## I Theology, Culture and the Church

Professor James Torrance is a man of wide and varied interests, but to my knowledge he has never numbered science fiction among them. Nevertheless, he did permit the present writer to embark on a thesis which involved some discussion of this apparently far from theological subject.

In this essay, I wish to propose that certain inherent features of this characteristically modern genre of literature (though many would deny such a title to what they regard merely as a form of written trash[2]) reflect specifically theological concerns. To express the basis of this enterprise: concern about such a subject is not self-indulgence, but a reflection of the theme of this book. Professor Torrance proclaimed through his teaching the truth of this theme, the patristic pronouncement that 'what is not assumed is not healed',[3] the incarnational basis to all our evangelism. If this means that we have to meet men where they are, then it entails a rigorous encounter in every age and time with the prevailing culture. To maintain that the Gospel has a timeless power is self-evident, but unless it engages in dialogue with that world, how then can it be heard?

In his book on homilectics, Professor Ian Pitt-Watson talks of

---

[1] Science fiction is often known by its abbreviation: sf. I have striven to reduce the references to stories to a minimum.

[2] For example, see John Wain's comment that an interest in science fiction is 'usually a reliable sign of imaginative bankruptcy' (JT Como (ed.), *C S Lewis at the Breakfast Table*, (London, 1980, p. 74). By contrast, D Suvin, *Metamor-phoses of Science Fiction: On the Poetics and History of a Literary Genre*, (London, 1979), p. vii f., produces a defence of science fiction as a form of 'paraliterature'.

[3] Gregory of Nazianzus, *Epistle* 101, 7.

329

the bowstring stretched 'between the text of the Bible on the one hand and the problems of contemporary human life on the other' as the essential mark of preaching.[4] Tillich's *Systematic Theology*, vol. 1, criticizes Barth for abandoning apologetics by a distorted emphasis on 'kerygmatic theology'.[5] The question of whether this attack is fair or not ignores the fact that the issue raised is crucial. Were Tillich to be correct, then he would be proving that Barth offends against one of his own central axioms - the real humanity of Jesus in which God adopts fallen human nature in the Incarnation.[6] Such an emphasis, argues Donald Baillie, breaks with Christian tradition.[7]

To assert this - rather than to adopt the more popular docetic position - is to say that wherever Christ seeks to be the Lord of life, the world that he came to save has to be taken seriously. By analysing science fiction, the present writer is attempting to spoil the Egyptians, to redeem that which God has made, which man is perverting and which God in Jesus Christ has saved. He came 'for us men, and for our salvation' - and this must surely include our works.

In his book *Rural Anglicanism*,[8] Leslie Francis gave what the present Archbishop of Canterbury describes as a 'devastating' analysis of the state of the Church of England in what is generally regarded as its heartland. The latter wrote that he welcomed Dr Francis' particular emphasis on specific pastoral strategies aimed at the young: 'if the Victorian country clergy

---

[4]I Pitt-Watson, *A Kind of Folly: Towards a Practical Theology of Preaching*, The Warrack Lectures for 1972-75, (Edinburgh, 1976), p. 57.

[5]P Tillich, *Systematic Theology*, vol. 1, (Digswell Place, 1960), pp. 3-9: 'Theology moves back and forth between two poles, the eternal truth of its foundation and the temporal situation in which the eternal truth must be received' (p. 3).

[6]K Barth, *CD* I/2, pp. 151-9.

[7]DM Baillie, *God Was in Christ: An Essay on Incarnation and Atonement* (London, 1961), p. 16f. 'Barth is quite conscious that he is adopting a position that has always been regarded as heretical' (p. 17).

[8]L Francis, *Rural Anglicanism: a future for young Christians?* (London, 1985).

rightly feared the alienation of the poor from the church, their successors must recognize the alienation of today's young from theirs'.[9] Elsewhere Leslie Francis synopsizes much of the problem: 'Recent research has highlighted the growing gap between young people and the churches. Nowhere is this gap more apparent than in public worship. Generally the young say that they are bored by church services. They are bored because much of what is happening is so completely different from what happens in the day to day culture of their environment ... Those of us who are familiar with Church services easily forget how large is the gap between ourselves and the uninitiated'.[10]

Pastors will recognize the signs of apprehension and even fear in families assembled for a Sunday afternoon baptism: such is the effect of being in a Church today. With the young, however, Francis argues, such a reaction is increasingly likely to be due to the secularization of society and marginalization of the Church. Scripture, psalms, hymns are all more and more unfamiliar. An approach to mission which assumes that people have to come *to* the church is thus intensely problematic, as well as being hopelessly untheological. The bandwagon now is often for 'mission, not maintenance', a slogan that seems unrealistic in many places where the whole organisation is geared to maintenance - to keeping going costly and time-consuming buildings, often attended by the 'safe' assumption that the Church is there to be used when people need it. Evangelism - going *out* - thus becomes seen as a threat, to congregations and to ministers.

If the basis of Christian behaviour, however, is the witness of Christ, it is easy to see that going *out*, however costly, is indeed the pattern of Christian Ministry. In Christ, God *went out* in the Incarnation. He did not, could not, remain where he was, but went out in order to bring in; and suchis our calling too. The connection of all this with a study of scence fiction is to argue

---

[9] *Ibid.*, p. 7.
[10] L Francis, *His Spirit is With Us: a project approach to Christian Nurture* (London, 1981), p. 9.

that Christians cannot afford to adopt a 'sniffy' approach to modern culture. It indeed needs redemption, but then so does everything. My contention, then, is that we are obliged by the logic of the Incarnation, by the fact that it was 'for us men, and for our salvation' that Christ became man, to take seriously modern culture - and for the purpose of my argument, this means science fiction. I shall leave here a justification of the importance of science fiction in modern culture, apart from merely pointing out the way in which its iconography now permeates just about everything from pop lyrics to yoghurt and freezer advertising.

All this, perhaps it should be added, does not go to an affirmation of the '60s dictum, 'the world writes the agenda', so abhorred by Professor Torrance - but rather that, because of God's action towards mankind in Jesus Christ, the world has to be loved just as God loved it. Charles Pickstone, writing in *Church Times*, observes well that whilst 'people must feel that the liturgy is theirs, ... even so, it goes on independently of them, even as God is independent'.[11] Indeed, we do not change the Gospel to make it more acceptable. However, we do find out about those to whom we speak, even as Christ did in the thirty years before He began His ministry. 'God so loved the world'![12] 'The language of Canaan' just will not do.[13] It is a tragedy that those of us who speak so eloquently of Jesus becoming Man so often remain indoors, and expect the world to come to us, rather than us going to the world: an irony Kierkegaard would have appreciated - the Kierkegaard who told the story of the eminent pastor preaching *with emotion* to an elect company in the magnificent cathedral on the text: 'God hath elected the base things of the world, and

[11] C Pickstone, 'Journey into Space' in *Church Times*, 10/7/87, p. 11.

[12] Jn 3:16.

[13] Pitt-Watson, *supra*, argues that we are in Babylon, not in Canaan, and the problem is how 'to sing the Lord's song in a strange land'. 'Much of our preaching gives the appearance of offering painstaking answers to questions which nobody is asking' (p. 52). The preacher tends to speak 'in a foreign language of which [many] understand little or nothing' (p. 53). Barth himself writes that 'the word of the preacher must be relevant to the immediate preoccupations of his hearers', *Prayer and Preaching* (London, 1964).

the things that are despised'. 'And nobody laughs', concludes
Kierkegaard.[14] Even the best ministers admit they become
caught up in this tendency.

Vincent Donovan's book, *Rediscovering Christianity*[15], is an
interesting account of an attempt amongst the Masai of East
Africa to go to them, rather than expect them to come to the
long-established mission corral. To do this requires courage, the
more so because Christians who follow the evangelistic
imperative risk criticism from those who do not. (Professor
James Torrance's own brother, Thomas Torrance, has made a
notable attempt in his study of theology and science.)
Evangelism means to investigate the culture to which you go, not
merely to be *amongst* it, bearing 'the Truth', untouched by it.
Bruce Reed's book, *The Dynamics of Religion*, notes the
phenomenon many Churches find - ecclesiasticism.[16] Converts
spend all their time in the Church, in services, Bible studies,
prayer meetings and the like. Their witness to the world is
hampered by the fact that, contrary to John 17:15,[17] they no
longer hardly encounter the world at all! They have ceased to be
part of one culture, and have merely become part of another.
When they do meet it, they go Bible in hand, armoured from
hearing. But, Barth said, read the Bible and the daily newspaper!
Robert Short's popular theological books on the comic strip
Peanuts (*The Gospel according to Peanuts*[18] and *The Parables of
Peanuts*[19]) are in some ways models of the kind of interpretation
which is possible; and they themselves give a justification for the
activity in Kierkegaard's 'wounding from behind' which is
possible: which assails non-believers at their weakest spot,

---

[14]S Kierkegaard, *Attack upon 'Christendom'*, W Lowrie (ET), (Princeton,
1968), p. 181.

[15]VJ Donovan, *Rediscovering Christianity: an Epistle from the Masai*
(London, 1982).

[16]B Reed, *The Dynamics of Religion: Process and Movement in Christian
Churches* (London, 1978), pp. 79ff.

[17]'I am not asking you to remove them from the world, but to protect them
from the evil one' (Jerusalem Bible).

[18]RL Short, *The Gospel according to Peanuts* (London, 1966).

[19]RL Short, *The Parables of Peanuts* (London, 1969).

where, unwarned and without their defences up, they are not prejudiced against the truth in advance.[20]

The context for my study of science fiction was a discussion of the way in which Christian truth is conveyed through story, and particularly the works of CS Lewis, aknowledged by Alasdair Heron to be 'still apparently the most widely read religious writer in English'.[21] One of the most characteristic elements of the appeal of Lewis was the way in which he interacted with the culture of his day - this despite the way in which he presented himself as an old-fashioned dinosaur. To read *The Pilgrim's Regress*[22] is to be presented with a list of philosophical adversaries as large as that which figures in between the lines of Karl Barth's *Dogmatics in Outline*.[23] Lewis wrote in the context of his times, even if he could be accused (as Barth has, occasionally) of an unashamed backwards-looking mentality. The immediate importance for our study, however, is the fact of Lewis' interest in science fiction - an interest that has been returned from the non-Christian practitioners of that literary genre, however ambiguously.[24]

In our own day, interest in the social and philosophical context of the Church is shown by the success of Umberto Eco's

[20]*Ibid.*, p. 14. The whole of the first chapter of this book is concerned with this issue. *The Gospel according to Peanuts*, *supra*, advocates a Kierkegaardian strategy of 'indirect communication'; 'If one is to lift up the whole age one must truly know it. That is why those ministers of Christianity who begin at once with orthodoxy have so little effect and only on few ... One must begin with paganism ... If one begins immediately with Christianity then they say: that is nothing for us - and they are immediately on their guard'. (Quoted, pp. 8-9, from Kierkegaard's *Journals*, ed. and tr. A Dru (ET and ed.), (London, 1938), p. 232).

[21]AIC Heron, *A Century of Protestant Theology*, (London, 1980), p. 130.

[22]CS Lewis, *The Pilgrim's Regress: an allegorical apology for Christianity, Reason and Romanticism* (London, 1977).

[23]K Barth, *Dogmatics in Outline*, GT Thompson (ET), (London, 1966).

[24]Cf. e.g., Brian Aldiss' fair-minded appreciation in his *Billion Year Spree: The History of Science Fiction* (London, 1975), pp. 222-9.

detective-cum-thriller novel, *The Name of the Rose*,[25] which is also an exercise in semiotics as well as a description of the appalling barbarity and bigotry of medieval Christendom. For our purpose, however, its interest resides in its startling presentation of Aristotelianism's impact on Christianity as a murder motive: it is for this reason that monks have been variously slaughtered and the Inquisition summoned. It is interesting too to find Eco's hero, the improbably named William de Baskerville, revering as his master the Franciscan Roger Bacon, pioneer of science. It is Roger Bacon, too, who figures as science fiction writer James Blish's hero protagonist in his *Doctor Mirabilis*,[26] concerned here with the relationship between culture and knowledge, the perennial science fiction theme of superstition and science. *Kerygma* and *paideia*, Christianity and Hellenism: such themes of the interface of faith with its culture have been the staple of theology since Harnack. Today's context is that of Carl Sagan and cosmology, the question of life beyond this world,[27] in other words, the very issue of science fiction.

## II Story and the 'other'

It is my contention that there is a formal resemblance between the essence of theology, and the way in which the science fiction story works. It is a resemblance that is common to every story, and is to be found in the human experience of attention to story. Here I am not concerned with the expression of 'our' stories (a popular concern of much modern theology), but with the way in which we, as we say, are 'drawn into' stories. To be 'moved' by a story is, to use conventional parlance, to be 'enthralled' by it, 'enraptured', to 'have a spell cast over one', to be 'carried away', to become 'hooked'.

Such expressions are generally used without explicit awareness of their significance, but they all emphasize the way in which stories make us *passive*. We are 'affected' and 'moved' by them.

[25]U Eco, *The Name of the Rose*, (ET), (London, 1984).

[26]J Blish, *Doctor Mirabilis* (London, 1984).

[27]The heroine of Carl Sagan's *Contact: A Novel* (London, 1986) is outraged by biblical inconsistencies as a child, pp. 29-31.

Such an experience of *capture* is not seen however, as bad, but as good. We recognize the way in which being caught up out of ourselves - in *ekstasis*, out of our own immediate experience, is not only enjoyable, but also enlightening and beneficial to us. We forget our own immediate problems in the light of some thing that 'takes us over'.

I recall a particular experience of being so moved by a William Golding book I was reading[28] that my anxiety at an approaching driving test was considerably relieved. It seemed insignificant by comparison with the elation I received through emotional engagement in the book.

Such disattention from ourselves as a result of external cause (distraction) is common to many human activities - love, education among them - and it can be argued that humanity consists in this potentiality for external reference. That is to say, an individual is not merely concerned about him or herself, at this particular moment, but about others, about other times, about, to put it bluntly, *the other*. Much attention in theology has been rightly concentrated on this aspect of the other in speaking of God: God is the 'wholly other'; God is the One who is 'other' within Himself in the Trinity; God is the One to whom we are called to relate in order to be truly ourselves. Indeed, according to Barth, man's imitation of God consists precisely in his sharing in God's own multiplicity, in His Being as Father, Son and Holy Spirit.[29]

Our life, then, consists of external reference, and this is not slavery or loss of ourselves, but the point at which we truly find ourselves. 'Whoever loses his life will save it', says Luke's Gospel.[30] Marriage is an obvious example of a relationship in

[28]W Golding, *Darkness Visible*, (London, 1979). In a similar way Hans Georg Gadamer discusses play as an anlogy to art, emphasizing 'the primacy of the game over the players engaged ... The attraction of a game, the fascination it exerts consists primarily in the fact that the game tends to master the players', *Truth and Method*, W Doepel (ET), (London, 1979), p. 95.

[29]K Barth, *CD* III/1, pp. 182-95 and ff.

[30]Lk. 17:33.

which people are intended to become more truly themselves by mutual giving. The Christian faith is that, by giving our allegiance to Christ as Lord, we become what we have always been meant to be: His service is perfect freedom.[31] Christian life then is contingent, both in creation and redemption: we have life by being orientated to the One who gave us, and continually gives us life - and who has given us new life through His Son.[32] Our Christian experience has to consist of a continual looking away from ourselves to the One who is our justifier, 'who of God is made unto us wisdom, and righteousness and sanctification, and redemption'.[33]

Bronowski argues that man's capacity for envisaging future possibilities - that is, imagination - is his most striking feature.[34] In these terms, science fiction becomes very significant, at least if the envisaging of future possibilities is basic to it. Michael Polanyi's emphasis on personal knowledge entails a passionate concentration through the particulars of apprehension to the object of interest.[35] And, as Barth put it, 'whoso means to rescue and preserve the subjective element shall lose it; but whoso gives it up for the sake of the objective, shall save it'.[36] This, too, is what CS Lewis meant by his 'law of inattention',[37] whether applied to the getting of friends or the relationship between heaven and earth or whatever.

### III Science Fiction - the 'alien' and the 'other'
In a way, it is obvious that science fiction is concerned with the other: often the other in time (generally the future, though, in rare cases, the past, or even alternate universes parallel to the present); with other worlds or beings (above all, intelligent beings on a par with humanity); with the other in mankind - the

---

[31]*The Book of Common Prayer*, Second Collect, for Peace.

[32]*The Alternative Service Book 1980*, p. 315 (Funeral Service).

[33]I Cor. 1:30 (AV).

[34]J Bronowski, *The Ascent of Man* (London, 1977), pp. 56, 60-6.

[35]M Polanyi, *The Tacit Dimension* (London, 1967), pp. 4-13ff.

[36]K Barth, *Dogmatics in Outline*, p. 16.

[37]JT Como, (ed.), *op. cit.*, p. xxxi. Cf. e.g., *Mere Christianity* (London, 1969), p. 116.

monster or the superman, or the supposedly inhuman but often all too human robot. These four variants: the alien, the robot, the monster and the superman are the categories under which one writer[38] has analysed the 'alien encounters' of science fiction. Above all, science fiction is concerned with *change*, often change brought about by scientific or technological developments, but with the common idea of a world which is significantly different in one or many ways to the one we take for granted. Because of this, various grandiose claims have been made by the genre, as might be expected by card-carrying members of it (JG Ballard[39] and Frederick Pohl[40]) as well as by more mainstream writers like Doris Lessing.[41]

The American science fiction writer Ursula Le Guin is notable for the way in which she has protested against the limitations of the genre, its concentration on the 'idea as hero' and its lack of interest in the individual and his or her character amongst other defects.[42] Kingsley Amis has defended the genre against such commonly made criticisms on the ground that it is unfair to rebuke it for failing to provide what is not its aim.[43] Nonetheless Le Guin interestingly (if not intentionally) responds to the critisicm in her books by integrating the other - the conventional ( in genre terms) 'alien' of science fiction - with the *human* other, the other who is met and known in love.

---

[38]M Rose, *Alien Encounters: Anatomy of Science Fiction* (Cambridge, Mass., 1981).

[39]JG Ballard claimed that sf is *the* characteristic art form of the 20th Century, it being a time of change, 'Book Four', Channel 4 TV., 24/11/82.

[40]Frederick Pohl quoted with approval Arthur C Clarke's description of sf as 'the only literary form which concerns itself with reality' at a meeting of the Cambridge Univeristy sf Society, 16/10/1982.

[41]D Lessing, *Shikasta* (London, 1981), pp. 10-11: 'the most original branch of literature now' (p. 10).

[42]'Science Fiction and Mrs Brown' by Ursula le Guin was published in *Science Fiction at Large*, P Nicholls (ed.), (London, 1976). There are two discussions of the issue in *Science Fiction: a critical guide*, P Parrinder (ed.), (London, 1979), by Scott Sanders and Patrick Parrinder.

[43]K Amis, *New Maps of Hell: A Survey of Science Fiction*, (London:, 1961), esp. pp. 132ff., 155.

Thus we find the difficulties between humans and non-humans in
her books ('I am a man and you are not. What likeness between
us?'[44]) answered: 'She, the stranger, the foreigner, of alien blood
and mind ... shared nothing at all with him, but had met him and
joined with him wholly and immediately across the gulf of their
great difference: as if it were the difference, the alienness between
them, that let them rest, and, in that joining together, freed
them'.[45]

This passage comes from *Planet of Exile*. Le Guin's books are
full of individuals alone on foreign planets who enter into an
intimate relationship with the inhabitants (so too *Rocannon's
World*, *The Left Hand of Darkness*, *City of Illusions* and *The
Dispossessed*). Love is frequently that which crosses the gap,
and one sentence from *Planet of Exile* sums up the theme: 'he
searched for the alien, the stranger, his wife'.[46]

In *The Dispossessed* the argument is even more strongly put as
one character contemplates her husband sleeping after a return to
her across space: 'We came, Tavker thought, from a great distance
to each other. We have always done so. Over great distances,
over years, over abysses of chance. It is because he comes from
so far away that nothing can separate us. Nothing, no distances,
no years, can be greater than the distance that's already between
us, the distance of our sex, the difference of our being, our minds;
that gap, that abyss which we bridge with a look, with a touch,
with a word, the easiest thing in the world'.[47]

This appreciation of otherness in science fiction is often revealed
in the treatment of the animal kingdom. As God is to man, says
one fantasy story directly,[48] so is man to the animal world.

[44]U Le Guin, *Planet of Exile* (published with *Rocannon's World*, (London,
1983), p. 200.
[45]*Ibid.*, p. 196.
[46]*Ibid.*, p. 238.
[47]U le Guin, *The Dispossessed* (Frogmore, 1975), p. 266.
[48]F Brown, 'Search' in *Angels and Spaceships* (New York, 1954), pp. 100-
1. Cf. also CD Simak, *City* (London, 1961), pp. 170-1 among other stories.

*The Dispossessed* sums up the theme yet again as the hero meets an otter: 'The otter sat up on its haunches and looked at him. Its eyes were dark, shot with gold, intelligent, curious, innocent. *"Ammar"*, Shevek whispered, caught by that gaze across the gulf of being - "brother"'.[49]

Similarly, CS Lewis, in the first of his interplanetary trilogy, *Out of the Silent Planet*, depicts the encounter of his hero with an alien being as 'the shy, ineluctable fascination of unlike for unlike',[50] 'the first tingling intercourse of two different, but rational, species'.[51]

The element of intelligence is indeed an added attraction. 'We are not alone', declared an advertising poster for Steven Spielberg's film, *Close Encounters of the Third Kind*.[52] And here the quest for the great Other, the otherness of God, is not absent. John Griffiths writes: 'stories about aliens by Western SF writers reveal three things: an ineradicable instinct for colonisation, an insatiable curiosity about the nature of man himself, and a great sense of loneliness ... above all, I believe, [sf about aliens] reveals a sense of loneliness, however dignified, which is bound to descend on man without religion'.[53] Kingsley Amis writes of alien beings of an 'unconscionable niceness' that 'it is in this way that emotions of humility and reverence most commonly make their appearance in sf, and I should not fight hard against a diagnosis of these as religious, or at least religiose'.[54] So, too, in Clifford Simak's stories aliens frequently are the bearers of

---

[49]*Op. cit.*, p. 131.

[50]CS Lewis, *Out of the Silent Planet* (London, 1971), p. 67.

[51]*Ibid.*, p. 63.

[52]In a very 'over the top' review of the film by Robert L Short in his *The Gospel from Outer Space* (London, 1983), p. 33. Another poster for Spielberg's film, *E.T.*, has the extraterrestrial's outstretched finger making contact with a man's in an obvious imitation of Michelangelo's painting of the Creation of Adam (J Pascall, *The Movies from 1930 to the Present*, (London, 1984), p. 282).

[53]J Griffiths, *Three Tomorrows: American, British and Soviet Science Fiction* (London, 1980), p. 156.

[54]*Op. cit.*, p. 82.

divinity for mankind, teaching them and transforming them.[55]

Thus we find 'otherness' a major concern in science fiction: the yearned for, if feared, otherness of other worlds, societies, intelligences, the introduction of the *novum* that is the essence of science fiction. Yet, this cannot be disassociated from the otherness of sex, of non-human creatures, of - in the last resort - God. Brian Aldiss has acknowledged both in novel and history the significance of the rejection of God for the development of science fiction.[56] The Enlightenment dream of a humanity freed from religious superstition gave birth to what he claims to be the first science fiction novel, Mary Shelley's *Frankenstein : or The Modern Prometheus* (1818).[57] Aldiss plausibly argues that science fiction is the work of mankind left alone in the universe, seeking to find his place in it without God. But man's creation, Frankenstein's monster, turns against its maker, destroying him. A thousand robot stories in which man's creation rebels against him lie in the future! Will mankind, left alone, bring in the vaunted earthly Paradise, or will a world come of age annihilate itself instead?[58] It is not insignificant that the final drama of Mary Shelley's novel is played out in the icy Arctic wastes, for many Romantics a symbol of man's terrifying new relationship to his environment.[59]

---

[55]E.g., CD Simak, 'Kindergarten' in *Portals of Tomorrow*, A Derleth (ed.), (New York, 1954), pp. 174-214; *Way Station* (London, 1976).

[56]Cf. *Billion Year Spree*, pp. 22-34; *Frankenstein Unbound* (London, 1982).

[57]*Classic Horror Omnibus*, vol. 1 (London, 1979), pp. 15-155.

[58]As occurs in Aldiss' novel *Frankenstein Unbound*.

[59]Fischer, *The Necessity of Art*, (p. 54) wrote that 'Romanticism arose from "a single I" opposed to an immense "not-I". This situation stimulated powerful self-awareness and proud subjectivism, but also a sense of bewilderment and abandon', (quoted in *Romanticism*, O Edwards and G Martin, (Milton Keynes, 1972), p. 18). Cf. also *ibid.*, p. 56 and plate 4 ('the Wreck of the "Hope"', 1821), showing a crushed ship dwarfed by the surrounding ice-floes. As Rose, *op. cit.*, pp. 69-75 points out, the invading Martians of HG Wells' *The War of the Worlds* (1898) are, in the end, not so much man's

The discussion of man's place in the Universe gives rise either to pride or terror, *praesumptio* or *desperatio*.[60] Sovereign, rebellious man doubts his own capacity. 'This swing to and fro between pride and anxiety is man's life', says Barth.[61] In science fiction terms, these alternative outlooks can be seen in the varying depictions of 'Man's' role in the universe (man is significantly given a capital letter in much science fiction). On the one hand, mankind is expanding, dominant, upthrusting: either the rulers of a Galactic culture, the seedbed of an interstellar civilisation, or the young and promising deposers of old static Empires; on the other hand, man is the exploiting villain of alien cultures, the victim of a socially-controlled or war-ruined future, or requiring guidance by mystical aliens towards interstellar maturity. Such contrasting visions may be partly rooted in national social and economic circumstances: Aldiss observes[62] that American science fiction is characteristically upbeat and expansionist - if with a lingering guilt about the treatment of the American Indian; British sf since HG Wells (with his description of the underground dwelling Morlocks of *The Time Machine*, 1895) is obsessed with political and social divisions, and global catastrophe. We may note in passing, the way in which science fiction serves to displace a vision of Earth, to give us the reflected 'view from a distant star', presenting earthly events in unearthly terms.[63]

Just as man displaces God in his role as the sole creator of life in *Frankenstein*, so too sf frequently depicts man in the manner of Genesis 3:5 ('you shall be as Gods') and 11:1-9 (the Tower of Babel). In fact in much sf, man becomes God, achieving self-transcendence in the conquest of the body (sf is much given to E.S.P., telepathy and creatures of 'pure energy'[64]), and, above

---

enemies as his companions, equally islands of life in an indifferent universe.

[60] J Moltmann, *Theology of Hope* (London, 1967), p. 23f.

[61] *Op. cit.*, p. 20.

[62] *Billion Year Spree*, pp. 131-2, 366 n2.

[63] An essential element in science fiction.

[64] The TV programmes *Dr Who* and *Star Trek* afford many examples. In van Vogt's 1968 story, 'The Proxy Intelligence' (*The Best of AE van Vogt*, vol.

all, of space. Typical sf book titles are *They Shall Have Stars*[65] and *The Stars My Destination*.[66] If science is the new religion, scientists the priests and science fiction writers the prophets, then space is the end goal: its heaven! For the *telos* of space, virtually any crime is justifiable, incuding murder.[67] Expansion through the universe is seen as man's 'manifest destiny'[68] which he must fulfil, and in which (in a rather ambiguous way) is seen his hope of avoiding nuclear holocaust: that is, if we blow up this planet, we can move on to the next one - *und so weiter*.[69]

Ben Bova speaks thus of a shuttle launch at Cape Canaveral: 'There is something about seeing a launch - the electric excitement of it, the overpowering grandeur of a giant rocket climbing into the sky slowly, inexorably, driven on by billowing tongues of flame - that's the closest thing to a religious experience that many of us have ever had. Hardened sceptics break into tears, when you see a 50-story tall column of intricate machinery detach itself from this planet and carry not only a few astronauts but also all the hopes and fears of the human race outward toward the infinite universe, you can never view your own life, the world or the space program in the same old way again'.[70]

Here man conquers the Universe, assails successfully 'the heavens' and becomes 'God'. Whether speaking of man as God, of aliens as god-replacements (saviours from beyond the sky - see

2, (London, 1984) a being reaches a state of invulnerability by reason of his high I.Q.!!

[65]J Blish (orig. 1952-4, published in *Cities in Flight*, (London, 1981)).

[66]A Bester (London, 1955), as Tiger! Tiger!.

[67]P Anderson, 'The Burning Bridge', in *Astounding Science Fiction*, 4/60, 68-87 (British edn.).

[68]James A Michener speaks this way of the space shuttle (*OMNI*, vol. 3.7, pp. 48-9, 102-40). Cf. also JF Kennedy's famous speech of 1961 to this effect (Lord Longford, *Kennedy*, (London, 1976), pp. 90-1).

[69]Ray Bradbury, *The Martian Chronicles* (London, 1979).

[70]*OMNI* , Jan. 1980, 2.4, p. 6 ('First Word').

*Superman!*), or of a divine Universe with which Man is merged in the fulness of time, religious ideas of one kind or another - and frequently dualistic and even Gnostic ones [71] - seem inseparable from sf.   The Christian contention, which is one of faith sustained by reason, is that such yearnings can be seen to echo our need for the great Other, who is the Creator of all.

Thus, it is the contention of this essay that the evangelistic imperative based on the command of our Lord (Matthew 28:19) requires us to take seriously the yearnings, fears and aspirations of the modern culture of which science fiction is a part; and as Christians, to respond to the sf dream of ascending to godhood in the heavens through space travel by the proclamation of the real God, 'who for us men and for our salvation came *down* from heaven'.

---

[71] Bob Shaw's *The Palace of Eternity* (London, 1980) features human souls ('egons') which float in space, attached to a 'world-mind' (p. 218).   Philip Jose Farmer's *Riverworld* books have a similar idea.

# 18

# Does God Suffer? Incarnation and Impassibility

ALAN TORRANCE

In the midst of his suffering Job gave expression to what might be regarded as the concrete form of humankind's cry of protest in the face of suffering: 'Hast thou eyes of flesh? Dost thou see as man sees?'[1] This is the ultimate question for those who suffer - the question of the extent of God's identification and solidarity with humankind in its unhappy situation. There is no theodicy which could appease Job. There is no explanation of why suffering must be a feature of the best of all possible worlds - and is therefore compatible with the existence of a God of love - which could be an adequate response to his questions. Indeed, any such answer would only serve to absolutize his suffering. It would make it ultimately and infinitely acceptable, something to be celebrated as constitutive of God's good creation. The only possible ground of meaningfulness for Job in his context is the address of the crucified Christ, not simply the Christ on the cross carrying out the painful work of redeeming humankind from its sin - this would be to refer to a suffering with a purpose whereas Job's seems to be meaningless - but the God who bears the cross in total and radical solidarity with Job in all his godforsakenness. This relates not only to the cross of Easter Friday but to the silence, the discontinuity and the rupture of meaning and language signified by Easter Saturday.[2]

In *The Brothers Karamazov* Fyodor Dostoevski offers a graphic description of human misery and suffering which further serves to

---

[1] Job 10: 4 (Revised Standard Version)

[2] Alan Lewis offers an excellent discussion of this theme in his brilliant paper, *The Burial of God: Rupture and Resumption as the Story of Salvation* presented to the joint Annual Conference of the Society for the Study of Theology and the Irish Theological Association, Belfast, 1986 in *SJT*, 40 (1987), pp. 335-62.

present the question as to whether God suffers as the most real question the theologian can ask.

'A Bulgarian I met lately in Moscow', Ivan went on, seeming not to hear his brother's words, 'told me about the crimes committed by Turks and Circassians in all parts of Bulgaria through fear of a general rising of the Slavs ... These Turks took a pleasure in torturing children, too; cutting the unborn child from the mother's womb, and tossing babies up in the air and catching them on the points of their bayonets before their mother's eyes. Doing it before the mother's eyes was what gave zest to the amusement. Here is another scene that I thought very interesting. Imagine a trembling mother with her baby in her arms, a circle of invading Turks around her. They've planned a diversion; they pet the baby, laugh to make it laugh. They succeed, the baby laughs. At that moment a Turk points a pistol four inches from the baby's face. The baby laughs with glee, holds out his little hands to the pistol, and he pulls the trigger in the baby's face and blows out its brains'.[3]

How do we conceive of the being of God in the context of this kind of event? What kind of solidarity with the suffering of the mother can we understand on the part of God? Does her suffering touch His Being in any way? The most, possibly the only, valid way of posing this question would be by recounting the story of the crucifixion but the force of that story has been undermined by the way in which the cross has been explained and categorized over two thousand years as theologians have struggled to reconcile it with their preconceived conceptions of the Being of God and to remove its foolishness before their Greek philosophical conceptualities. Accordingly, its reality has been tragically lost for much theology by way of its translation into the ideal world.

---

3*The Brothers Karamazov*, C Garnett (ET), (New York, 1933), pp. 245-6, quoted in A Plantinga's book, *God Freedom and Evil*.

## I  A Brief Discussion of the Historical Origins of the Debate - Patripassianism and Theopassianism

The notion that God suffers was systematically rejected by the fathers of the Church and its assessment fell under two closely related headings: 'patripassianism' and 'theopassianism'.

Patripassianism was a monarchian heresy articulated by Noetus of Smyrna. He affirmed that there was only one God, that is, the Father and as a corollary of this concluded that it was the Father therefore who suffered and who was the subject of Christ's other human experiences. In Kelly's words, 'if Christ was God, as Christian faith took for granted, then He must be identical with the Father; otherwise he could not be God. Consequently, if Christ suffered, the Father suffered, since there could be no division in the Godhead'.[4] Noetus was condemned and left protesting, as Hyppolytus tells us, 'what wrong have I done, glorifying one only God, Christ, Who was born, suffered and died?'[5] The primary objection was to their denial of the Trinity, in that 'they believed not in the Triad, but only in the Monad'.[6] The Patripassian heresy was a consequence of a weakness in their doctrine of God and was condemned along with other Trinitarian errors in the canons of the 'Tome of Damasus' which emerged from the Council of Rome (382): 'If anyone says that in the passion of the cross it is God Himself who felt the pain and not the flesh and the soul which Christ, the Son of God, had taken to Himself - the form of servant which he had accepted as Scripture says (cf. Phil. 2.7) - he is mistaken.'[7]

The issues here were raised very early on with Clement of Rome revealing the theopaschite leanings reflected in the teaching of the Patripassians before the end of the first century. By the second century theopaschite statements abounded. Prestige provides several examples. Ignatius, the prophet-bishop of Antioch, leads the way. 'Our God, Jesus the Christ, was

---

[4]JND Kelly, *Early Christian Doctrines* (5th edn.), (London, 1977), p. 120.
[5]*C. Noet. 1* (quoted in Kelly, *op cit.*, p. 120)
[6]Cf. AH Strong, *Systematic Theology* (Philadelphia, 1907), p. 327.
[7]*The Christian Faith in the Doctrinal Documents of the Catholic Church*, J Neuner and J Dupuis (eds.), (London, 1983), p. 147

conceived by Mary' (*ad Eph.* 18.2); 'by the will of the Father and Jesus Christ our God' (*ib. proem.*); 'permit me to be an imitator of the passion of my God' (*ad Rom.* 6.3.). Tatian (*ad Graec.* 13.3) speaks of the minister of the God that has suffered. Melito (fragment 7, Goodspeed, p. 310) says that God suffered at the hands of Israel ... Clement (*Protrept.* 10, 106.4) cries, 'believe, O man, in Man and God; believe, O man in the living God that suffered and is worshipped'.[8]

Theopassianism was systematically asserted and espoused by certain Monophysites and was first maintained in an extreme form by Peter Fullo, the Monophysite Patriarch of Antioch. It is said that he altered the Trisagion ('Holy God, Holy and mighty, Holy and immortal, have mercy upon us') which featured so prominently in Eastern liturgies, to the form 'Holy God, Holy Mighty, Holy Immortal, thou who for our sakes was crucified, have mercy upon us'. This formula enjoyed fairly widespread use and the Emperor Justinian even issued an edict directing its adoption. This, incidentally, was after the Council of Rome in 382 where it had been asserted (canon 166) that 'if anyone says that in the passion of the cross it is God Himself who felt the pain and not the flesh and the soul which Christ, the Son of God, had taken to Himself ... he is mistaken'.[9]

Whereas patripassianism was rejected because it betrayed confusion on the part of its advocates with regard to their grasp of the Triune being of God,[10] theopassianism interpreted more

[8]GL Prestige, *God in Patristic Thought*, 2nd edn., (London, 1952), p. 77.
[9]Cf. JH Blunt, *Dictionary of Sects, Heresies, Ecclesiastical Parties, and Schools of Religious Thought*, 'Theopaschites', (London, 1874), p. 594. Here is quoted another church canon to emerge from Rome which condemns theopassianism decreeing that the Godhead of Christ could not suffer and that he 'sustained the suffering of the cross to as great an entent as was in accordance with the flesh'.
[10]St Augustine makes this particularly clear in *Tractate 36*, 'On the Gospel of John Chapter 8:15-18' sections 8-9 where he exhorts his readers to be 'sane' and to avoid the Patripassian form of Sabellianism arguing that we must distinguish though not separate the Father and the Son thereby avoiding the Scylla and Charybdis of theology. His particular concern here, however, is to emphasize the absolute 'togetherness' of the Father and the Son throughout the

generally was rejected because it confused the two natures of Christ. This immediately poses the question however as to *why* the suggestion that God suffered on the cross should involve such a confusion. Why must the suggestion that God suffered betray a confusion between the two natures? Is there not the possibility that suffering relates to some common ground - something which, like love, could be predicated of *both* the human *and* the divine natures of Christ? The answer is simply that for the theologians of the time it was believed that God *cannot* suffer and that therefore the suffering of Christ must be localised accordingly by being predicated of his human nature alone.[11] The concern which emerges here is whether this eagerness to deny that God can suffer does not begin to undermine the very integrity of the incarnation - an integrity which was taken for granted in much of the earliest theological reflection and was often reflected, as we have seen, in the prayer and liturgy of the early church. We are now led to consider therefore to what extent we are required theologically to perpetuate this denial that God can or does suffer.

---

incarnation. 'The Son carried flesh, the Father was with the Son. If the Father was in heaven, the Son on earth, how was the Father with the Son? Because both Father and Son were everywhere; for God is not in such a manner in heaven so as not to be on earth'. This section reflects the extent to which suffering was connected in Augustine's mind with human flesh and, as should become clear later on, this was because his metaphysical categories were not adequately 'personal'. This is further seen in his Sermons where he writes: 'The Father indeed suffered not, but the Son, yet the suffering of the Son was the work of the Father and the Son'. Sermon 2, section 8 (*The Nicene and Post-Nicene Fathers, vol. 6*, P Schaff (ed.), (Grand Rapids, 1974), p. 261a) Augustine sought to emphasize the 'togetherness' of the Father and the Son but this was construed in spatial terms i.e. as omnipresence or in terms of common work or intention in order to avoid theopassian categories. The question with which one is left concerns the extent to which his notion of the Holy Spirit as the *vinculum caritatis* between the Father and the Son has been allowed to inform his thinking here. If it had been would he not have found himself having to say more about the character of this togetherness in the context of the fleshly suffering of the Son?

11 There is not space to go into the philosophical and sociological background of the apperception which could not connect suffering with the being of God but clearly one would have to discuss the influence of the neo-Platonism of Plotinus on the fathers and also the correlation of suffering with sin and the understanding of life as the 'school of suffering'.

*Does God Suffer?*

We have hinted at the extent to which a negative answer to the question, 'Can God suffer?' has played a profoundly important rôle in the development of doctrine, we must now look at the kinds of arguments, and their underlying methodologies, which have operated to support a negative answer to the question.

## II Arguments grounded in the Concept or Definition of God

Traditionally the unity of God has been adopted in the Judaeo-Christian context as an unquestioned axiom. Aquinas presented the traditional argument in support of this axiom suggesting that if there were two gods one would possess what the other lacked and therefore the notion of divine perfection necessarily involves divine unity. For the same reasons divine indivisibility, i.e. divine simplicity, was affirmed.[12] If God is in any sense divisible those parts which constituted the being of God would have to be lacking in some way and would therefore be less than perfect. As Eusebius had argued in the fourth century, the unity of the deity makes it superior therefore to any compound body. And as Gregory of Nyssa had suggested about the same time,[13] it is the compound character of bodily nature which necessarily leads to passions and infirmities. Suffering is grounded in the tension between conflicting desires and capacities - the desire for happiness and the perception of its negation.

Immutability was similarly affirmed because change implies imperfection - if one is changing in any way then one must be involved either in progression towards or retrogression from perfection and both of these alternatives involve some point where the being involved is less than perfect. Impassibility was seen to be equivalent to immutability since it suggests that God cannot suffer change or be affected by any cause or influence be it external or internal. As Nels Ferré summarizes the traditional argument, 'after all, if everything is perfect, why should there be suffering on the part of the perfect author? If God as suffering is

12Plotinus interpreted this simplicity as a bare, characterless, self-identity. Aquinas however held that God actually possesses the perfections we ascribe to him and that these coalesce in an unimaginable unity.
13 *Or. Cat.* 7. cf. Prestige, *op. cit.*, p. 10.

imperfect, however, He certainly is not sovereign in the final sense. Certainly He must in that case be limited from within by this condition'. [14] And he adds that this was taken to mean that God cannot therefore experience pain.

The concern throughout these traditional forms of reasoning was to maintain the reality and unity of God and this, as Prestige argues, involved adherence to a notion of divine self-consistency which excluded the possibility of divine passibility.

Parallel to the doctrine of divine unity is the equally important doctrine of divine self-consistency. This doctrine is also closely allied to that of impassibility and on it the latter logically depends. As has been stated already, there is no sign that divine impassibility was taught with any view of minimizing the interest of God in his creation or his care and concern for the world that he had made. In fact, any such theory is manifestly absurd. Impassibility, though affording an obvious line of approach to the wider doctrine, is a department of the larger question of self-consistency.[15]

Therefore traditionally there has been advocated a tightly interwoven web of concepts which serve to support each other and together to exclude any notion of divine suffering.

However, this obviously raises the question, as HP Owen points out,[16] of the apparent contradiction between the supposition that God cannot experience pain and the biblical descriptions of God's love. Of course, this apparent contradiction classical theologians attempted to explain away at least in relation to christological references, by appealing to the two nature interpretation of the person of Christ arguing that although Christ experienced pain in his human nature, God cannot experience it in himself, for being wholly perfect, he is pure joy.

---

14*The Christian Understanding of God* (London, 1952), p. 118.

15Prestige, *op. cit.*, p. 11.

16'Concepts of God' in *The Encyclopaedia of Philosophy*, vol. 3, P Edwards (ed.), (New York, 1967), p. 346.

*Does God Suffer?*

As we have seen this whole concern can be traced to a particular approach towards defining God's nature and his necessary simplicity and unity which, as Nels Ferré rightly points out, stands in danger of translating the living Agape into some static, mathematical One. He continues, 'often this One, too, must statically remain so, and cannot, therefore, recur in history without being considered relative or less than absolute. With the right conception of the ultimate these problems evaporate. Love then becomes seen as the nature of the changeless which yet affords the richness of continual creative change. The nature of love, however, is to become involved with those who need - the sinful and the sufferer. Love identifies itself with sorrow and shares it. Love sympathises'.[17]

But there is a danger here and that is to add a new concept, namely *agape*, to the list produced by this metaphysic and simply reinterpret the attributes in accordance with a prior human definition of love. To do this is to fail to grasp the extent of the methodological fallacies in the traditional approach. The fundamental question here is: 'to what extent does this approach really seek to define God out of God's own Self-gift in the incarnation?' Any approach which fails to do this at the most fundamental level must in the final analysis be interpreted as offering a *de facto* denial of the incarnation. The only way of accepting the incarnation or indeed taking it into account is to allow it radically to redefine all one's prior concepts of God. If Christ becomes simply 'another word' or an 'extra word' he becomes a postscript to metaphysics and ceases therefore to be The Word. For this reason in Christ all our prior forms of human wisdom and definition must be submitted to the Truth, not to be revised by us in the light of the extra information which Christ may or may not provide about God but to be redefined and restructured in the light of his *person*. This is surely the only way we can begin to work out the implications of, for example, the first two chapters of 1 Corinthinians for theological method.

17*Op. cit.*, p. 119.

### III The weakness of the traditional 'metaphysical' approach

Over the last millenium some of the arguments of the Church
Fathers have been taken up and recast within a metaphysics
(which the Greek fathers in particular would have found quite
foreign and which has ignored their christological insights)
whereby a quasi-deistic conception of God was developed and it is
on the denial of divine passibility on these grounds that I now
wish to concentrate.

Jürgen Moltmann sees the approach exemplified by Aquinas in his
five ways as one that defines God *for the sake of* the world and
finite being.[18] Following Luther, Moltmann argues that we must
oppose the knowledge of God in the cross to the natural
knowledge of God from his works.  This is not to dispute the
*possibility* of natural knowledge of God but rather to dispute its
*reality* and this is disputed on the basis of 1 Cor. 1: 21 which he
interprets in the following way: 'Because men and women did not
know God from creation' - but perverted this truth into the lie of
idolatry - 'it pleased God through the folly of what we preach (the
crucified Christ) to save those who believe'.  Natural knowledge
of God is potentially open to men but in fact they misuse it in
the interest of their self-exaltation and self-divinisation.[19]

When, on the metaphysical approach, the divine being is
conceived for the sake of finite being 'it must embrace all the
determinations of finite being and exclude those determinations
which are directed against being.  Otherwise finite being could not
find a support and stay against the threatening nothingness of
death, suffering and chaos in the divine being'.  Accordingly, 'for

---

18Moltmann writes of Aquinas: 'He calls God that which must be conceived
of as the first, the all-embracing, the origin and the principle, if the finite
world is to be conceived of as a unity.  That is, he conceives of a last, first,
unconditioned and final principle for the sake of the concept of the world as a
whole.  God is then not thought of for his own sake but for the sake of
something else, for the sake of finite being.  The heuristic interest is that of
'securing' God in and for finite being'. *The Crucified God*, (ET), (London,
1974), p. 211
19*Ibid.*, p. 211.

metaphysics, the nature of divine being is determined by its unity and indivisibility, its lack of beginning and end, its immovability and immutability'.[20] Characterised in this way the metaphysical approach was driven to conclude that 'the God who was the subject of suffering could not be truly God'.[21]

The underlying motivation here may seem to be incidental but what is of material importance is that God was defined in terms of *a priori* categories of unity and indivisibility and therefore of a logically necessary impassibility which, as Ferré has pointed out, is grounded in a mathematical conception of the One rather than the living Agape known reverently through divine Self-disclosure to the finite mind. Such a notion of unity quickly becomes a Procrustean bed into which God is shaped to fit.

What emerges from the 'panlogicism' of this kind of metaphysics as it developed after Aquinas is a conception of God which is highly anthropomorphic. God is interpreted in monadic terms as the ultimate, rational, self-contained *Individuum* - the extrapolation and projection *ad infinitum* of the human person of medieval scholasticism for whom love was not seen as of the essence of the self but as an extrinsic attribute. *Persona est naturae rationalis individua substantia.*

It is on the grounds of what is best described as the unselfcritical 'foundationalism' manifest in this manner of defining God that the Christian theologian must reject such 'metaphysical' approaches. In addition to being methodologically invalid, the foundationalism operative here is programmed by prior categories which are materially inappropriate.

Foundationalism in its most general form is characterized by the presupposition that the philosopher can define, in advance of investigating any particular subject-matter, the general shape which the methods, the theory of knowing and indeed the conclusions will have to take on the basis of certain universal and absolute foundations without which, it is believed, there could be

---

20*Ibid.*, p. 214.
21*Ibid.*, p. 215.

no human knowledge, discovery or scientific conclusions. The genius of the chief reformers lay in their ability substantially to break with this way of approaching theology. Both Luther and Calvin were determined, in their various ways, to allow Christ and the cross to interpret their own theological significance and revise our metaphysical apperceptions such that they became neither subsumed under nor conditioned by any prior scholastic categories and concepts.[22]

It was with Karl Barth, however, that the refusal to adopt a 'foundationalist' approach was worked through with the most radical thoroughness. Indeed, this concern characterizes the whole method and structure of his dogmatics and receives explicit theological expression both in *Church Dogmatics* 1/1 and in his controversy with Emil Brunner over natural theology where he rejected what we are referring to here as the 'foundationalism' inherent in natural theology (rather as Martin Luther had done before him in the Heidelberg disputation) but where in total consistency with himself he also refused, to engage in any *a priori* rejection of natural theology![23] Any such *a priori* rejection would have been to submit to a new form of *a priori* theologizing or foundationalism. Knowledge of God must be, as

22 Alister McGrath's definition of scholasticism conveys something of the 'foundationalist' nature of medieval thought. He defines it as 'a method of theological and philosophical speculation that seeks the rational penetration and systematisation of revealed truth on the basis of philosophical concepts'. *The Science of Theology*, G Evans, A McGrath and A Galloway, (Basingstoke, 1986), p. 155. Although Luther did manage to move substantially from medieval scholasticism one still witnesses in some of his thought, not least his interpretation of the Lord's Supper, the hangover of scholastic metaphysics. Calvin was much more successful than Luther here due both to the remarkable genius of his insights into theological method and also to the influence upon him of the humanist school of thought. In his discussion of predestination, however, we witness at times an unfortunate flashback to a doctrine of God which owes less to the Word than to scholastic conceptions of God.

23 This is a point rarely appreciated by Barth's critics but of fundamental importance. The rejection of natural theology is purely the corollary of grace - David Hume's *Dialogues* offer, for Barth, *neither* the reason *nor* the ratification for his rejection of natural theology. It is the incarnation alone which offers both.

Brunner also argued, 'through God alone' and is grounded therefore solely in God's Self-bestowal as Word to us and for us. Barth went on, however, to insist that this Word is not to be regarded simply as material provided to take the shape of prior human *forms* but as creating its own forms of understanding, its own space and its own grammar. There can be no divorce between form and content here which would allow a synergistic form of Divine Self-communication whereby human beings were responsible for fifty per cent of the process holding up vessels which would define the shape (and therefore in this case the content) of that 'revelation' which would fill them.

What it is important to appreciate here therefore is that it was the failure, in the medieval period, to grasp these issues of fundamental importance for theological method which led to the seductive influence in the West of a 'foundationalist' theological approach - which operated with preconceived arithmetic notions of oneness and unity - and which resulted in the profoundly detrimental conditioning and individualising of God and the human subject. This occurred by virtue of the attempt to define the nature of the God of revelation by way of a methodology formed *in advance of* the content of this revelation. And it was this which led to a notion of divine impassibility which was ultimately incompatible with the God of the incarnation. This resulted on the one hand in a widespread denial of the incarnation on *a priori* grounds and, on the other, in an accompanying conception of God which could be nothing more than the projection *ad infinitum* or 'divinisation' of concepts (such as oneness, indivisibility, impassibility) grounded ultimately in the operations of the human mind.

The strength of the grip in which this approach held (and still holds) the theological debate lies in a circular form of self-support which this model has lent to itself by way of the conception of revelation and action of God in the world which it engendered.

**IV The atomism inherent in the foundationalist model of God's engagement with humanity**

One of the universal confusions which radically moulds and conditions theology is grounded in an inadequate conception of the grammatical form of revelation. It is naïvely accepted that if there is to be divine revelation it will be of the form: $S^1$ (the divine subject) reveals P (propositional truths or 'ideas') to $S^2$ (the human subject) where an absolute distinction and disjunction can be made between the being of $S^1$ and the being and nature of P. What is more, a further distinction can be made between the being of $S^1$ and the extrinsic and external act of 'revealing'. If there is any correlation between P and $S^1$ then this must be 'referential' in form and not therefore 'ontological'. There is also presupposed a kind of parallelism about the revelation axis such that we can say similar things about $S^2$. For example $S^2$ is regarded as receiving revelation P in such a way that the act of receiving the revelation is extrinsic to the being and constitution of $S^2$. Receiving revelation P might conceivably influence $S^2$ such that s/he acts differently in the future on the basis of additional information gained through the act of revelation. However, this does not relate to the form or being of S which is presupposed as determined in advance of (since it is historically prior to) the revelation occurrence.

This revelation model profoundly influences the redemption/ sanctification models of God's activity in relation to humankind. Here it is acknowledged that the acts of redemption and santification on the part of God touch the human subject - specifically their will.[24] However, this is rarely construed as relating to the mind and intellectual structures of the 'rational subject' for the simple and fallacious reason that our intellectual structures are again presupposed by and therefore 'foundational to'

---

24 I might add here that too often sanctification is conceived as self-sanctification in response to divine revelation i.e. where it is interpreted not as a relational act of God in grace focussing our minds on the one in whom 'all parts of our salvation are complete' (Calvin) - such that, by the Holy Spirit, that mind which was in Christ Jesus might be realised in us - but as a strenuous (*incurvatus in se*) act of the human subject performed on him/herself!

*Does God Suffer?*

any activity on the part of God toward us which can (rationally) be recognized to be such. In other words, God's actions are regarded as necessarily 'external' to the rational essence of the (thereby 'individualized') subject. Furthermore, in accordance with the forementioned parallelism around the revelation axis, the being of God receives similar treatment and is conceived as quite independent of God's actions and 'communiqués' which are perceived accordingly to be external actions of grace ('graces') and mercy which are responses to external affairs extrinsic to the being of God.

In the Reformation this model began to break down, first, from the side of God in Martin Luther and his theology of the Cross where he rediscovered the very Being of God in the suffering of Christ and, second, from the side of the human subject in John Calvin when he began to work out the implications of redemption for the working of our minds. Calvin was enabled, thereby, to perceive the extent of the effect of sin upon the operations of the mind, that we are 'alienated in our minds' and that we are therefore radically and fundamentally (i.e. *foundationally*) corrupt. For this reason, Calvin's approach to the knowledge of God was radically new in the West, and is still rarely appreciated and fully understood! Reconciliation is the *sine qua non* of knowledge of God and there can be no divorce therefore between revelation and redemption - for God is known *in a reconcilinga c t*. It increasingly became clear therefore that there could be no atomistic divorce between the being of the one receiving revelation (S2) and the whole event of revelation itself, and that nor could there be a disjunctive compartmentalising of revelation and reconciliation. The carcinogenic fragmentation which had occurred as a result of the foundationalist individuation of God (by way of the absolutisation of a mathematical conception of Oneness), of his activities and consequently of the human subject was finally being interrupted as a much more holistic, and indeed Pauline, understanding of the being of the human person began to emerge.

It is not until Karl Barth, Eberhard Jüngel and Jürgen Moltmann,

358

however, that we see the reversal of this process fully realised. Karl Barth expounded the identity of the Word and Act of God in such a way that the totality of the nature, structure and content of revelation was seen to *be* God. He writes: 'When God speaks, there is no point in looking about for a related act. The fear that talk might be "only" talk is, of course, only too apposite in relation to human speech. When a human being speaks, then his/her misery, the rift between truth and reality in which he/she lives, is plainly exposed ... The distinction between word and act is that mere word is the mere self-expression of a person, while act is the resultant relative alteration in the world around. Mere word is passive, act is an active participation in history. But this kind of distinction does not apply to the Word of God. As mere Word it is act. As mere Word it is the divine person, the person of the Lord of history, whose self-expression is as such an alteration of the world, whose *passio* in history is as such *actio*'.[25]

Barth's interpretations of the Triunity of God as the Revealer, the Revelation and the Revealedness - where the Being, Word and Act of God are interpreted together as a total and integrated unity - exposed once and for all the absurdity of the traditional models of revelation and methods of interpreting the being and revelation of God. Accordingly, the theologian is liberated to interpret God out of God in the Spirit of God whereby the very activity of this interpretation becomes part of the redeemed and sanctified life of the Church theologian who is compelled by silence and reverence before God to proclaim Christ, to utter the Word and therefore, in Bonhoeffer's words, 'to speak within the context of the silence of the church'.[26] It is this prior human silence which is disallowed by foundationalism in all its forms. And it is this silence which allows our questions about the being of God and the prior apperception which frames these to be questioned and accordingly restructured by God himself.[27]

---

25 *CD I/1*, pp. 143-4. (I have made minor changes to the translation to remove 'exclusive' language which is not there in the German.)

26 D Bonhoeffer, *Christology*, J Bowden (ET), (London, 1966), p. 27.

27 Cf. TF Torrance, *Theology in Reconstruction* (London, 1965), Ch. 7,

This new (for the West) interpretation of revelation is expressed brilliantly by Eberhard Jüngel in his exposition of Barth. First, he shows that '*the revelation of God itself is the enabling of the interpretation of revelation*'.[28] And second, he expounds the implications of the fact that in God's revelation God's word is identical with God himself. Since in revelation the fulness of the original self-existent being of God's word reposes and lives, then 'revelation is that event in which the *being of God* itself comes to word'.[29] This leads to a new understanding of the oneness of the Being of the God of the Christian faith - a oneness which is very different from the mathematical One which Ferré witnessed in scholastic theology. 'In revelation, therefore, we have to do with *one* internally-distinguished being of God. The *oneness* of this internally-distinguished being of God is grounded in the fact that revelation is "not an other over against God" but "a reiteration of God"'.[30] This reiteration denotes the fact that in God's taking form God is in his revelation his own double. God's taking form is thus not an *accidens* of God but an *event*: 'an event which presupposes a self-distinction in God, "something new in God, a self-distinction of God from himself, a being of God in a mode of existence ... in which he can also exist for us"'.[31]

This tracing of revelation into the very being of God does not lead us to deprive God of freedom. Jüngel does not introduce necessity into revelation. And this is of importance for us as we finally come to answer the question, in the light of this discussion, as to whether God suffers as we shall be arguing that this suffering is a free suffering. He writes, '"*Revelation* always means *revealing*"; for "God's presence is always *God's decision to be present*'. The God who *can* reveal is not *obliged* to reveal himself ... God as the subject of revelation *remains* distinguished from revelation. Were this not so then revelation

'Questioning in Christ'.
28Eberhard Jüngel, *The Doctrine of the Trinity: God's Being is in Becoming*, H Harris (ET), (Edinburgh, 1976), p. 15.
29*Ibid.*, p. 15.
30*Ibid.*, pp. 16-7.
31*Ibid.*, p. 18.

would cease to be revelation. For it is not '*the form* which reveals, speaks, comforts, works and aids, *but God in the form*".[32]

In God's self-revelation we have the self-gift of the God who is irreducibly triune. He can be our God only because he is eternally triune and as such he is our God 'in advance'. In other words, the revelation of God is both a radically free act of grace grounded in the free decision of God to be God for us and yet also one which emanates from the eternal being of God. God *is* love and his being-as-event *is* love. Jüngel explains this in the following way:

The self-giving in which God is already ours *in advance* is the self-giving in which *he* belongs *to himself*. This self-giving is the self-relatedness of God's being within the modes of being of the Father, the Son and the Spirit, which must be differentiated. In the self-relatedness of God's being the relational structuring of this being *eventuates*. As the mutual self-giving of the three modes of God's being, the being of God is event. Because the being of God as threehood is self-giving (love), this being may not be thought of as something abstract. Where it becomes abstract it is not comprehended as God's being. For 'being is actually something abstract only where it is abstracted from love'.[33]

What is of supreme importance here is that on this model 'the self-interpretation of God is also the self-identification of God and where accordingly there is no *identity* separable from the *event* of self-identification between the being of God and a being understood as revelation'.[34] As Jüngel himself points out, this has a profoundly anti-metaphysical and anti-mythological significance and frees us to think God as the God who reveals himself - not as something concealed behind the revelation but *as* the revelation.

32*Ibid.*, p. 19.
33*Ibid.*, pp. 28-9.
34*Ibid.*, p. 26.

Here Jüngel (following Barth) has finally broken the grip upon theology of the 'atomistic' model of God's interaction with humankind in revelation and reconciliation where the Subject of revelation (S1), the revelation and the receiver of revelation (S2) are each conceived as self-contained and distinct entities. Now we have a theological perspective which refuses to engage in a naïve 'construction' of God's unity by the projection on to God either of fallacious anthropological models of the self as a self-contained, rational individual or of mathematical models of simple, monadic One-ness - in terms of which it is questionable as to whether God could in any way be thought.[35] We have a dynamic conception of a God who has his Being in loving and where this is grounded in internal relations constitutive of God's self-revelation *ad extra* but where the *Deus ad extra* is the *Deus ad intra* in such a way that God's being *toward us* is not something external to (and thereby different from) God's own being but *is* God's *being* in the profoundest sense - where God's being is *in becoming*.[36]

In many ways this emphasis parallels that of John Zizioulas as he discusses the revolution in ontology which took place in the Church Fathers but which was tragically lost sight of in the West. This revolution in thinking can be characterized by the discovery, shaped by their ecclesial experience and contemplation on the Trinity, that 'it is communion which makes things "be": nothing exists without it, not even God'.[37] 'There is no true being without communion. Nothing exists as an "individual",

---

[35]In a private conversation with Eberhard Jüngel he suggested that if God's being were 'simple' he could not be thought. This connects with the comment of John Zizioulas that 'the being of God is a relational being: without the concept of communion it would not be possible to speak of the being of God', *Being as Communion*, (London, 1985), p. 17.

[36]*Ibid.*, p. 64. See also p. 102 where Jüngel adds that this 'becoming' is the becoming of relationship which is 'a becoming of itself but not from itself'. If this important point is not understood then God's being becomes the *panta rhei* of the process theologians where it is mistakenly thought that the being of God can be understood in dynamic terms by working with that same model of divine substance and divine unity but by conceiving of it in organic terms.

[37]*Op. cit.*, p. 17.

conceivable in itself. Communion is an ontological category'.[38] What was of decisive significance here, accordingly to Zizioulas, was the discovery of Athanasius that *'Communion belongs not to the level of will and action but to that of substance'.*[39] Accordingly, 'the substance of God, "God" has no ontological content, no true being, apart from communion'.[40] What is true of God here becomes true of creation as a whole: *'To be* and *to be in relation* become identical. For someone or something to be, two things are simultaneously needed: being itself *(hypostasis)* and *being in relation* (i.e. being a person). It is only in relationship that identity appears as having an ontological significance'.[41] What is being argued is that communion between persons is not an external relationship between individual, self-contained substances. Rather a person is constituted by communion, by love. A person has his/her *hypostasis* in *ekstasis*.[42] Persons only *are*, therefore, to the extent that they have their being in communion. This understanding finds ultimate ontological grounding in the being of God who 'is' communion. 'The Holy Trinity is a *primordial ontological concept* and not a notion which is added to the divine substance or rather which follows it, as in the case of the dogmatic manuals of the West'.[43]

Zizioulas spells out the implications of this for our understanding of God in the clearest terms: 'The expression "God is love" (1 John 4:16) signifies that God subsists as Trinity, that is as person and not as substance. Love is not an emanation or "property" of the substance of God ... but is *constitutive* of His

---

38*Ibid.*, p. 18.
39*Ibid.*, p. 86.
40*Ibid.*, p. 17.
41*Ibid.*, p. 88.
42Cf. 'Human Capacity and Incapacity: A Theological Exploration of Personhood', *SJT*, 28 (1975), p. 420 where Zizioulas makes the point that the notion 'person', if properly understood, is 'perhaps the only notion that can be applied to God without the danger of anthropomorphism'.
43*Being as Communion*, p. 17.

substance, i.e. it is that which makes God what he is, the one God. Thus love ceases to be a qualifying - i.e. secondary - property of being and becomes *the supreme ontological predicate*. Love as God's mode of existence "hypostasises" God, *constitutes* His being. Therefore, as a result of love, the ontology of God is not subject to the necessity of substance'.[44]

The implications of the emphases of Jüngel and Zizioulas for the question whether we can conceive of God as suffering are profound. A proper theological ontology grounded in the relational being of God as love compels us to break radically with the impersonal conceptions of divine (and human) substance which have shaped Western thinking on the matter. It is at the same time no longer valid to define the divine 'substance' (*hypostasis*) in terms of impersonal (anti-personal) models of unity, simplicity and necessary impassibility. To approach the being of God in terms of *a priori* (foundationalist) categories constituted by a foreign, secular ontology or metaphysic of substance is not only methodologically unscientific and irrational (if a rational investigation is one which allows the nature of the object of an enquiry to prescribe the modes of its investigation) but theologically inappropriate. There are at least three reasons for this. First, being must be comprehended ultimately in terms of the being of God not *vice versa*. Second, central to the Christian Gospel is the discovery that human being is constituted by the being of God in the dynamic of revelation as God's gracious act of reconciliation and redemption. Third, God's being cannot be conceived as existing apart from (behind) God's act of revelation. Such a conception neither does nor can make any sense of the nature of divine revelation for the reasons we have expounded above. Rather, the being of God ek-sists in the act of revelation, that is, it *is* in the act of self-communication for communion. God *is* in the event of revelation.

**V Can God suffer?**
Clearly, the person of Christ, as the eternal Word made flesh and the One in whom the fulness of the Godhead *dwells* bodily (ek-

---

[44]*Ibid.*, p. 46.

statically) and *is* bodily (hypo-statically), must serve as the control on our answer to this question. It should become quite clear now that we cannot sidestep the question of God's identification with the sufferings of Christ by appealing to the two natures of Christ and defining the divine nature in accordance with a 'metaphysical' conception of divine substance. A blithe assertion that the suffering relates only therefore to Christ's human nature would be unacceptable for all the reasons discussed above. At the same time we cannot fuse the Divine and human in such a way as to eternalize the suffering which characterizes the historical world and to make divine suffering a necessary suffering. This would be simply another way of perpetuating a static conception of divine substance by interpreting it as infinitely suffering substance. Such a notion again could owe nothing to the dynamic of personal communion stemming from the free Person of God.

An invalid way of predicating suffering of God is to define God as eternally loving and then, by defining love as participation in the suffering of others, to define God as necessarily, eternally suffering. This approach has some appeal to those who would romanticize suffering and God's participation in it. To use the concept of suffering of God's essence in this way would mean that we would have to say with Aquinas that, like love, suffering must be predicated analogically of God by being attributed archetypally, intrinsically and primarily of God (*unius ad alterum* and *per prius et posterius*).[45] This would be to make suffering an essential perfection of God's eternal being in which humankind would ideally participate in and through communion with God - and, incidentally, this could offer no hope to those who suffer. To say that God suffers in this way would ultimately be to make precisely the same mistake as those who deny God's suffering on grounds of ontological necessity - it would be to support a *material* fallacy deriving from mistaken *forms* of reasoning.

Rather, if we approach the hypostatic union in common with the Greek fathers such that the starting-point of our Christology

45Cf. B Mondin, *The Principle of Analogy in Protestant and Catholic Theology* (The Hague, 1962), chs 2-4.

becomes the hypostasis, the person of the God-man then we interpret Christ's sufferings as God's ek-static sharing in the sufferings of humankind not as a necessary co-distribution of suffering but as a free act of love. God's suffering would then be seen to be a suffering *in* communion - a communion which, when fully and ultimately realised, will be eternally free from suffering (I might add that this would be to reject categorically the 'all is now fair' approach whereby some have sought to escape the theodicy question by suggesting that God and humankind suffer the misery of God's creation equally and together!).

Does the refusal to predicate suffering as a necessary dimension of the eternal nature of God undermine the reality of God's sharing or 'participating'[46] in human suffering by implying that God does not suffer in his being? Surely not! As we have seen, God *is* in his engagement with creation and he has his *hypostasis* in his 'ek-static' engagement with humankind. This means that in God's identification with humankind in love we do not have a form of relation which is extrinsic to the being of God. It means we have the eternal being of God *in* or indeed *as* this event. When Barth, Rahner, Moltmann and Jüngel affirmed an absolute two-way identification between the immanent and economic Trinities they were asserting that what God *is* toward us he *is* in his innermost being and what he *is* in his innermost being (as love constituted by the eternal trinitarian relations internal to the Godhead), he *is* toward us. There could be said to be therefore a two-way reiteration in God which receives trinitarian expression when we expound the priesthood of Christ. What the Father is toward us, Christ is to the Father in our humanity, and what Christ is toward the Father in our humanity, the Father is toward us. This is the ground of our adoption and being taken up by grace into the Triune life of God.[47]

---

46I am using the term 'participation' here in a loose sense. Theologically speaking, there is of course an asymmetry in the relation of participation between God and humankind which meant that the Fathers could never have used it of God in his relation to creation.

47By way of a tribute to my father and teacher, James B Torrance, in honour of whom this *Festschrift* has been produced, it is expressive of the outworking of his theological perceptions in his life and teaching that he

This expression of salvation makes it quite incoherent to suggest that God cannot and therefore does not suffer. It is however equally incoherent to eternalize suffering and create a 'pauper' God by describing God's sharing in our suffering as a necessary expression of the divine substance. This is the weakness of a 'process' approach to the issue where it is believed that nature becomes dynamic if it is understood as 'moved nature'.

Rather, God suffers by virtue of the fact that he *is* in his sharing in our suffering but this is a free (though not arbitrary), gracious act of love. If one denies the hypostatic freedom of God then God's free *ekstasis* is dissolved into a determined *hypostasis* and the being of God is reduced to the static substance of Western scholasticism. For precisely this reason it is not strictly correct to say that the divine hypostasis suffers, as this is to treat God's personhood in terms of some prior hypostasis rather than the other way round and it would fail to convey the fact that God's suffering is always an 'alien' suffering - a 'Personal' sharing in the suffering of that which is not God. It must be emphasized here, however, that far from detracting from the notion of God's sharing at the level of his being in human suffering this affirms it for the divine sharing in human suffering stems from the being (hypostasis) of the God who has his *hypostasis* in this ekstatic 'participation' in human suffering. God's suffering is not to be construed as the suffering of the divine nature but rather in terms

---

begins his first year lectures by expounding the nature of worship grounded in the priesthood of Christ. By doing this, he breaks with the customary 'ways into' theology adopted in the West whereby students are first grounded in method, epistemology and the proofs of the existence of God. Rather, theology is communicated as participatory knowing in the most complete and holistic manner. Following the prayer at the beginning of the lecture the students are brought to discover theologically what worship is - that it is 'the gift of participating through the Spirit in the (Incarnate) Son's communion with the Father'. In this way, the theology student is taken up into a contemplation of the personal being of God in such a way that he or she is liberated from the confusions and distortions of the foundationalism which has so characterized our Western heritage. Accordingly, the 'way into' theology through which the students are introduced to the discipline is radically more coherent and appropriate to the Being of God.

of God's becoming where God is understood as having his being *in becoming*. When this is spelled out in terms of the relation between the Father and the Son in the incarnation we can say with Barth that, 'it is not at all the case that God has no part in the suffering of Jesus Christ even in His mode of being as the Father. No, there is a *particula veri* in the teaching of the early Patripassians. This is that primarily it is God the Father who suffers in the offering and sending of His Son, in His abasement. The suffering is not His own, but the alien suffering of the creature, of man, which He takes to Himself in Him. But He does suffer it in the humiliation of His Son with a depth with which it never was or will be suffered by any man - apart from the One who was His Son'.[48]

This brings us finally to the question: how does one respond to the person who suggests that this approach offers too naïve a theory of God's all-pervasive presence and fails to take seriously the God-forsakeness of Auschwitz or Easter Saturday? This cannot be answered at the level of theology, as it cannot be addressed with any theological 'idea'. Christ alone can speak here as he alone addresses the kind of suffering which ruptures language and meaning - not as the one who suddenly introduces meaning into stark meaninglessness but as the one in whom God enters into and takes to himself the very God-forsakenness of men and women, the very depths of Hell and the absence of God. Here he asks our questions for us and on our behalf such that when they are answered in the resumption of communion in the resurrection there might be the ultimate and final realisation of presence-without-absence projecting toward the consummation of God's Kingdom as the joyful, all-pervasive ek-stasis of God in communion with the whole of his creation.

---

48*CD* IV/2, p. 357.

# 19

# The Goodness and Dignity of Man in the Christian Tradition[1]

THOMAS F TORRANCE

In the Christian tradition we do not think and speak of the goodness and dignity of man merely in moral or social terms, but in terms of 'the truth as it is in Jesus'. Moral and social factors cannot but enter into our understanding of the nature of man, but they are considered only within the perspective of the Gospel. Christian judgments about man are properly formed in the light of the humanity of Christ and in accordance with his redemptive purpose in the regeneration of mankind. But since Jesus Christ is none other than the Incarnate Word of God by whom all things were made and in whom they hold together, a truly Christocentric approach to our theme must surely keep in view the place that man *in Christ* must have within the whole created order of visible and invisible realities.

In our discussion here we must first give careful attention to the Hebraic understanding of man's creation and nature found in the Scriptures of the Old Testament, which is not, however, restricted to the Old Testament for it permeates the whole biblical tradition. Although quite distinctive conceptions of God and man arise with the New Testament revelation, they cannot be properly understood without due consideration of their presuppostions and roots. It is not my purpose, then, in this first part to concentrate on the teaching of the Old Testament by itself, but rather to offer an account of the basic tenets and presuppostions of the Judaeo-Christian biblical tradition as a whole. Only then will I turn to offer an account of specifically Christian teaching, while seeking at the same time to draw out some of its most significant implications for us today.

[1] A paper presented at the Lam Chi Fung Memorial Symposium on *Christianity and Chinese and Culture*, Hong Kong Baptist College, Kowloon, 23-25 October 1986.

## I  The Biblical Tradition

A   Man has been created by God, in body and mind, out of nothing, and affirmed by him as 'good'. He is respected by God as his own handiwork, to which he has committed himself. God has given man a unique reality, utterly different from his own transcendent Reality, but endowed with an integrity of its own, and with a real measure of creaturely independence over against him. That very integrity and independence, however, are themselves dependent upon God, for it is in him alone that they have their sustaining ground and sufficient reason, and in his approval that they have their actualisation. This is what we mean by the *contingent* nature of creaturely being - a contingence which applies, not just to man's physical but to his mental or intelligible nature. All creaturely being is contingent, but there is a fundamental difference between the contingent nature of human being and that of any other creaturely being, physical or animal. God created all things by his Word - he commanded and they came into being. But God created man in a more intimate way, not only by the command of his Word but by calling man into a relationship with himself through his Word, for his Word and in his Word in such a way that the Word of God is made to echo in the innermost being of man as man. This means that the distinctively contingent nature of human being is grounded in the direct address of God to man which has the effect of sealing and destining him for communion with God.

B   God has created man in such a way that as a physical and rational being he is not body and mind but body of his mind and mind of his body, a unitary whole. It is as such that he lives and moves and has his being in God, for he is made to exist within a relation that God establishes with him through the immanent presence and power of his transcendent Spirit. The activity of Spirit of God in creation is the freedom of God to be present to the creature, sustaining it in its creaturely being and realising the relation of the creature to himself, so that the creature may reach its true end beyond itself in God. While this applies to all created beings, physical and animal as well as human, it is distinctive of

God's relation to the human creature through his Spirit that he is
not only present to him upholding him from below in his bare
contingent existence, but present to him in such an intimate way
as to sustain him in his contingent openness to God and the
address of his Word - that is what belongs to the created
constitution of man as man, as what we call *homo sapiens*. The
Bible speaks of this relation of man to God constituted through
his Creator Spirit as 'spirit'. Hence the 'spirit' that is in man is
to be understood, not as some spark of the divine Spirit that he
possesses in himself, but rather as the creaturely pole of the
spirit/Spirit relation. It is creative Spirit at God's end and
creaturely spirit at man's end. It is the relation of man to God in
which his distinctively human being consists, unifying his nature
as body of his mind and mind of his body before God. Damage
introduced into that spirit-relation with God would bring about
decay in the unification of his nature and engender a dualism of
body and mind within him. Here too, then, it is apparent that
man must be regarded as an essentially relational being, who is
what he is as man through subsisting in the being-constituting
relation of the Creator with him. If God were to withdraw the
sustaining presence of his Creator Spirit from him, man would not
only lose all openness to God but would simply vanish, mind as
well as body, into nothing. It must also be added here that man
is the creature who lives on the boundary between two 'worlds',
the physical and the spiritual, the visible and the invisible, or
what the biblical tradition speaks of as the earthly and the
heavenly. What makes him so distinctive in this respect is that,
as a unitary being who is body of his mind and mind of his body
uniquely related to God through the presence of his Spirit, man
spans both 'worlds'. He is thus the one constituent of the
universe through whom the creation discloses its astonishing
order and harmony and comes to expression in such a way as to
praise and glorify God the Father Almighty, Creator of all things
visible and invisible.

C Human beings have been created by God, not as solitary
individuals, but as male and female, in such a way that they need

each other to be human and to be what each is over against the other and what both are in their ordered unity. That is to say by 'man' the biblical tradition means 'man-and-woman', for it is man and woman who constitute in their union the basic unit of humanity. This fellow-humanity or what is sometimes called 'co-humanity' belongs to the essential fabric of human existence. It is understandable, then, that an essential place should be given to marriage, to becoming 'one-flesh' by act of God, in the structure of humanity. This basic man-woman relation generates a dynamic ontological relationship within human existence. As we have seen, man is constituted a relational being basically through a 'vertical' relation to the Creator, but within his God-given existence as man and woman. Through procreation this intra-human relation within the family reaches throughout the human race generating the intrinsic social structure of humanity around the family.

D  It is in respect of this intra-relational structure of man as man and woman that man is said in the biblical tradition to have been created after the image and likeness of God. There can be no doubt that in the Bible the concept of the image of God does not have anything to do with the idea that man is constituted a rational being through sharing in the eternal reason let alone the essence of God. Rather does it have to do with the way in which the basic inter-human relation, called into existence by the Word and Spirit of God, is made to reflect in its creaturely difference a transcendent relation within God, and also to exhibit the basic covenant-partnership between God and mankind. It is not man or woman individually or as such that is said to be created after the image and likeness of God, but 'man' as man and woman in their reciprocal and complementary relationship, that is as man-and-woman in unique analogical relation to God. The horizontal relation between them grounded in their vertical relation to God is a contingent reflection of God and represents a created correspondence to uncreated relations within God himself. In being thus created after the image of God man is singled out from all other creatures to be what he is destined to be as man in this created correspondence to him, and thereby to be locked into a transcendent end that reaches out far beyond the whole created order. It is in this respect that man is traditionally spoken of as 'the crown of creation', for in a significant sense he has been given a central and unique role in covenant-partnership with God in virtue of which he is to exercise a 'dominion', but not unrestricted lordship, over his fellow-creatures in the world.

E  The enigma of man, however, is that he has 'fallen' from this state in which God created him and thus exists in contradiction to the very end for which he is destined as man, and yet far from being abandoned by God he continues to be claimed and accepted by God as his own good handiwork.  The human nature created by God as such is not evil but essentially good in its determination for fellowship with God, and perfectly adapted for the fulfilment of his will and purpose in the creation.  Although the contradiction into which man has lapsed is judged by God, the very fact that God sets his 'No' against it means that God will not allow man to escape from the primary 'Yes' of God in his creative affirmation of him as good, and so man must always be regarded in the light of God's promise that he will make good his claim. The effect of this strange fall and God's endurance of man is presented in a very vivid and profound theological account in the opening chapters of the Old Testament.  The breach introduced by the inexplicable emergence of evil into the relationship between man and God, results in a state of affairs in which man and woman are estranged from one another, in which each becomes alien to himself or herself, and in which both find themselves at odds with nature.  That is to say, the breach between man and God enters into the inner being of men and women, so that they are no longer the beings they ought to be either in relation to God on in relatio to one another.  Even their physical existence in the world has become dislocated.  The fact that human beings ought to be what they are not, now qualifies their very existence as human beings.  They are ontologically so deeply split within themselves that they are trapped within that split and cannot escape from it. They have become so inverted in their nature, so inextricably curved in upon themselves in the very roots of their being, that no matter how much they exercise their free-will they are quite unable to escape from their self-will. Try as they may to be what they ought to be, they remain aware that they still ought to be other than they actually are - they cannot overcome the disruption in their constitutive relations with God or fellow human beings which inexorably imposes that obligation upon them for it belongs to the ontological structure of what they now are.

F It is thus that what we call 'conscience' has arisen - the inner warning that is soundlessly voiced within us, or the red light that flashes in our minds, when we come into conflict with God and with one another. Conscience has a primary reference to the vertical relation of man to God through which his being is constituted, but also a secondary reference to the horizontal relations in which he exists along with other human beings. It functions at the intersection of those references, where the inarticulate but compelling claims of God written on our hearts meet with the claims of our neighbour upon us. The term 'conscience' literally means 'knowing with', that is, a conjoint knowing with God and our neighbour, for in it the claims of God and the claims of our neighbour upon us interlock and bear upon each other. As such, conscience now belongs to the ineradicable make-up of human being. It is, so to speak, the 'sounding-board' where we somehow echo the Voice of God at whose command we came into being and are continuously sustained in being, but because of our broken relation with God the awareness we have of God through conscience is inevitably refracted. Hence conscience tells us nothing positive about God, but at best signals that we are 'in the wrong' with him, and with our neighbour. Moreover, conscience easily becomes twisted, so that its signals can be taken over by evil and be used as subtle cover for further and greater evil.

G Since fallen man exists in contradiction to God and to the end for which he was created, his whole being partakes of that inner contradiction - his sin and guilt are thus rooted in the ontological depths of his existence before God. Nevertheless God continues to claim man and affirm him as good and refuses to allow that claim and affirmation to be thwarted by man's disobedience or compromised by the contradiction within which he has become trapped. That is powerfuly expressed in the biblical tradition in terms of the covenant of grace in which God has grounded his creation upon his own eternal faithfulness and with which he ceaselessly undergirds its reality and maintains its integrity before him. This applies to the whole of God's creation but in a special way to man whom God has created in order to share fellowship with himself and thus even in his contingent creatureliness to reflect his own transcendent Reality and Integrity. The covenant means that while the Righteousness of God is brought to bear upon man in uncompromising judgment of his sin and guilt, nevertheless God's affirmation of man as good undercuts the disruption in his existence and undergirds the divinely given integrity of his being. In the steadfastness of his Covenant Love God refuses to let him go but holds on to him and redeems him from the evil that menaces his reality and integrity as a child of God. Thus it is one of the quite distinctive features of the Old Testament tradition that God is concieved as a just God and *therefore* a Saviour. His holiness is far from being merely condemnatory for it is supremely self-imparting and redemptive; indeed God's Holiness is the purity of his everlasting Love with which he has bound man to himself and will not let him go. God's relations with Israel in the redeeming and renewing force of his steadfast Love constitute the paradigm case of his relations with all humanity.

The astonishing revelation of God in the biblical tradition is that God does not wish to exist alone, and has freely brought into being alongside of himself and yet in utter distinction from himself another upon whom he may pour out his love, with whom he may share his divine Life in covenant-partnership. That is the relationship in terms of which the ultimate secret of human nature is to be sought, and with reference to which therefore the essential goodness and dignity of man are to be understood. Hence everything about man and his history must be seen in the light of God's determination of man for fellowship with himself, and of his positive affirmation of man that underlies all human existence and triumphs over all the contradiction of evil and wickedness entrenched within it. While the biblical traditon does not allow us to overlook the fearful depth of sin and wickedness in the human heart, it will not allow us to forget that in making man for himself God approves of what he has made and affirms its goodness as well as its reality before him. In spite of all its depravity and distortion through sin, human nature is not, and cannot be, effaced or destroyed, for man's creation after the image and likeness of God continually stands sentinel over him as the divinely given law and truth of his human being, even in the face of everything that contradicts it. It is a man's destiny to live in covenanted relation to a ground and goal in God that transcends all the brokenness and tensions in his actual existence, and in reliance upon God's promise to make good his creative affirmation of the goodness and dignity of human being. For man to live like that beyond himself in God, is to live in goodness and in the infinite worth that God has conferred upon him. What greater dignity could man have than to be the covenant-partner of God, the being of whom God is for ever mindful, the one to whom he addresses his Word and whom he enlightens as no other creature, and indeed the one with whom God wishes to share his own life and love and glory?

## II The Christian Tradition

The absolutely decisive factor in the Christian tradition is, of course, Jesus Christ. In him the whole biblical tradition has its climatic fulfilment and its controlling centre. In him as God and man in one Person the ground and goal of the Covenant and of the whole creation have been embodied within actual human existence. He is the eternal Word of God by whom and for whom all things were created and in whom they all hold together. He is the incarnate Son of God in whom God reconciles the world to himself and through whom he sends forth his Spirit to dwell with human beings in order to bring their creaturely relations to their destined end in unrestricted access as children to their heavenly Father. It is in Jesus Christ, therefore, and in him alone, that the real truth of human nature is to be found, for in him God has made good his original claim in creation, when he affirmed the goodness and integrity of man before him. Jesus Christ is the

376

Word by whom, for whom, and in whom we have been created in the image of God, so that in his Incarnation as Immanuel, God with us and for us and in us, he is the key to the secret of our creation and redemption - in him we may now penetrate through all the distortion, depravity and degradation of humanity to the true nature of a man hidden beneath it all.

We must direct our thought here above all to the reconciliation of man with God in the sacrificial death of Jesus upon the Cross, for it is there that God both justifies man and justifies his own claim for man. It is there that the truth of man's fearful sin and guilt and disgrace is exposed and he is judged, but it is precisely in that exposure and judgment that the infinite Love of God for man is revealed and thus the true form and worth of human being as the object of that Love. Moreover, in the crucified and resurrected humanity of Jesus it became finally established that for man to live apart from God is to lapse into monstrous inhumanity, but for man to live in union with God is to become fully and perfectly human. Thus it also became established that the evil and wickedness of man have nothing to do with his creaturely nature, but with the perversion and corruption of that nature due to rebellion against the creative source of human nature in God.

Our particular concern here, however, is not with the sin and inhumanity of man as such, which brought Jesus to the Cross, but with what the incarnation, crucifixion and resurrection of Jesus, and God's forgiveness of the sin and inhumanity of man, have to tell us about the real goodness and dignity of man.

A  The Love of the Father
The Cross of Christ is a window into the Divine Heart. 'God so loved the world that he gave his only Son'. 'He who did not spare his own Son but gave him up for us all, will he not also give us all things with him?' I suppose that in the Christian tradition the central focus of attention has generally been on the sacrifice of Christ on which all our hopes rest, but the sacrifice of Christ is in reality God's sacrifice. The supreme significance of the Cross as atoning sacrifice through which our sins are forgiven

377

is to be traced back to the act of God the Father. What is absolutely decisive is the Deity of Christ - if he were not God but however exalted only Man, then we could not believe either in God or in humanity. The Cross would then be a revelation on the one hand of an indifference in God toward the desperate plight of humanity, and on the other hand of the ultimate antagonism and hatred of the human race for the only perfect human being that ever existed. If God is quite separate from Jesus, then the Cross stands for nothing but unrelieved darkness and despair. But if Jesus Christ is God incarnated, God himself come to be one of us and to make our lost cause his own, then the Cross is something altogether different, the mighty act of God bearing and vanquishing in atoning sacrifice all the wickedness, hatred and violence of mankind. That is to say, we must think of God as directly present in Christ on the Cross, suffering along with him, and suffering not less than he. So that we must look through the sacrifice of Christ to the sacrifice of God, through the passion of the Son to the passion of the Father. The self-abnegating Love of God the Father is surely the supreme truth that lies behind everything else in the Gospel and gives it its decisive meaning and redemptive power. It is the utterly astounding and awesome fact that God forgives our sins at *infinite cost* to himself in the sacfrifice of his own Son. It means, in fact, that *God loves us more that he loves himself.* Such is the immeasurable worth, the infinite value, that God puts upon man in the price he has chosen to pay in order to share with him his own divine Life and Love. In view of what God has done for man in the sacrifice of his beloved Son on the Cross, and therefore in view of the incredible dignity he has conferred upon man in Jesus, we are unable to set any limits on the worth of our fellow human beings. That is the major premise of everything else that must be said here.

B  The Grace of the Lord Jesus Christ
'The Word became flesh and dwelt among us, full of grace and truth, and we beheld his glory, the glory as of the only Son of the Father'. 'You know the grace of our Lord Jesus Christ, that though he was rich, yet for your sake he became poor, so that by his poverty you might become rich'. I have brought these verses

from St John and St Paul together in order to focus attention upon two interrelated facts about the Incarnation. In Jesus Christ the very Word of God through whom all things were created and who is the life and light of men, has himself become man, thus embodying in his humanity the creative source of all human being. From beginning to end, however, the Incarnation of the Word or Son of God took the form of a vicarious intervention in our poverty-stricken human existence in which Jesus Christ took our place in atoning exchange, making our lost condition his own, that we might be given his place and be endowed with the riches of God in him. That is to say, in Jesus Christ the Son of God penetrated into the dark depths of our alienated, enslaved and distorted human existence, making it his own in order to heal, sanctify and renew it in himself throughout the whole course of his vicarious human life, death and resurrection and thus restore us to perfect filial union with God the Father. It was not by assuming some neutral human nature but by assuming our actual fallen human nature, thereby taking our place under the judgment of God's Holiness and Love, that he effected our salvation and transformed our human being in himself, bringing it into conformity with his own perfect obedience as incarnated Son of the Father.

Thus in Jesus Christ the Word of God has himself become Man, and as such is not the ground and source of our human being within the actualities of our human existence. In him the dehumanizing breach between man and God has been healed, for he is the perfect Man in whom there is no split between what he is and what he ought to be. If to be truly man is to be with God and to be wholly determined in his humanity through fellowship with God, then Jesus Christ is the one true Man for he is perfectly one with God. He is the one Man who is properly and completely in the image of God, but he is much more that that - he is the only One who is both the Image and the Reality of God, for in his incarnated Person God and Man, divine and human nature, are inseparably united. Jesus Christ is that, however, precisely as *our* fellow-man, as *our* brother, for it is *our* actual human being and nature that have been taken up in him and been perfectly

379

united to his Divine Being and Nature. That is the astonishing way in which God has justified his original claim in the creation of man to be 'good'. And so it is in the human being and nature of Jesus that the true nature and dignity of man are ultimately disclosed and established.

Now since in Jesus Christ the Creator Word of God has become man in such a way that in him Divine Nature and human nature are indivisibly united in his one Person, the humanity of every man, whether he knows it or not, whether he believes or not, is ontologically bound up with the humanity of Jesus, and determined by it. Jesus Himself, then, is the true secret of the nature of every human being. Moreover, if he is both the Image and the Reality of God, then he is the unique image-constituting Image of God, and it is by reference to what he is that we must now think of human beings as created after the image of God. It may well be wholly concealed under their sin and disobedience, defaced in the distortion of their humanness, but the image of God nevertheless remains sealing their human existnece through their ontological bond with Jesus Christ the Incarnated Word. Even if we cannot discern it, he acknowledges it, as he made clear when he taught that in all our relations with our fellow human beings it is ultimately with *him* that we have to do, and that whatever we do to one another we actually do to *him*. We must not forget, however, that in having to do with him we have to do with the One who interposes himself for us, who gave himself for us, who substitutes himself in our place that we may have his place before God. And as such Jesus is the one human being in whose existence we have to do immediately and directly with God.

It belongs to the Grace of the Lord Jesus Christ that he has been given to us as *humanizing Man* and as *personalizing Person*. He alone is Man in the full and proper sense, for in him the creative Source of human being and the perfect actualisation of human being are one. He is not only Man *par excellence*, Archetypal Man, but the one humanizing Man, the fount from which all that is truly human is derived. We on the other hand are but humanized men and women, for we are not human in virtue of

380

some essence of humanity that we have in ourselves but only in virtue of what we receive from his Humanity which embodies the Life that is the Light of Men. For us really to be human, therefore, is to be in Christ. Likewise Jesus Christ is Person in the full and proper sense, for in him God the creative Source of personal being and the one perfect human person are wholly and indivisibly one. In the strict sense God only is Person, for he is in himself the fullness of personal Being - he is personalizing Person. In the Incarnation, however, God himself has become one with us and one of us in such a way that Jesus Christ is now the fount of all that is truly personal among us. We on the other hand are but personalized persons, for we are not personal in virtue of some personal substance inherent in ourselves, but only through what we receive from Jesus Christ and become in union with him and indeed in communion with the fullness of personal Being in the Holy Trinity. For us really to be personal, therefore, is to be in Christ. To be truly human is to be truly personal, and to be truly personal is to be truly human - that is the kind of human nature that God has embodied in Jesus Christ. 'And from his fullness have we all received, grace upon grace'.

This immensely humanizing and personalizing force of our Lord Jesus Christ must be understood in terms of the fact that he is the incarnate embodiment of the infinite self-abnegating Love of God. As we have already seen, God loves us with such measureless Love that he has given us his own beloved Son at infinite cost and agony to his Father's heart in atoning sacrifice on the Cross. This means that God actually loves us more that he loves himself - that is the love of God that is embodied in Jesus Christ and actualized in the midst of our sinful humanity through his own selfless self-giving for us and to us in coming 'not to be served but to serve and to give his life a ransom for many'. Thus Jesus Christ loves us to the uttermost, without any reserve, and loves us unconditionally, more than he loves himself. That is the essential nature of his Divine Love which bears upon us in Jesus with all the compelling claims of God upon us and with the undiluted imperative that we love God with all our heart, and with all our soul and with all our mind, and love our neighbour as ourselves. That is such a new kind of love that a new word *agape* had to be coined in the New Testament to express it. It is the kind of love in which we love others objectively for their sakes and not for our own sakes, in which we let the objective 'other' be the Archimedean point, as it were, beyond ourselves for the humanizing and personalizing power of Jesus to be actualized in our daily existence and life with one another. It is here, then, that there becomes manifest what in the Christian tradition the real goodness and dignity of man is: our loving others objectively for their own sake, and being accounted as the object of such selfless love for our sake. That is why in his Epistles St John focusses attention so much upon the *new* commandment to love others with the very love with which we ourselves are loved by God in the self-giving of his Son on the Cross.

C The Communion of the Holy Spirit
We recall that in general the biblical tradition thinks of man in a non-dualistic way as a unitary being who is body of his mind and mind of his body. As such he is related to God through his spirit which is not a third thing in man but rather a dynamic correlate to the Spirit of God by whose creative power he is determined and sustained in his distinctive existence as a human being before God in relation to other human beings. This is to be understood in connection with the biblical teaching that the Spirit of God, although infinitely exalted above and beyond all creatures, is nevertheless free to be present to the creature and to realise and bring to completion the purpose of God for the creature. While this holds good for all God's creatures, animate and inanimate, it applies in a special way to man who has been created by the Word of God for fellowship with himself, and to whom the Spirit is present in such a way as to make him open to God and capable of responding to him. Here the Spirit is to be thought of as acting not only from God toward man but from man toward God by bringing his human relations with God to their proper end in him, and thereby undergirding and upholding man in an enduring ontological relation to God. This means that while man does not have any continuity in relation to God inherent in his own creaturely being, he does have a relation to God which is

continuously given and unceasingly sustained by the creative presence and power of the Spirit. In this event, as we have seen, man is not to be understood from an independent centre in himself but only from above and beyond himself in a 'transcendental' relation to God - and therefore also, of course, in a transcendental relation to his fellow-men.

Now to this general teaching in the biblical tradition about the relation of the Spirit of God to man, there must be added certain other factors that are absolutely decisive for the Christian tradition: that the Holy Spirit is the Spirit of the Father and of the Son, and that he is mediated to us through the Person and Work of the Incarnate Son.

With the Christian doctrine of God as three Persons in one Being, the concept of the Holy Spirit became intensely personal. The Holy Spirit is the sovereign divine Subject, the creative, life-giving personal Presence of God who addresses man in his Word, actualizing knowledge of God within man and creating in him the capacity to respond as a rational subject and agent to himself. It is through this inter-personal mode of his Presence to him that the Spirit brings man's human relations to their true end and fulfilment in God, for coming from the inner Communion of Love in the Holy Trinity he effects communion between men and God in Love, that is in the Love that God himself *is*. In the Holy Trnity the relations of Love between Father, Son and Holy Spirit are personal relations subsisting within his One Being. God is thus to be understood as the Fullness of Love and of Personal Being. That is to say, the relations of Love between the Persons of the Holy Trinity belong essentially to what the Divine Persons are. It cannot be stressed enough that is was this trinitarian doctrine of God that actually gave rise to the concept of *person*, which was quite unknown in the world before, and to the realisation that God has created human beings in such a way that their inter-human relations are meant to be inter-personal, and as such are meant to reflect on the level of the creature the inter-personal relations in God himself. Thus while it is uniquely true

383

of God that the relations between the divine Persons are essential to what the Persons are, so it is true on our human level that the relations between persons belong to what persons really are.

We cannot enlarge now upon the effect of this Christian concept of the person upon the whole development of thought in human civilisation. However, let us note that it is in the light of this concept of the person deriving from the Holy Trinity, that we are to understand the humanizing and personalizing impact of Jesus upon human nature. Moreover, as in an altogether transcendent way in God the Love that God *is* belongs to the inner personal relations of his Triune Being, so with us on our creaturely level, in spite of our utter dissimilarity, love belongs to the essential equation of the personal - but love in the profound ontological sense that derives from the Holy Spirit, the love between persons which belongs to what personal beings really are. That is what takes place when the Holy Spirit dwells in our hearts and floods them with the Love of God which he himself is, so that as he is the bond of Oneness in the Holy Trinity, he may also be the bond of oneness and love and thus of intensely inter-personal relations among us. It is thus that in our frail contingent human nature we may even be 'partakers of the Divine Nature' as through the Communion of the Holy Spirit we are allowed to share in the very Love that God himself is.

This intimate indwelling of the Holy Spirit in the human heart was made possible only through Jesus Christ, the one Mediator between God and man. While the Holy Spirit is the freedom of God to be present to his creatures and sustain them in their creaturely being and reality, and thus to realise their relations with himself, this immanence of the Spirit inevitably means that the Holiness of God is brought to bear upon the ontological roots of our sinful being in a fearful judgment which we are quite unable to bear, for it threatens our very existence, that Jesus Christ has made himself one with us, making our lost and damned condition his own, in order to redeem us by his atoning exchange, and restore us in forgiveness to communion with God. Thus through his vicarious life, death and resurrection he has made himself the dwelling place of the Holy Spirit within our human existence and now mediates him to us in the fulness of his divine presence and power. In other words, through the reconciling sacrifice of Christ the profound ontological tension between our human being and the Holy Spirit has been healed so that the Holy Spirit is now freely given to us in all the fulness of his life-giving and sanctifying presence. This is the new spiritual and ontological condition of people which the New Testament refers to by the expressions 'in Christ' and 'in the Spirit'. While this is true in a distinctive and intimate way only of those who believe in the Lord Jesus Christ as their Saviour, it has a wider application. Just as all men, whether they believe or not, whether they know it our not, are ontologically dependent upon the humanity of Jesus Christ, so they are also ontologically dependent in a new and profounder way upon the immanent presence and power of the Holy Spirit, who on the ground of the atoning and reconciling work of Christ, has been poured out 'upon all flesh'. While we cannot understand all that this being-constituting relation of the Spirit of God to man involves for one who is 'without Christ', it certainly means for a man 'in Christ' that his human nature as body of his mind and mind of his body is affirmed with a spiritual wholeness and a new ontological interrelation with others that transcends his original creation, for now he exists not just alongside of the Creator, but in such a way that his human being is anchored in the very Being of God. No wonder that the Greek Fathers were fond of citing in this connection those words of Jesus recorded by St John, 'the Scripture calls "gods" those to whom the Word of God came' - such was the exalted status they felt obliged to accord to man 'in Christ' and 'in the Spirit'.

In concluding our discussion let me point back to the utterly stupendous event of the Incarnation: in Jesus Christ God himself became man, the Creator became a creature, yet without ceasing to be God. The Incarnation is the divine-human axis which God has thrust through the centre of the creation in such a way that everything in heaven and earth, eternity and time, is made to revolve around it. As very God and very man for ever united in his own Person, the ultimate foundations of being are lodged in him, and all the eternal purposes of God are gathered up and consummated in his life and work. Jesus Christ is not only the cardinal reality upon which all history turns, but constitutes in his Person the very hinge and pivot of the universe. The breathtaking import of all this for our theme is that our human nature has been taken up and in Jesus to the top and summit of being, and that with him and in him man has been located in the very centre of all things!

With this understanding of the Incarnation everything in the Christian view of the universe and man's place is deeply affected. It will not allow us to go along with the dualist outlook that cuts the universe in two, a physical half and a spiritual half, and then argues that the former is a closed mechanistic system governed by rigid laws of nature, and that the latter is only a subjective realm which is not open to intelligible, let alone scientific, apprehension. On the contrary, the Christian Gospel proclaims that as there is only one Lord God revealed in Jesus Christ who is both Creator and Redeemer, so there is only one Kingdom in which he rules over the whole universe of physical and spiritual reality. The Incarnation tells us that in spite of the contradictions introduced by sin and evil, the Creator and the creature, God and man, are for ever one in Jesus Christ, and that through his Cross all things are reconciled to God whether they be on earth or in heaven. In the Person and Work of Christ creation and redemption are so completely integrated that every part of the universe comes under his providential control. He who triumphed over all the contradiction and disruption of evil in the atoning death and resurrection of Christ is he who is omnipotently at work throughout all space and time, making everything serve the eternal purpose of his Love. Far from being a closed mechanical system hostile to divine intervention, the whole empirical and intelligible universe is the scene where the kingdom of Christ actualizes itself and subjects every evil or refractory element within it to the will of the heavenly Father.

It is in the centre of this universe under the overarching sovereignty of God that man has been appointed to serve the Lord

386

Jesus Christ as his covenant-partner. With the Incarnation the original relation between the covenant and the creation has been reaffirmed by God and fulfilled in such a way that the whole creation has been redeemed, sanctified and renewed in Christ. It is not the role of man in union with Christ to serve the purpose of God's love in the on-going actualisation of that redemption, sanctification and renewal within the universe, and not least in the inner coordination of visible and invisible, earthly and heavenly reality. Thus man is called to be a kind of midwife to creation, in assisting nature out of its divinely given abundance constantly to give birth to new forms of life and richer patterns of order. Indeed as the covenant-partner of Jesus Christ man may be regarded as the priest of creation, through whose service as a man of faith and a man of science the marvellous rationality, symmetry, harmony and beauty of God's creation are being brought to light and given expression in such a way that the whole universe is found to be a glorious hymn to the Creator.